Resowing the Seeds of War

RHETORIC AND PUBLIC AFFAIRS SERIES

Resowing the Seeds of War

of War

PRESIDENTIAL PEACE RHETORIC SINCE 1945

Stephen J. Heidt

MICHIGAN STATE UNIVERSITY PRESS | *East Lansing*

Michigan State University Press
East Lansing, Michigan 48823-5245

LIBRARY OF CONGRESS CATALOGING-IN-PUBLICATION DATA
Names: Heidt, Stephen J., author.
Title: Resowing the seeds of war : presidential peace rhetoric since 1945 / Stephen J. Heidt.
Description: East Lansing : Michigan State University Press, [2021] |
Series: Rhetoric and public affairs series | Includes bibliographical references and index.
Identifiers: LCCN 2020020827 | ISBN 9781611863840 (paperback)
| ISBN 9781609176594 | ISBN 9781628954180 | ISBN 9781628964196
Subjects: LCSH: Communication in politics—United States—History—20th century.
| Communication in politics—United States—History—21st century.
| Presidents—United States—Language—History—20th century.
| Presidents—United States—Language—History—21st century.
| Peace-building, American—History—20th century.
| Peace-building, American—History—21st century.
| Rhetoric—Political aspects—United States—History—20th century.
| Rhetoric—Political aspects—United States—History—21st century.
Classification: LCC JA85.2.U6 H43 2021 | DDC 327.1/720973—dc23
LC record available at https://lccn.loc.gov/2020020827

Book design by Charlie Sharp, Sharp Designs, East Lansing, MI
Cover design by Erin Kirk New
Cover art: War Versus Diplomacy, by freshidea. Used with permission, Adobe Stock.

Visit Michigan State University Press at *www.msupress.org*

Contents

———•◆•———

Acknowledgments

———•◆•———

On March 20, 2003, I sat on the couch in my studio apartment in Washington, DC, and watched my country launch an ill-advised and unpopular invasion of Iraq live on CNN. Helpless to arrest the war machine, I joined millions of others shocked at the brazen, crooked, and hapless case for war. What followed moved past folly into catastrophe, war crimes, boondoggle, and the undoing of American influence in the world. Barack Obama's election offered hope that the country could escape quagmire and restore the promise of American idealism. But wars once begun are not easily ended. The inability of democratic politics at home to stop the war, and the incapacity of the military to pacify and rebuild Iraq altered how I understood politics, power, and policy. Fundamentally, I grasped that both democratic politics and American power have distinct limits that rhetorically adept political actors can exploit. While I cannot draw a straight line between

9/11, the Iraq War, and this book, I can attest to the first decade of the twenty-first century as its genesis point.

This book, and the argument it contains, owes much to those who read, reacted to, or otherwise complicated my views of war, presidents, and the rhetoric they seek. David Cheshier, the ever dispassionate interlocutor, helped me discover embedded nuggets in early versions of this project that became the essence of the book I have now completed. Carol Winkler pushed me to go back to the evidence. Robert L. Ivie pointed out notable gaps and incongruities. Nate Atkinson urged me to drill down. And Mary Stuckey did her utmost to keep me on task, talked me down when I wanted to blow the manuscript up for a fourth time, and has been an ideal mentor-scholar-colleague-friend. I will forever be grateful for her quick and insightful criticism, her faith in my ideas, and her friendship.

Discussing and writing this book has demonstrated the deep generosity of this community of scholars. At every stage of this process, I found colleagues interested in the project, willing to give feedback on ideas that I could barely express cogently. Jason Jarvis made sure I always remembered the stakes. Jason Derby chided me for taking so long, even as he welcomed any and all conversations about the project. Lisa Corrigan expressed trust, confidence, energy, and enjoyment at my ideas, not to mention plenty of opportunities to decompress. Michael Lee helped me navigate the publication process. Paul Johnson and John Lynch offered friendship and citations for some of my wilder research needs. David Cratis Williams, as my chair at Florida Atlantic University, listened as the argument for this book flourished and materialized. Joel Lemuel and Joe Bellon kept me focused. Neil Blackmon joined me for many coffee breaks. I am deeply indebted to these colleagues and the conversations we have shared, and feel deeply privileged to have the opportunity to share with and listen to the diverse voices, perspectives, and experiences that constitute this academic community.

Three colleagues deserve special mention. Rob Mills has been a colleague, friend, and co-conspirator since we first ran into each other. I think about the presidency, rhetoric, and the world differently because of him. Similarly, without the friendship of Andrew Barnes and Nicole Barnes, I never would have been in position to finish this book. Andrew has proven to be an able and nimble foil, sharpening many of my ideas as well as laying out research terrains too arduous to traverse. Nicole, who listened, offered feedback, and commiserated even though she's not terribly interested in presidential rhetoric, has served as my primary literary consultant. If this book contains any of the best words, it is only because she was willing to provide them.

This book reflects the influence of a number of important individuals, including Melissa Wade, Eric Kessler, Dan Fitzmier, Larry Heftman, Victor Tabak, Jamie McKown, and Paul Kerr. I will always have deep gratitude for having learned from them along the way. The years might have pushed us apart, but the lessons learned on the Emory debate team last forever.

A William M. Suttles Graduate Fellowship for Doctoral Research grant at Georgia State University and a Morrow Fund grant at Florida Atlantic University supported the research for this book. I am indebted to the ways both institutions supported me and this project.

Presidential libraries are strange places that I have still not yet figured out how to navigate. Fortunately, Randy Sowell at the Truman Library and Mary Burtzloff at the Eisenhower Library understood what I needed and helped me find it.

I am deeply privileged to have had the assistance of Martin Medhurst and his attention to detail in preparing this manuscript. His incisive and pointed comments on the original draft helped direct and manage the revision process.

David Zarefsky, as I know now, was one of the anonymous reviewers of this project. The work is better for it. His careful and pointed review helped compact and narrow my argument to the one contained in the coming pages. Similarly, I am grateful for the two anonymous reviewers whose comments helped make the argument and the prose more efficient and coherent. It has been a delight to work with Catherine Cocks, Bonnie Cobb, Amanda Frost, Anastasia Wraight, and the entire editorial staff at Michigan State University Press.

Finally, I can never thank my family enough for the love and support they have provided over the years of this project. My mother, Patricia, has endured countless "conversations" in which I have discussed many of the finer points contained in this book. My brother, David, patiently listened and provided intellectual and emotional support as needed. But, from the outset, Diana Barreto has empowered, trusted, and believed in me. It's not easy to live apart from one's spouse for an extended period of time, especially when separation crosses international borders and time zones. But with her love and support, this project made it through a long-distance relationship, moves across six metropolitan areas, and the arrival of two rambunctious and energetic boys, Santiago and Samuel. In the end, our motivations are multitude, our passions amplified by those who love us and who we love. I hope this work reflects as much trust and confidence they have in me as I have in them.

Preface

————•◆•————

In 1914, H. G. Wells published a short volume titled *The War That Will End War*. The book opened with a brief description of the cause of the war before moving from the particulars of German aggression to a more general thesis of war and peace. As declared in the title, Wells's central claim averred, "the greatest of all wars, is not just another war—it is the last war!"[1] He argued that defeating Germany would send a resounding message that the world would not tolerate aggressive statecraft, creating the conditions for a long peace. That message would underscore the benefits of democracy as a means for resolving conflict peacefully and for avoiding the consolidation of power that allowed a few power-hungry leaders to lead nations into military expansion. Becoming a dominant justification for the war, Wells's thesis framed and shaped public attitudes about the conflict in Europe and the United States.[2] Woodrow Wilson echoed his position shortly after U.S. entrance into the war, explaining, "we are fighting . . . for the future peace and

security of the world."[3] John Dewey lent his voice as well, basing support
for American entrance into the war on the notion that it was a "war to
end all wars" and would "make the world safe for democracy."[4] After the
armistice agreement in November 1918, Wilson declared, "Armed imperialism . . . is at an end, its illicit ambitions engulfed in black disaster . . .
The great nations . . . have now united in the common purpose to set
up such a peace as will satisfy the longing of the whole world."[5] Ralph
Pulitzer, publisher of the *New York Times*, adopted the frame to argue for
consensus at the Paris Peace Conference.[6] Arthur Derrin Call, editor of
the journal *Advocate for Peace*, recalled that "we were fighting a 'war to end
war,' . . . we were struggling to 'make the world safe for democracy.'"[7]

Twenty-one years later, Germany invaded Poland, unleashing a second world war and a cataclysm of death previously unseen in human
history. Rather than abolish the force of "mental and material corruption" that led nations into war, the postwar era had fueled them, dashing
hopes for a long peace.[8] Upon the advent of war, Franklin D. Roosevelt
again imbued the nation with noble purpose, stating, "It seems clear to
me, even at the outbreak of this great war, that the influence of America
should be consistent in seeking for humanity a final peace which will
eliminate, as far as it is possible to do so, the continued use of force between nations."[9] Reflecting the deep commitments to the highest ideals
of peace, freedom, and equality, the message echoed principles enshrined
in the nation's founding documents, previewed Roosevelt's elaboration
of the Atlantic Charter and the charter of the United Nations, and fit
with American views of national character. Yet, American history, like
that of the world, is replete with violence. The violence of nationhood
and expansion, conducted against slaves, Native Americans, and foreign
powers, underscores a central paradox of American politics. A nation
committed to some of the highest principles continually violates those
principles in pursuit of the national interest.

Paradoxes between the ways presidents speak of the nation and the
policies they enact are not unusual in the history of war. Presidents have
always scapegoated adversaries to justify national violence, depicting
Others as savage, uncivilized, irrational, and aggressive.[10] In the lead-up

to the War of 1812, for example, James Madison employed decivilizing vehicles to portray the British as "criminal" and "crazed."[11] James K. Polk claimed Mexico had invaded national territory and "shed American blood upon American soil" to sell the conflict as a defense against barbaric aggression.[12] For William McKinley, the United States had to defend itself against Spain's "cruel, barbarous, and uncivilized practices of warfare."[13] Accompanied by a dialectical vision of American character as rational, civilized, peaceful, and acting in self-defense, the savage idiom perpetuates the nation's drive to war, ingrains the nation with a belief in the necessity of war, and undermines dissent.[14]

Scholars have addressed the paradox between American desires for peace and continuity of war from a variety of perspectives. Some argue situational factors ensure that peaceful international relations remain elusive. Factors outside the president's control, they suggest, undermine even the best-laid plans for peace.[15] Others contend that national violence has become a sort of culture imbued by history and context. They explain that enmity has become a pervasive condition or a learned habit of thought animating the continuous turn to war.[16] Pointing to the centrality of war to American national identity and politics, these approaches mark American history as having resorted to violence to achieve the goals of statecraft when expedient. War rhetoric, these scholars argue, grafts tropes of American exceptionalism onto a savage idiom to characterize military intervention as defensive, filled with noble purpose.

While situational factors and war culture have existed to some degree since the nation's inception, World War II marked a turning point. For much of the nation's history, America existed as a regional power, intent on consolidation. Having experienced war in the homeland with the attack on Pearl Harbor, political arguments designed to keep the country out of world affairs became unfeasible.[17] The wreckage of war collapsed European empires, fundamentally altering the dynamics of the geopolitical system and creating an opportunity for the United States to assume global leadership. At the same time, military technology became symbols of national pride and exemplars of technological achievement, abstracting the connection between military armaments and violence. The symbolic resonance of this specific form of power fueled American claims to global hegemony by equating military might with the right to govern.[18] As military industries and security concerns comingled, the use of violence as a legitimate form of statecraft moved into a prominent, visible position in American public culture.[19] Cementing a new form of militarization in American culture, World War II sparked a military buildup and consolidation of power that justified war as an agent of change.[20]

War culture, as a broad ideological critique, helps explain the structuring of public attitudes and the normalization of a militarized foreign policy, but it doesn't pinpoint the ways and means by which a nation finds itself routinely engaged in a policy of violence. Prior studies have sought to fill that gap by focusing on the president's role in making the case for war. While rich and sophisticated, these approaches have focused on rhetorical actions that induce the nation into war, leaving the end of war mostly unexamined. The lack of attention to the end-of-war discourse is startling because exiting a war is almost always a tricky affair requiring significant rhetorical maneuvering by the political leadership.[21] War rhetoric produces a viscous layer of discourse political leaders have to finesse at the end of conflict in order to resolve the tension between representational residues and the practical need to terminate war. Typified by what Roger Spiller called "an impenetrable wall of enmity," complex domestic debates inflamed by images of the enemy as a savage, barbaric force aggravate efforts at conciliation.[22] The interaction between declared victory conditions, strategic goals, operational possibilities, and public opinion further challenge presidents because they can't just end wars; they have to win them.[23] This dynamic has only worsened with the proliferation of non-state actors and the rise of ethnic conflict in the post–Cold War era as the level of animosity generated among participants hardens attitudes against reconciliation.[24]

This end-of-war context occludes presidents from abandoning war, even if they pledged to do so, and instead requires them to resolve the paradox of power by reframing and redefining the discursive context related to the enemy, the stakes of the conflict, and the terms of victory. This reframing must also end the war in ways that preserve, if not amplify American presence in world affairs. While prior studies have pointed to the challenges presidents face in overcoming metaphors of savagery and public insistence on victory, they have also infused depictions of the enemy with a stability that ignores the inherent slipperiness of the savage image and the inevitable slippage between the symbol and the symbolized.[25] Yet to be addressed is how presidents resolve the tension between archetypal figures of the enemy and the need to conclude war, recuperate relations with the enemy, invest in reconstruction, and develop a postwar rationale for a continued U.S. mission in world affairs. This book fills that gap.

Displacing Savagery at the End of War

Ending war poses one of the most significant and complicated rhetorical challenges a president can face. In addition to political and policy constraints, the language utilized by presidents and political culture to characterize the enemy during the war produces its own impediment to peace. For instance, in the lead-up to war with Iraq in 1991, George H. W. Bush declared, "Saddam Hussein systematically raped, pillaged, and plundered a tiny nation . . . and murdered innocent children."[26] While the claim was fact-checked endlessly, the wide acceptance of Saddam as a barbarous dictator intent on dominating Iraq's neighbors impeded the peaceful settlement of the conflict since no president could make peace with such an enemy. In most cases, presidential characterizations of enemies prior to war produce thorny rhetorical complications in the conflict's aftermath. Archetypal metaphors of savagery endure and manifest a significant hurdle for making peace because, to get out of a war, the enemy must be redeemed or otherwise dealt with.

While the savage idiom is protean in nature—it shifts and transforms over the course of the war—I will argue that periodically, particularly at the end of wars, depictions of the enemy become disrupted, fluid, and precarious. In those moments, presidents can overcome representations of the enemy and work toward peace by displacing savage depictions with a political language flexible enough to satisfy policy demands and public opinion.[27] This political language seeks to unmoor, dissolve, or recontextualize a singular meaning of the enemy constructed at the start of the war in favor of fluid representations that can displace tropes of savagery and realign policy to postwar contexts. Constituting a central, if previously unexamined component of end-of-war decision-making and postwar planning, acts of displacement by presidents and their staff provide a rhetorical exit strategy from war. That exit strategy facilitates transitions to peaceful international relations, justifies massive financial investment in rebuilding former foes or affected allies, and reveals the decisive role presidential communication strategies have on postwar outcomes.

Yet, refiguring the metaphoric field that has defined the enemy and the war incurs unexpected consequences for the president and the policy bureaucracy. Principally, the inconstancy of the enemy image in these moments—induced and facilitated by presidential speech—liberates a specific antagonist from the conflict at hand, but it also amplifies the necessity of American leadership in the postwar era. Far from an optimistic narrative about the possibilities for ending war or for identifying authentic discourses of peace, this book tells of how presidents confront past renditions of savagery, redefine them or mutate them, and recast representations of savagery to rationalize a continuing American mission in the world. Rather than resolving the problem posed by enduring metaphors of savagery, then, metaphoric shifts at the end of the war entrap speakers into the confines of the representational elements advanced by the metaphor. This entrapment takes the form of presidential claims about postwar insecurity and the potential for additional antagonists to extend an epistemology of otherization that sets the stage for subsequent U.S. military action. Thus, even while cultivating the conditions for an immediate peace, presidential end-of-war rhetoric authorizes policies that maintain, if not amplify, American power in ways that foster the conditions for the continuation of war.

American interests align in specific ways and, since at least the publication of Hans Morgenthau's classic *Politics among Nations*, have generally fallen along economic, security, and ideological lines.[28] While interest is an ever-shifting form of mimicry, evolving with international contexts, shifts in leadership, and public opinion, the pursuit of the national interest in the post–World War II era has entangled the United States in regional and global political institutions that present opportunities and constraints for American power. These entanglements fuse with presidential efforts to align interests and policies in ways that balance security concerns with economic goals, raising concerns about presidential management of foreign policy.[29] Critics have pointed to America's deep penetration into world affairs as producing a recurring pattern in which interests and policy fall out of alignment due to leadership changes, shifts in balances of power, and the inevitable instability of international contexts.[30] This problem manifests in its most extreme form after war, in which the international scene is highly unstable and requires significant realignment of policy and interests to fit the new parameters of the postwar order. It is from this backdrop that presidents displace the savage at the end of war to establish or sustain policy in response to shifting contexts. At times the discourse of displacement is opportunistic—it serves as a means for articulating U.S. power; at other times it operates as the mechanism by which presidents escape unfavorable conditions on the field of battle. The essential point, however, is that displacing savagery enables presidential agility in a quickly shifting context. While this does not guarantee successful policymaking, displacing savagery provides the president the rhetorical resources necessary to modulate policy in a shifting security environment.

Presidents employ four rhetorical strategies to revise representations of the enemy at the end of war: recivilization, mobility, erasure, and disembodiment. Strategies of recivilization refigure enemy character by portraying the citizens of enemy nations as victims of their leadership. These strategies dissociate definitions of the enemy from nation to antidemocratic ideologies that seek wars of aggression to consolidate power. Strategies of mobility relocate the source of savagery from the actual antagonist to an alternative source. That source could be a distant land or an ideological force. At other times this rhetoric refers to the antagonist as a client state acting on the behest of a more powerful one. Strategies of erasure shift the focus from international actors to the international scene itself, deemphasizing the antagonist's role in causing war in favor of a more generalized critique of international politics itself. Displacing attention from the enemy to the system, these strategies seek acts of melioration to structural fault lines. Finally, strategies of disembodiment distribute the savage across international space, displacing focus on any given antagonist in favor of an unlimited number of potential antagonists. Disembodying the enemy rationalizes continuous American military presence in world affairs even as it displaces attention from any given field of battle.

The strategies of displacement identified in this book enabled presidents to escape the rhetorical legacy of savage imagery, convert defeated foes into friends, and resolve concerns about the effectiveness and necessity of war generally. Beyond those immediate policy concerns, re-representing the enemy at the end of war also managed American power in times of systemic change. Rather than reflect a discourse of peace, presidential end-of-war discourse facilitated the continuation of war by other means and, in doing so, shifted the balance of war power toward the presidency, normalized public attitudes about the necessity of war, laid the foundation for the next war, and institutionalized war as a necessary component of the foreign affairs bureaucracy. Thus, this study of the rhetoric of savagery elucidates the structuring logic that animates presidential articulations of the enemy at the end of war to reveal the way linguistic choices rationalize a specific set of power relations that define and determine postwar policy.

To make the case, I trace presidential end-of-war discourses orchestrating the endings of World War II, Korea, Vietnam, and Afghanistan—the War on Terror—to mark the influence this discourse had on the development of U.S. foreign policy.[31] Each of these cases represents a different type of war conclusion. As I will discuss in more detail, World War II reveals the possibilities of recuperative rhetorics in the ideal case of complete submission. Korea relates the outcome of a limited deal—a cease-fire—and the sustained animus such an outcome produces. Vietnam examines the rhetorical gymnastics of a bad deal, difficult to explain to the public, and at cross-purposes with American foreign policy. And the War on Terror demonstrates how end-of-war rhetoric finesses policy when there is no possibility of a formal peace deal. While these cases may not exhaust all possible outcomes, they do represent archetypal examples of the types of wars presidents have ended.[32]

A chapter about Afghanistan and the War on Terror in a book about end-of-war discourse may generate concerns that the war has yet to conclude. These concerns, while understandable, hinge upon implicit disagreements between how one defines a war and the continuously violent practices of American statecraft. I take up this theme in the conclusion, but briefly, the term "war" invokes both a legal category and a colloquial description of a type of military practice. This distinction matters because by all measures the war in Afghanistan is over. U.S. military activities continue in Afghanistan and beyond, of course, but those activities cannot be properly referred to as war any more than the brutal occupation of the Philippines after the end of the Spanish-American War. The problem, here, is rooted in the very term. War represents a particular type of irruption, a shift away from the norm of "peace," and implies that the use of force is a limited, occasional tool of statecraft.[33] Employing a broad categorical definition of "war" to describe any and all military activities creates confusion about the types and forms of state-sponsored violence, undermines clarity about the types of discursive activities required to justify such actions, and risks masking critical inquiries that can unravel the complexities of American foreign policy. As I argue in the conclusion, the endless war thesis participates in this problem by inferring that the current era of violent statecraft is somehow new, different, and atypical, when in fact it is in the mainstream of the history of American foreign policy.

The rhetorical archive of this book derives from all of the end-of-war speeches by Harry S. Truman, Dwight D. Eisenhower, Richard Nixon, George W. Bush, and Barack Obama. While inelegant, I employ the that mass media shifted who presidents talked to and how they crafted those appeals.[37] While communication scholars have challenged Tulis's argument, they have also endorsed one of its central premises—that presidents have increasingly employed deliberative rhetoric to argue for their policy agendas.[38] Indeed, the dominant form of criticism parses presidential texts to center attention on the persuasive power of the president.[39] This approach has produced a broad catalog of the types of presidential persuasion, focusing on the rhetorical dynamics of the text and its relationship to place, audience, genre, context, and materialities.[40] By zeroing in on presidential utterances, this scholarship isolates the importance of presidential speech beyond the narrow confines of popular support and public persuasion.

Complementing this tradition, this book foregrounds the importance of the institutional setting as a site for policy deliberation. Concordant with Roderick P. Hart's claim that "public speech . . . is governance," the ways presidents articulate problems, opportunities, situations, and challenges in public and private implicate the administrative mechanisms used to implement policy.[41] Two things motivate this direction. First, relying on public comments to accomplish policy goals may not be the driving mechanism of postwar policy. While there are certainly some aspects of the policy agenda at the end of war that require congressional action, war authorization has already granted the president wide latitude to negotiate truces, design and implement strategies of occupation, or otherwise shift away from a war footing. In essence, the end-of-war context requires bureaucratic leadership rather than public persuasion. Other disciplines, of course, have attended to these needs, advancing studies about diplomacy, leadership style, and more.[42] But this book isolates presidential communication as an important, and overlooked, aspect of bureaucratic leadership.

Second, identifying the institutional components of presidential rhetoric raises rather than reduces the significance of presidential rhetoric. The presidential bureaucracy underwent a massive expansion immediately before, during, and after World War II. As John M. Murphy pointed out, "the 1939 Administrative Reorganization Act authorized the Executive Office of the President and arguably institutionalized 'the presidency.'" After the war, the 1946 Employment Act, 1946 Atomic Energy Act, and the 1947 National Security Act all acknowledged presidential responsibility for vast portions of the civilian and military economies, with the latter creating a security infrastructure that remains mostly intact today. Murphy argued, "the acts granted the president a dominant place when it came to the development and implementation of economic and defense policies."[43] While the president remained the public face of government, the position at the top of an expansive bureaucracy shifted the role from persuasion to administration. In that vein, presidential speech serves as "a resource that frames issues, creates institutional capacities, communicates with elites, provides inventional resources, balances" institutional power with public norms and expectations, and represents the executive to the public.[44] Recent scholarship has pointed to ways that the institutional presidency advances deliberation, buoys existent policies, provides campaigns with rhetorical resources, influences public attitudes about controversies, works against deliberation, undermines the policies of a prior president, and institutionalizes public discourse in the implementation of policy.[45] This study adds to present research by demonstrating how administrative actors adopt the president's linguistic strategies in ways that influence the implementation of policy.

Presidential speech impacts the functioning of the foreign-affairs and military bureaucracies by articulating and distributing worldviews or rationalities for how, when, and under what conditions war should end. These worldviews or rationalities—what Wendy Brown described as "normative political reason"—govern how the end of war can be understood and discussed.[46] While presidents enjoy significant latitude in speech and action, particularly given America's pliable vision of itself and Others, political rationalities are limited by the nation's "histories, traditions, memories, and typical discourses."[47] As Ned O'Gorman discerned, a successful rhetorical strategy "depend[s] in part on aligning the worldview of the strategy with the norms of those who [need] to be persuaded."[48] In practice, this give-and-take between institutional actors manifests as complex negotiations that see participants forward arguments that, according to Karlyn Kohrs Campbell, render them "points of articulation" rather than authors.[49] That is, presidents articulate specific types of political logic at the end of war within definitive and confining parameters. That logic operates as a technology of governance that guides how the executive bureaucracy approaches, understands, and responds to the challenges posed by a war's ending.

The significance of presidential rhetoric to this project, then, is not in its originality or its publicness, but rather in how presidents select and elevate certain theses about war and peace as parameters of governance. To paraphrase Edward Said, presidential administrative discourse disciplines policy debates by establishing criteria that map any given policy conversation. The disciplinary function polices the boundaries of what can be talked about, how it can be talked about, and under what situations one thing should be talked about instead of another. The power to perform that function is derived primarily from the unique position presidents enjoy as the principal administrative actor in the policy domain. Presidents, by speaking and directing others, generate vast quantities of administrative discourse. In this sense, they hold significance as "individual writers upon the otherwise anonymous collective body of texts constituting a discursive formation."[50] Behind any presidential articulation is a wide body of anonymous articulations in the form of policy memos, public comments, and policy guidelines that influence and are influenced by presidents. The authorial input of the president via executive, administrative speech provides rules, norms, and procedures for governance and, as Mary Stuckey put it, their rhetoric "resonates (or not) within the executive branch as an institution."[51]

Methodologically, I center inquiry on specific texts, and how those texts operate in their historical context and "within the networks of power that produce" them.[52] Presidential speech has become what Said called a "specialized language or discourse."[53] The public, the media, and the bureaucracy expect presidents to speak in certain ways, about certain topics and not others, and to perform the role of administrator, spiritual leader, commander in chief, and many other potential personas depending on contextual and personality factors. These expectations mesh with cultural precepts about the country, what O'Gorman called the "terms of nationhood," to complicate and constrain presidential latitude at the end of war. Presidents are expected to orchestrate an exit from war, in ways that fit cultural norms and expectations of a nation convinced of its own invincibility. The inability to express goals, strategies, and values with precision—best exemplified by George Kennan's lament that the policy bureaucracy had misunderstood his Long Telegram by implementing containment—drives presidents and administrative actors to search for and find an expressible vernacular that aligns strategic orientations with national expectations. O'Gorman refers to this as a "moral language" that shapes and frames policies.[54] This book locates the public shape of that moral language in the metaphoric economy presidents employ to articulate the challenges and opportunities present at the end of war. Gradually, that metaphoric economy shapes a presidential persona—"self-images, or identities"—that typifies the strategic approach to former enemies, the postwar era, and international relations themselves.[55]

Centering attention on the president's authoritative role in deliberations on enemy character and postwar policies demonstrates how presidential rhetoric reconfigures policy away from the practices of war even while extending wartime institutional arrangements into the postwar era and cultivating a bureaucratic attitude predisposed to managing international problems with violence. While there are problematics bigger than the president—things like war culture, the historical conditions of militarism, and the constraints imposed on any president by prior administrations, Congress, and public opinion—this genealogical approach isolates the decisive influence presidential rhetoric has on how the federal bureaucracy determines a war's outcome and manages the postwar era. Due to the president's constitutionally imbued role or persona of commander in chief, presidential rhetoric produces a textual authority by which policy agents and mass publics understand the enemy, war, and the terms of peace.[56] Even as the persona shifts at the end of war, the president's position as insider amplifies their institutional significance. The public and the bureaucracy continue to look to the president for rhetorical leadership and policy guidance, even if they disagree with or dispute the president's account.[57] Productive of an entire apparatus of administrative discourse, with dozens of subsequent agents who rearticulate the disciplinary boundaries articulated by the president, this rhetoric, as Stuckey argued, is "most effective when it is supported by institutional mechanisms" that articulate the implementation of policy.[58]

Enemies, Presidential Identities, and Concluding War

Resowing the Seeds of War centers end-of-war discourses of the enemy in the history of otherization as a continuously available rhetorical resource. This history highlights the fungibility of constitutive identities that contain what Chantal Mouffe called "multiple and contradictory" elements, are "always contingent and precarious, temporarily fixed," and subject to constant movement and displacement.[59] Temporarily constitutive representations of the Other are inherent to the symbol system because they are the building blocks of national identity. By defining Others, we define ourselves. As Michael Shapiro explained, this act of negotiation replicates processes of negation in which leaders seek out "dangerous forms of disorder, various Others . . . in attempts to produce an ideology of national coherence."[60] The need to distinguish between us and them predisposes leaders to seek out the next danger or next enemy as a means for extending coherence and meaning to representations of the nation.[61] In the early years of the republic, representations of the Other invoked what Jeremy Engels termed "enemyship" to recast public views about the British and establish a unique American identity.[62] The War of 1812 served this purpose by outlining distinctions between the two nations on the basis of their approach to politics and economics. Shapiro argued that the Indian Wars provided a powerful set of representations that consolidated American national identity on the basis of race and ancestry. Said revealed how Western representations of Middle Eastern and Asian people effaced difference and distilled non-European identities into dangerous and sexy archetypes.[63] And, Stuckey identified the ways presidents employ representations of the Other inside the country to reform understandings of national identity.[64] In short, the history of otherization points to the ways presidents and public figures employ representations of Others to articulate the nation's identity and mission.

Prior accounts of otherization at times of war have argued symbolic representations of the enemy ranging from barbaric to uncivilized or animalistic. Identifying the metaphoric forms that typify this discourse, studies have cataloged a narrow topoi or core images of the enemy, and inferred conceptions of enemy character modulate minimally during war.[65] Scholars like David Campbell, Robert Ivie, and more have argued that these discourses animate the nation to war by inflaming fears, passions, and racist attitudes. Presidents adopt and reiterate archetypal metaphors of savagery because they are familiar and accepted. They give force to policy that alternative arguments could not. As the discourse blankets public culture and gets taken up by policy elites, alternative conceptions for understanding the international situation and resisting the war drive become politically impractical. This account of savagery has repeated across American history, and in addition to the role it plays in defining national identity, it continues to serve as a rhetorical resource for presidential foreign-policy-making.

Rather than focus on how metaphors of savagery mobilize publics to respond to specific threats, in this book I examine the ways presidential acts to displace metaphoric representations of the enemy impact public comprehension of the enemy, alter the policy landscape, and create the conditions for peace, or not. Tropological and discursive representations of the enemy at the end of war reclassify enemy character in ways that enable the end of armed confrontation. This reclassification displaces totalized conceptions of the enemy in favor of more nuanced ones capable of distinguishing between the leaders and the people in order to blame the leaders and forgive the people. In the ideal situation, the fluidity instituted by these displacements provides presidents the discursive space necessary to rationalize investment in the foreign entity after the war in ways that beget a long-term relation between the ex-belligerents and would have been unthinkable in the early stages of the war. This thesis nuances current understandings of how political leadership talks about enemies by demonstrating the flexibility of representations, the conditions in which a foreign evil can give way to the good, and the pathway for citizens of enemy countries to rise from the ashes of war and constitute a democratic, American-friendly nation respectful of international law.

This analysis focuses on metaphor because of the trope's centrality to discussions of Others and the ease by which metaphors enter the vernacular while avoiding close scrutiny. Powerful representational devices, metaphors erode distinctions between the real and the perceived, melding the social world into a composite that actors can accept. To put it differently, metaphors advocate for "understanding and experiencing one kind of thing in terms of another," and derive strength by virtue of "being implicit and unexamined."[66] The definitional power of metaphor is such that totalized representations of danger enable the application of old tropes to new situations. Presidents incorporate metaphors to portray enemies; to characterize, contextualize, and explain the end of war; and to justify postwar policies. But this rhetoric is not deliberative in content. Rather, since metaphoric representations of the enemy at the end of war emanate from a position of absolute authority and, by nature, restrict understandings of the antagonist, they implicate public understandings of the international scene in a rhetorical economy from which there is no escape.

While public conceptions of the enemy play an important role in the execution of war, this book focuses on the ways presidential metaphors entrap policy elites with a specific understanding of the enemy and the implications that has for policy. Since, per Kenneth Burke, some forms of rhetorical discourse contain their own compulsion to see things out to their logical conclusion, the metaphoric economy that forms the basis of presidential end-of-war rhetoric prefigures the policy debates that arise at war's termination. The narrowing of options results from the orientational aspects of the set of associations articulated by the metaphor. Once circulated, metaphors extend the logical implications of their depictions—what Michael Osborn and Douglas Ehninger termed "extensions."[67] For example, if finance is understood as a high-stakes game, then audiences interpret economic success or loss in terms of winners and losers, and opportunity as equal. This narrowing process, as Kathleen Hall Jamieson put it, "simultaneously create[s] inventional possibilities and impose[s] inventional constraints."[68] One only has to recall presidential depictions of the enemy as an unruly, aggressive barbarian to get the point. The nation cannot negotiate with the uncivilized. Tropes of savagery create the possibility of national violence to remedy the problem of insecurity, even as they close off the potential for diplomatic resolution.

In institutional settings, metaphors connect disarticulated fragments of meaning and drive understandings of events, situations, and the necessary response. As an inventional resource in policy debates, metaphors have become what Ronald Walter Greene called a "technology of governance."[69] This rhetorical technology "defines a discursive field in which exercising power is 'rationalized,'" and "structures specific forms of intervention" into the defined field.[70] For example, articulating a dispute with China as a trade war shifts the bureaucratic focus from negotiation to retaliation. This materialist conception of metaphor suggests that metaphors penetrate bureaucratic settings to produce "new institutional arrangements by bringing together divergent discursive domains."[71] Institutional actors, particularly presidents, imprint the contours of the master metaphor upon the institutions in which they operate, establishing a sort of *phronesis* or practical wisdom about how government should address a given problem. By associating commonplaces that link and limit meaning, the president's rhetorical act provides one-way designations for guiding institutional actors on how to respond to emergent policy challenges.[72]

As the rhetorical material of policy, the routine ways of thinking enacted by metaphor also reflect back on the speaker, producing a persona or identity that guides and orients their approach to the policy problem. In times of war, depicting the enemy as barbaric induces a presidential persona of commander in chief. The investiture of the commander-in-chief persona reduces the policy approach from a broad array of options—including negotiation—to a singular one: the use of force.[73] By establishing a persona that the speaker is bound to embody, metaphors invest the presidency in a discursive circuit in which the metaphoric depiction of the problem resolves disagreements about the security threat and induces a line of policy response geared toward discovering the best remedy to the asserted danger. For example, NSC-68 articulated the Soviet Union as a "slave state" out to dominate the world, and Soviet policy as representative of a "fanatic faith, antithetical to our own," totalizing the danger posed by the enemy as a means for engaging a substantive policy discussion.[74] Framing the challenge in terms of good versus evil pitted the United States in spiritual contest with the Soviets. In doing so, the framing shifted foreign-policy debates from deliberations about insecurity to questions of containment. In this way, the metaphor avoided deeply rooted questions about empire, danger, and America's position as provocateur.

Presidential metaphoric choices, then, narrow the horizon of policy possibility and assign to the speaker an identity mirroring the metaphor's entailments. When presidents extend new metaphors or revitalize old ones to displace representations of savagery, they constitute a persona that orients postwar policy. Those displacements shift characterizations of the enemy from barbarian to victim, animal to immature subject, or evil to afflicted, constructing new identities for the Other to confront prevalent, racist attitudes toward the enemy. Without exception, the presidents examined in this book employed metaphoric choices that finessed pervasive fears, recast racist depictions, and diagnosed facets of international conditions relevant to American interests. But, each act of depiction reflected back onto the presidency and the policy bureaucracy, binding the speaker to a persona implied by the articulated metaphor. That presidential persona constrained and directed policy, encouraging presidents to carry out a policy program suitable for the reconfigured security challenge.

By focusing on this important but understudied discourse, this book attends to the rhetorical means by which presidents and their bureaucracies articulate the postwar challenge to reshape policy. This analysis indicates how presidents manage fraying control of agenda, framing, context, and policy by assuming a role consistent with their ideology, their party, and the political and cultural context in which they emerge. Parsing these choices offers a means for evaluating presidential leadership and speech at the end of war. Some presidents manage complicated postwar contexts involving domestic and international factors. Others don't. And the difference is largely a function of the presidential persona adopted and how that role fits the postwar context. This book encourages scholars of presidential rhetoric to think of the significance of presidential speech outside the confines of the instrumental/constitutive divide and instead conceive of presidential speech as operative upon the president, the party, the institution, and the public—to see presidential speech as indicative of a logic structure that it helps establish.

Finally, this study explains the permanence of American power in the postwar era. Institutionalists note the installation of American power in postwar institutions like the United Nations, the World Bank, the International Monetary Fund, and other international bodies that are located in the United States and influence international economics and power distribution. They argue that American power became a permanent fixture in international relations because of American leadership of those institutions and American military expenditures, interventions, and the nuclear arms race. Concentrating on the presidential logic that shaped American policy engagement with those institutions, across distinct periods, nuances rather than contests this analysis. It also demonstrates the truth of George Kennan's claim that "the aftermaths of wars are the decisive moments of foreign policy" by pointing to the ways discursive choices provide policy with new energy and new direction.[75] Highlighting the transition points when one discourse flows into another demonstrates how the management of peace mobilizes constituent identities in ways that facilitate the reproduction and the continuity of American power, even when war undermines or jeopardizes national standing in the world.

Examining the discourse of the enemy at the end of war is a critical act that seeks to uncover the ways metaphoric shifts blur distinctions between war and peace, influence postwar policy, and lay the foundation for the next war. The portrayal of savagery presented here amplifies conventional views of archetypal metaphors by examining the ways representations of the Other modulate depending on political and security calculations at the end of war. This project isolates transitional representations of the Other as a process vital for sustaining the politics of representation in international relations. More succinctly, my thesis suggests that avenues for change, modulation, and transition constitute one reason distinctions between "us" and "them" endure as a discourse. These acts of transformation shift conceptions of the enemy, but they don't banish discourses of otherization. Instead, this work underscores how the systemic and regular use of otherization as a primary tactic for justifying postwar policy inscribes the nation in cycles of war from which we have yet to escape. The metaphoric movement elaborated—sometimes occurring instantaneously—reflects the episodic nature of war rhetoric and the continuity of the history of otherization. There is always another enemy, another savage.

The cases that follow bear out the point. Chapter 1 argues that Truman's selection of disease metaphors at the end of World War II finessed attitudes toward the defeated foes by explaining the cause of war as the symptom of weak German and Japanese body politics. This rhetoric contextualized the rise of fascism as the outcome of fixable flaws, justifying occupation and reconstruction in the process. By assigning the cause of the war to the disease of Nazism and militarism, Truman's end-of-war rhetoric enacted the president-as-doctor persona, limiting presidential management of the postwar era to policies associated with observation, diagnosis, treatment, and follow-up. These metaphors and the flexibility they instituted seeded the postwar era with an organizing principle or framework for understanding the rise of enemies generally. That framework interpreted the rise of antagonists as an outcome of anti-democratic and anti-capitalist diseases that pervert and twist the minds of enfeebled citizens to support aggressive forms of militarism. When confronted with Soviet intransigence and hostility, the doctor metaphor found new life in Truman's articulation of his policy to contain Soviet power.

Chapter 2 charts shifting metaphoric conceptions of the enemy and danger in Korea from the domain of the disease/doctor metaphoric pair to metaphors of competition. That movement began with Truman's depiction of the invasion as a criminal action, enabled by the Soviet Union. The crime metaphor consigned American efforts to the domain of police action, which became problematic after Truman authorized General Douglas MacArthur to cross the 38th parallel and attempt to re-unify the peninsula. With China's intervention in the war and the stale-mate that followed, Truman sought to escape the conflict by rhetorically transferring the savage from Korea to the Soviet Union. Hamstrung by diplomatic impasses, however, the task ultimately fell to Dwight D. Eisenhower. Upon assuming the presidency, Eisenhower found pur-chase with the metaphor of competition, depicting the conflict in Korea as but one of several struggles across a global field of contest. Entailing the president in the persona of the game player, this metaphoric shift facilitated a negotiated settlement in Korea while setting the stage for the next confrontation in Southeast Asia.

For both Truman and Eisenhower, ideological orientations evoked metaphoric pairs that guided and constrained their end-of-war rheto-ric and, in consequence, the national-security bureaucracies tasked with implementing presidential visions. Richard Nixon's belief that he could win the war in Vietnam, too, shaped his end-of-war rhetoric and his policy approach. Chapter 3 charts two rhetorical displacements in Nixon's rhetoric of the enemy. First, Nixon explained the cause of the conflict not as ideological, but as the outcome of a poorly structured or fractured set of international relationships. Second, Nixon abandoned the competition metaphor used to explain the danger posed by commu-nism—specifically the metaphor of falling dominoes—in favor of meta-phors of architecture that spoke to the structure of international relations themselves. This new political language of the war erased the figure of the enemy, rendering the North Vietnamese a mere manifestation of the true, spectral danger of power imbalances. Entwining the president in the persona of architect, the metaphoric economy of architecture echoed across the foreign affairs bureaucracy to articulate peace as something planned, built, and transacted. While Nixon left the White House in disgrace prior to the end of the war, the discursive imprint of his rhetoric of absence detached the nation from the particulars of Vietnam, justified the establishment of diplomatic relations with China, and enabled rapprochement with the Soviet Union. It also pointed to foundational elements employed by George W. Bush and Barack Obama to represent the enemy in the War on Terror.

Chapter 4 contends that Obama's end-of-war rhetoric sought to disembody the enemy by cloaking its identity in mystery and emphasizing the disembodied structures used by the enemy to endanger the West. While the parameters of the disembodied enemy were present at the inception of the War on Terror, Obama's discourse diffused and distributed the enemy across time and space, rendering the modern antagonist a precarious sort of fighting force with an ever-shifting membership, unbound by nationality or race. This movement diminished the importance of Afghanistan in favor of a systematic rebalancing of the War on Terror to focus on the sanctuaries and digital networks used to plot and orchestrate attacks. The chapter maps the rhetorical depiction of the savage across the Bush and Obama administrations to demonstrate how the same metaphors gave rise to different presidential personae and policy attitudes. For Bush, the existence of terrorist sanctuaries and organizational networks signaled the existence of a disordered, ungoverned world that needed frontier justice. His depiction of the enemy represented the danger as emerging not from the terrorists themselves, but rather from two conditions that made terrorism possible—ungoverned territory and nations hostile to the West willing to harbor terrorists. Embodying the persona of the sheriff on the lawless frontier, Bush sought to occupy and democratize the frontier as a means to prevent the danger posed by terrorism. Obama, having pledged to end the war in Iraq and win in Afghanistan, also employed the discourse of the safe haven and the metaphor of the network to depict the danger posed by terrorism. But, rather than signify the need to bring the law to the lawless, Obama instead characterized the nation as an international sentinel, always on the lookout for danger. Embodying the persona of the watchman justified the gradual end of the occupations, but it also reordered the national-security bureaucracy away from democratization and pacification and toward efforts to seek, find, and destroy terrorists before they could launch deadly attacks. This rhetoric, an end-of-war discourse committed to the withdrawal of ground forces but not an end of national violence, underwrote the rise of aerial bombardment as the preferred policy for addressing terrorists in ungoverned or hostile territory.

This study of savagery, as the iconic rhetorical vehicle for the implementation of foreign policy, identifies how fluid depictions of the enemy amplify presidential power at the end of war while authoring a postwar policy regime that ensures the continuation of American hegemony. Each of the selected cases demonstrates how metaphoric displacement aligns policy to fit the rearticulated enemy and indexes the new entailments those metaphors enact upon the president. The flexibility afforded by shifting depictions of the enemy provides presidents with a crucial resource at the end of war—options. Presidents who enjoy multiple rhetorical options enjoy greater latitude of action when confronting diverse and unstable rhetorical and geopolitical contexts. Presidents who find their options significantly constrained have difficulty developing and justifying policies capable of addressing the new complex of power that appears at the end of war. Counterintuitively, enacting strategies to displace savagery reduces and restricts the domain of possible policy actions. The fluidity of representations of the enemy at the end of war, then, expands and contracts presidential policy options as metaphoric choices entrench a governing logic that regulates and justifies the president's views of the international situation, the policy approach required, and the articulation of continuing danger.

While *Resowing the Seeds of War* is a story about the inherent flexibility of representations of the enemy, it is also a story about the continuity of political violence in statecraft. Unraveling this political language amplifies our understanding of why America preaches peace but engages in policies that ensure the continuation of war. Indexing presidential articulations of the enemy provides a snapshot of a broader process in which presidents employ figures of savagery at the end of war to serve political and policy goals. Principally, this discourse mobilizes depictions of the enemy, international relations, and the potential for new threats to extend, deepen, and perpetuate the rationale for American leadership in the world. As a primary rationale for the expansion of American power, these metaphors establish the terms and outlooks by which to understand additional challenges in the postwar era, making continued confrontation with foreign adversaries inevitable. In other words, *Resowing the Seeds of War* concludes that the language used to depict the defeated foe extends and amplifies the discourse of otherization, while establishing the conditions for the next episode of armed confrontation with foreign Others. Institutional discourses of peace have always been discourses of war.

CHAPTER 1

The Recivilized Savage:

HARRY TRUMAN AND THE VICTORY
OF THE GOOD WAR

———•◆•———

rom Trafalgar Square to Times Square, millions of people around the world celebrated the end of World War II. First with Germany's surrender on May 7, 1945, and then with the end of the war in the Pacific on August 14, masses of people flooded the streets of Europe and North America, euphoric at the end of a civilization-shaking conflict. In New York, a photographer for *Life* snapped a picture of a uniformed sailor kissing a nurse in what became one of the most celebrated images of the twentieth century.[1] For many Americans the image symbolized the end of the war and the dawn of a new era of peace.[2] Public eagerness to demobilize spiked with the end of the war in the Pacific.[3] After a decade of economic catastrophe, the rise of fascism and dictatorship, and a devastating global war, the nation wanted to return to normalcy.[4] Secretary of State James Byrnes put it simply, "Families want the boy[s] home."[5] Yet, the end of the war didn't herald a return to normalcy. With much of Europe and Asia in ruins, political leaders worried economic and human

1

insecurity would create "fertile ground for the spread of extremism," contribute to the rise of a new fascism, and heighten the risk of another global war. Germany and Japan had been central to European and Asian economies, and their destruction undermined the global economic landscape.[6] Rivalry between the United States and the Soviet Union during and after the war warned of a return of international politics governed by competition over spheres of influence.[7] And, Franklin D. Roosevelt's death on April 12, 1945, combined with Winston Churchill's electoral defeat to Clement Attlee a few months later, left an immense leadership vacuum in the management of the war and beyond.[8]

Harry S. Truman, inexperienced and uninformed in matters of foreign policy, inherited the awesome responsibility of winning the war and securing the peace. That responsibility involved maintaining national unity after V-E Day, developing a rationale for occupation and reconstruction of Germany and Japan, and communicating the necessity for American leadership in the postwar era.[9] After initial gestures toward cooperation with the Soviets, the Red Army's plundering of Eastern Germany soured Truman's attitude toward the wartime alliance and the long-term potential for cooperation. Concerned about the potential for a similar division in Asia, he increased efforts to force Japan's concession prior to Soviet acquisition of territory in the region and, after the war, resisted Soviet attempts to partition Japan.[10] The danger of geopolitical rivalry in a new era in which American scientists had "harness[ed] the basic power of the universe" hung over these concerns.[11] In the immediate aftermath of the war, the prospect of an atomic age contributed to America's decision to occupy and rebuild Germany and Japan to counterbalance Soviet power. But the bomb also fundamentally altered the structure of international relations by rendering all nations vulnerable to utter annihilation, generating deep public anxiety about the viability of ever achieving global peace.[12]

While these shifts in power, vulnerability, and fear complicated the policy agenda, the postwar futures of Germany and Japan posed a more immediate challenge. By the end of the war, the circulation of stories detailing Germany's "ghastly war crimes . . . triggered a deep, worldwide revulsion that darkened the German name for decades," raising questions about Truman's occupation and reconstruction program.[13] The shock of these revelations reverberated deeply across the American foreign-policy bureaucracy, leading even moderate policymakers to favor a hardline approach toward Germany. Secretary of Treasury Henry Morgenthau, in particular, argued that occupation must force Germans to understand "that the whole nation has engaged in a lawless conspiracy against the decencies of modern civilization."[14] More pragmatic members of the administration objected to a Carthaginian peace, warning it "would resemble what the Nazis had done to their victims, namely 'be a crime against civilization itself.'"[15] While Truman's moderate, pragmatic voice ultimately won out, the internal debate underscores the profound impact the war and evidence of concentration camps had on policy debates. Anti-German attitudes presented a serious and enduring hurdle to his attempts to rhetorically recast Germany as a civilized nation.[16]

In Asia, the intensity of racist animosity directed at the Japanese represented a significant hurdle for ending the war and for recuperating amicable relations.[17] Unlike in Europe, a war that inflicted damage primarily upon European nations, the Japanese attack at Pearl Harbor penetrated national territory, humiliated the nation, and exposed an inherent vulnerability of the era.[18] As one historian put it, the union of vulnerability and racism "reinforce[ed] pressure for a hard-line policy toward Japan."[19] Government propaganda contributed to public attitudes by portraying the Japanese as less-than-human vermin out to rape and plunder. One such image, "The Barbarous Jap," for instance, depicted an ape-like figure wearing a Japanese military uniform with the word "Tojo" on the arm, clawing at the corpse of a dead American airman. Tojo's face perfectly demonstrated the blurring of man and ape, and the image represented an archetypal depiction of the Japanese in World War II by the American press, soldiers, citizens, and politicians.[20] Racial animosity contributed to the internment of close to 100,000 Japanese Americans in 1942 and reached its apex near the end of the war with talk in public and government that it would be better to exterminate the entire Japanese race than to negotiate a settlement.[21] The desire to destroy Japan remained strong even after the war when at least one public opinion poll claimed that "nearly one quarter of those polled . . . regretted that the U.S. did not have the opportunity to use more atomic bombs before the Japanese surrender."[22] For Truman, dehumanizing discourse and public calls for Japan's extermination impeded efforts to justify the occupation, reconstruction, and restoration of a sovereign Japan.[23]

Pressed to overcome these discursive obstacles by the pragmatics of strategic rivalry, Truman needed a vernacular that could rationalize the reconstruction of Germany and Japan and, eventually, facilitate their reintegration into the world as sovereign, democratic nations. With the geographic and economic importance of both regions impossible to ignore, and archetypal, racist depictions of the Axis deeply embedded in perceptions of the enemy, Truman shifted the figurative economy to revise enemy character and give purpose to American actions abroad. His rhetorical strategy recuperated the enemy via two overlapping tactics: dissociating the enemy from the people to the leaders and articulating the German and Japanese people as contaminated by toxic ideologies that had driven them mad for power. Both tactics advanced nuanced portraits of the Axis powers, amplified German and Japanese victimhood, and justified American assistance as the appropriate remedy to the disease of totalitarianism. This transformation of enemy character bridged policy demands with political realities by positing the possibility that the Axis powers could be saved. Becoming the fabric that bound together interest and ideology to recivilize the Axis, rationalize reconstruction, and enable their readmission to international society, it also redefined the international scene as perpetually in need of the type of oversight and intervention Truman could provide, inaugurating American power as a permanent fixture in global affairs.

At its base, Truman's recivilizing discourse employed a form of the body politic metaphor to establish a set of parameters for determining the true nature of the enemy. This metaphor finessed representations of enemy character and provided a basic, paradigmatic orientation for postwar understandings of the Axis by articulating Germany and Japan as bodies-in-distress. While metaphors equating the polis to the body have existed since virtually the origin of advanced human thought, the metaphor resurged in the form of disease metaphors to depict the Axis powers during and after World War II.[24] For Truman, disease metaphors contextualized the rise of fascism in Europe and Asia by representing the German and Japanese people as patients infected by an anti-democratic ideology.[25] Such rationalizations imbued the discourse of the enemy with a figurative body, susceptible to contagion and in need of prophylaxis. It also activated a lexicon of metaphors linked to notions of the body enfeebled by disease and suffering from disorders of the mind. Depicting the Axis as physically and mentally debilitated displaced savage representations of the enemy by identifying the ways an externally imposed ideology had bent the will of a malleable people. Orchestrating a representational shift from savage or subhuman to infirm or guileless patients, these metaphors claimed that proper, democratic governance could treat the symptoms of the disease, inoculate the people against external sources of savagery, and address the patient's mental incapacity. The nation-as-weak-body-politic metaphor and its progeny personified the Axis polities in terms of health and sickness, strength and weakness, and labor and rest. In doing so, these metaphors provided a linguistic currency that urged collective action to reincorporate individuals into the national corpus.[26] In the years after the war, the embedded coherence of this metaphoric economy recivilized Germany and Japan and served as the primary rationale for occupation, humanitarian relief, reconstruction.

Truman's recivilizing rhetoric rationalized reconstruction of the Axis powers, but it also constituted a postwar persona of the doctor and figured the nation as caretaker of the international community. His displacement of savagery structured postwar international relations by articulating nations-as-bodies, vulnerable to outside forces that could take advantage of puerile impulses. This act of diagnosis prepared the nation for the full recuperation of postwar relations, but it also reflected back on the speaker to justify a treatment regimen up to the task of curing that which had infected the world. Constitutive of the postwar persona of the doctor, these metaphors rendered the Axis as patients in need of American medicine. The doctor persona—implicit in Truman's definition of the enemy and the cause of the war—figured the president as a benevolent, paternalistic physician engaged in a custodial relationship with the Axis powers.[27] Establishing a relationship between the physician and the patient typical for the 1940s, the persona positioned Truman in the role of absolute "authoritarian and sacerdotal" authority.[28] Obligating Truman to take decisions based on the patient's best interests, the persona initially entailed the provision of humanitarian relief to ensure their survival.[29] But it also articulated the president's role in the postwar era as to observe, diagnose, and treat the causes of disorder. Permeating the foreign-policy bureaucracy, the persona bonded the presidency with an obligation to tend, protect, and nurture the Axis powers until their eventual reintegration into the civilized society of nations.

The paradigmatic reorientation enacted by the embodied persona of president-as-doctor also stimulated new possibilities for American power in the postwar era. Invested with a paternalistic obligation to ensure the good health of all nations, the metaphoric displacement charted in this chapter merged with Truman's efforts to build a liberal international order abroad, and his efforts to convert wartime military departments into permanent fixtures.[30] The doctor persona synced with concerns about the potential return of toxic political ideologies and competition with the Soviets to prescribe a specific role for American leadership after the war. Marking a permanent shift in how the United States understood and interacted in the world, the metaphoric entailments of the disease-doctor pair provided the principal rationale for material changes to the foreign affairs bureaucracy, most importantly the National Security Act of 1947, which created the Department of Defense, the National Security Council, and the Central Intelligence Agency,[31] and the reorganization of the State Department, the creation of a Policy Planning Staff, and a fivefold increase in area experts.[32] Those metaphors also served Truman's call to quarantine and contain the dangers posed by communism in 1947.

To be clear, Truman's displacement of the enemy did not cause this shift. Rather, his recivilizing rhetoric and the institutional shifts that accompanied that discourse participated in an ongoing discourse of seeing threats in medical terms and American power as remedy. By relying on that discourse to qualify American policy in Germany and Japan, Truman rationalized reconstruction and extended the regime of surveillance and treatment to the parts of the world most damaged by the war. He also strengthened his case for the wholesale reorganization of the government and aligned the policy bureaucracy to act collectively to identify areas of danger in the world, propose and administer remedies, and ensure the peace.

Displacing Enemy Character at the End of World War II

At the end of World War II, recivilizing the savage involved narrowing the scope of depictions of the enemy from national identities—Germans and Japanese—to national leaders and their anti-democratic ideologies. This movement, what Murray Edelman termed a "displacement of resentments onto personified targets," refocused culpability for the war from the people to leaders in preparation of a more complex postwar discourse designed to manage representations of the Axis powers.[33] Truman signaled this movement in his first presidential address. He reiterated the justification for the war, pointed to progress, and claimed, "America, along with her brave allies . . . are assisting in the liberation of entire nations. Gradually, the shackles of slavery are being broken by the forces of freedom . . . The armies of liberation today are bringing to an end Hitler's ghastly threat to dominate the world. Tokyo rocks under the weight of our bombs."[34] This rhetoric signaled the recuperative potential of the savage in two ways. First, Truman displaced blame for the war from the German and Japanese people to Hitler and Tokyo. The synecdochic movement distanced German and Japanese citizens from their role in the war by diagnosing the true cause as the consolidation of power in the hands of a few power-hungry leaders. At the same time, this rhetoric articulated nations as bodies in bondage. American efforts sought to shepherd the victimized into an era of peace by unshackling the people from dictatorial regimes. This depiction of bodies in bondage deprived the nations affected by the war of agency, rendering them victims of an ideology that prioritized government by the few at the expense of the many.

Blaming leaders for war instead of the people is common for presidential war rhetoric. James K. Polk blamed the Mexican-American War on the failure of the Mexican government to establish a democratic government.[35] William McKinley claimed he sought every avenue to avoid war with Spain, but the Spanish government had left him no choice but to request a "formal declaration . . . of war."[36] Woodrow Wilson distinguished between the Kaiser and Germans to rationalize American entrance into World War I.[37] Roosevelt claimed beating Germany "would open the door for a thorough remaking of German popular attitudes," including the complete eradication of the militarized culture responsible for the war.[38] Truman extended this strategy, but with two caveats. First, as Michael Dobbs noted, "hatred could not be turned on and off, like a tap."[39] The American public desired to punish the enemy, saw no distinction between the people and the Axis powers, and no amount of rhetorical alchemy could transmute such animus. Second, insisting on unconditional surrender sustained the war rhetoric necessary to impassion the American public. Attempts to distinguish the leaders from the people, as with Roosevelt's declaration that the German leadership had implemented a war against the interests of their own people, could not recivilize the enemy when there was still fighting to be done.[40] This recuperative rhetoric gained new life after the war, when the president claimed the Germans and Japanese had been victims of their anti-democratic governments, led astray by noxious notions, to elicit interest in occupation and reconstruction. With the nation primed for a return to normalcy, conceptions of the enemy as victims, rather than as partners in the crime of war, facilitated reconstruction and the eventual normalization of relations.

Germany's unconditional surrender on May 8, 1945, innervated Truman's dissociation of the people from their leaders. Abandoning totalizing characterizations of the enemy and refocusing attention on eliminating the last vestiges of Nazism, he noted the country had paid a "terrible price . . . to rid the world of Hitler and his evil band," and maintained that the Allies proved "stronger by far than the might of the dictators or the tyranny of military cliques."[41] This iteration distinguished between the leaders and the people by blaming a small group of dictators for the war. These groups or cliques—by definition anti-democratic—had exerted their will without regard to the interests of the people. Underscoring the distinction between the Nazi-as-enemy and the German people, Truman claimed that surrender "of all the armies of Nazidom" had freed "the oppressed people of Europe from . . . Nazi barbarians."[42] These specifications disarticulated the German people from tropes of savagery and prepared for the end of the war when it would be incumbent upon the nation to invest in the reconstruction of Europe. Truman continued the theme at a news conference a week later, declaring, "There can be no restoration of a free German press in Germany until the elimination of Nazi and militarist influence has been completed. We are not going to lose the peace by giving license to racialist Pan-Germans, Nazis and militarists, so that they can misuse democratic rights in order to attack Democracy as Hitler did."[43] Crediting German civil society with a strong desire to play a productive role in rebuilding the nation, the statement warned of the danger of the Nazi ideology persisting and circulating in postwar Germany. Giving a strange kind of agency to the ideology, characterized as an aspect of the disease metaphor, this rhetoric warned of the communicable potential of Nazism itself. Since most Germans were members of the Nazi party, the act of division also conditioned the possibility for the recivilization of the German people on the complete elimination of a worldview responsible for the war.[44]

Distinguishing between the Nazi ideology and German citizens marked the people as victims while burdening them with the responsibility for their own rehabilitation. Displacing the onus from Germans to Hitler's mad desire for power didn't exonerate the people, however. Hitler's madness had permeated German society, after all. Instead, this redefinition of the enemy released the people from a degree of responsibility, while demanding they participate in their own recovery. The Allied statement at Potsdam, for example, formalized the recivilizing elements implicit in this redefinition by targeting the danger of militarism and

Nazism. The report pledged to "dissolve all Nazi institutions," punish war criminals, and ensure "the German people . . . atone for the terrible crimes committed under the leadership."[45] Almost exculpatory in nature, the rhetoric constricted the definition of the savage to the Nazi Party, its leaders, and its institutional arrangements. Placing Germans in opposition to their leadership pitted the inhumanity of Nazism against the innate humanity of the people and implied the Germans were worth saving. But they had to show their commitment to peace with action. These arguments established Nazism and its penetration into German society as a primary target of postwar occupation efforts, justifying denazification and demilitarization in the postwar era. While denazification proved controversial and ineffective, narrowing the scope of savagery to the German leadership raised the possibility of eventual forgiveness, charted a course for German recivilization, and opened a path for the reintegration of the German people and government into democratic life.

In the Pacific theater, where the war continued apace, Truman contended with widespread bureaucratic and cultural antipathy toward the enemy. The sneak attack at Pearl Harbor, news reports of Japanese barbarity against Allied forces and the Chinese, the "rape of Nanking," and propaganda describing "Japanese mistreatment of American prisoners" all contributed to a level of American hatred toward Japan "exceeding even their antipathy toward Germans."[46] These views created two specific problems for Truman. First, administration officials worried that notions of the Japanese as subhuman, nonthinkings beings underestimated the challenge in the Pacific.[47] In much private deliberation, policymakers fretted that underestimating the Japanese jeopardized Truman's ability to achieve unconditional surrender.[48] Truman addressed this concern in his announcement of Germany's surrender by foregrounding the danger in the Pacific and blaming the "treacherous tyranny of the Japanese" for the genesis of the war.[49] While this rhetoric muted the most racist versions of the savage image, it extended archetypal elements of public war rhetoric to evoke awareness about the continuing nature of the Japanese threat. In doing so, it created a secondary problem for Truman: unleashing and energizing anti-Japanese war rhetoric in the short term could help the nation win the war, but it would impede his ability to argue for postwar occupation and reconstruction.

Over the last three months of the war, his public depiction of the Japanese resolved this tension by extending nuanced explanations of their character to nourish the war drive while leaving space for postwar occupation efforts. In a radio address celebrating unconditional surrender on September 1, 1945, he asked the country to not forget Pearl Harbor and the "evil done by the Japanese war lords." Attending to public passions opposing assistance to Japan, the message extended the dissociation between Japan's leaders and its people. It also hinted at long-term occupation as capable of ensuring their successful transition to democratic capitalism. Claiming "it is our responsibility" to ensure the peace lasts, he reminded the nation that "victory always has its burdens and its responsibilities as well as its rejoicing."[50] The setting did not invite additional remarks, but the point remained. Truman's immediate postwar position inferred that the mission to achieve the peace had not concluded, that he had a responsibility to ensure that war did not recur. Indeed, the next day he commended the armed forces for their efforts, but warned the end of combat didn't signal the end of the effort. Instead, he explained, it signified that "we can turn now to the grave task of preserving the peace . . . a task which requires our most urgent attention."[51]

The initial move to induce distinctions into German and Japanese character shifted depictions from flat, one-dimensional portraits of national bodies enraged by savage passions to more nuanced versions reflecting distinctions between the leadership and the people. To extend this rhetorical trajectory, Truman disarticulated the German and Japanese people from their responsibility for the war by diagnosing corporal and mental disorders that had infected the national body politic. By framing totalitarianism as a disease, Truman could explain the irrationality of the Axis commitment to war in the face of sure defeat as a feature of the contagion of ideology. This metaphoric maneuver, combined with nuanced articulations of the enemy people, recivilized the savage and fostered the conditions for the renewal of friendship and the ultimate inclusion of the Axis powers into the postwar, anti-communist power structure. In public speeches and internal deliberations, Truman returned to the language of medicine to explain the postwar situation, his policy approach, and his attitude toward the defeated foes. Doing so reaffirmed the president's postwar identity of doctor and American-style capitalism the cure.

At the end of the war, Truman's metaphoric economy specified Nazism and militarism as etiologic agents that had infected the German and Japanese body politics and required immediate treatment. These metaphors reconstituted the enemy's national publics by amplifying distinctions between the "true" Germans and Japanese and the internal and external elements that threatened those identities. A central aspect of this rhetoric relied on a thesis that nations of mental fitness make rational calculations about their best interests, leading to good decision-making. In this context, the failure to capitulate when faced with utter destruction signaled the enemy's disorder of the mind. As Truman put it on the event of Germany's surrender in Italy, the Axis "must recognize the meaning of the increasing, swifter-moving power now ready for the capitulation or the destruction of the . . . arrogant enemies of mankind." Their failure to do so could only be attributed to them being "lost in fanaticism or determined upon suicide."[52] Attributing German responsibility for the war to the madness of fanaticism explained the war drive as a sort of mental disease that could occur to anyone, anywhere, given certain material factors. It also shifted depictions of the enemy from a "single representation of the body politic" to a more nuanced one that envisioned national bodies as masses of diverse citizens.[53] Figuring the Axis nations as bodies in mental distress underscored the need for treatment rather than punishment and provided a rationale for purging the undesirable elements thought to contaminate the body politic—in this case, Nazism and warlordism.[54] Doing so scapegoated the militarist ideology and leadership for the war while freeing the people from a degree of personal responsibility.

The diagnosis of madness—manifest in the form of an unreasonable commitment to war and self-slaughter—extended to the Japanese as well. Truman's call for unconditional surrender mapped this discourse by isolating the source of aggression as a character flaw exploited by Japan's leaders. As with Germany, this rhetoric displaced representations of the enemy in two ways. First, Truman posited rationality as the guidepost by which international conduct should be governed. He claimed the commitment to fight in spite of "the striking power and intensity of our blows" and the inevitability of utter destruction, and demonstrated the cavalier and arrogant attitude of Japan's leaders. Warning that "our blows will not cease until the Japanese military and naval forces lay down their arms in unconditional surrender," this rhetoric represented the enemy as vainglorious and irrational.[55] For Truman, violations of reason evidenced the mental distress of Japan's leadership, and their inability to see the truth of his argument underscored the depth of their defect. A rational, sane government would anticipate the futility of the war, seek to protect civilian populations, and act to avert the devastation to come.

Even while warning of utter destruction, this rhetoric shifted the source of savagery from the realm of national defect to a defect of leadership. Where leaders and the people had once been lumped into a single group, Truman now lamented the "suffering and hardships which the people of Japan will undergo—all in vain" because military leaders will not give up the "vain hope of victory."[56] Elevating vanity to explain an irrational commitment to the war highlighted a character flaw that impaired rationality. Japan's leaders, so afflicted, were irredeemable. But, charging that the United States did not seek the "extermination or slavement [sic] of the Japanese people," Truman contended that unconditional surrender served Japan's own good because it would liberate the people from the clutches of dictatorship.[57] Rather than punishment, unconditional surrender meant "the return of soldiers and sailors to their families, their farms, their jobs. It means not prolonging the present agony and suffering of the Japanese."[58] Complicating simplistic depictions of the Japanese as vermin to be eliminated and conveying concern for the Japanese people in the face of escalating violence, this rhetoric humanized the enemy and evoked sympathy for their situation. The Japanese, Truman assessed, were victims of the vice of vanity. While they merited some blame for allowing the nation to act irrationally, Truman's

stance deprived the Japanese people of agency for the infamy of the war.
It also implied that Japanese soldiers could demonstrate a civilized form
of reason by laying down their arms and returning to civilian life.

By June, with the outcome of the war all but certain, Truman's depiction of the Japanese isolated madness as the source of their continued
will to fight. In announcing his strategy for winning the Pacific war, he
claimed Japan was "animated by desperate fanaticism," and posed the
problem as facing a "fanatical enemy" in the throes of the "delirium of
. . . suicide attacks" and "continuing resistance beyond the point of reason."[59] To Truman, Japan's refusal to capitulate proved cultural madness
that had infected and poisoned the body politic. This view implicated
the people in an either/or equation. They either suffered from a mental
illness that propelled them to continue to fight a lost cause beyond reason or they would anticipate their utter destruction and concede defeat.
Thus, continuing the fight signaled Japan's incapacity to discern reality
from illusion. But, by framing Japan's option as an either/or choice, Truman signaled that reason could once again govern the enemy's behavior,
heralding the possibility of the return of sanity and the potential for
recivilizing the savage after the war.

By August, Truman's patience had run out. No longer willing to
wait on Japanese capitulation, concerned that Japanese defenses could
inflict heavy casualties to the point of forcing a negotiated peace rather
than unconditional surrender, and likely seeking to head off Soviet influence in Northeast Asia after the war, he approved of the use of the
atom bomb on Hiroshima.[60] Having already threatened the Japanese
government with destruction, he posited the use of the atom bomb as a
rational action when confronted with an irrational enemy. Making the
case at Potsdam on August 9, he claimed the atomic bomb served as a
just retaliation to "those who attacked us without warning at Pearl Harbor, against those who have starved and beaten and executed American prisoners of war, against those who have abandoned all pretense
of obeying international laws of warfare." Raising the memory of Pearl
Harbor and connecting it to subsequent acts of deception, barbarism,
and lawlessness justified the bomb as rational when confronting a

dishonest, demented enemy, bent on violence. It also implied that the United States could never trust Japan's military government to negotiate honestly. They had deceived before and, short of complete capitulation, could never be trusted to keep the peace. The depth of Japan's irrationality made sensible his claim that atomic retribution aimed to "shorten the agony of war" and "to save the lives of thousands and thousands of young Americans."[61] This humanistic concern extended to Japanese civilians as well, who he urged to "leave industrial cities immediately, and save themselves from destruction."[62] Navigating the contradiction of bombing a people in order to save them, Truman surmised that speeding up the end of the war would spare many more the long-term agony of invasion. This frame shifted responsibility for the bomb from Truman to Japan's feral leadership while explaining atomic retribution as in the interests of mercy, rather than vengeance. Doing so established an essential faith in Japanese humanity and signaled the potential for a recuperative discourse in the postwar era.

Six days after dropping a second atomic bomb, the war was over. Emperor Hirohito, the imperial ruler of Japan, announced on the radio his decision to unconditionally surrender to the Allied forces. Citing the deteriorating situation and the "new and most cruel bomb," he warned that continued fighting would "result in an ultimate collapse and obliteration of the Japanese nation and lead to the total extinction of human civilization."[63] Reason had prevailed at last. In its aftermath, Truman reiterated the role the "war lords of Japan and the Japanese armed forces" had played in this "cruel war of aggression."[64] The defeat of Japan marked, in Truman's vernacular, "the end of the grandiose schemes of the dictators to enslave the peoples of the world, destroy their civilization, and institute a new era of darkness and degradation."[65] Isolating Japan's anti-democratic government as responsible for the war and the target of American retribution carved out space for new representations of the Japanese people. Truman reiterated this distinction in announcing the signing of the unconditional surrender agreement on September 1, attributing the war to "Japanese militarists," "Japanese war lords," and "forces of tyranny."[66] The rhetoric insinuated that the people were victims, subject to the aggressive tendencies of the anti-civilizational impulses of the military leadership. The Japanese leadership may have been the responsible party, but the people paid the price at Hiroshima, Nagasaki, and beyond. In acknowledging and sympathizing with their suffering at the hands of warlords and militarists, Truman's comments conveyed a basic humanistic presupposition about the Japanese. Deceived by poisonous ideas rather than committed to them, they could be saved.

Curing the Disease of Totalitarianism after the War

Metaphors of disease and mental illness served as powerful rhetorical resources at the end of World War II because they explained the cause of the war while authenticating the redemptive potential of the enemy. Typically, rhetors employ the disease metaphor "to frame conditions of weakness in the state." According to Michael Osborn, ancient usage situated the imagery as a niche metaphor that served specific situations, but due to the improbability of a cure, did not appear in deliberative contexts.[67] Truman's metaphors of disease at the end of World War II, however, shifted valences for understanding the enemy because, as Osborn argued, "Depictions of disease imply often not so much a judgment of guilt as an opportunity for dramatic healing. People are simply afflicted, not convicted, by their condition." Within the metaphoric frame depicting Nazism and militarism as toxic ideologies that had poisoned the minds of Germany and Japan lurked a recuperative potential. The Germans and Japanese were sick, and sick individuals should be treated, not punished. And, as enfeebled subjects, they had the capacity to "effect their own restoration to social and political health."[68] They could participate in their own recovery. Doing so would indicate their return to civilized international society.

More fundamental than the prospect of redemption, sketching the disease of totalitarianism as a form of mental and bodily illness inferred a presidential orientation to the madness of the age. This orientation, what I term a persona, elevated the ethos of Truman as one of "the heroic champions of needful patients," inscribing the executive in a doctor-patient relationship with the Axis powers.[69] The doctor persona articulated the enemy body as sick, the condition curable. As such, it implied the Axis could be saved with the appropriate application of American power, conditioned the occupation of the enemy on the eradication of the disease that had infected the Axis, and presumed Truman's personal investment in their rehabilitation. Infusing the president with a paternalistic role typifying doctors of the era, the persona conferred a relationship of responsibility for others that framed and shaped the immediate nature of occupation and reconstruction, while also engaging the nation in the long-term good health of the defeated foes. This medicalized approach to policy, moreover, isolated and treated the whole patient, rather than individual symptoms, tasking the presidency with the comprehensive assessment and rehabilitation of the enemy.[70] In doing so, the doctor persona permeated the foreign affairs bureaucracy more generally, binding American foreign policy to diagnose and prescribe remedies to problems wherever they might be found in the world.

The rhetorical collaboration between representing the Axis powers as infirm body politics and Truman's postwar identity as paternalistic doctor gave way to a diagnostic and treatment regimen befitting the depth of the challenge facing Europe and Asia. With his diagnosis pointing to the rise of totalitarian and militaristic influences, the initial treatment called for identifying and removing or cutting out the mephitic agents that could forestall the return of national health. In addition to excising noxious elements, Truman argued he had an obligation to provide for the basic needs of the occupied territories. This obligation typical for the era—connected the provision of basic needs to the medical interests of the patients and the conditions that led to war.[71] This synthesis between empirical causes and immediate needs rationalized humanitarian aid to the Axis as part of a comprehensive treatment regimen designed to prevent the recurrence of the disease of totalitarianism. A final aspect of treatment prescribed democratization as the appropriate intervention of the mind, a measure that would ensure the long-term mental and emotional health of the occupied countries.

OCCUPATION, EXCISION, AND REHABILITATION

A doctor sustains a practice by correctly identifying the causes of a malady, prescribing an appropriate remedy, and maintaining an affable bedside manner. For Truman, the first act of rehabilitation required cutting out the tyrannical influences that inhibited the Axis powers from becoming civilized states. According to the logic of the disease metaphor, national propaganda, party membership, and the military leaders of each nation had served as the mode of transmission. As such, any attempt at remediation required freeing the national body from those elements, even if doing so inflicted harm upon the occupied nations. Only the full removal of the malignancy could enable the "true" spirit of the Germans and Japanese to emerge. Truman explained that occupation sought to "rid Germany of the forces which have made her so long feared and hated . . . to eliminate Nazism, armaments, war industries, the German General Staff and all its military tradition . . . to rebuild democracy . . . to make Germany over into a decent nation, so that it may eventually work its way . . . back into a place in the civilized world."[72] This pragmatic explanation invoked the contours of the doctor persona by defining the task as identifying and excising the influences that had contaminated and corrupted the national body. It also recalled the memory of World War I and helped clarify that even if Congress did not favor foreign aid to the defeated foe, placing savagery in permanent remission required that assistance. The force of the World War I analog bolstered the case. As one scholar explained, Truman was convinced that "the United States must not repeat the mistakes that followed the first" war and must "act in accordance with the most essential 'lesson' that Wilson's experience taught."[73] That meant investing in Germany, rebuilding the nation and its economy, ensuring the recuperation of the German soul, and minimizing the factors that risked the reemergence of war and jeopardized the next generation.

This planned treatment applied to Japan as well. The first act of occupation, as Truman put it on September 2, 1945, began with maintaining a "force in the Pacific to clean out the militarism of Japan, just as we are cleaning out the militarism of Germany."[74] Again diagnosing militarism as a contaminant—a corrupting agent dirtying the Japanese and German body politics—the statement inferred the potential for metastasis absent complete excision of the noxious elements. The formal policy statement on the occupation of postwar Japan also articulated the postwar mission in terms of quarantine and excision. Representing the true enemy as the "ultra-nationalist and militarist organizations," Truman dictated that those involved would be "removed and excluded," the institutions "dissolved and prohibited."[75] Like a doctor lecturing an infected patient on the need for surgery, Truman implied that the continued presence of these infectious agents would expose the Japanese body politic to further contagion. And since the disease had penetrated all aspects of Japanese society, as the president put it, the "existing economic basis of Japanese military strength must be destroyed and not be permitted to revive."[76] Imagining militarism as a noxious influence that has to be removed, militaristic organizations as terminal cases that had to be euthanized, these orders represented first steps. With them as part of the broad package of rehabilitation, Truman contended that "tyranny must be rooted out from the very soul of the enemy nation before we can say the war is really won."[77] Like a surgeon, excising a tumor from a diseased body while prescribing postsurgical rehabilitation, the metaphor established the central task of occupation as delving beyond the physical and into the essential habits and practices of the enemy populations in order to locate and eliminate the pathology of tyranny.

As doctor, Truman sought the revival, recovery, and rehabilitation of enervated national bodies in the aftermath of war. Beyond social, political, and economic surgery, this goal materialized a broad package of policy programs encapsulated by the term "rehabilitation." At the level of discourse, rehabilitation extended the figure of broken national bodies in need of medical or psychiatric intervention while conferring an obligation upon the foreign affairs bureaucracy. For the victors, Truman explained, winning the war invoked a duty "to do our share in supervising former enemy governments, enforcing the peace terms, disarming and repatriating enemy troops, taking care of hundreds of thousands of displaced persons . . . [because] the victors must make sure that there will not be a recurrence of enemy aggression and tyranny."[78] Humanizing the former enemies by identifying them as targets for medical intervention, rather than discipline or punishment, this discourse directed American postwar efforts. In the short term, the nation had an obligation to ensure the factors that caused the war had been completely removed from the body politic. Figuring that cause as a tumor, deeply embedded in the national corpus, Truman pledged to excise it, but also to see the patient through to recovery to prevent relapses. At the same time, the patients had to do their part, since, according to Truman, the efficacy of the rehabilitation program—including reconstruction and a return to sovereignty—would "depend entirely on how well the Germans [and Japanese] rehabilitate themselves on the democratic way of life."[79] Subtly shifting the disease frame from the immediate treatment to systematic efforts to remake the Axis powers rested the ultimate prognosis on the patients' commitment to the tough labor of melioration.

The president's biological terminology spread throughout the foreign-policy intelligentsia, both inside and outside the administrative bureaucracy, to justify American vigilance and commitments to European and Asian recovery. As early as January 1945, Arthur Vandenberg, the Republican senator who urged isolation prior to the war, adopted the essential biological framework. In a speech delivered to the Senate advocating prolonged American engagement in world affairs, he explained: "I do not believe that any nation hereafter can immunize itself by its own exclusive action . . . This Second World War plagues the earth chiefly because France and Britain did not keep Germany disarmed."[80] Conceiving of the danger posed by dictatorship, and later communism, in terms of a disease to which there could be no natural resistance, Vandenberg's rhetoric coincided with the president's conception of American power in the postwar era. Only aggressive steps to contain anti-democratic impulses could protect the nation.

Vandenberg's address signaled the distribution of the disease/doctor metaphor across and through the national and international bureaucracies tasked with reconstruction efforts in the postwar era. Written into the very terminology used to describe the postwar mission, biological metaphors shifted conceptions of the Axis powers from savage to that of victims in need of medical attention. Domestic and foreign leaders commonly referred to the postwar mission in biological terminology. This terminology claimed the need to provide relief, recovery, or rehabilitation to nations impacted by the war. For instance, Truman's initial directive to Dwight D. Eisenhower, supreme commander of Allied Forces in Western Europe, restricted the mission of occupation forces to the provision of "relief for the benefit of countries devastated by Nazi aggression."[81] The United Nations Relief and Rehabilitation Administration, the primary organization tasked with reconstruction, incorporated the biological frame in its title. The U.S. program responsible for administrating emergency assistance to Germany, Japan, and Austria was titled the Government Aid and Relief in Occupied Areas program. Internal deliberation about how to best govern Japan debated the prospect of rehabilitating the nation.[82] Immediately after the war, the *New York Times* reported on efforts to rehabilitate Japan to ensure the nation's recovery.[83] Byrnes, in remarks explaining the provision of U.S. assistance to Germany, stated that the occupation "envisaged that Germany will gradually recover."[84] And a year into occupation of Japan, the *New York Times* warned that "Japan's recovery has not been fast."[85] Echoing the nation-as-body metaphor, these depictions posited war-torn nations as bodies in need, injured but not destroyed. Inclusive of Germany and Japan, the metaphoric frame plotted a course for the recuperation of friendly relations.

Having embraced the president-as-doctor persona, this rhetoric expanded beyond the Axis to reorient the foreign affairs bureaucracy toward overseeing the state of the world and prescribing remedies for the ills of war. Internal State Department memorandums describing the European Recovery Program exhibit the adoption and penetration of the metaphoric framing. One such document claimed the policy would "foster Europe['s] recovery as a whole" by emphasizing "short-term recovery rather than long-run development." The logic implied that the first step was to heal the patient before focusing on rehabilitation. The report went on to argue that the "breakdown in normal monetary exchange is to considerable extent symptom rather than cause" and that American policy had to remedy the factors producing economic crisis rather than just treat the symptoms. Throughout, the report articulated Germany as an important member of Europe, in need of treatment.[86] These representations of nations as sick—laid out by the disease of war and economic stagnation—and in need of the proper medicine populated the public and private comments of the foreign affairs bureaucracy. By extending the nation-as-body metaphor, they facilitated the rehumanization of Germany and Japan, making the recuperation of normal relations probable.

As 1946 waned, Truman's recivilizing rhetoric merged with a deeper theory of war to justify American leadership in the world. This merger extolled the benefits of the four freedoms and economic prosperity to the long-term recovery of the Axis powers while warning of the dangers of economic dislocation. Doing so justified American leadership while distinguishing it from colonial occupations of the past. The nation sought German and Japanese recovery, rather than territorial acquisition. Truman's United Nations address given on October 23, 1946, exemplifies the shifting sands of his foreign-policy discourse. The address, which marked the opening of the first General Assembly of the United Nations in New York, laid out the policies Truman deemed necessary for ensuring peace in Germany and Japan, as well as globally. He explained, "So far as Germany and Japan are concerned, the United States is resolved that neither shall again become a cause for war. We shall continue to seek agreement upon peace terms which ensure that both Germany and Japan remain disarmed, that Nazi influence in Germany be destroyed and that the power of the war lords in Japan be eliminated forever."[87] Like much of his rehumanization rhetoric, this excerpt rearticulated the true enemy as an extreme few who had taken charge of the Axis powers. While this fit with prior claims about American efforts to save the German and Japanese people from their dictatorial overlords, Truman placed fluid notions of savagery within the contours of a broader narrative about danger in global affairs. According to the president, the failure of all nations to commit to "four essential freedoms . . . freedom of speech, freedom of religion, freedom from want, and freedom from fear" endangered the postwar peace and the potential of the United Nations.[88] Putting it this way gave agency to savagery itself and warned of its recurrence. During the war, savagery had been located in Germany and Japan. With those forces defeated, savagery had shifted from the particular to the unknown. Constitutive of a long-term role for American leadership, the speech foreshadowed the confrontation to come, but it also pointed to the true source of conflict and the nation's role in addressing the root causes of conflict.

NATIONAL HEALTH AND THE PROVISION OF BASIC NEEDS

Articulating the Axis as unwell and the president-as-doctor represented the war as one way to treat the violent outbursts of the sick and deranged. This metaphoric reconfiguration extended Truman's thesis that war derived from the existence of vulnerable, feeble bodies exposed to toxic ideologies or influences. As doctor, Truman's duty and obligation toward the patient extended beyond observation, diagnosis, containment, and treatment, and included the compositional dynamics of the foreign body itself.[89] Successful treatment required attending to the basic corporeal necessities of the patient—the provision of food, clothing, housing, and so on—as well as to cognitive, emotional, and spiritual development. These obligations, of course, began at home, as he explained in his message to Congress on postwar economic reconversion, but extended to "the other members of the family of nations" since all "are facing the hazardous transition to a peace economy in a world grown acutely sensitive to power."[90] While much of the immediate postwar reconstruction assistance went to Allied nations, the implicit set of obligations rationalized the provision of basic needs, reconstruction, and reeducation for occupied nations, including emergency food aid and development assistance.[91]

Truman's diagnostic discourse posited material distress and the lack of basic necessities as the root cause of disorder, warlordism, militarism, and evil. This rhetoric responded to those "who have come to believe that wars are inevitable," while framing the prospects for a durable peace around the provision of food aid and economic recovery.[92] He had learned of the immediate needs in a memo circulated prior to Nazi surrender that warned, "Food is the great need—food for the displaced persons, food for liberated Europe, food for the Germans."[93] Less than three weeks after German capitulation, he tasked the war agencies with addressing the grave humanitarian situation in Europe, stressing that "the future permanent peace in Europe depends upon the restoration of the economy . . . a chaotic and hungry Europe is not a fertile ground in which stable, democratic and friendly governments can be reared."[94] Once again inferring that the German turn to totalitarianism had been a product of economics rather than racism, this rhetoric warned that the long-term health of the patient depended on recovery packages that addressed the physical needs of the Axis nations.

Emphasizing the provision of basic needs rationalized the continuation of American military presence abroad, because military occupation, he contended, would establish order and address humanitarian concerns, preventing the return of insecurity and aggression. Warning of the potential of resurgent savagery, he declared, "We must do all we can to spare [America] from the ravages of any future breach of the peace. That is why . . . we are going to maintain the military bases necessary for the complete protection of our interests and of world peace. Bases which our military experts deem to be essential for our protection."[95] Coming a week after the Potsdam Conference, this declaration hinted at fractures in the wartime alliance between the United States and the Soviets.[96] Rather than highlighting those divisions, he instead pointed to the inherent danger of a "cold and hungry" Europe and the risk to the "foundations of order" and "the hope for worldwide peace" that such factors entailed.[97] These dangers, he contended, warranted an expansive American role in world affairs. American leadership, he argued, could remedy the material conditions that made nations vulnerable to the rise of savage elements. This was especially the case for Asia, where Truman sought to cement American power in the Pacific. As he wrote on the margins of a memo from Byrnes, "I [am] very anxious that our place in Pacific affairs should be a dominant one in the peace as it has been in the war."[98] In response, Byrnes held off on pushing forward a formal peace treaty with Japan because "the only way in which we could have a dominant position in Japan in the days following the adoption of a peace treaty would be to provide for the continued occupation by our troops."[99] While these statements did not allude to direct confrontation with the Soviets, forward basing foreshadowed the confrontation that would convert Europe and Asia into armed camps.

Beyond immediate humanitarian concerns, Truman's diagnosis about the root causes determined that economic failure had made the German and Japanese body politics susceptible to corruption. As he put it in April 1946, "the madness and desire for world conquest" originated from the "material distress and spiritual starvation born of poverty and despair. These evil forces were seized upon by evil men to launch their program of tyranny and aggression. The danger of war will never be completely wiped out until the economic ills which constitute the roots of war are eliminated."[100] This rhetoric located the genesis of World War II in the economic circumstances of both nations and implied the present remission could be temporary, that the disease of totalitarianism could recur. Referencing an implicit mutability of all body politics displaced the unique responsibility for the war from the Germans and Japanese to fundamental conditions of human existence and the opportunists who seized upon bleak material circumstances to lead nations into disaster. Far from mere savages, the Germans and Japanese became the latest, and worst, victims of the ills of poverty. Their number had been called and there was no telling who was next.

Truman's diagnosis of root causes and his embodiment of the doctor persona connected basic needs to the cultivation of democratic governance. With presidential oversight and management situated as central to the recovery and rehabilitation of the defeated enemies, the provision of basic necessities provided a crucial demonstration of American commitment to the long-term health of Germany and Japan. When the food problem in Europe and Asia blossomed into a full-blown crisis, he reminded the press, "we can't afford to see our enemies starve" because it would be "un-American."[101] By 1947, the responsibility to feed, as Truman put it, existed as part of "our policy of encouraging the growth of democracy in these occupied countries."[102] This rhetoric reflected the synthesis of Truman's thinking about the former enemies. Like a doctor, concerned about a patient's recuperative environment, Truman worried about the ex-belligerents' ability to commit to peace. A crucial aspect of that process involved the provision of basic biological needs and a safe environment for the patient. The stakes for the postwar era provided their own compulsion. Either Germany and Japan completed the treatment regimen, demonstrated their mental fitness, and reentered civilized society, or war would recur.

Truman's fixation on the long-term health of Germany and Japan expanded to justify a global mission for presidential leadership. Claiming "rumors of war still find willing listeners" that, if unchecked, "are sure to impede world recovery," he claimed "an early improvement in living conditions throughout the world" would determine the prospects for a true peace.[103] This rhetoric mobilized the biological metaphor to justify foreign assistance beyond the Axis because the conflict had wreaked havoc on all nations. As weakened bodies in need of sustained assistance, all nations became potential targets for Truman's treatment plan. To turn away from that task would turn away from fundamental American ideals and risk the return of militarism and all its attendant dangers because, as Truman put it, peace could never take hold "from a soil of poverty and economic distress."[104] This rhetoric signaled the importance of American hegemony in the postwar era and authorized presidential power to manage the challenge of rooting out tyranny because the task required leadership above and beyond mere reconstruction funds. It required presidential leadership.

DEMOCRATIZATION, REEDUCATION, AND OTHER INTERVENTIONS OF THE MIND

Having plotted a metaphoric course for the return of international health and situated his role as doctor, Truman connected improvements in material conditions, as well as economic and spiritual growth, to the adoption of democratic capitalism. Up to this point, figuring nations-as-bodies permitted the elaboration of disease metaphors that charged the foreign affairs bureaucracy with observing, diagnosing, containing, and treating biological threats to the national body. As an inventional resource, however, Truman's foundational metaphor postulated intertextual possibilities beyond that of bodies exposed to disease. Those possibilities materialized via warnings about the need to care for disorders of the mind. Revisiting notions of German and Japanese irrationality and fanaticism during the war, Truman's postwar metaphor of mental disorder represented anti-democratic notions as a philosophy of suffering that mapped a specific pathology of power onto the enemy's body. This representation moved policy attention beyond immediate material needs and targeted the wholesale reeducation of the German and Japanese people. As the logic went, the judicious exercise of American power could cure the disease of war because U.S. engagement could spread "universal" American ideals, enable the "roots of democracy" to take hold, and create the conditions for a lasting peace.[105] The final aspect of the treatment plan, then, argued that democratization would ensure the ultimate destruction of the "Nazi influence" and prevent the recurrence of the disease of aggression.[106]

Truman's initial call to democratize the Axis powers came on June 26, 1945, in a speech at the United Nations Conference. Establishing a set of guidelines for how the world should understand the rise of discord after the war, Truman identified the seeds of discord as fascism, the "ideas, which gave [aggression] birth and strength," and manifested in the "evil spirit which has hung over the world for the last decade."[107] Extending the biological metaphor, the rhetoric identified ideological causes of conflict. In form, the speech argued for the creation of the United Nations—a democratic institution—in order to prevent (or manage) future moments of discord, but it also centralized the importance of American power. For Truman, only the adoption of an Americanist system of economics and government could prevent future wars. Producing an image of a diffuse but opaque danger "trying . . . to divide and conquer . . . to make one Ally suspect the other, hate the other, desert the other," the speech inferred that anti-democratic ideas that had infected the hearts and minds of the enemy with an "evil spirit" were now at work generating fractures between East and West.[108] This discourse hinted at a growing divide between the United States and the Soviet Union while asserting agency for savagery itself as a highly mobile, communicable condition.

A secondary aspect of Truman's turn to democracy identified a central component of the Axis infirmity as an outcome of puerile conduct. This rhetoric posited the Axis powers—or any nondemocratic nation—as immature and in need of cultural reeducation.[109] Blaming the rush to war on an anti-democratic ideology, Truman claimed the application of American guidance and education could push naive nations away from the philosophies of militarism. An Office of War Information document strategizing a media campaign for maintaining public support for the war after V-E Day signaled the beginnings of this movement. The document depicted Japanese soldiers as highly intelligent and well educated, "having been trained since birth to believe that the highest glory attainable by man is death in battle for the glory of his emperor . . . This fanatic nationalism makes them dangerous adversaries who pit their desire to die against our desire to live. The Japanese soldier is no superman, but his courage and aggressiveness are beyond question."[110] Rather than inculcate tropes of mindless savagery, the document explained the character flaw of Japanese fanaticism as a product of cultural education. The Japanese commitment to a nondemocratic leader, the fanatic willingness to sacrifice the self for the emperor without hesitation, and the stubbornness to continue fighting "even when eventual defeat stares them in the face," including "utter physical destruction," outlined the parameters of the character flaw.[111] This version of savagery imparted fluidity in its very definition: the solution to unreason is reason; the solution to a fanatical worship of the monarchy is democratic education. Far removed from archetypal depictions of the Japanese as animalistic or subhuman, the administration's internal analysis validated the human features of the Japanese. In emphasizing the enemy's autonomy, it also plotted the course for American efforts to guide and reeducate the Japanese in democratic forms of government.

Truman's postwar democratic prescriptions relied on two arguments. First, by pointing to the vitality of "free government" as "the most efficient government," and therefore, the best government, Truman attributed American victory to the nation's commitment to democratic capitalism.[112] As he put it on October 7, 1945, "our victories over Germany and Italy and Japan and their allies" and the end of the war conclusively proved the superiority of the American system of government.[113] These remarks gained new poignancy with Truman's Navy Day address on October 27. This speech, his first major foreign-policy address after the end of the war, publicly acknowledged a real divide between the United States and the Soviet Union. Marking a shift from conciliation to challenging negotiation, Truman claimed that the "differences of the kind that exist today . . . are not hopeless or irreconcilable" and that "there are no conflicts of interest among the victorious powers so deeply rooted that they cannot be resolved." Publicly acknowledging cleavages between the United States and Russia, the speech urged for continuing "forbearance and firmness" and "undying patience" in "building a peace."[114] Coming so soon after the end of the war, this rhetoric made public the prospect of the postwar failure of cooperation and the return of geopolitical rivalry. And with sudden territorial vulnerability brought on by modern warfare and the atomic bomb, the consequences shook the nation.[115]

Second, Truman justified German and Japanese democratization as representing the only means for neutralizing totalitarian manipulation of the Axis nations. As he expounded in a series of speeches in 1946, the Axis recovery hinged upon their adoption of an American system because, as he put it, only democratic capitalism could prevent a "return to the kind of narrow economic nationalism which had poisoned international relations and undermined living standards between the two World Wars."[116] Articulating international relations in biological terms, the rhetoric claimed that failure to produce economic opportunities raised the specter of a return of the political disease that gave way to war in 1939. The appropriate remedy to the problem of totalitarianism necessitated democratic governance because "democracy is the rallying cry today for free men everywhere in their struggle for a better life."[117] Replicating the nation-as-body metaphor to depict the Allied powers as victims, the Axis as oppressors, this statement emphasized the singular importance of democracy. "Encourag[ing] the growth and spread of democracy and civil rights," including the "revival of economic activity and international trade," he argued, was crucial to the "rehabilitation and development of the Far Eastern countries" and for preventing "recurrence of enemy aggression and tyranny."[118] Pledging to continue the occupation until the Axis had adopted democratic capitalism, Truman rationalized a long-term relationship between the United States and Germany and Japan, as well as significant sums dedicated to the task of democratization.

The cultivation of a democratic outlook, like any pedagogic endeavor, requires time, and Truman's public case for reeducation both sharpened and elongated the mission. In doing so, it risked augmenting national desires for a vindictive peace. Truman finessed those expectations by articulating enemy character as inherently malleable, the people as capable of comprehending the received wisdom of American experience. The significance of his democratic reeducation program came into focus at the opening of the National Archives exhibit of Japanese surrender documents. Led by Congressman Sam Rayburn and broadcast live over radio, the presentation figured the end of the war in bodily terms. The archivist related the end of the war as forcing bodily submission, in which America had "brought the Japanese to their knees," but the messages during the ceremony also spoke about the importance of a reeducation program that could instill Western, democratic values to facilitate Japan's political maturity. Truman appended a brief note that expressed satisfaction with the end, but concern about "the evil ideologies" still present in the world. "Those ideas must be wiped out," he explained, "and the German and Japanese people must be taught, with sternness but with justice, to live in a world where there is respect for the rights of nations and of men."[119] As a whole, the ceremony figured the

Germans and Japanese as mentally feeble in need of a firm hand, Truman as clinician tasked with their reeducation. The metaphoric relation dictated a policy program premised on reeducating the Axis nations, but again it represented the former enemies as autonomous actors who had to accept the tenets of political liberalism in order to demonstrate their maturation.

Truman's policy statement on the occupation of Japan, published on September 22, 1945, amplified the administration's focus on the mental health of the defeated foes. The report established the boundaries of Japanese territory, pointed to militarism as the cause of the war, identified the reeducation of the Japanese as the principal task for ensuring the peace, and posited economic growth as the central goal for the country's future. Stating that "the Japanese people shall be encouraged to develop a desire for individual liberties and respect for fundamental human rights . . . [and] to form democratic and representative organizations," the report established the defect in Japanese character as conformity and impressibility.[120] Truman's thesis implied the need for a fundamental reconfiguration of the Japanese outlook—one premised on establishing independent thought. It also imagined Japan as a singular body with a homogeneous worldview and Truman as doctor, concerned with treating his patient's mental health. While Truman left the particulars up to the occupation forces and foreign-policy bureaucracy, the important thing, he said, was for the Japanese to "renounce all military aims and apply themselves diligently and with single purpose to the ways of peaceful living."[121] This statement ceded agency to the Japanese people, granted the civilian population responsibility for transitioning to the postwar peace, and positioned them as victims, miseducated but pliable. It also rearticulated the mutually reinforcing relations between doctor and patient. Those relations resolved into a mutual responsibility to rebuild the country, American obligations to provide necessary goods and services to the occupation force, and Japanese dedication to learn to appreciate democracy and human rights.[122] Inferring a fundamental capacity for learning, development, and maturation, the message offered Japan the opportunity to demonstrate its commitment to American ideals. Such a commitment, Truman implied, would enable Japan to reintegrate into the family of nations.

In addition to its textual elaboration, the tone of the policy statement asserted a rhetoric of personal responsibility akin to a lecture one would deliver to a patient. Placing the blame for the war on the policies of Japan, Truman enjoined the Japanese to recognize their plight as "the direct outcome of [their] own behavior." As they had caused the problem, they would have to make the necessary changes. These changes included "physical reconstruction" of the country along with "reform[ing] the nature and direction of their economic activities and institutions."[123] Wartime depictions of the Japanese as vermin rendered them bodies-in-motion, mindless and vicious. Here, Truman figured the Japanese as having control over their own bodies and future. They had agency—a capacity to learn from their mistakes—and their fate would be determined by how they reformed themselves. The displacement of Japanese character exhibited here is stunning in its quickness. A month earlier, Truman had authorized the use of atomic weapons against the country because of their incapacity to exercise reason in the face of "utter destruction."[124] Now, he expected the Japanese to recognize their failures and work to overcome them—he expected the Japanese to act on the basis of higher-order reasoning.

By investing the people with marginal forms of democratic agency over their own lives, Truman inverted the logic of state power popularized by the German and Japanese dictators. German and Japanese participation in their own rehabilitation would reveal a true, democratic nature present in everyone. As the occupations stretched on in 1946, Truman clarified that their political and economic reorganization required a transition to democratic capitalism. He contended that the former enemies' commitment to the treatment regimen would cultivate a system of government rooted in "our American tradition" and "the belief that the state exists for the benefit of man."[125] Absent their rejection of the "false doctrine that man exists for the benefit of the state," the provision of American assistance could only do so much.[126] And, in language that could only refer to the Soviet Union and its system of government,

Truman explained that "promoting those liberties and principles which the word 'democracy' implies" is the best "bulwark of peace."[127] By implication, Truman flattened all forms of nondemocratic government as opposed to the individualism manifest in democracy and invested in the corruption of the body politic. At once diagnostic and prescriptive, this rhetoric rationalized American hegemonic leadership in Europe and Asia as a direct counter to the recurrence of war.

Truman's call to democratize the Axis powers represented a subtle shift in public postwar discourse by identifying democracy as an a priori necessity for permanent peace. This discourse displaced and diminished the significance of German and Japanese savagery by representing their aggression as the outcome of a temporary infection, made possible by the lack of individualism, human freedoms, and market economics. Placing the American way of life on a pedestal, his remarks to the United Nations General Assembly in October 1946 prioritized democratic ideals as central to the prospects for permanent peace. The speech identified the source of discord and danger in the world as "propaganda that promotes distrust and misunderstanding," the lack of "respect [for] the legitimate interests of all states," and the failure to "act as good neighbors toward each other."[128] While not naming the Soviets, this rhetoric incorporated Truman's private thoughts about the need to counter Soviet power. Peace, he posited, relied upon "justice for all—justice for small nations and for large nations and justice for individuals without distinction as to race, creed or color—a peace that will advance, not retard, the attainment of the four freedoms."[129] This language defined postwar tranquility in function of the expansion of liberal ideals and inferred only American leadership could counter those who opposed those ideals. And, by universalizing American political sensibilities, Truman warned that war could recur by "differences in economic and social systems . . . by different political philosophies."[130] Echoing the displacement of the savage present in much of his end-of-war rhetoric, this message suggested that the toxic philosophies capable of contaminating or brainwashing national bodies persisted. With the United States serving as the material home of the United Nations and as the only powerful country immune to the ravages of the Great War, the message signaled a singular truth. America had an obligation to extend the four freedoms globally as the only rational prophylaxis from the disease of totalitarianism. Such a declaration brought East-West relations into sharp relief—the ideological struggle, already begun, would become a global contest governing the human soul.

Disease Metaphors and the Bureaucratization of the Peace

Representations of nations as sick—laid out by the disease of war and economic stagnation, and in need of the proper medicine—populated the public and private comments of the foreign affairs bureaucracy. By posing the postwar mission as treating and rehabilitating national bodies, Truman's rhetoric entailed the foreign affairs bureaucracy in a set of practices designed to provision, educate, and develop Germany and Japan. Internal documents reflected the contours of the metaphor and mimicked the metaphoric economy enacted by the president-as-doctor persona. A memorandum written by Byron Price shortly after the war, for example, warned of the potential for Germany to slide back toward fascism if the "mounting bitterness [of] their situation becomes more desperate." Highlighting the circulation of stories explaining the plight of postwar Germany and the danger of anti-American and anti-democratic propaganda, the memo noted the risks of denazification and expressed concern that American "propaganda . . . to instill a sense of collective German guilt has fallen flat." This warning about the cognitive state of the German people indulged a view that the German problem was one of miseducation and the solution one of reeducation. Indeed, the concern expressed related to the failure of American reeducation policies, not the failure of economics. It stressed German confusion about democracy, "the German's traditional aversion to thinking for himself," and the "widespread and apparently genuine questioning of any political system where more than one name appears on the election ballot." The principal problem, then, referred to a failure of understanding—of education. Problems of economics and starvation—significant and urgent—took a backseat to the broader issue of the German mind. Successfully converting the former enemy into a partner nation, the Truman administration explained, required "win[ning] converts to democracy." It required "instilling hope—hope that Germany can rise from the dust and become a respected nation." It required "more books in tune with democratic concepts." And it required centralized control of "publications, broadcasting and theaters" to ensure consistency of the American message.[131] Only these things could ensure the long-term reeducation of the German people.

The risks posed by the political reorganization of Japan extended and amplified these aspects of the doctor-patient metaphor. A missive from George Atcheson Jr., acting political advisor to Japan, to Truman dated January 4, 1946, claimed that the "speed and completeness with which our final objectives can be realized will depend on the healthy development by the Japanese people of a democratic political consciousness." Articulating Japanese responsibility in their own formation, the message emphasized politics as developmental. As if referring to an enfeebled patient, grasping with a new ideology, Atcheson warned that "full development is still far away," but that initial signs were encouraging. The message also worried about the difficulty of inculcating democratic norms from the outside. Those norms were necessary to ensure Japanese pacifism in the long run, but, like all forms of psychic therapy, they had to grow on their own. Still, even while warning of the danger that Japanese political development could result in nondemocratic outcomes, the message stressed the necessity of continuing American policies, concluding that the "country will eventually develop into a reasonably decent member of the family of nations."[132] Again, the reiteration of the goal of occupation identified Japan as a wayward subject, on the path to eventual reintegration into normal society.

The basic logic of the doctor-patient metaphor manifested in State Department documents as well. A State Department report described the need for "the reeducation and reorientation of the Japanese people," and noted the "fundamental responsibility of the Allied authorities in

Japan" to identify Japanese citizens most likely to facilitate national reeducation.[133] A memo from Max Bishop to the secretary of state expounded upon the differences in Japanese "psychology," claiming reeducation was feasible because the Japanese were "fundamentally unlike . . . any western people." Assistant Chief of the Division of Japanese Affairs John Emmerson added in an additional memo that American influence on "the now very malleable Japanese will be decisive."[134] As a recivilizing discourse, this rhetoric ascribed agency and intelligence to the Japanese. But it didn't provide them with equality. Instead, it echoed prevalent racist stereotypes about the Japanese to justify the likelihood of their reeducation. They were different, alien, backward, but could be brought around. And General Douglas MacArthur, in public remarks pointing to progress of the occupation, contended that occupation had resulted in "progress and retrogression as the forces of liberalism and reaction have fought to establish a common ground for Japan's salvation." The statement reiterated the educative function of occupation, but also warned that "the success of these and other projected reforms" depended on how the Japanese "people themselves discharge their new political responsibilities . . . and proceed resolutely in the exercise of that power to build upon the ashes of decadence a new and enlightened social system."[135]

By September 1946, the rhetoric of responsibility isolated the importance of additional policy measures directed toward Germany. Inferring the danger posed by the consolidation of Soviet power in Europe, a top secret memo sent by Byrnes to Truman made the case for Germany's importance to European stability and long-term peace. In doing so, the memo articulated the tenets of a dual responsibility. The United States, on the one hand, "was not unmindful of the responsibility resting upon it and its major allies to maintain and enforce peace under law." On the other hand, demilitarizing Germany instituted an obligation upon the German people, an "opportunity, if they will but seize it, to apply their great energies and abilities to the works of peace . . . to show themselves worthy of the respect and friendship of peace-loving nations." Much like with Japan, the argument invested confidence in the German people's abilities to learn about and commit to democratic, peaceful existence. The message reminded the president that "it was never the intention of the American Government to deny to the German people the right to manage their own internal affairs . . . in a democratic way with genuine respect for human rights and fundamental freedoms." And, in a veiled reference to the Soviet Union, Byrnes suggested the "purpose of occupation did not contemplate a prolonged alien dictatorship of Germany's peacetime economy or a prolonged alien dictatorship of Germany's internal political life." Ultimately, Byrnes concluded by expressing a desire for Germans to embrace peaceful, democratic life as dictated by the American occupation so the country could "win their way back to an honorable place among the free and peace-loving nations of the world."[136]

Byrnes's rhetoric, mirrored in Truman's speeches and public comments about Germany, embodied the contours of the doctor persona. As benevolent clinician, the United States committed to feeding the German people and providing them protection from the elements. U.S. occupation served as a security measure—enforcement against strife and outside influence. And U.S. policy existed to restructure German economic and political life in order to facilitate the country's return to civilized society. But, in doing so, American occupation imposed a mutual obligation on Germans. They needed to choose democracy and peace. They needed to demonstrate their commitment to human rights. And their war crimes required fair punishment in the form of reparations and criminal prosecution of the guilty. Like a strict counselor establishing the components of a punishment regime, the Truman administration's rhetoric defined the contours of how Germany could rehabilitate itself, while expressing measured respect for the German people. The implications of the dissociation between the leaders and people is notable here. Prior to the end of the war, Truman depicted Germans as barbarians, unsuited to negotiation and only understanding the language of force. After the war, the rhetoric shifted. Now, Germans were thinking, reasonable individuals with the capacity to choose the appropriate course of action.

Infused with the language of medicine, Truman's end-of-war rhetoric entailed the American mission in an elongated and intense occupation. With militarism as the disease and American power the cure, only a long-term commitment to Germany and Japan could keep the disease in remission. Doing so would excise the external agents that had infected the German and Japanese body politics and ensure they recovered from the war and fully rehabilitated themselves. Like the doctor who had diagnosed the problem, prescribed the proper remedy, and urged the patient to see the treatment through, the rhetoric maintained the importance of monitoring and follow-up as a means to prevent recurrence. But rhetoric is not easily contained, and having found purchase in Germany and Japan, Truman's disease-doctor pairing enacted fundamental shifts in the organization and use of American power in the postwar era. With postwar American leadership "no guarantee,"[137] stressing the importance of occupation as the cure for the social disease that led to the war became a powerful argument for the Truman administration's efforts to stave off the return of isolationism. Beyond its use as persuasive resource, however, the metaphor framed and circumscribed the role of American postwar policy because it imparted the wisdom of surveillance, response, diagnosis, and treatment. Beyond occupation, reconstruction, and rehabilitation of the Axis powers, the metaphoric entailments of the doctor persona—totalitarianism as a disease, democracy as the cure—directed the foreign affairs bureaucracy to act as international monitor ever vigilant against the reemergence of the madness of fascism and militarism. As explained in the next section, it also foreshadowed the ultimate confrontation with the Soviets because his prescribed solutions extended an economic and political ideology hostile to Soviet-style communism.

The Recivilized Savage and the Containment of Soviet Power

Truman's management of the immediate postwar era marked a dramatic rise in American power and presidential leadership. Codifying presidential management of the occupied countries and extending the terms of occupation to an indefinite future, the rhetoric concentrated the task of vigilance during the occupation under the office of the presidency.[138] Between 1945 and 1947, Truman argued from this basis that the proper role for the United States in world affairs was to observe, diagnose, and treat those conditions in order to prevent the spread of hostile, aggressive ideologies. By conceiving of the threat to international relations in organic or biological terms, Truman figured the response as one of containment and treatment. This rhetoric circumscribed the policy agenda by narrowly confining U.S. leadership to an initial role of diagnostician and therapist before eventually ceding to the Cold War's dominant framework of containment and quarantine.[139] It also rationalized the forward positioning of military forces, security alliances, and the construction of an international economic system designed to prevent the types of competition that gave rise to war.

Articulating the need for U.S. primacy in the world and extending an Americanist system of politics abroad cemented American postwar leadership, but it also put the country on the path to confrontation with the Soviet Union. By 1947, the groundwork for the Cold War had been laid. The Red Scare of 1919 had convinced many in government that communism was incompatible with capitalism.[140] The press had compared the Nazis and Soviets in 1939, identifying an "essential similarity of the two regimes." Both were totalitarian governments. Even as references to the USSR as totalitarian faded once the Soviets joined the Americans and British, the resonance sustained.[141] One of Truman's first declarations upon assuming the presidency stressed the need to "stand up to the Russians," implicitly criticizing Roosevelt for going "too easy on them."[142] After Germany's capitulation, Dean Acheson worried about the devastation of Europe and the potential for the Soviets (or a revived Germany) to fill the power vacuum. This fear of Soviet or German control of Europe, one study found, "undergirded every aspect of postwar American policy from the time World War II ended."[143] And, even though Truman may have been reticent to name the Soviets as an antagonist, his administration identified diplomatic failures and

U.S.-Soviet tension in the immediate aftermath of the war. Press accounts of the Council of Foreign Ministers meeting in September 1945, for example, warned of a "two bloc world," pitting the former allies against each other.[144] Truman's discourse on the dangers of totalitarianism revived latent associations between the Soviets and the Nazis.[145] His Navy Day address in October 1945 declared a refusal "to recognize any government imposed upon any nation by force of any foreign power," a line "widely interpreted as a response to Soviet actions in Eastern Europe."[146] And Josef Stalin's claim on February 9, 1946, that capitalism and communism would inevitably clash "drew a surprisingly alarmed response from American pundits and officials," who called the speech a "declaration of World War III."[147] In short, tensions between the United States and the Soviet Union materialized in the same moment that Truman sought to shift the policy bureaucracy away from war and toward rehabilitation and reconstruction.

Truman grappled with the best approach for addressing the Soviets after the war when his policy gradually drifted toward "get[ting]-tough-with-Russia."[148] By 1946, Soviet intransigence in Eastern Europe had complicated postwar peace plans. As Truman put it in a handwritten memo written to Byrnes on January 5, 1946, Soviet policy in Poland and Iran was an "outrage" that proved the communist nation was a clear danger to world peace. "There isn't any doubt in my mind that Russia intends an invasion of Turkey and the seizure of the Black Sea Straits to the Mediterranean," he wrote. "Unless Russia is faced with an iron fist and strong language another war is in the making. Only one language do they understand—'How many divisions have you?' I do not think we should play compromise any longer . . . we should maintain complete control of Japan and the Pacific. We should rehabilitate China and create a strong central government there. We should do the same for Korea."[149] These thoughts cohered into a get-tough approach toward the Soviets in early 1946, when "diplomatic gestures, notable statements by Kennen, Vandenberg, Byrnes, and Churchill," combined with "hard-line policy over Iran" marked a dramatic shift in the way the nation engaged the Soviets.[150] Only Secretary of Commerce Henry Agard Wallace upset the growing consensus in the administration. His September 12, 1946, speech at Madison Square Garden, widely interpreted as "go soft on the Soviets," proposed a nuanced and pragmatic approach to rivalry that ran counter to the administration's emerging "get tough with Russia" policy.[151] Calling him "notoriously 'soft' on communism," Truman fired Wallace on September 20.[152] With his departure, the president's cabinet united in favor of a policy of confrontation with the Soviets and sent a message to other would-be dissenters: the Truman administration was committed to a specific policy direction and would not waver.

Restraint gave way to open confrontation with the Truman Doctrine speech. The message to Congress on March 12, 1947, called for economic assistance to Greece and Turkey by characterizing the danger posed by communism in terms of the disease-doctor metaphoric frame. It warned that the "disease" of communism could infect Greece and Turkey, depicted those nations as victims, and called for urgent relief. Embodying the persona of doctor, Truman figured the United States as the only "country to which democratic Greece can turn," and U.S. assistance as necessary to "keep that hope alive" for "a better life."[153] This rhetoric recalled Truman's convictions that economic insecurity enfeebled national bodies, and presented American assistance as a sort of final defense against the communist contaminant. Profoundly affecting U.S. foreign policy, the address finalized the gradual evolution of policy in Truman's discourse.[154] Vandenberg portrayed the policy as "a plan with numerous precedents" with "broad implications," and contended that it reflected what "we have always done" to oppose Soviet power generally and communism specifically.[155] Walter Lippmann popularized the term "Cold War" to describe relations between the two powers.[156] And a series of crises in Eastern Europe led to the creation of the North Atlantic Treaty Organization and the collective defense of Europe. In short, the hopes of a lasting peace ceded to the reality of prolonged confrontation.[157]

Shortly after the Truman Doctrine speech, the president explicitly depicted totalitarianism as having many names but an essential likeness. "There isn't any difference in totalitarian states," he told the press.

> I don't care what you call them Nazi, Communist or Fascist, or Franco,
> or anything else—they are all alike . . . The police state is a police state;
> I don't care what you call it. I have tried my level best to get along with
> our friends the Russians . . . But when I make straight out and out
> agreements with a government . . . and not a single one of those agree-
> ments is carried out, I have got to use other methods. They understand
> one language, and that is the language they are going to get from me
> from this point.[158]

This declaration coincided with Truman's claim that "Japan has been
handled because we had control of it" but Germany had become a hot
spot for the return of conflict because of the lack of economic unity generated by Soviet malfeasance.[159] In later speeches, he depicted rehabilitation as designed to return European nations to a "self-supporting basis"
because doing so would provide a bulwark against the "other ideology"
in the world that "believes that the individual is a slave of the state."[160]
This rhetoric actualized the displacement of the savage in two ways. On
the one hand, the rhetoric posited that successful rehabilitation would
reintegrate the defeated enemy into civil (international) society. On the
other hand, the proximity of the nondemocratic Soviet Union jeopardized Germany's recovery. These displacements rearticulated Germany
as victim while pinpointing the source of German—and European—mal-
aise in a toxic ideology that, if unchecked, could contaminate the entire
European body.

Truman administration officials echoed the framing of the Truman
Doctrine speech, posing the problem of Soviet power as the recurrence
of the disease of totalitarianism. Benjamin V. Cohen, from the Department of State, argued that American policy "must deal with the causes of
unrest in the world and not merely their symptoms," and urged Congress
to pass direct financial assistance to Europe or risk a "body blow to security, political stability, and economic progress the world over." Doing so,
Cohen claimed, would ensure "the vitality, strength, and will to maintain
peace and freedom under the law."[161] In May 1947, Under Secretary of
State Dean Acheson highlighted political instability as jeopardizing

the revival of European and Asian countries.[162] Later, in an address at Wesleyan University, he identified the Soviet Union as endangering the "whole course of recovery."[163] Secretary of State George C. Marshall, in proposing his plan for economic assistance to Europe, described the Axis activities leading up to and during the war as feverish, and posed the postwar mission as pursuing the "recovery" and "rehabilitation of the economic structure of Europe." The immediate problem, according to Marshall, was "to assist in the return of normal economic health" with American foreign policy directed at "the revival of a working economy," both of which were prerequisites to individual freedom and a lasting peace. In order to "place Europe on its feet economically," concluded Marshall, American policy had to "provide a cure rather than a mere palliative."[164] Typifying the administration's conceptual framework, this rhetoric replicated the neutral tones of Truman's doctor persona, depicting Europe as still recovering from the sickness of war to justify economic assistance. Doing so extended the basic elements of the Truman Doctrine without the inflammatory anti-communist rhetoric.[165] Even muted, however, the Soviets called the plan "economic imperialism."[166]

Press accounts of these speeches, most of which endorsed Truman's policy and commended his administration for striking the appropriate tone toward the Soviet Union, replicated the biological metaphors put forth by the administration. Coverage of Acheson's speech stated "a healthy, solvent and friendly Europe" was necessary "to avoid an insane competitive scramble." The logic put forth generally supported the disease/doctor metaphor as well. Much like a doctor tapering off the medicine as the patient improves, press accounts rationalized continuing aid as temporary and eventually disappearing as the nations recovered. The *Washington Post*, for example, equated American assistance to Europe as existing on a sliding scale, claiming "our resources will, no doubt, diminish as rehabilitation goes forward." A general, universal fear of chaos in Europe and the danger posed by disruption supplemented these accounts. Raymond Swing at ABC argued, "A ruined Europe, which we've not adequately aided, will go communist in its chaos, the communism is not the danger, the chaos is the danger and the way to stave off the communism is to stave off the chaos."[167] The administration, of course, sought to frame press accounts of the policy. Toward that end, they circulated the doctor/disease metaphor. In a letter to Walter Lippmann, sharing Acheson's address at Wesleyan, Joseph Jones explained the necessity of the economic assistance package to Greece and Turkey as a remedy for the "conditions of economic anarchy in which Communism inevitably breeds."[168] The framing worked. Lippmann repeated the metaphor before praising Acheson for striking the right "tone and temper."[169]

Truman's disease metaphors to describe Soviet danger reflected the broad penetration of biological metaphors as continuously available rhetorical resources in the postwar era. The president employed those resources to justify the Marshall Plan, as well as the continuation of occupation and recovery efforts. But he also fused metaphors of disease with the rhetoric of containment to underscore the need to continue to occupy and rehabilitate Germany and Japan. With Congress espousing isolationist views, this discourse underscored the need for occupation and for recovery efforts throughout Asia and Europe. As Truman explained, his policy sought to "assist free men and free nations to recover from the devastation of war," an effort especially important as both Europe and Asia faced serious difficulties, particularly in Germany, Japan, and Korea.[170] He further explained those difficulties as the result of Soviet aggression in his annual message to Congress in 1948. Warning that "economic distress . . . [was] a disease whose evil effects spread far beyond the boundaries of the afflicted region," he represented the Soviets as the malignant agent intent on subverting capitalist nations and undermining "a healthy world economy [which] is essential to world peace."[171] The financial aid package to Greece and Turkey, along with the reconstruction and recovery activities in the occupied countries of Germany, Austria, Japan, and Korea now served as the primary policy out to contain the spread of the Soviet disease. Figuring nations as a body-at-risk, the rhetoric warned that failure to fully revive the former enemies would risk contaminating the region anew.

The rise of Soviet savagery also fueled Truman's exhortations about the need for democracy and capitalism. Rearticulating his special responsibility to ensure the occupied nations transitioned to democracy and capitalism, particularly "Germany, Austria, Japan, and Korea,"[172] he later linked the failures of the German people after World War I with the failure of American leadership to inculcate democratic norms in the defeated nation. The key lesson pointed to the impermanence of character. A love of freedom did not provide protection from the "powerful reactionary forces which are silently undermining our democratic institutions."[173] Truman leveraged the fluidity of German and Italian character to warn against the dangers of communism and urge vigilance and a commitment to leadership. "Other people have also loved freedom, but have lost their liberty with tragic suddenness," he explained. "It happened in Italy 25 years ago. It happened in Germany 15 years ago. It happened in Czechoslovakia just a few months ago. And it could happen here."[174] By reiterating the conditions under which democracy gives way to dictatorship—"when people are hungry—and homeless—and frightened—they are easy victims for clever demagogues"—he explained the potential for additional nations to lose "their freedom to men who made promises of unity and efficiency and security."[175] Truman's rhetoric carefully articulated the German story as one of corruption by skilled orators who "used anti-Semitic propaganda as a way of stupefying the German people with false ideas."[176] Rehistoricizing the war implied that democratic nations, educated in the tenets of liberalism and reaping the benefits of capitalism, could discern between truth and falsehood.

As the war faded into memory and crisis solidified the Cold War era, Truman's rhetoric gradually incorporated Germany and Japan into the broader ideological framework that defined the competition between East and West. As allies, the former enemies were strategically located on both sides of the communist power base. And, as democracies, they served American interests in containing the expansion of the Soviet Union's sphere of influence. In a message responding to claims that U.S. policy "is deliberately following a course that leads to war" with the Soviets, Truman expounded upon the benevolent and beneficent aspects of occupation, reconstruction, and rehabilitation. He claimed his efforts only sought "the economic revival of Germany" and the prevention of the rise of "new forces of destruction" wrought by the advent of "atomic weapons and bacteriological warfare." Germany's inclusion marked the Axis powers' passage from confinement to reintegration into civilized society.[177] No longer did Germany appear as ill and in need of continuous intervention. Instead, the former enemy had become valuable members of civilized society. Their value, of course, existed in relation to the growing danger posed by the Soviet Union and "the recovery of all Western Europe," but the point remained. Truman deemed that Germany's physiological fitness warranted their readmission to civilized society. Equally, Truman's remarks announcing the official end of the war with Japan in 1952 credited the Japanese people with "build[ing] a democratic and peace-loving nation." Japan's transition to fully sovereign state, he claimed, "strengthened the essential bonds of friendship between our two peoples" and afforded the ex-belligerent the opportunity to play a positive role in heading off the dangers posed by "Communist imperialism."[178] The short message reflected the tenets of the doctor-patient metaphor. Having overseen Japan's passage from infirmity to health, insanity to sanity, Truman ended the occupation. Because recovery, ultimately, involves release.

The Legacy of the Recivilized Savage

Truman's end-of-war rhetoric constituted the postwar era as one requiring the correct identification of the causes of war and an American strategy up to the task of preventing future conflicts. Metaphors of disease invested the presidency with the persona of doctor, and in doing so, bound American foreign policy to diagnose problems and prescribe remedies. Since rehabilitation of the Axis powers was a long-term program that required monitoring and follow-up, the persona ensured a long-term relationship between the United States and Germany and Japan. But, while victory had put the world on the path, peace could only be achieved through the "same devotion to the essential freedoms and rights of mankind which sustained us throughout the war and brought us final victory."[179] The treatment regimen, then, called for actions above and beyond reconstruction of Germany and Japan. Indeed, Truman's metaphoric economy called for an international program designed to boost national immunities to the forces of totalitarianism, to watch for additional outbreaks of tyranny, and to prepare to respond rapidly to the transmission of pathogenic ideologies. Positing the United States as first among equal democratic partners, his rhetoric identified a unique role for the nation in the postwar era and portended the rise of permanent American hegemony.

At the end of war, presidents come under enormous pressure to forgo war powers and abandon the role of commander in chief. While some war powers are designated emergency or temporary and expire automatically, presidents often retain discretion over when to declare the crisis over and dispense with the war powers they possess. But the arc of presidential power bends toward consolidation, not diffusion.[180] With the president thinking of future threats and interested in conserving the unfettered potential for military action within the discretion of the presidency, war powers never return to prewar configurations. In the postwar era, Truman delayed peace treaties with Germany and Japan by extending the nation-as-body metaphor to request patience while the Axis patients were cured, educated, and rehabilitated. These rationales enabled Truman to maintain temporary war powers until 1951, placing the occupation and the stationing of U.S. military forces in the defeated nations under the penumbra of the president's power as commander in chief. They also facilitated construction of a national-security state and the most significant and permanent increase in presidential power in U.S. history.

No matter the motivation, however, Truman's metaphoric economy displaced the savage at the end of the war and enabled the rhetorical rehumanization of Germany and Japan. In spite of initially harsh peace terms, both nations became closely allied to the United States, providing important economic if not security benefits. Still, rather than usher in an era of peace, Truman's rehumanizing rhetoric facilitated the rise of the Cold War by positing the forces of savagery as ever present, ready and able to infect or persuade vulnerable body politics. In particular, Truman's use of the disease metaphor to motivate foreign-policy decisions locked the nation into the role of international doctor. The persona positioned the presidency in the role of surveyor, overseeing the globe, watchful for the spread of the communist disease, and mindful of vulnerable bodies in danger because, as Ivie put it, "disease itself is never conquered."[181] While Truman's successors would modify foreign-policy strategy and tactics, the framing of international relations as perpetually endangered would not change. However, the return of savagery in Korea complicated Truman's discourse of the enemy, requiring an entirely new lexicon to characterize the Cold War, America's adversaries, and the nation's role in the world.

CHAPTER 2

The Mobile Savage

HARRY TRUMAN, DWIGHT EISENHOWER, AND STALEMATE IN KOREA

———— •◆• ————

The communist invasion of South Korea on the morning of June 25, 1950, caught Harry Truman unaware. Having delegated policy related to Northeast Asia to others so he could focus on Europe, the president rarely engaged Asia policy prior to the attack.[1] For these reasons, North Korean aggression surprised the president and left him with few options. Afterwards, he received daily briefings on battle reports and "insist[ed] that all directives regarding the war come to him for approval."[2] The scattered information contained in initial battle reports warned he could lose Korea, just like he had lost China, a development that would undermine his plans to rebuild Japan as a democratic, capitalist nation; threaten his policy of containment; and jeopardize the future of the United Nations (UN) as keeper of the peace in world affairs.[3] Confronted with these risks, Truman secured a UN resolution authorizing a military response to the invasion and mobilized the military under the command of General Douglas MacArthur to defend South Korea.[4] Even with quick American intervention, however, the North Korean invasion maintained its advance until they reached Pusan, the very southeastern tip of the Korean peninsula.[5]

The addition of U.S. forces eventually proved decisive. By September 1950, American forces gathered with sufficient strength to take the war to the North Koreans, rather than merely engage in defensive action. MacArthur's counterattack at Inchon—a port town southwest of Seoul—collapsed the enemy's supply lines, split the communist forces in half, and gave the upper hand to the UN coalition.[6] Had the president stuck to the tenets of the original UN Resolution and sought a settlement based on the prewar borders, the war might have gone down as a footnote in Cold War history. Unfortunately, Truman heeded MacArthur's advice and gambled that passing the 38th parallel could achieve the unification of the peninsula and defeat the communist government in North Korea.[7] The decision backfired, precipitating a massive Chinese invasion and more than two years of stalemate.[8] During that time, thousands died for minor shifts in position that never altered the trajectory of the war. Truman initiated peace talks in December 1950, but achieved little progress in formalizing an agreement during the rest of his term. Finalizing a settlement fell to Dwight D. Eisenhower, who made the issue a core component of his campaign for the presidency in 1952.[9]

As with World War II, Truman's rhetoric of the enemy hampered his ability to rationalize an end to the war short of total victory. Contemporary accounts of the stalemate identify political, policy, and diplomatic roadblocks that impeded negotiations with the North Koreans. Yet, once inflamed, the savage idiom is not only difficult to extinguish, it prolongs the motive force for conflict. Casting the invasion as lawless and unprovoked, Truman depicted the enemy as a criminal enterprise willing to use whatever means available to achieve their goals. His initial statements described a willful, lawless antagonist bent on unprovoked aggression and engaged in activities endangering "the peace of the world."[10] Internal documents echoed this depiction, with one memo explaining, "The Army of North Korea launched a completely unprovoked general invasion . . . a surprise attack."[11] Identifying North Korea as a criminal element gave way to a more general portrait of a communist conspiracy. A month into the war, the State Department issued guidance requiring all officials to refer to the enemy as "international Communist invaders . . . rather than more neutral phrases like 'North Korean forces' and the 'Korean War.'"[12] By December 1950, Truman pointed to the Soviet Union as culprit in Korea "when he declared a state of national emergency . . . 'has been created by the rulers of the Soviet Union.'"[13] This rhetoric made explicit connections between the war in Korea and generalized fears of communism. It also signaled to the Soviets that the democratic powers of the world would defend against communist incursion in Korea and beyond.

Framed this way, Korea raised material and rhetorical stakes for Truman and Eisenhower. Yet, linking Korea to the broader context of the Cold War complicated domestic attitudes toward the conflict and communism. While the American public had already become disillusioned with aspirations of global peace, Korea cemented the new reality of a Cold War that could become hot. From the Truman Doctrine to the fall of Czechoslovakia to Korea, Americans both inside and outside the administration became convinced of the communist ideology's aggressive desire to conquer the world.[14] Stalin's decision to block all attempts at a negotiated settlement kept the war going, exacerbating American debates about the war and complicating Truman's war strategy.[15] These factors made it, as Elizabeth Stanley put it, "virtually impossible to extricate [the nation] from these 'sticky' policies and the war itself."[16]

The Korean challenge required both Truman and Eisenhower to escape the quagmire in a way that could sustain and strengthen the American position in the world. Under normal circumstances, presidential rhetoric favors continuity over rupture. The presidency, as a fundamentally conservative institution, builds upon its rhetorical tradition by reproducing similar rhetorical forms over time.[17] End-of-war rhetoric is no different. Presidents enact similar forms in different situations. The metaphors presidents select to enable the transition out of war enjoin the foreign affairs bureaucracy to devise postwar policy around the structures endorsed by the metaphor. In situations of surrender, like World

War II, presidents can draw on the body-politic metaphor as a means for explaining the rehumanization of the enemy. Most antagonists don't capitulate, however. Unconditional surrender is the exception, not the rule, and presidents have to anticipate situations in which no clear exit from armed conflict exists. In those situations, presidents seek strategies that can facilitate an exit while placating public and congressional concerns.

The inability of the allies to force a decisive resolution on the field of battle stymied the prospects for a redemptive rhetoric during the Korean War. With no prospect of victory, neither Truman nor Eisenhower could employ the rhetorical frames used to characterize the German and Japanese people at the end of World War II. The antagonists continued to antagonize. Additionally, representing Korea as a flashpoint driven by the spread of Soviet designs highlighted the Soviet role in precipitating the conflict and hindering negotiations. For most of the conflict, discussions of the enemy invoked the figure of Soviet sponsorship. For those reasons, Truman and Eisenhower opted for a strategy of mobility, positing the enemy as comprised of secret agents, testing the West on multiple fronts, driven to conquest, and originating from the Soviet Union. By underscoring the ways that communist danger flared up around the world, Truman and Eisenhower made the case for policies that could adapt to a secretive, mobile antagonist. This rhetoric reinscribed American policy into the broader ideological conflict with the Soviet Union and set the stage for additional confrontations.

While both presidents emphasized the mobility of the savage to shift focus from Korea back to the USSR, the means by which they achieved transference differed. Truman, from the beginning of the war, defined the conflict as a criminal act, the intervention as a United Nations police action, and, in effect, the president as global policeman. Initially limiting his characterizations of the danger to the Korean theater, he gradually began to rely on more general references to "the communists." This shift abstracted depictions of the enemy, enabling the movement from Korea to China and, eventually, the Soviet Union.[18] The portrait of the enemy in Truman's rhetoric reflected the complex danger posed by criminality. Echoing the logic of the disease metaphor, that danger required vigilance and engagement in the world and a commitment to respond to emergency wherever it appeared. Representing the enemy as a mobile, criminal force articulated the need for rapid response to emerging crises generated by the conspiratorial impulses of a criminal communist ideology, oriented U.S. foreign policy to the logic of policing, and set the stage for the next crisis.

Eisenhower, alternatively, characterized international politics as a competition and the president as a game player. Participating in a certain rhetorical trajectory, his rhetoric spoke to many of the same themes expressed by Truman—particularly about the potential for communist insurgency to appear, suddenly, anywhere—but his metaphoric choice enabled a set of policy options beyond the limited scope of police work.[19] Where Truman characterized the war in Korea as a manifestation of a criminal conspiracy planned and orchestrated by the Soviet Union, Eisenhower placed the story of Korea into the broader picture of great power competition. His pivot deemphasized the importance of Korea as a site of competition, while pointing to the war as the example that demonstrates the rule about Soviet intent. Arguing that the Soviets competed for power with a specific type of strategy, one that included war by proxy, Eisenhower defined an international situation that required attention to multiple areas of the globe at once. And, in the role of game player, confronted with an intractable opponent intent on jeopardizing national bodies across the globe, the Eisenhower administration pointed to Indochina—Vietnam—as the next front in the contest for control of the world.

This chapter indexes the metaphoric economy utilized by Truman and Eisenhower to articulate the nation out of stalemate via a rhetoric of mobility. Mobilizing the savage enables presidents to close a war by displacing tropes of savagery from the conflict at hand, and in the process, redirects the foreign-policy bureaucracy to a new antagonist. Previous presidents have rhetorically transferred savage imagery from one enemy to another by taking advantage of the enduring strength of prevalent archetypal metaphors utilized to justify war.[20] This strategy remedies the discursive problem produced by stalemate by displacing and redirecting fears of the Other. In doing so, strategies of mobility sustain the war drive while offering a means to close the present conflict. Truman's and Eisenhower's rhetoric of mobility overcame public opinion and budgetary pressure, facilitated armistice, and placed the nation on the path to additional confrontation. Charting Truman's depiction of the threat posed by the communists explains how his crime-police metaphoric pair constituted American policy in ways that undermined efforts to implement containment globally. Similarly, Eisenhower's refiguration of the Cold War as a contest for control of the world facilitated an exit but came with a steep price for policy.

Defining the Enemy with a Rhetoric of Police Action

The way Truman talked about the war mattered just as much as his quick move to deploy air and naval forces to aid South Korea. From the first moments, his public comments displayed metaphoric confusion. While not fully abandoning the disease-doctor frame, he designated the conflict a police action, setting into motion a network of metaphoric entailments that defined the enemy, the war, and his thesis of the broader confrontation with communism. While the term police action" first appeared publicly when Senator William Knowland (R-CA) used it on the Senate floor discussing American assistance for Korea, it came from a U.S. Army contingency plan. That plan had predicted that any UN Security Council Resolution would be vetoed by the Soviet Union and thus proposed a police action as a more limited form of intervention involving "the dispatch[ing of] a task force that could include US troops to restore order in South Korea."[21] When a reporter put the term to Truman on June 29, 1950, the president eagerly accepted it.[22] Quickly becoming "the soundbite everyone would remember," the term stuck and became official government language to describe the conflict.[23]

Articulating the war as a police action enacted an array of crime metaphors to define the enemy, the war, the UN response, and the danger posed by communism generally. That rhetoric displaced metaphors of disease with tropes of criminality. Those tropes depicted the enemy's actions as designed to obstruct the forces of peace and intimidate South Korea, revealing their true outlaw character. For example, Truman's first national remarks on the war on July 19, 1950, a speech heard by "an estimated 130 million Americans," depicted the communists as engaging in lawless aggression and explained his decision to intervene as necessary to restore the "rule of law of nations."[24] Labeling the North Koreans as the true culprits with oblique references to communists, the rhetoric fit with his prior pronouncements of the enemy as bandits conducting a raid.[25] Characterizing the enemy as criminals, bandits, and beholden to a broader communist conspiracy raised two problems. First, the rhetoric understated the nature of the threat posed to South Korea and the region. Bandits don't conquer, they steal. Depicting the invasion as a criminal act and the enemy as a criminal element seeking to exploit weaknesses in international law limited the scope of the danger and undermined claims to national crisis.

Second, depicting the conflict as the outcome of criminal elements called for a limited response by fast-moving police forces with limited goals. Bandits are targeted for "capture and incarceration by the police," not elimination by military forces, because all police actions, by definition, are not sustained activities.[26] The police arrive, sort out a mess, and leave. Truman's rhetoric restricted the scope of policy options to that of a defensive action with minimal strategic goals. Indeed, he spoke to these limitations in private deliberations of the National Security Council on June 29, making clear "he only wanted to restore order to the 38th parallel."[27] Like the police officer quelling a riot, the military response sought to use the minimum force necessary to reintroduce the legal boundary between the two countries. In a broad sense, then, Truman's crime metaphors failed to credibly represent the enemy while placing significant limitations on the military response. The visual "images of tanks, airplanes, and infantry" that followed American intervention reflected incongruity between the metaphoric depiction and actual representations of the enemy.[28]

Emphasizing the criminal component of the war and its antagonists constituted Truman in the role of president-as-policeman, reorienting his policy agenda away from containment and toward emergency response to crises. Containment, as the master frame of the Cold War, served Truman's policy goals of reincorporating Germany and Japan into the domain of the democratic family, while providing a firewall against communist imperialism.[29] Truman's articulation of the crisis in Korea via crime metaphors displaced this metaphoric framing of the communist danger and entailed the nation in the role of policeman, rather than physician. Completing a movement begun with NSC-68, which "mapped out the US role in the Cold War . . . as global policeman," Truman's policeman persona refined containment to focus on crisis response.[30] This shift inferred the likelihood of additional criminal acts and the need for additional acts of remediation. And indeed, his letter to Congress on August 1, 1950, requested funds for a global response to the "communist assault . . . challeng[ing] the authority of the United Nations and jeopardiz[ing] world peace.[31] Figuring the invasion as the work of a mobile, criminal force that would create future problems, the letter sketched the U.S. role as that of global policeman. As Truman put it, Korea demonstrated the need for "preparedness to defend the principles of international law and justice for which the United Nations stands."[32] Again premising policy on the tenets of the crime metaphor, the request posited collective defense as essential to the preservation of law itself. Congress granted the $4 billion request on September 27, 1950.[33]

At the same time the police-officer entailment limited the scope of the engagement, it also collapsed the distinction between war and peace. The symbolic order instituted by war rhetoric identifies hostilities as occurring abroad—that war is something that happens somewhere else—between sovereign powers left with no recourse for resolving differences short of violence. Truman's adoption of the policeman persona, however, related the conflict as something occurring within sovereign space, necessitating a form of mediation enacted by law enforcement. Truman made this distinction explicit in December 1950, claiming, "Our problem is more than a military matter. Our problem and our objective is to build a world order based on freedom and justice. We have worked with the free nations to lay the foundations of such a world order in the United Nations . . . That is the only way out of an endless circle of force and retaliation, violence and war—which will carry the human race back to the Dark Ages if it is not stopped now."[34] This rhetoric figured the stakes of the conflict as juridical. Success in Korea, in this view, would demonstrate the existence of a global sovereign space instituted by the regime of international law. But, conceiving of Korean territory as coextensive with a global sovereign order rendered the police action as existing in a domestic space. As Deborah Cowen has argued, reimagining conflict as occurring within sovereign space alters the ways military interventions function. An external war invests the military with the norms of a campaign, including enemy definition, strategies of attack and counterattack, and the "violent economies of space" enabled by the logistical frameworks that make military campaigns possible.[35] An internally situated conflict reduces the scope of war while escalating the conditions of insecurity felt by those involved. The paradox of Truman's police action is that in articulating a "modern political spatiality," in which historical distinctions between war spaces collapse, it also rendered the conflict as an event happening in a distant neighborhood.[36] Far from invoking public fears about communist expansion to enjoin the nation to war, the rhetoric of a police action instead provoked limited, provisional public concerns. This symbolic collapse—and the evaporation of the idea of a separate, distinct field of battle where conflict would occur—figured the military response as that of assistance, prolonging the war and undermining public support for the effort.

COMMUNIST CONSPIRACY

As the war stretched on, Truman's crime frame expanded beyond Korea to represent the conflict as one component of a broader communist conspiracy. Beyond mere law-breaking, the invasion demonstrated that the communist conspiracy rejected the authority of law entirely. As he put it on October 17, 1950, after returning from a meeting with MacArthur, the

"North Korean communists . . . refuse[d] to acknowledge the authority of the United Nations." Their use of force, he continued, demonstrated the "evil purpose" behind the communist conspiracy and its willingness to use "unlawful military force" to achieve political goals.[37] Korea demonstrated how communist forces enabled law-breaking and how this conspiracy sought to subvert the law in order to threaten the viability of the only international body capable of policing the peace. This rhetoric extended the discourse of mobility by claiming that the communist conspiracy could endanger any area, at any time, and that the United States had to remain ready to respond to disruptions of the lawful order. Additionally, by equating the invasion to blackmail, Truman implied that the use or threat of force was a core tactic of communist governance. As blackmail can be used on anyone, anywhere, the depiction mobilized the danger, paving the way for additional police activities in response to an emboldened, global conspiracy against freedom.

Depicting the Korean War as a product of a conspiracy at work behind the scenes enabled Truman to displace the savage from the theater of war to the globe, while also solidifying the president-as-policeman persona. Having initially avoided publicly naming the Soviets as responsible for the invasion in order to preserve the possibility of a quick negotiated settlement, Chinese intervention in October shifted the narrative context of the conflict.[38] The conspiracy frame penetrated policy conversations at the start of war, establishing the basis for the rhetoric of mobility by locating the source of savagery in an ideology and not a people or a nation. Over the course of his tenure, Truman employed legal terminology to describe that ideology and the conflict, envisioning communism as a criminal enterprise with a global reach. This legal vernacular mobilized the figure of the enemy, shifting it from a regional problem to a global one, and, as he contended, required expanding efforts to provide military equipment in defense of "free nations" around the world.[39] But Chinese intervention raised the rhetorical stakes by forcing the administration to acknowledge the presence of an additional conspirator. In a nationally broadcast address on December 15, 1950, Truman claimed "the communists . . . threw their Chinese armies into battle against the free nations," a phrase simultaneously highlighting the mindlessness of Chinese barbarism while inferring an additional driving force behind the invasion.[40] Four months later, he explained the fight in Korea was a proxy for the more important confrontation with the Soviets. In reminding the public why it is "right for us to be in Korea," Truman pointed to a "monstrous conspiracy" orchestrated by the "communists in the Kremlin . . . to stamp out freedom all over the world."[41] This depiction completed the rhetorical movement by focusing entirely on the Soviet Union and the mysterious prospect of communist effort to undermine and eliminate democracy.

Truman's extended legalistic discourse of conspiracy enacted a metaphoric logic—that all conspirators share equal liability for the criminal act—to suggest that even if the Soviets hadn't launched the invasion, culpability extended to them. Definitionally, conspiracies are organized attempts to commit crimes or jeopardize public welfare.[42] Secretive, unlawful, and obscure, they involve multiple actors, all of whom conceal their identities. The clandestine nature of conspiracy means they can involve many actors across international borders, some unaware of their involvement but liable for the criminal activities undertaken. As a rule, conspiracies are also mobile, flexible, and contingent; difficult to track; and highly responsive to law enforcement. These factors make demonstrations of proof difficult, and circumstantial inferences rather than more direct forms of evidence often determine culpability.[43] By describing the Chinese intervention within the contours of a broader criminal enterprise, Truman inferred that the police action in Korea had revealed a criminal enterprise that stretched beyond Northeast Asia and thus merited a more sophisticated investigation of communist designs.

As negotiations to end the conflict stretched on, the conspiracy metaphor continued to frame Truman's understanding of the war. Claiming the defense of Korea was "exposing the evil objectives of the communist conspiracy," he posited the American mission as both educational and juridical.[44] Stopping the "Kremlin conspiracy" from succeeding in Korea would send an important signal to the world, he claimed, and would bring "new hope and courage to free men in Europe, and in the Middle

East, who face the Soviet menace across their frontiers."[45] In Truman's discourse, the war demonstrated the dangers of the conspiracy, but having defined the cause of the war as a network of criminal elements, the police work required to combat an international conspiracy transcended the response in Korea. Instead, the metaphor entailed pursuing the investigation wherever the conspiracy appeared, and expanding police activities from Northeast Asia to other regions of the world. Truman made the case in a national address in 1952, explaining, "We have been blocking the Kremlin's conspiracy to undermine and take over the free countries around the world . . . We have put a lot into this struggle. It has called for American troops and arms in Europe, and American fleets on the seas, and American bases in foreign lands, and a hard, bitter conflict in Korea."[46] Having mobilized and articulated the danger in such a way that it could only be understood as roving, international, and constant, Truman's rhetoric used those depictions to rationalize conventional military deployments around the globe.

Representing the enemy and the defense of South Korea with tropes of criminality, even when linking the conspiracy directly to the Soviets, limited the scope of the mission, undermining the president's containment doctrine in two ways. First, tropes of criminality place violence outside of the bounds of the law. Rather than conceiving of the North Korean attack as a colonial war or a war of territorial acquisition, Truman represented the outbreak of violence as a failure of the law to police unlawful parties and deter violations of the legal regime. Second, designating the perpetrator of international violence—North Korea—as criminal circumscribed the UN mission as policing the violence, repelling the invasion, and restoring the rule of law. By constituting the mission as the restoration of a legal order, Truman's discourse of criminality resituated the foreign-policy response as punitive, rather than a host of other possibilities.[47] This orientation theorized international law as a regime of punishment in which the collective defense of South Korea could deter "future calculated outbreaks against the peace."[48] Appropriately punishing an individual or group who transgressed the law carries a symbolic resonance that warns others of the consequences of their actions. In a single stroke, then, tropes of criminality delegitimized the violence and judged those responsible for that violence as unlawful, criminal elements in need of punishment. Rather than task the bureaucracy with developing strategies to prevent additional outbreaks of violence, these entailments limited how the government understood the problem in Korea and narrowed the landscape of remedies to police action.

In addition to directing the war effort, the rhetoric of criminality and the persona of the president-as-policeman also guided the president's end-of-war strategy. Public speculation about "how to bring the 'police action' to a successful conclusion" played a role in this dynamic by raising two possibilities—atomic escalation or a return to the 38th parallel.[49] China's intervention caught Truman in an unwinnable conflict, leading MacArthur to propose atomic warfare to break the stalemate. While Truman never intended to use nuclear weapons to settle the war—they were unlikely to alter the landscape of the conflict—these discussions pointed to the improbability of military solutions.[50] They also indicated how framing the war as a police action precluded escalatory options entirely. The embodied role of global policeman established the terms of victory as the restoration of the international legal order, not the complete obliteration of the enemy. American allies participating in the UN mission, concerned about the potential for escalation, emphasized the constraints implicit in the term "police action." Raising objections to the possible use of atomic weapons, they contended that "this is a United Nations police action, and we do not want to kill thousands of civilians and create a radio-active shambles, but with the minimum loss of life and expense on either side, to restore the *status quo* and the integrity of South Korea."[51] Regardless of strategic inefficiencies, the terminology of the war ensured it would remain a conventional conflict.

Unable to negotiate a return to prewar borders, Truman instead asserted that the defense of Korea proved the success of his efforts to beat the global conspiracy. As he put it in September 1952, "We've stopped the advance of communism all over the globe. We moved into Korea to make it plain to the Kremlin that the free countries of the world don't plan to engage in appeasement—for we have learned from bitter experience that appeasement is the road to total war. The Communists have been stopped cold in Korea. And the Communists haven't crossed another frontier since, anywhere in the world."[52] Embodying the tenets of the police-action metaphor and the Truman-as-policeman persona, the rhetoric marked the conflict of Korea as something less than war, but that could eventually lead to war. Implicitly analogizing the communist invasion in Korea to Germany's invasion of Poland in 1939, Truman's remarks claimed crisis response as the appropriate remedy to aggression. The rhetoric also figured the United States as lawman, tasked with corralling the danger posed by the anti-democratic ideology. As lawman, his job wasn't to end crime; it was to establish the rule of law by policing its worst elements.

IDENTIFYING NEW SITES OF COMMUNIST CRIMINALITY

In his final year in office, Truman featured Korea as one incident in a wider field of Soviet-sponsored criminality. This rhetorical shift facilitated the geographic expansion of the Truman Doctrine to Asia while reasserting Korea's displacement from *the* site of confrontation to *a* site of confrontation. This displacement pointed to the global motives of the crooked forces responsible for the war. In a message to George C. Marshall, Truman confirmed the crime-police thesis underwriting his view of the international situation. In the telegram, he claimed the "lawless aggression of communist forces in Korea, and . . . the menace of still further communist attacks against other free nations" justified the buildup of American military might. The broader confrontation, he continued, would be won by the "armed forces we are building, and the supplies for them which our factories, farms, and mines are turning out," all of which exist "for the protection and preservation of our freedoms."[53] Truman's definition of armed forces as inclusive of civilian technology and materials, from factories to farms, served to erode distinctions between the military and civilian spheres of the economy and, most importantly, the federal budget. In doing so, it raised the possibility that the military and civilian spheres could never be delinked. Raising the potential for enemy forces to pop up anywhere rationalized military preparedness and expansion as the logical response to criminal elements probing the international order. Korea, as the example that demonstrated the truth of the criminal conspiracy endangering the globe, compelled the United States to prepare for confrontation anywhere at any time. And, as with his more explicit renderings of the police-action metaphor, Truman characterized the danger posed by communism as a threat to the fair and legal order itself. American preparedness against "further communist attacks against other free nations," as he put it, constituted the American mission as that of protectorate, armed and ready to respond to additional violations of international law.[54]

As the 1952 campaign got underway, Truman's discourse of the enemy maintained the tenets of the crime-police metaphor while specifying the need for sacrifice at home and abroad in millennial, transcendent terms. Recalling that the selection of Warren Harding in 1920 had led to a more isolationist foreign policy in the 1920s and, eventually, the outbreak of World War II, he claimed "the present moment" exhibited the same potential. Truman warned that as the most powerful country in the world, an undisputed leader, and the primary combatant in Korea, "the course America chooses in 1952 will be even more important than the choice in 1920. This is because of the great change which has taken place in our position among the nations of the world." He offered success in halting Soviet encroachment in free Europe as evidence and noted, "We have thrown back lawless aggression in Korea. We have curbed the creeping menace of Communist subversion that was attacking one country after another around the world." Again the rhetoric embodied the tenets of the president-as-policeman persona by figuring the attack as lawless and Truman's efforts as restoring the legal order. To bow to the pressures of the isolationist wing of the Republican Party would risk abandoning the national role of policeman, replicating the same circumstances that produced the Second World War and undermining the tangible gains made under his presidency.[55] For Truman, his policies "can and will be successful in preventing another world conflict" that will result in "a great age—an age of great achievements for mankind."[56] Once again, Korea served as empirical evidence backing his proposition that American leadership could check communist imperialism even if it reappeared. By placing Korea in the context of a thirty-year trajectory of U.S. foreign policy, Truman bound together the disparate notions of rearmament, confrontation, encirclement, and deterrence into a long-term vision for success in the "true" war—the war for a peaceful, lawful world order.

After Eisenhower's victory, Truman sought to ensure continuity of his policy of deterrence with conventional military strength. He contended that the proper defense of democracies from aggression could sustain the international legal order and forestall future wars. In his final State of the Union, Truman claimed, "The free nations may have to maintain for years the larger military forces needed to deter aggression. We must build steadily, over a period of years, toward political solidarity and economic progress among the free nations in all parts of the world."[57] This strategy mattered, he said, because the danger of global war remained. Only sustained cooperation with allies to encircle and deter the Soviet Union, he warned, could "sav[e] the basic moral and spiritual values of our civilization."[58] By placing Korea in this context, Truman not only bolstered his defense of containment as a strategy and the risk of communist imperialism generally, he also validated the role of president-as-policeman. Korea, in Truman's final iteration, represented one incident in a broader criminal enterprise orchestrated by the Soviet Union. By emphasizing the enterprise over the incident, the rhetoric suggested his efforts—in spite of the failure to achieve armistice—had been appropriate and successful. Equating the war in Korea to the "desperate struggle that George Washington fought through to victory," Truman's closing argument elevated the importance of preparation, crisis response—police action—to the long-term stability of the global, legal order.[59] Perhaps attempting to constrain the Eisenhower administration, this rhetoric urged continuity in American efforts to counteract illegal communist activities, by force if necessary.

Truman's quick move to support South Korean troops saved the Asian nation from utter ruin and forced unification with the communist north. Yet, like many of his actions, the instinctual response lacked the deep, strategic thinking of his predecessor or that of Eisenhower. His subsequent decision to cross the 38th parallel and seek the unification of Korea by force resulted in a foreign-policy calamity that sank his presidency amidst the mire of war and strategic failure. While his discourse of mobility altered the terminology that constituted the Cold War, his inability to negotiate a conclusion undermined his claims about the efficacy of his policeman strategy. Even in displacing savagery from Korea, his administration remained bogged down in the conflict, the policeman who could never leave the scene. The task of concluding the war fell to Dwight D. Eisenhower. As detailed in the next section, his shift from president-as-policeman to president-as-game-player embraced the concept of mobility to facilitate the rhetorical conclusion of the Korean War. It also blossomed into a full-blown theory of international affairs premised on the potential of falling dominoes. This strategic reorientation elevated the importance of communist insurgency and set the table for American military involvement in Vietnam.

From Korea to the World: Eisenhower and the Metaphor of Competition

All presidents inherit rhetorical frames from their predecessors, but not all frames produce problems for policy. For Eisenhower, he faced immediate challenges involving public strife about a stalemated war, economic stagnation, rising budget deficits, and a domestic witch-hunt for communists.[60] As candidate, he blamed Truman for failing to adequately prepare for the communist threat, for allowing China to fall to communism, and for not deploying U.S. military forces in Korea to deter invasion.[61] He understood the political stakes of the war, declaring, "I shall go to Korea," but offered no new policy proposals to extricate the nation from the conflict.[62] As president, Eisenhower needed a war policy up to the task of grappling with the material circumstances of the war. And, since stalled negotiations made progress on the battlefield unlikely, he sought to shift the language of the war away from Truman's

war-as-police-action frame and produce new terminology capable of
recapturing the essence of the policy problem.

Ending the war was Eisenhower's highest priority.[63] His basic strategic calculation—as described by his advisors in private memos and briefings—argued that Truman had bogged the nation down in Korea while
the Soviet Union had sponsored communism in many other regions in
the world. A memo from American Legion National Commander Lewis
K. Gough to the president-elect elaborated the basic point: containment
as a policy had to attune strategic and tactical efforts to the mobility of
the communist danger. American response to communism, Gough argued, should "fulfill a defensive mission of containment in Korea" while
attending to growing danger in Southeast Asia.[64] John Foster Dulles
concurred, identifying "four separate battlefronts of the cold war: (a) in
Korea . . . (b) in Southeast Asia, Indian [*sic*], Africa and the Middle East
. . . (c) in Western Europe . . . (d) in Eastern Europe."[65] Korea, he argued,
was the "proving ground for America's ability to corrupt the enemy
command and dissolve his armies with political warfare." On that basis,
Dulles recommended publication of "mass defection from Communist
armies" as a means for demonstrating the failure of the ideology.[66]

Seeking an exit to the war, Eisenhower recontextualized the concept
of limited war to justify a negotiated settlement as part of a broader
strategy for confronting communism. He could not anticipate, obviously, that Josef Stalin would expire in early 1953, freeing North Korea to
negotiate an armistice.[67] Under pressure from media and policy elites to
define his Far East policy and distinguish it from Truman's, Eisenhower
sought a political language that could reframe the war and America's
involvement in it.[68] For reasons obvious and implicit, Truman's crime-
police metaphor could not serve. At a most basic level, the frame did
not fit the new president's policy interests because it called for limited
engagement, where Eisenhower sought more direct confrontation with
the Soviets. Eisenhower's own support for intervention in Korea added
an additional complication to the rhetorical legacy of a police action.[69]
His statement in September 1950 that military force in the postwar era
should operate on a "'fire department' basis" contradicted his criticism

of Truman's strategy in Asia.[70] The similarity between Eisenhower's fireman and Truman's policeman constrained his ability to recast Korea as a single site in a larger contest against communist savagery. And, the crime-police metaphor conflicted with Eisenhower's broader concerns about the state of the Cold War and the risk of communist expansion in Southeast Asia and beyond if the French abandoned Vietnam.[71] By January 1953, Eisenhower's decision to base the nexus of his foreign policy on confronting and containing Soviet power globally excluded the crime-police metaphor. New language was required.

Because of the widespread implications war has on the nation's foreign policy, the rhetorical choices of presidents who rise to power during an ongoing conflict deeply penetrate the bureaucracy. In this situation, Eisenhower's abandonment of the police-action metaphor coincided with a discourse positing foreign relations as a continuous competition for power, with East and West striving for control of a global board. At its base, the politics-as-competition metaphor derives from Thomas Hobbes's state of nature thesis and his claim that human relations are "marked by competition and prone to hostility and violence."[72] The underlying notion, popularized by "Darwinian and Spencerian concepts of 'survival of the fittest,'" posited life in the international sphere as inherently competitive, if not always fair.[73] By the 1950s, these concepts were deeply ingrained in American political thought and had partially underwritten Truman's approach to the war, and reappeared in policy domains as diverse as outer space, missiles and nuclear weapons, and free enterprise.[74] Elmer E. Schattschneider's pivotal text encapsulated these themes, arguing that competition lay at the base of politics. As such, would-be losers act preemptively to widen the scope of a conflict in order to even the odds of success.[75] At its base, this conception of politics raised the likelihood that calculation, rather than ideology, drove political decision-making.

Eisenhower's embrace of the competition metaphor encouraged a type of strategic thinking in which calculating actors engaged in diverse public and private tactics to accrue economic and security benefits abroad.[76] This orientation invested the nation in three basic paradigmatic

orientations: that the winner-takes-all, that the nation was involved in
a no-holds-barred-dogfight, and that the policy should focus on winning.[77] These orientations ask participants to establish goals, methods for
achieving goals, and an attitude focused on victory. They also infer that
participants make "quick and effective decisions . . . to assess opponents
(and teammates) and react to their strategic decisions."[78] In addition
to evaluating material factors like armaments, this thinking entailed a
territorial focus—an emphasis on locating strategic zones and holding
or defending them. Focusing on the position or location of a state in
the broader context of the great game treats states as pieces on a grid—
simultaneously undervaluing and overvaluing their existence. In this
metaphoric relation, an individual state held no value on its own other
than its role in the broader elements of international competition. But,
since individual states could be linchpins that upheld the entire international order and sustained the prospect of winning the game, strategy
required anticipating the importance of any given nation in relation to
the great power contest.[79] Any act of danger to a single state had to be
weighed and calculated to determine its importance in the overall strategic position of the game so that actors could devise appropriate and
effective tactics. Conceiving of states as pieces on the board—or politics
as international competition—justified alliances with unsavory regimes,
sacrifices in some areas to achieve gains elsewhere, and control of key
resources as a means to leverage an advantage over the opposition.[80]

While the competition metaphor may have fit the personality of a
world-famous general turned president, it also entailed Eisenhower in
the persona of the game player.[81] That persona served the president's
desire to refocus foreign policy on the Soviets and away from Korea
by describing a strategic posture oriented toward a calculating, mobile
adversary. The metaphor and the persona extended the logic of competition as a means for distancing policy from Korea via three primary
claims: fronts, geography, and strategy. Emphasizing the geography of
competition, the metaphor justified a proactive strategy up to the task
of countering Soviet power. Competitions require agility and a willingness to shift course in order to achieve goals. Claims about geography

implicitly criticized Truman's strategy and reoriented the foreign affairs bureaucracy away from viewing Korea as a focal point to that of a hot spot on a wider board of danger. For Eisenhower, effectively addressing each of the fronts in the global competition required divesting from Korea. Doing so would generate a sustainable strategy that could cope with Soviet pressure and provide a reliable defense of allies. While this rhetoric did not produce significant shifts in war policy—diplomacy determined the outcome, not battlefield tactics—it established a postwar paradigm for competing with the Soviets. That discursive shift refocused foreign affairs on a broad set of problematics while preparing for a form of confrontation that was both less costly and, in Eisenhower's view, more effective. His strategy would rely on proactively identifying zones of concern, building collective defense operations to stave off Soviet incursions, and relying on nuclear weaponry as the ultimate deterrent. Thus, while both presidents understood the need to end the Korean War, defend allies, and deter communist advances, Eisenhower's discourse shifted the conceptual framework that underwrote those policies by depicting the Korean War as a distraction from the global competition for control over territory, resources, and people.

INTERNATIONAL RELATIONS AS COMPETITION

A principal difference between the presidents appeared in the way that Eisenhower defined the events in Korea and how that definition implicated questions of strategy. Internally, the administration conceived of the conflict as one aspect in a global competition. A brief titled "Victory with Honor in Korea," attached to a memo Dulles sent to Eisenhower on November 20, 1952, laid the groundwork for the metaphor and the game-player persona. Claiming the Cold War had already been "won" by the West, it pointed to the possibility of mass defections from communist armies both as depriving those forces of the bulk of their military power and as orchestrating a public relations victory that would have significant psychological effects. With a significant number of Korean and Chinese prisoners of war refusing repatriation, holding up peace talks, the brief claimed allowing defections would add to the "box score" between East and West, and bolster the forces of democracy around the globe.[82] While the claims of victory amounted to little more than fantasy, they underscored the basic thesis of competition that defined the administration's approach to Korea. Even modest achievements—points scored—in Korea added up to victory in the great game.

Orienting foreign policy as a competition and Korea as one aspect of the contest, moreover, meant rejecting the police-action metaphor. Toward that end, Eisenhower talked about the conflict in millennial terms that defied any notion that Korea marked a limited engagement. This rhetorical campaign began with his inaugural address when he noted that the conflict

> joined no argument between slightly differing philosophies. This conflict strikes directly at the faith of our fathers and the lives of our sons. No principle or treasure that we hold, from the spiritual knowledge of our free schools and churches to the creative magic of free labor and capital, nothing lies safely beyond the reach of this struggle. Freedom is pitted against slavery; lightness against the dark. The faith we hold belongs not to us alone but to the free of all the world. This common bond binds the grower of rice in Burma and the planter of wheat in Iowa, the shepherd in southern Italy and the mountaineer in the Andes. It confers a common dignity upon the French soldier who dies in Indo-China, the British soldier killed in Malaya, the American life given in Korea.[83]

Far from describing a criminal act requiring a return to law and order, Eisenhower's depiction of the danger raised the prospect that a global competition for the soul of the world had already begun; only the form of confrontation was yet to be determined. The rhetoric emphasized the mobility of the savage by pointing to the struggle beyond Korea, rendering Korea as one front in that broader conflict. By extending Truman's rhetoric of mobility to emphasize the interconnectedness of the challenge, Eisenhower doubled down on the idiom of savagery to explain and justify his policy approach. Unlike the end of World War II, victory in Korea couldn't excise savagery from the world. Instead of thinking that way, the nation had to think strategically about the best way to counter emerging savagery. Only the proper form of strategic management, he implied, could ensure success beyond the bloody conflict in Korea. Far removed from depictions of the enemy as an unscrupulous criminal mind, this speech articulated the savage as a global, secretive force driven by an artful game player, testing the West on multiple fronts at once.

Eisenhower reiterated the metaphoric shift from police action to global competition against communism in his first State of the Union. Identifying the war in Korea as "the most painful phase of Communist aggression," he connected Korea to the struggle in Indochina and in Malaya and communist incursions in Western Europe.[84] Distinguishing his approach from Truman's, Eisenhower explained the danger as part of a shrewd scheme to undermine the West's position in the world. Korea was a phase, one set of tactics used by a wily opponent committed to eventual victory over the West. In spite of progress, he explained, the forces responsible for the Korea invasion now challenged Laos, where "a new act of aggression has been committed which might have serious consequences for Thailand and the whole of Southeast Asia . . . [and] must cast doubt on Communist intentions."[85] Beyond refocusing attention away from Korea or mobilizing the enemy, this statement transformed conceptions of danger by relocating it within an ideological struggle between competing worldviews. The pivot capitalized on the collective terror generated by the communist ideology and, in concert with his inaugural address, implied that only a certain type of strategic thinking could recognize the depth of the danger and execute solutions up to the task of countering it.

Eisenhower's reconceptualization of international relations as a global competition underwrote a shift from crisis response to long-term strategic planning. In the first months of his presidency, he warned that Truman's response to the Korea crisis reflected a strategy "of sudden, blind responses to a series of fire-alarm emergencies" that failed

to grapple with communism's desire for "destruction of freedom everywhere." The crisis in Korea was a war, he told reporters, "a particular
kind of war—but it is a war."[86] Pinpointing the cause of the conflict as
derived from an essential rivalry between the United States and the
Soviet Union, he represented it as the first battle in a global contest for
freedom everywhere. This rhetoric precluded the possibility that Korea
could be understood in any other terms. As he put it after armistice,
"a police action is not war . . . a police action is restoring order." This
rhetoric asserted the basic politics-as-competition metaphoric framing
by designating the war as an exercise of "force for reaching a decision
in a particular area."[87] Articulating war as one form of competition in international relations, what Clauswitz called the "continuation of policy
by other means," Eisenhower recast the significance of Korea in terms
of its cost to American strategy.[88] The American response to the Soviet
gambit demonstrated the shortsightedness of Truman's police-action
strategy. War weighs heavily on national policy to the detriment of trade,
diplomacy, cultural exchanges, and many other actions constitutive of
foreign policy. Eisenhower's critique implied that overinvesting in a
faraway conflict had unbalanced the board, risked conceding position
to the true enemy, and made the task of international competition more
difficult. These arguments recast the nature of the war and rationalized
Eisenhower's comprehensive military spending package by focusing on
the real player in the great game—the Soviet Union.

The international politics-as-competition metaphor also theorized
the existence of an audience monitoring the outcome of the great game.
This discourse apprehended the symbolic value of Korea and sought
to conclude the war in a way that appeared as if the United States had
gained something, prior to shifting attention to the Soviets. The target of
this symbolic shift, beyond the American public, involved all the nations
of the world. As a memo by Douglas MacArthur put it, "The Korean war
has now grown to symbolize in the eyes of the world the struggle between the Soviet and the United States in which every facet of disagree-
ment in every sector of the world is a part of the correlated whole."[89] The
statement reflected conceptions of the enemy as inherently mobile while

figuring the world as divided into discrete sectors upon which the two nations vied for position. The symbolic value of the Korean War, then, linked the conflict to the broader context of the Cold War, distributing the savage to the farthest reaches of the world.

RESITUATING KOREA AS ONE FRONT
IN A GLOBAL CONTEST

Shifting attention from Korea to the world played a crucial role in the Eisenhower administration's rhetorical displacement of the enemy, internal assessments about the war, and American strategy. In both public speeches and policy documents, the administration referred to Korea as one battle in a wider, global conflict. A memo from Dulles to Eisenhower, for example, explained the failure to negotiate an armistice as an outcome of "the dominant will with which we have to deal . . . the Soviet Union," which worked through the "Chinese Communist Party" to obstruct a conclusion to the war.[90] The logic of this declaration led to a significant conclusion: communist strategy was based on "global considerations and not considerations limited merely to the battle in Korea or the desires of the North Korean or Chinese Communists. There is no doubt that Moscow looks on the Korean war as only one of many fronts."[91] This passage, provided to Eisenhower prior to his official swearing in, formed the basis of the rhetorical strategy of displacement and mobility. For the new administration, Korea represented a tactical defeat in an emerging conflict between East and West because the Soviets had bogged down American forces on one battlefield. As Dulles observed, the outcome produced a "bad strategic disposition of U.S. land forces" and "an advantage to Soviet Russia" since the lingering Korean War "weakens our resolution with respect to other actual and potential areas of conflict."[92] Those areas included Western Europe, Formosa (Taiwan), Vietnam, Manchuria, and Japan. Worse, Dulles argued, the Korean War "slow[ed] down the rearming of Western Europe," served as a source of Soviet propaganda, generated "serious friction between the U.S. and the other NATO powers," and continued to threaten Japan.[93] With victory impossible, Dulles's brief portrayed the international situation in late 1952 as extremely precarious and requiring a broadening of strategy from Korea to the multiple fronts of communist challenge.

Dulles's first nationally televised address extended these themes. It featured a map behind the man that he used as a prop to distinguish between the free and enslaved worlds. As an expression of the geographic thinking infused in the administration's foreign-policy discourse, Dulles pointed to areas "which our enemies control" and identified the strategic benefits those areas provided. In doing so, he articulated Korea as a pawn in a larger game. Korea, he said, "naturally comes first to our minds because of the cruel and bloody war." But, from the Soviet perspective, Korea only matters because of Japan. Pushing back the communists in Korea, Dulles argued, would keep Japan out of the "Communist pincers" and deprive the enemy of the "great industrial power" found in the island nation.[94] As Dulles's speech moved around the map of the world, each area he highlighted contained some strategic reserve of minerals, oil, or other raw materials that explained Soviet intentions. Thematically, the speech posited Soviet intent as hostile, Soviet goals as pragmatic, and Soviet methods as diverse. Taken as a whole, the presentation outlined the contours of the administration's foreign-policy discourse and the presumption that international relations were always competitive and strategic. The strategic faults across the globe, moreover, appeared in specifically geographic ways that suggested the need for policy decisions based on the elements of competition.

For his part, Eisenhower rarely spoke about just Korea and instead placed the conflict in the context of democratic struggle in Southeast Asia, the Middle East, Africa, and Europe. This rhetoric recontextualized the Korean War as one front in a global struggle for freedom and evoked the embodied persona of the game player. For example, in his second State of the Union, Eisenhower argued:

> Some developments beyond our shores have been equally encouraging. Communist aggression, halted in Korea, continues to meet in Indo-china the vigorous resistance of France and the Associated States,

assisted by timely aid from our country. In West Germany, in Iran, and in other areas of the world, heartening political victories have been won by the forces of stability and freedom. Slowly but surely, the free world gathers strength. Meanwhile, from behind the iron curtain, there are signs that tyranny is in trouble and reminders that its structure is as brittle as its surface is hard.[95]

As with Truman, this statement classified Korea as a success because American efforts had stopped the communists. But, Eisenhower's metaphoric economy governed the evaluation of the outcome in relation to long-term strategic calculations. On the one hand, the rhetoric reiterated the basic metaphoric framing of politics-as-competition by revealing his suspicions about the other side. A central feature of strategy games, particularly card games, involves hiding vital information from one's opponent.[96] Equally, one of the tasks of the astute strategist is to make determinations about the other side's capabilities. In this excerpt, Eisenhower embodies the role of the game player by making public his judgment about the other side's capabilities. With the other side cloaked behind the Iron Curtain, however, those judgments approximated informed evaluations and not actual statements of fact. Policy decisions, then, amounted to informed wagers designed to account for the totality of the opponent's options.

On the other hand, by articulating the contest as ongoing, the rhetoric posited Korea as an early maneuver in a great competition. This claim extended the president-as-game-player persona and the postwar conceptual order because it signified that the West didn't have to defeat communism—it only had to halt its advances. The game would not be won or lost on a single hand. The failure of the armistice to halt the advance of the other side proved Eisenhower's point. Korea was one front of many in an international contest, a communist feint designed to draw American attention to Northeast Asia while making other fronts invisible. The idea implied in this discourse—that the true enemy used American fixation on Korea to advance in other regions of the world—constituted one basis of Eisenhower's metaphor. But it also prescribed a form of strategic thinking that could anticipate where the enemy would next press its advantage. Such thinking postulated the need for strength in armaments and preparations as a means for staving off future incursions.

An additional aspect of the competition metaphor emphasized the sides in the global game for control. While the Iron Curtain had materialized those divisions, physically dividing East from West, Eisenhower frequently spoke of "our opponents," "two world camps," and "the Communists."[97] These utterances reinforced the notion that there were only two sides—East and West, communism and democracy. For Eisenhower, pointing to the other side called for an orientation toward competition itself, rather than a specific strategy. This orientation, he explained, called for "vigilance, energy, and loyalty" because, as with any competition, players had to monitor each other in order to parse strategy, understand motivations, and identify weaknesses.[98] By recasting the divide between the East and West as a global competition, then, he displaced attention from Korea in favor of a more generalized stance of monitoring and containing communism, wherever it manifested. This reorientation played on prevalent fears that the communists sought to probe the weaknesses of the West and that attending only to Korea might distract from other, more important activities.[99]

Rapid change appeared as another feature in this logic of competition. Explaining that the world had transformed in the aftermath of World War II, Eisenhower argued that policy had to be responsive to new velocities. Noting that "every single day things change in this world," the president explained his role as "re-examining . . . the whole situation, geographic and otherwise, of our country and of others, to see what is it that we now need most to insure our security and peaceful existence."[100] As the principal competitor for the West, Eisenhower needed to continuously monitor and observe the world situation in order to devise policy strategies up to the task of countering the enemy's next move. Claiming that "a policy that was good six months ago is not necessarily now of any validity" because the world changes rapidly, Eisenhower identified a fundamental task of political leadership as to respond with equal speed.[101] Like the consummate game player three moves ahead of the competition, he argued the policy apparatus had to be forward thinking to get "ahead of the problem. We must see its major parts. We must get its critical factors set up . . . and then we must pursue a common course vigorously, persistently, and with readiness to make whatever sacrifices may be demanded."[102] Global, proactive, and constant, Eisenhower's rhetoric constituted the principal role of the foreign affairs bureaucracy as anticipating the opposition, awaiting their moves, and responding appropriately. Like the chess player continuously revising strategy while monitoring the opponent's moves, Eisenhower's strategic orientation hinged upon Soviet actions.

ARMISTICE, COLLECTIVE DEFENSE, AND THE GEOGRAPHIES OF COMPETITION

Cease-fire with North Korea presented the Eisenhower administration an opportunity to reiterate claims that the West was winning the competition against communism. Ten days before signing the agreement, Assistant Secretary of State Walter S. Robertson claimed, "The enemy we face in Korea is the same ruthless evil force which threatens free people along the perimeter of the globe. It seeks to destroy not only Korea but the entire free world as well."[103] This rhetoric enacted many of the tenets outlined by the president, but it also pointed at the trajectory of the administration's foreign policy by rearticulating the idea that multiple fronts required a broader gaze. Explicitly mobilizing representations of the enemy by pointing to endangered zones around the periphery of the world, Robertson singled out Korea as one crisis among many that had transpired since 1947. Rather than mark a unique incidence of savagery, the war demonstrated the tactics of a savvy opponent. Embracing the game-player persona, this rhetoric directed postwar foreign policy to attend to the geographies of competition that defined the era.

Embodying the role of the game player attacking a complex problem, Eisenhower reinstituted geographical thinking to divide up the world into zones of freedom and zones of slavery. This was necessary because Roosevelt had presided over an era where the significance of geographic distance appeared to be at an end. The attack at Pearl Harbor and the calamity that followed shattered the illusion of security provided by geographic isolation from Europe and Asia. In defense of U.S. engagement in world affairs, Roosevelt had argued that World War II demonstrated the futility of depending on isolation for security.[104] Paradoxically, the Eisenhower administration returned to prewar conceptions of geography to highlight the fortitude of the country's location. This rhetoric treated the globe as a grid or board upon which a great game of power appeared. His toast to the president of Turkey typified this discourse. As he put it, "in the world today, there is a free world—and its opponent is a world that is ruled by dictatorial processes behind the Iron Curtain."[105] The figure of borders—and notions of who lay inside and outside of the communist zone—coupled with the representation of the enemy as an opponent inscribed Eisenhower, and the nation, in a global competition for space.[106]

The geographic thinking instituted by the metaphor of competition differed substantially from that of the prewar era, however. Between World War I and World War II, geography appeared as a form of protection from European rivalries and entanglements. The lead-up to the war, the attack on Pearl Harbor, and the use of atomic weaponry forever banished that conception of geography from national-security discourse. Instead of reviving tired notions of isolationism, Eisenhower's competition metaphor advanced the notion that geography marked important zones for attention and protection. The finalization of armistice in Korea extended these conceptions to rationalize the postwar mission. In a nationally broadcast address announcing the cease-fire, Eisenhower welcomed peace with sober satisfaction, explaining, "We have won an armistice on a single battleground—not peace in the world. We may not now relax our guard nor cease our quest . . . we and our United Nations Allies must be vigilant against the possibility of untoward developments." Far from reassuring, the message placed peace as the endgame—the ultimate quest—but vigilance and deterrence as the means for getting there. Even without mentioning the Soviet Union by name, the speech implied that the inherently competitive nature of international relations made future clashes with Soviet power likely.

Still, even while admonishing the communists for the aggressive game they played and the human costs incurred, Eisenhower adopted an attitude toward the opponent that raised the possibility of an end to competition. Concluding his remarks with echoes of Lincoln's Second Inaugural, he stated, "With malice toward none; with charity for all; with firmness in the right as God gives us to see the right, let us strive on to finish the work we are in . . . to do all which may achieve and cherish a just and a lasting peace, among ourselves, and with all nations."[107] Ostensibly a quiet pause for peace, the quotation reaffirmed American purpose as beneficent, divinely driven, and respectful of other nations. It reminded the audience that peace required continuous efforts to prepare, watch for, and defend against aggression. But it also imagined an end to competition with the Soviets by implying the possibility of peaceful relations. As a player in a great game, the United States held no malice for the other side, even if they had erred in sponsoring war in Korea.[108] Remarkably forgiving, the speech closed one front while offering the possibility that both sides could agree to end the competition entirely.

The overture was short-lived. After armistice, the administration continued to characterize policy in terms of the competition metaphor. This rhetoric figured Korea as an outcome of the great power contest driven by the competitive nature of international relations, pitting opposing ideologies against one another, spread across the globe. Dulles activated these figures to demonstrate the viability of collective security and to establish "the principle of political asylum" for prisoners of war who desired to defect. As an important phase of American foreign policy, he claimed the stalemate demonstrated the capacity of the administration's anti-communist strategy. They had stopped the communists in Korea, a small, distant place. Armistice was a type of victory, one that heralded the need for a global, strategic plan to confront a crafty opponent.[109] Naming different locations where the opponent had probed the West provided the postwar rationale for collective defense and nuclear competition.

Dulles's articulation of the Soviet danger in globalist, strategic terms amplified the geographic logic of competition. Painting a picture of the Soviets assessing and challenging the West on multiple fronts, the secretary of state placed Korea, Vietnam, Germany, Austria, and the Soviet satellite states in a chronology that demonstrated Soviet intransigence and dishonesty. Figuring his role as the president's partner in the game, Dulles's claims about Soviet dishonesty signaled that the American side had pierced the fog of Soviet intent and knew the cards they held. As he explained in September 1953, the fighting in Indochina derived from Communist China and Soviet Russia and demonstrated the continuing danger posed by a mobile savage intent on world domination.[110] Dulles's "The Moral Initiative" speech, delivered on November 18, 1953, added to the competition thesis by conceiving of the entire world as a series of fronts dividing Soviet and American power. Pitting the two sides in a dramatic contest, the speech articulated the West as a zone of freedom in moral and spiritual contest with the tyrannical forces of the Soviet Union. Dulles argued that the Korean War demonstrated the rewards for persistence and strength, and that the commitment to win in Korea reflected the type of commitment necessary to pursue the quest of freedom in the world. The rest of the address embodied the strategic components of the competition metaphor by identifying the different fronts in the war and the need to act on each one of them to stave off Soviet power.[111] Consistent with Eisenhower's view that the contest between East and West involved ideological and spiritual components, Dulles's pivot to the next front—Southeast Asia—set the stage for the incidence of hot war.

Eisenhower also extended the competition thesis after the armistice to identify fronts endangered by the mobile savage. He claimed in the lead-up to the 1954 midterm elections, for example, that "two years ago, war was raging in Korea and Indochina. All Asia lay exposed to the steady advance of the Reds. Iran . . . was in deadly danger. Suez and Trieste posed constant threats to peace . . . Europe had foundered . . . even in the Western Hemisphere, communist imperialism had ominously appeared."[112] On another occasion, he reminded audiences that he had ended the "futile waste of American life and treasure" on the Korean peninsula.[113] This rhetoric embodied the essence of Eisenhower's enactment of the competition metaphor. On the one hand, it depicted communism as a global force and the nations of the world as endangered. On the other hand, it implied Truman had failed to recognize the global nature of the contest. Korea, as one front in a multiple-front battle, mattered less because players could not get bogged down in a single place when there was an entire board to engage. Exiting Korea, then, enabled "crisis . . . to give way to promise" and demonstrated the truth of Eisenhower's policy agenda.[114] Only clear-eyed assessments of national capacities and interests could result in triumph.

The politics-as-competition metaphor and its attendant persona produced a strategy premised on dividing the world up into sectors, applying the appropriate remedy to each sector, and not letting a single sector become a policy obsession. By articulating the structure of international relations in geographic terms, in which different regions or sectors comprised areas of concern in geopolitical competition, Eisenhower enacted a form of containment that did not overinvest in any given place. In an address close to the end of his first term, he spoke of breaking the globe into important sectors that faced "direct assault . . . by the disciples of communistic dictatorship."[115] Like the bridge player at auction identifying vulnerable tricks, the rhetoric assessed certain zones as defensible while calculating others were already lost. In Asia, for example, Eisenhower distinguished between Japan and China by their geographic location. Japan lay "outside the Iron Curtain" and that meant it had to be protected.[116] The designation allowed the application of the right tactics to defend the American position in Northeast Asia. It also involved prudent judgment about the prospects for successful intervention.

Eisenhower's geographic thinking also provided the president with political cover in a time of fear and uncertainty about communist capacities. Acknowledging that dividing the globe into corners left some concluding "we are losing the cold war," he cited the armistice in Korea, support for the French in Vietnam, the resolution of the Iran crisis and the difficulty in Egypt, and the practical solution to the Trieste problem as proof his policies were winning and did not necessitate great change. This geographic appraisal connected diverse events across the globe to the zero-sum competition between East and West. As Eisenhower put

it, these examples demonstrated the nature of "cold war victories, because the purposes of the Russians were defeated." In that context, the
Armistice generated "reason for cautious hope that a new, a fruitful, a
peaceful era for mankind can emerge from a haunted decade. The world
breathes a little more easily today."[117] Redefining victory in terms of an
opponent's goals embodied the tenets of the metaphor. With fronts of
contest across the globe, even small accomplishments demonstrated the
necessity to stymie Soviet power in every sector. Eisenhower returned to
these themes in 1958, contending that his efforts in Korea and beyond
demonstrated that "aggression, direct or indirect, must be checked before it gathered sufficient momentum to destroy us all."[118] Articulating
Korea as one contest between East and West reiterated the fundamental
mobility of the enemy while justifying American actions to impede Soviet designs. Such was the nature of great power contest.

THE SOVIET UNION, COLLECTIVE DEFENSE, AND NUCLEAR COMPETITION

The emergent portrait of the enemy in Eisenhower's discourse—generally
focused on Soviet power but not always explicitly—infused the foreign-
policy bureaucracy with an emphasis on strategy and positionality.
While this emphasis, in many ways, mirrored Truman's policy of containment, Eisenhower disarticulated his approach from Truman's policies
by noting the differences in strategy and tactics. Truman, he claimed,
had merely reacted to "crises provoked by others." Eisenhower's ascen-
dance to the presidency, however, marked "a great strategic change in
the world" that allowed the development of foreign policy "along lines
of our choice."[119] This strategic shift represented a fundamental reordering of policy. As the president explained, his administration "sought a
rebirth of trust among nations—an enduring foundation for a coopera-
tive peace—not a mere breathing space free from imminent crisis."[120] In
explaining his foreign-policy goals in this way, Eisenhower enunciated a
common thread running through all of his actions. Correctly identifying
how the game is played and understanding the enemy's commitment to

positionality proved integral to the "honorable armistice in Korea; a free and united Germany, a liberated Austria; a secure Indochina and southeast Asia; [and] atomic energy harnessed for peaceful purposes."[121] This rhetoric again connected diverse fronts in the game and linked them to competition with the Soviets. But, in envisioning those distinct sites as connected, it also underwrote the strategic distinction between Truman and Eisenhower. For Eisenhower, every contest mattered, but not every one had to be won. The game was bigger than the hand.

Taken as a whole, Eisenhower's post-Korea rhetoric articulated the danger posed by the Soviet Union as manifest globally, cementing a Manichean narrative pitting the United States against the Soviet Union. As David Halberstam has stated, "In the years that followed the 1952 campaign, the Cold War deepened exponentially as a political issue, even as the outer limits in terms of real power alignments were largely settled."[122] Eisenhower used that narrative to leverage congressional support for his Mutual Security Program, a foreign-aid allocation that included military and economic assistance to at-risk nations. In January 1954, Senate accession to a Mutual Defense Treaty with South Korea finalized security arrangements and assured a long-term U.S. military presence in the country.[123] The treaty, the president explained, sought "to deter aggression by giving evidence of our common determination to meet the common danger."[124] The common danger, of course, referred to the risk of communist aggression. The treaty, perhaps more than any other move, institutionalized presidential military authority and power over the Korean peninsula and gave Eisenhower and future presidents wide latitude in determining the practice of military activities in the region. Combined with the permanent military presence in Japan, ending the war in Korea enabled Eisenhower to lock in American military power in Northeast Asia as a means for securing and sustaining threats of deterrence and mutual security against the communist powers. It also established a blueprint for the extension of American military power as a response to a highly mobile enemy force.

Eisenhower made the case for extending this strategic blueprint in an address to Congress advocating his Mutual Security Program.

The program provided military assistance to allies, particularly in Asia, as a means to deter communist incursions.[125] Due to its high cost, the program was politically contentious. Eisenhower navigated the politics by extending the competition metaphor. To move forward without the program, he claimed, risked enabling the "communist strategy [that] seeks to divide, to isolate, to weaken." Authorizing the mutual security program, however, "helps us bolster strength in remote areas which are, nevertheless, vital to our own security."[126] Imagining the existence of a Soviet strategist, plotting the ways to capture certain sectors of the world, this rhetoric justified an expansive policy agenda that included treaties, forward basing, and economic and military assistance around the world. Only such an agenda, Eisenhower argued, could address an adversary committed to challenging multiple fronts across the globe at the same time. The antagonist's speed, moreover, amplified the need for comprehensive action. As Eisenhower put it, "the continued ruthless drive of communist imperialists for world domination places an especially high premium on our maintenance of close relations with friendly nations."[127] The Mutual Security Program could meet "rapidly changing conditions" in the world, he contended, if Congress empowered the president to "transfer, for use in another geographic area," the funds allocated for assisting nations he deemed at risk from communist incursion. Doing so would enable the president to act with "the utmost speed and precision to accomplish our goals under the swiftly shifting circumstances of the world."[128]

Beyond speed and geography, the role of the antagonist in forcing competition with the West played a dominant role in Eisenhower's rationale for the Mutual Security Program over the course of his presidency. Typified by a speech he gave to the American Society of Newspaper Editors in 1956, this rhetoric pointed to Soviet material assets as providing competitive advantage in the contest for global power. The growth in Soviet military power, he claimed, justified "a strong military establishment" and "the bonds of collective security" among allies. Shifting responsibility—agency—for the contest from the scene to the actor, the speech lamented that the post-Stalin leadership sought to continue

U.S.-Soviet competition, rather than seek conciliation. Soviet policy had left Germany "divided . . . the satellite nations of Eastern Europe . . . ruled by Soviet puppets . . . Korea remains divided, and stable peace has not yet been achieved."[129] The consistency of the Soviet approach, moreover, meant "we must be tireless in our efforts to remedy these injustices and to resolve the disputes that divide the world."[130] Three years removed from hot war, Eisenhower pointed to successful "systems of common defense" that "advances our own security interests" and prevents "a war which . . . could result in the virtual destruction of mankind."[131] The collective defense established in Korea made up the form of this strategy—forward basing in strategic locations as a deterrent to military invasion by the Soviet Union. With the antagonist ensconced in the Kremlin and the competition between the United States and the Soviets global, Korea demonstrated the significance of the struggle and the appropriateness of Eisenhower's policy.

Atomic weapons composed the final element of Eisenhower's discourse, displacing and diminishing Korea's importance in the grand competition for global peace. Unlike "conventional" war, the rise of atomic weapons threatened the entire globe and raised the stakes for a contest immersed in a nuclear arms race. They also raised the stakes of great power competition, putting the complete annihilation of the planet on the table. Eisenhower's competition metaphor resolved the tension between his rhetoric of peace and the deployment of atomic weapons by shifting agency for proliferation to the Soviets. His new look strategy justified the development of atomic weapons as a logical response to nuclear competition begun by the Soviets, and cemented nuclear deterrence as an essential, if unfortunate, component of the contest for the globe.[132] Justifying that strategy relied on the politics-as-competition thesis advanced to rationalize the end of the Korean conflict and demonstrates the deep penetration of the thesis across the foreign affairs bureaucracy.

Two speeches exhibit the way Eisenhower's competition metaphor diverted attention from Korea and toward nuclear deterrence. The "Chance for Peace" address, spurred by the occasion of Stalin's death, reiterated the basic tenets of the metaphor, characterizing the nation as participating in a competition with global stakes and requiring strategic leadership. The speech articulated two theses or paths of international relations—cooperation or competition. The first path, Eisenhower argued, reflected an American approach to global affairs. It sought "a common hunger for peace," security via effective cooperation, self-governance of all nations, and peace from "just relations and honest understanding," rather than a "race in armaments." Unfortunately, the Soviets had chosen another path, one defined by self-interest, the notion that "security was to be found . . . in force: huge armies, subversion, rule of neighbor nations," a goal of power superiority, and a zero-sum notion of politics in which Soviet "security was to be sought by denying it to all others." Even while calling for armistice, the president noted the futility of any peace deal "that merely released aggressive armies to attack elsewhere."[133] In this sense, armistice represented an opportunity to alter the rules of the game—for the Soviets to demonstrate their interest in abandoning a theory of politics that imagined power as zero-sum and instead opt for cooperation and mutual benefit.

At the same time, the address served as a guidepost for determining Soviet character after Korea and a barometer for future interactions with the communist power. He warned the Soviets that if the end of the war in Korea signaled a mere pause in the competition, then the Soviet orientation to international politics would force the West to develop and deploy conventional and atomic weapons. For Eisenhower, "the amassing of Soviet power . . . forced [free nations] to develop weapons of war now capable of inflicting instant and terrible punishment."[134] In essence, the Soviets changed the rules of the game, and absent some interest in cooperation, the West had to follow suit. To not invest in nuclear armaments would abandon a central axis of competition that defined the Cold War. This shift of agency—blaming the Soviets for American atomic weapons—leveraged the tenets of the politics-as-competition metaphor and legitimized nuclear deterrence as strategically sound. As Robert L. Ivie has argued, the address "launch[ed] a determined crusade against communism under the legitimate guise of a quest for peace."[135] That is, a message ostensibly oriented at elaborating the rationales for peace also articulated the necessity of competing with the Soviet Union up to and including the deployment of nuclear weapons.

After armistice, Eisenhower's "Atoms for Peace" address reiterated this ontology of international politics while identifying the heightened stakes of a nuclear competition. The axis of cooperation and competition again framed much of the address, this time with Eisenhower proposing more expansive and direct forms of "constructive, not destructive" interactions, "agreements, not wars," and an end to a world divided. Two things stand out about this approach. First, he repeated the basic themes of the "Chance for Peace" address, in particular claiming American nuclear weapons were defensive, developed only because of Soviet tactics. Second, and more importantly, the address demonstrates the deep penetration of the politics-as-competition metaphor. The deployment of atomic weapons was a race, pitting one side against another in a global contest for military dominance. Signaling that the competition had expanded beyond ideology and geography to include technology, the address warned that the outcome of that race would determine the fate of the world. With stakes set so high, Korea was little more than a footnote that proved the episodic nature of the contest.

The move to highlight the danger of nuclear war, above and beyond the risks associated with communism, became Eisenhower's signature when discussing foreign affairs.[136] In the years after armistice, he returned to these themes periodically, raising the memory of Korea to justify nuclear proliferation. In October 1954, for example, he reminded Americans that "the war in Korea . . . was a costly war, allowed to become futile, and seemingly without end." The remarks implied that under his management, the United States had better deployed resources to avoid a recurrence of futility in combating the communist threat. Instead, he offered a bright-eyed diagnosis of the problem—the danger of "penetration by the communist conspiracy" at home—and claimed his leadership had resisted "the futile sacrifices in Korea" in favor of a comprehensive, proactive program aimed at containing communist advances.[137] The first and primary pillar of his strategy sought to build a "collective shield against aggression."[138] The figure of a shield—an object designed to protect a body in combat—common in Eisenhower's rhetoric, reinforced the notion that American actions were defensive. It also recycled the president-as-game-player persona, this time as engaged in perpetual jousting with a communist opponent. Moreover, Eisenhower's shield incorporated allied nations as fellow game players, collectively grouped together "to guard against aggression, and to ensure that the world remains at peace."[139] This version of containment—allied strength as a means for deterring Soviet power—could not win the game by itself, but it could prevent the advance of additional communist moves.

From the Great Game to the Domino Theory:
Vietnam and the Next Front

Having displaced attention from the region to the globe and shifted policy toward direct competition with the Soviet Union, Eisenhower's discourse following the end of hostilities in Korea resolved into the outlines of what became known as the domino theory of international politics. Particularly over the course of 1954, the president's version of the domino theory posited the movement of the enemy as a feature of a failure to adequately resist aggression. Originating from the Soviet Union, communist antagonism took on its own agency in this discourse. It was active, purposeful, and moved between states effortlessly. Specifically in relation to Southeast Asia, the president claimed U.S. national interest required assisting the French in Indochina because "along this line, this must be blocked. It must be blocked now."[140] Echoing Eisenhower's days as a football coach, this discourse enacted the president-as-game-player persona by depicting the challenge as a series of blocking strategies. Raising the specter of a highly mobile force intent on encircling India and then Vietnam, the rhetoric also marked the beginning of a rhetorical campaign spanning several years that positioned Vietnam as the next front in the global contest for the economic and political makeup of the world.

The danger in Vietnam, however, differed from that posed by Korea. In the Korean conflict, Eisenhower had argued, the Soviets sought to bog down the United States to diminish American attention to other areas of the globe. In Vietnam, Eisenhower worried that Soviet strategy had shifted from creating quagmire to seeking the collapse of weak democracies. Employing the metaphor of competition to explain the stakes of Vietnam, Eisenhower asked the nation to ponder the strategy of the communist opponent. That strategy sought to push weak nations, one at a time, toward communism to build momentum toward the collapse of many. As he explained in a news conference in 1954, "When, each standing alone, one falls, it has the effect on the next, and finally the whole row is down. You are trying, through a unifying influence, to build that row of dominoes so they can stand the fall of one, if necessary."[141] The logic of competition and the linguistic currency of falling dominoes justified the U.S. defense of Vietnam against communist insurgency not because of the significance of the country, but because of its importance to the region. This rhetoric also reiterated the United States' role as a strategic player in a contest for the fate of the world, capable of acting in support of the domino nations. Standing together, in support of allies, became the central strategic element necessary to contain the creep of communism. A conference in the Oval Office hosted by the president and involving top officials from the State Department and the military on May 28, 1954, made the case. Declaring unconditional American commitment to Vietnam at the start of the meeting, Eisenhower stated that a successful defense of Indochina depended on "certain political prerequisites" because a military strategy by itself could not arrest communist insurgency. He directed the participants to develop an appropriate set of military and political measures up to the task of defending anti-communist forces in the region. After a discussion by Dulles about the prospect of a limited war against China—the party presumed most responsible for insurgency in Vietnam—Eisenhower "intervened to say that the US should conduct itself as not to lose to the free world side the 400,000 French Union forces now in Indochina." Explicitly committing the country to defending Vietnam, he stated "the US would be the

principal supplier of sea and air power," an "approach [that] would flat-
ter the French vanity, and buck them up."[142] While this assistance proved
incapable of saving the French, Eisenhower's rhetoric asserted American
support for anti-communist forces as de facto policy.

While not explicitly repeating the domino metaphor, Eisenhower's
discourse interpreted communist strategy as seeking to colonize free nations via a piecemeal strategy. This strategy, what he called a "doctrine
of divide and conquer," added to the portrait of a global threat, continuously active and highly mobile.[143] Again, attuned to the geography of
the contest, the rhetoric expressed foreign-policy strategy as a synthesis
between position and tactics. Rather than specify allies and enemies, as
is typical of war rhetoric, this discourse rendered those specifications
irrelevant by pointing to the competitive elements of international relations as determinative of policy. Controlling communist power, the logic
suggested, depended on strategic deployments and not the character of
our allies. Entailing the bureaucracy to act on this basis, the rhetoric
extended the mobility thesis by pointing to the growth and deployment
of communist military power as indicative of their desire to continuously
test the West, search for and exploit weaknesses, and generally expand
their spheres of control by any means necessary.

As usual, Dulles amplified Eisenhower's metaphoric framing. In
this case, he spoke about the danger in Southeast Asia as a "classic example of this Communist strategy." Describing how the Soviet Union
educated and trained Ho Chi-Minh before sending him back to Vietnam, Dulles claimed the insurgency demonstrated how Soviet power
sought to foment rebellion and produce "dependence upon external
Communist support" by insurgents around the globe. Doing so could
expand the realm of Soviet power while ensuring that new communist
states remained in the "communist orbit under a ruthless dictatorship."
Defining communist strategy as part of an "evil design" to conquer the
world justified the parameters of America's strategic response, including
foreign aid, collective defense agreements, and direct military intervention as necessary.[144] At each turn in the address, the communist appeared
as a strategic thinker engaged in a global plan for domination. And,

the rhetoric implied a zero-sum competition in which gains on one side necessarily meant losses for the other. Consigning Vietnam to a single location on the board, this rhetoric raised the stakes for U.S. policy in Southeast Asia.

As a manifestation of the interplay between the organizing metaphor and the mobility of the opponent, Eisenhower's public comments depicting the rise of communism in Indochina extended and amplified his thesis of international relations as inherently competitive. This thesis, articulated in his discourse about the Korean War, now mobilized Korea as the example that proves the rule. In public comments to local and national audiences, Vietnam appeared as the next front in the global competition between the East and West. Reenacting the contours of his Korea discourse, he claimed Indochina proved "the Communists have added new groups to their already great expanse of people that they are enslaving with the hope of destroying all of us." The solution to this danger, as in Korea, required the United States to arrange their forces in a line past which "the Communists will not dare attack."[145] It was far from a friendly contest, and this rhetoric isolated the deadly stakes. It demanded the utmost attention from the president to develop strategy for addressing a highly mobile force located in multiple regions of the world. In design, his policy sought to block communist plans by identifying boundaries upon which Western forces would mount defenses. In articulating the solution this way, Eisenhower segmented the world into a series of blocs akin to spaces on a board. His exhortations did not seek to capture communist blocs. Rather, they sought to consolidate the free world into a defensible terrain. Building on that theme, Eisenhower told the nation of the need to build "a strong concert of free nations" because, in doing so, "the Communist menace will be stalled—stopped—in this world, and finally driven back to where it belongs, to its own country."[146]

Near the end of his term, Eisenhower reiterated the geographic thinking of the game player to justify the continuation of his Mutual Security Program. As he explained in a message to Congress, the Soviet Union was the center and the at-risk states were those "adjoining the areas of Communist power."[147] This spatial thinking—mapping the proximity of danger onto diverse nations—was reflected in Eisenhower's policy choices. As a matter of focus, his policies emphasized a "strategy of general defense . . . by the powerful defensive forces" deployed to deter aggression aimed at countries "on the border of the Communist world."[148] Once again embodying the persona of the game player, simultaneously calculating the opponent's strategy while developing his own, the logic inferred that borders could shift in response to successes or failures. The doctrine of strategic positioning, then, depended not on holding set territory but rather on encircling the danger as a matter of course. The Mutual Security Program, a policy that had deployed military forces on "some 250 bases in the most strategic locations," implemented this logic.[149] Given the nature of communist aggression, he explained, the majority of the budgetary allocation for the policy resulted in support for "Turkey, Viet-nam, Taiwan, and Korea . . . strategically located nations . . . directly faced by heavy concentrations of Communist military power."[150] These examples demonstrated the logic of mobility running through Eisenhower's discourse. Korea had driven home a central lesson—communism sought to penetrate and conquer everywhere at once. To get bogged down in a single field of battle risked communist success elsewhere. Eisenhower's strategic leadership, then, served as the best remedy for limiting the damage done by the communist opponent.

Ultimately, figuring the nation as engaged in a zero-sum competition for control over the world rationalized a type of foreign policy that made intervention in Vietnam all but inevitable. Eisenhower, as the consummate game player, determined that Soviet strategy sought to win the game step-by-step, rather than in one fell swoop. This strategy required a step-by-step response because the alternative implied losing "the weak and the most exposed" to "aggression or subversion." Losing a small, out-of-the-way nation like Vietnam to communism, he contended, would endanger the strongest nations and make the communist threat increasingly menacing. The outcome of this positional orientation led to Eisenhower's declaration that "the inescapable conclusion [is] that our own national interests demand some help from us in sustaining in Viet-Nam the morale, the economic progress, and the military strength necessary to its continued existence in freedom. Viet-Nam is just one ex-ample. One-third of the world's people face a similar challenge."[151] While Eisenhower resisted the call to commit military forces to Southeast Asia, or perhaps ran out of time to do so, subsequent presidents escalated the conflict with disastrous results.

CHAPTER 3

Erasing the Savage

RICHARD NIXON, THE ARCHITECTURE OF PEACE, AND THE ETERNAL VIETNAM

———— •◆• ————

In spring of 1970, Richard Nixon faced a difficult decision. Having campaigned on a promise to end the war in Vietnam, he had formally announced his policy of Vietnamization on November 3, 1969, to an audience of 72 million Americans. The address, written by Nixon with input from Henry Kissinger, focused on the president's plan to bring about a "just and lasting peace."[1] Politically, the policy promised progress—the speech itself organized Vietnamization on the basis of time, marking steps or benchmarks on the way to peace. In an atypical war address, Nixon blamed the problems in Vietnam on poor planning rather than enemy activity. Even without solidifying a timeline for withdrawal, he sold the nation on the conceptual framework of his plan—that pressuring the North Vietnamese to make concessions while training the South Vietnamese to defend themselves would bring an end to the war. Doing so, he explained, would enable American withdrawal

from the war while maintaining U.S. interests in the region. Vietnamization's promise yielded great expectations by a country exhausted by the
war. One poll showed 77 percent favored the policy, over 50,000 tele-
grams and 30,000 letters arrived at the White House in support, and the
House and Senate passed resolutions "expressing confidence in Nixon's
handling of the war."[2]

When progress did not materialize, pressure rose on the president
to identify tangible outcomes. The failure of negotiation coupled with
no measurable advances in South Vietnamese capabilities reignited public distemper. The tactical dynamics of the battlefield posed additional
problems. The North Vietnamese had become adept at using base camps
in Cambodia to stage cross-border attacks. Nixon "ordered secret bombing raids" to address this danger in March 1969, but didn't go public
with the campaign until April 30, 1970.[3] This address, drafted by Pat
Buchanan and watched by 60 million Americans, justified the bombing
of Cambodia as necessary to clean out Viet Cong sanctuaries.[4] To make
the case, Nixon claimed the North Vietnamese had rejoined American
overtures for peace with "intransigence at the conference table, belliger-
ence in Hanoi, massive military aggression in Laos and Cambodia, and
stepped-up attacks in South Vietnam, designed to increase American
casualties." To not act, Nixon claimed, would expose the South Vietnamese "to the same slaughter and savagery" the communists "inflicted
on hundreds of thousands of North Vietnamese."[5] Representing the
enemy as disposed toward acts of barbarity, as war rhetoric often seeks
to do, backfired. After expanding the war into Cambodia, Nixon could
no longer blame Lyndon Johnson's mismanagement of the war for the
continued barbarity of the North Vietnamese. Nixon had designed
and implemented a program to end the war and, in contravention to
its purpose, had expanded and escalated it. As H. R. Haldeman put
it, Vietnam was now Nixon's war.[6] With eroding public support for his
management of the war, increased mobilization of antiwar activists on
college campuses, the violence at Kent State and Jackson State, and Senate revocation of the Gulf of Tonkin Resolution, Nixon faced increasing
pressure to end the war or suffer calamitous political consequences.[7]

Attempting to end a war that could not be won presented Nixon with a political and policy challenge similar to that of Korea. As a slow-motion conflict gradually unfolded across four presidencies, public understanding of the American mission in Vietnam remained unsettled. Relocalizing conflict in a specific region undid much of Eisenhower's efforts to articulate international relations as a global competition with many fronts. The North Vietnamese stonewalled virtually every overture, agreed to certain parameters or principles in secret while disputing those parameters in public, and generally frustrated Johnson's and Nixon's attempts to force a resolution to the conflict on terms favorable to the United States.[8] In addition, the domino theory of international relations permeated both the State Department and the Department of Defense, conveying an understanding of Vietnam as the linchpin to stopping communist aggression throughout Southeast Asia, if not the world, and warning of the dangers of abandoning South Vietnam.[9] The force of the domino metaphor, propelled by both Nixon and Kissinger, raised the stakes for the Nixon administration and elevated the conflict's importance. Due to these factors, ending the war required reorganizing public understandings of Vietnam and the Southeast Asian nation's importance in the world.[10]

Like all presidents exiting a war, Nixon sought a political language to rationalize his approach to Vietnam, resituate characterizations of the enemy, and explain his exit strategy. This political language needed to address figures depicting the North Vietnamese enemy as savages and claims related to Vietnam's importance to regional, if not global, security. Lacking the affability of Truman and the cold, calculating mind of Eisenhower, Nixon could neither rehabilitate the enemy nor rhetorically transfer images of savagery from Vietnam to the communist powers. Any attempt to blame the Soviets or the Chinese would upset his attempt at détente and rapprochement, achievements he sought to notch in the run-up to his reelection campaign in 1972. Nixon's solution to this quandary resolved into a discourse of strategic erasure, in which his rhetoric submerged representations of the actual enemy—the Viet Cong—into a broader narrative of international politics.[11] This erasure vacated the importance—if not existence—of the North Vietnamese by offering a substitute vocabulary for understanding the conflict. Substitute vocabularies, as Richard Morris and Mary E. Stuckey have argued, enable speakers to shift the focus of a controversy via a set of rhetorical tactics designed to dodge the "ethical consequences of action" by "maintain[ing] the appearance of integrity in abstract principles while engaging in conduct that otherwise would be perceived as antithetical to those same principles."[12] These tactics include silence, containment, definition, and reduction, rhetorical moves that exclude, isolate, marginalize, and dismiss, respectively. But, most important to Nixon, substitute vocabularies enable speakers to erase histories, contexts, and agents, producing "a blank slate onto which 'American' history can be written."[13]

While not entirely eliminating representations of the enemy—erasure always leaves residues—Nixon displaced representations of savagery via two interrelated rhetorical moves. First, he foregrounded political realism as an ideological guide to understanding international politics. Realism, an epistemology that explains all aspects of international relations via a narrow prism of power, flattens actors, renders them agents of power itself, and in the process, diminishes the importance of any given actor. Emphasizing a realist critique of the conflict redefined the cause and consequence of the war, shifting the focus from actor to scene. Rather than condemn the North Vietnamese, Nixon's critique blamed confrontation and containment for producing situations of conflict. Arguing for a policy shift from containment to détente, this discourse recessed figures of the enemy by abstracting and effacing differences between and among nations, contexts, and conflicts. Isolating the dangerous elements of international relations themselves dispensed with Viet Cong agency and responsibility, while producing a spectral enemy of the scene—the phantasmic danger of power politics inferred by realism itself. Doing so moved Vietnam from agent-driven flashpoint to the most extreme example of how political misalignments produce violent outcomes. It also invoked the specter of aggression without naming the ideological forces motivating enemy behavior.

Nixon's second movement reconfigured the central metaphoric frame explaining and justifying American intervention in Vietnam—the metaphor of falling dominoes—and replaced it with a new master metaphor of construction.[14] This metaphor centralized and organized a symbiotic network of metaphors into a distinct discourse. Where the domino metaphor implied that secretive ideological forces sought a chain reaction of falling dominoes, the construction frame intensified the movement from actor to scene by articulating the problem of conflict as the outcome of structural weaknesses in international relations themselves. Deeply penetrating the president's discourse, the logic of the construction metaphor served as a central vehicle for erasing figures of the enemy. By defining the conflict as a weak link in a broad, structural plan for peace, Nixon diminished Vietnam's significance, obscured representations of the enemy, and reoriented policy attention toward his vision of the international order. Peace in Vietnam, he claimed, would be an important fix to the international system and would demonstrate the essential truth of the president's vision for peace in the world. The metaphor provided its own remedy—the president's policies would address systemic problems, inclusive of Vietnam but globally oriented. Conjointly, this rhetoric constituted Nixon-as-architect, a presidential persona invested in establishing Nixon as both visionary and sensible, a man with a desire for peace and the faculty to see it materialize. Nixon's self-fashioning as architect focused his attention on building a structure of peace that could resolve the conflict in Southeast Asia and endure the ravages of time and politics. This discourse superimposed a vision of world politics that identified the need to resolve Vietnam as a precursor to peace while distancing itself from the intricacies of the conflict.

Generative of a broad metaphoric economy, Nixon's architect persona echoed across the foreign affairs bureaucracy by establishing a set of parameters capable of guiding foreign-policy decision-making. Addressing Vietnam and his other major foreign-policy initiatives, the metaphoric economy present across public and private documents cohered into a worldview that understood peace as something to be planned, built, and transacted. Each of the metaphoric forms discussed in this chapter articulated the problem of peace—either in Vietnam or more generally—as the inevitable outcome of national rights to property. This discourse figured the international situation as a neighborhood, nations as neighbors, and division and conflict the outcome of a failure of communication. Echoing Roosevelt, this discourse displaced, disappeared, or refigured the enemy from an ideological force into that of a client or ornery neighbor.[15] Their complaints, Nixon contended, could be satisfied with the appropriate negotiated settlement.

At the same time, Nixon's end-of-war rhetoric got absorbed into a larger body of discourse out to reconfigure the ways the country and the bureaucracy understood foreign relations as a whole. Echoing Truman, Nixon's construction metaphors emphasized the need to organize international relations in ways that balanced the demands of force with the needs of diplomacy. Isolating Vietnam as the example that proved the downside of containment, he shifted focus from peripheral conflicts to alliances and diplomacy as mechanisms that could induce stability and peace. This rhetoric sought a stable global structure, run by a few elites who understood the real issues of the world, that would restrict the likelihood of additional flashpoints.[16] The policy shifts orchestrated by his administration, most notably détente with the Soviets and opening diplomatic relations with China, served as evidence for his commitment to this new strategy for peace. But, as reflected in his foreign-policy messages, Nixon placed these achievements in the broader context of a shifting international structure. The frequent and consistent theme that runs through his foreign-policy discourse explained his presidency as a unique historical moment that signaled a point of departure from the policy trajectory of the postwar era.

Nixon's rhetorical reimagining of the war, American foreign policy, and the president's role in managing national power facilitated the displacement of the enemy and the rhetorical erasure of the North Vietnamese. Providing an organizing logic for policymakers and the public, Nixon's movement from actor to scene, the consonant metaphoric economy enabled by the master metaphor of construction, and the president's embodiment of the persona of the architect structured understandings of the end of Vietnam by "hiding features that could potentially be used to define" the enemy and promoting scenic solutions to the problem.[17] While this movement from place to structure, from savage presence to figurative absence, ultimately failed to quell public discontent with the war, secure an independent and democratic South Vietnam, and negotiate a new security architecture in Asia, Nixon's rhetoric demonstrates the possibility for metaphoric displacement even in situations of significant constraint.

The Rhetorical Erasure of Savagery

Nixon's path to erasing images of savagery was neither seamless nor direct, but it began long before he assumed the presidency. His *Foreign Affairs* essay "Asia after Viet Nam" marked his first significant attempt to erase the figure of the enemy. While explicitly committing to victory in Vietnam, the essay displaced representations of the enemy from communist or Soviet savagery in favor of a postcolonial explanation. Claiming the end of colonialism reignited ancient nationalisms between the Montagnards and the Han tribes, Nixon supplanted ideological motivations for war with tribalistic ones. This discourse redefined the cause of the conflict in Southeast Asia, and the origin of savagery, from externally imposed insurgency to internecine primitivism. Putting it this way effectively erased the figure of the true enemy by orchestrating an erasure of time. Depicting the Vietnam War as the outcome of "old resentments and distrusts" made new again, the essay shifted the focus away from the actual combatants, the ideological motivations for war, and the present moment.[18]

This attempt to historicize the war sought to erase the enemy, but also reflected the desires of an ambitious man, intent on the presidency, seeking to establish his authority on one of the thorniest issues in American politics. Several factors constrained this effort, however. The enemy was ethnically and nationally indistinct, making the demonization of the North Vietnamese without implicating the South Vietnamese difficult, if not impossible. Appeals to tribalism could not sustain given American commitments to South Vietnam and presidential characterizations of the South Vietnamese as democratic and, thus, civilized. And, Nixon campaigned on ending the war. Once he became president, this rhetoric forced his hand by escalating the political presence of the intractable conflict. He had no choice, ultimately, but to seek a rhetoric of accommodation. As Carol Winkler explained, Nixon refrained from visceral depictions of the enemy, preferring to allow subordinates to make the case for continuing the war. Selecting softer terms like "aggression" to describe North Vietnamese action, his subordinates referred to the same actions as terrorism. This bifurcated approach distinguished Nixon's discourse from that of the State Department, which "made explicit and repeated reference to Viet Cong terrorism at the Paris peace talks."[19] Perhaps it is for that reason that, as president, Nixon rarely referred to the enemy in any terms outside of noting their intransigence at the negotiating table.

Rather, Nixon displaced the figure of savagery by giving presence to structural factors contributing to conflict across the globe. In essence, Nixon rehistoricized the war to identify its cause as structural rather than related to factors inside the Southeast Asian nation, colonialism, or political ideology. This form of erasure worked in two capacities. On the one hand, it mirrored common neocolonial tropes of displacing the Other "from their stories—and replac[ing] them with Westerners."[20] That is, Nixon's rhetoric of the enemy removed the North Vietnamese and the political issues motivating the conflict from the story. In its place, he identified Western failure as the cause of the war—namely, the nation's failure to recognize shifts in the balance of international relations. By positing structural faults as the cause of the war, Nixon emptied depictions of the enemy of any relevance by converting them, in Bruno Latour's terms, "into mere intermediaries," as actors recognized but deprived of significance beyond the performance of their role as antagonist.[21] This discursive shift rendered the North Vietnamese as in motion but lacking agency over the process.[22] The logic of this discourse muted the question of motive, expunged legitimate grievances, and implied that the outcome of the war had little to do with North Vietnam.

The second component of this discourse abstracted the enemy by homogenizing all contexts and actors as essentially the same. Erasure by homogenization neglects "context and diversity in favor of familiar, often negative images."[23] In doing so, it denies the complexity of context and replaces it with flat, simple depictions of a people, country, or continent. This form of erasure is akin to what Stuart Hall termed a "simplistic . . . difference that doesn't make a difference," manifest in "the old internationalist grand narrative" that has eroded with the increasing dislocation of people from their places of origin.[24] This form of erasure can take the form of "forced invisibility, exclusion, subjugation, and repression," similar to the way designations of illegality erase the legal personhood of the undocumented immigrant.[25] Abstracting and homogenizing the Vietnamese enemy served that goal because it effaced differences across conflict zones, positing a one-size-fits-all type of policy remedy. As discussed below, this proved important for Nixon as he attempted to hold up his Vietnam policy as a model for the world to follow.

Nixon's explanation of the failure in negotiations bears out the point. Typically, he blamed the North Vietnamese for the failure to break the deadlock in negotiations. For example, in a national address on January 25, 1972, explaining his plan for peace, he claimed, "The only reply to our plan has been an increase in troop infiltration from North Vietnam and Communist military offensives in Laos and Cambodia. Our proposal for peace was answered with a step-up in the war on their part."[26] The rhetoric, even in blaming Hanoi for the failure of peace, left absent the figure of the enemy. By bypassing more sustained archetypal depictions of the enemy, Nixon instead implied the enemy refused to communicate. While an attentive audience might have noted that North Vietnam's tactics mirrored Nixon's desire to use force to extract concessions at the negotiating table, the discourse delinked enemy actions from the context in which those actions were undertaken. Nixon did not engage in a discussion of motive or provide an explanation for Viet Cong activities. Instead, the North Vietnamese appear as bodies-in-motion, deprived of agency, and resorting to violence as a primary communicative form. While not an absolute erasure, this fragmented depiction—savagery in abeyance—exculpated Nixon for the failure to broker a peace deal, while also stripping metaphors of savagery of their potency. To put it another way, most archetypal depictions of savagery equate the enemy to a known, and often brutal, animalistic force. Here, Nixon deprives the enemy of even minimalist depictions. They are simply there.

Simultaneously denuding the North Vietnamese of agency and motive while flattening and erasing depictions of the enemy, Nixon's rhetoric rendered the conflict as an inevitable outcome of the structural fault lines of the Cold War. By fixating on the structure, this rhetoric dissociated the conflict from savagery, relieved the president of the burden to explain enemy character and motivation, and rolled back savage characterizations. It also recast the enemy as a rational actor out to maximize its interests. Displacing savagery with rationality attributed the cause and continuation of the war to worldview, rather than intransigence and perfidy. Realist actors would seek to maximize gains, the logic went, and the absence of a security architecture that could balance desires versus consequences made violent outcomes inevitable. This discourse implied that the remedy to the problem of Vietnam—and beyond—lay in the structure of global politics itself and required a fundamental reorientation of the nation's approach to international politics. To orchestrate this orientational shift, Nixon had no choice but to unravel, refigure, and replace the dominant metaphoric frame buttressing the American commitment to the conflict.

Games, Dominoes, and the War in Vietnam

The Vietnam War, from the first moments, was fought under the umbrella of the game metaphor. Portraying the armed struggle as a contest between adversaries, war discourse enacted a wide network of game metaphors including allusions to dominoes, football, poker, chess, wrestling, boxing, and more. Portraying the danger as a "Red Tide of Communism," John F. Kennedy claimed that regional interconnectedness justified American presence in Southeast Asia. As president, he compared the war in Vietnam to a football match, but also used poker metaphors to more generally describe international politics.[27] Senator Lyndon Johnson analogized the war in Korea to a boxing match, claiming the country could handle Indochina and maybe even "a bout in Iran or Yugoslavia."[28] As president, Johnson also relied on game metaphors to describe the conflict and justify his management of it. While he frequently spoke about the need to score "a touchdown," he preferred boxing metaphors to describe unfolding conflict.[29] Those metaphors depicted the United States as facing off against communist challengers, positioning the country as a "veritable Rocky Marciano, an undefeated world champion holding forth in an international arena."[30] As vice president, Nixon explained international politics themselves as a game of poker.[31] As president, he used a combination of poker, football, and boxing metaphors to describe the fight in Vietnam. Other administration officials, such as General William Westmoreland, also used various forms of the game metaphor to describe both the fighting and the failure of the United States to notch decisive victories.[32] While these metaphors varied in usage, primarily by the affinities of the speakers deploying them, their consistent appearance to frame, justify, and explain the Vietnam War, from 1954 to 1973, speaks to the power and elasticity of the game metaphor.

As with metaphors of disease and crime, game metaphors rely upon the nation-as-body schema by articulating both sides of a conflict as singular entities capable of striking knockouts, scoring touchdowns, or bluffing without the cards. As Paul Chilton wrote, the recurrence of these metaphors across the executive bureaucracy extends a "conceptual system [that] crystalize[s] and spread[s]" an orientation to international relations, military preparedness, combat operations, and total war.[33] This orientation apprehends international politics as a contest between individuals, figuring enemies as players rather than monolithic evil forces. For policymakers, this metaphoric schema entails two outcomes. First, articulating enemies-as-players assumes a universal rationality that governs where and how the game will be played. That rationality assumes the existence of a level playing field, governed by a basic set of rules, which all players will follow in the pursuit of calculable gains. Second, and of equal importance, the schema distances audiences from complications associated with their policies. For example, representing bombing as moves in a game anesthetizes decision-makers to the real impacts those decisions have on the enemy population.[34] Combined, these twin outcomes undercut the ability of policymakers to respond to situations in which enemies break the rules or otherwise step outside of the expectations built into the rationality of competition.

The dominant form of the master metaphor of competition analogized the stakes in Vietnam to falling dominoes. Figuring countries as pieces arrayed in a row, the metaphor warned of the potential chain reaction sparked by a single nation falling to communism—the domino effect. As one observer put it, the metaphor "evokes the image of an interconnected system, the elements of which aid and determine one another."[35] Appealing to political leaders and bureaucrats because it resonated with understandings of the cause of World War II, the metaphor rendered complex situations simple and actionable.[36] That is, the metaphor organized and directed allied efforts in Vietnam, giving motive force to the intervention. Providing what Jerome Slater called "surface plausibility," the domino theory became the dominant reason for American involvement in the Vietnam War.[37] As Slater detailed, each of the key moments in American involvement in the war produced internal "reassessments of American policy and each resoundingly reasserted the domino theory as the essential reason for either dramatically expanding the American commitment or . . . continuing existing policy in a new form."[38]

Simple in form, the history of the metaphor is rather more complex. In Frank Ninkovich's account, Woodrow Wilson "articulate[d] the fundamental principles underlying the domino theory" as an alternative to prior theories of European power balances.[39] Franklin Roosevelt revitalized the tenets of the metaphor when describing the dangers posed by the Axis powers.[40] The metaphor provided Truman a lexicon for the basic logic of containment prior to its formal articulation.[41] He based his containment policy on "the logic—if not the analogy—of dominoes to describe the disaster that would befall the eastern Mediterranean if communists seized Greece and Turkey."[42] Secretary of State Dean Acheson used the metaphor of a rotten apple spoiling a bushel to depict intrinsic linkages between states, and the danger losing Greece to communism posed to other states. And, during the crisis, officials inside the administration and Congress worried about the potential domino effect, with Senator Arthur Vandenberg warning of a "chain reaction which might sweep from the Dardanelles to the China Sea." Collectively, Norman Graebner explained, this rhetoric convinced Americans of the veracity of the domino theory as "a self-evident truth" that needed no further explanation.[43]

Over time, these articulations cohered the metaphor into a theory expository of international politics, rather than descriptive of an immediate danger posed by a hostile state. Becoming one of the central conceptual artifacts of the Cold War, the theory drew adherents like George Kennan and Paul Nitze.[44] And in 1950, the National Security Council (NSC) warned that the fall of China substantiated the danger posed by "the coordinated offensive directed by the Kremlin" and aimed at the rest of Southeast Asia.[45] NSC-68 argued that defeat in small, faraway countries endangered the United States because it "would cause its allies to doubt U.S. leadership, lose morale, and give in to Communism."[46] This rationale justified Truman's intervention in Korea, while also stymying his efforts to extricate the nation from the conflict. Cumulatively, the metaphor penetrated the thinking of American policymakers and commentators engaged in understanding international relations and America's place in the world. By providing a broad metaphoric economy that quickly spread through policy and public circles, the logic of falling dominoes became the go-to explanation for addressing most foreign-policy challenges during this era.

After the Korean armistice, Eisenhower made the latent metaphor explicit in comments about the situation brewing in Vietnam. Referring to the potential of a falling domino in April 1954 to depict the strategic importance of Indochina, he reiterated the metaphor over the course of his presidency to justify his policy of limited support to South Vietnam.[47] Even while he opted not to intervene with military force, the

domino metaphor established a paradigmatic framework that defined
the problem in Southeast Asia as crucially important to American security interests, compelling his successors to embody a similar discursive
stance. While resisting an expansive military role, Kennedy endorsed
the domino theory in September 1963.[48] Johnson viewed communist aggression in Vietnam as evidence of "naked expansionism . . . part of a
worldwide conspiracy" that had to be checked even if that meant significant U.S. military assistance, up to and including intervention.[49] Others
inside and outside his administration reiterated the domino theory as the
primary rationale for intervention in Vietnam. And, National Security
Action Memorandum 268 (NSAM-268), drafted in the lead-up to massive American intervention in the war, warned that if the United States
failed to establish a democratic South Vietnam, "almost all of Southeast
Asia will probably fall under Communist dominance." The document,
which provided the primary "explanation and justification for the American war," claimed the war was a "test case of U.S. capacity."[50]

By linking Saigon to the security of the region and, thus, U.S. interests, the domino metaphor became superimposed on institutional
debates favoring intervention and escalation across the Eisenhower,
Kennedy, and Johnson administrations.[51] John Foster Dulles, for example, warned of the chain reaction across the region that would follow expansion of communism into Indo-China.[52] Robert McNamara
and Dean Rusk, two of the most influential policymakers of the era,
frequently relied on the metaphor to justify U.S. policy in Vietnam.[53]
McNamara, in particular, when confronted with evidence that the "war
was going poorly," worried that after withdrawal, "dominoes would clat-
ter down and Southeast Asia would be 'gone.'"[54] In sum, the metaphor
ruled the policy conversation for twenty-five years, involving "high U.S.
officials, on both the civilian and the military sides, in both Republican
and Democratic administrations, [and] linked the outcome in Vietnam
to a chain reaction of regional and global effects."[55] As an intellectual
and policy resource, the rhetoric of falling dominoes underwrote the
provision of assistance to the French, as well as the gradual amping up
of direct military support once the French retired from the conflict.[56]

Bipartisan, ubiquitous, and universal, the domino metaphor became "axiomatic [of] American policy."[57]

For his part, Nixon was "one of the original proponents of the domino theory."[58] Having long held hawkish views on Vietnam—as vice president he urged Eisenhower to use atomic weapons—he applauded Kennedy's deepening involvement and publicly endorsed Johnson's escalation of the war. When the intervention went poorly, he criticized both Kennedy and Johnson for having mishandled the war.[59] This bellicose approach to Vietnam, a small and out-of-the-way country, stemmed from his conviction that the "war [w]as part of a global struggle against communist aggression," principally sponsored by the USSR and China.[60] He posited in 1965 that failure in Vietnam would tip over Cambodia, Laos, and Thailand, but also "Japan will eventually be pulled irresistibly into the Red orbit."[61] He reiterated these claims during the 1968 campaign, stressing the importance of winning in Vietnam to stave off Soviet and Chinese aggression. After becoming president, his hawkish stance drew support from other foreign-policy thinkers, even after it became clear that victory was impossible. For example, Walt Rostow, out of government but still an active commentator on American foreign policy, claimed in 1969 that all of Asia understood "that if we pull out of Vietnam, we'd have to pull out of all of Asia, the place would fall."[62] And notable conservatives like Bill Buckley, William Rusher, Barry Goldwater, and James Burnham identified Vietnam as a "historical turning point" and warned U.S. withdrawal risked World War III.[63]

The metaphor of falling dominoes rationalized Vietnam policy during Nixon's first term in two ways. First, summarizing and clarifying the stakes of the conflict, the metaphor served as an "organizing concept, providing an internal anchor" that decision-makers employed to discuss, debate, and design war policies.[64] Orienting policymakers to see Vietnam as a linchpin to all of Asia prescribed a "range of action . . . limited to options that are implied by" falling dominoes.[65] This narrow scope, buttressed by fears of regional insecurity, provided policymakers incentives to continue to fight the war, even after it had clearly been lost. Second, the metaphor implied an enemy, secretive but forceful, awaiting its opportunity to trigger a chain reaction across the region, if not the world. This recessed enemy—the communist—retained force in the American national imaginary both inside and outside government and acted as a primary impetus for most of Nixon's foreign-policy program. Both of these factors impeded conversations about ending the war, but Nixon finessed the conceptual system by shifting the meaning of the metaphor while displacing it with construction metaphors. This metaphoric shift echoed across the foreign affairs bureaucracy and encouraged actors to understand international tensions generally, and war specifically, as a structural failure, rather than the inevitable outcome of a contest of competing ideologies. As a consequence, replacing dominoes with structures displaced figurations of the enemy, moving representations of the enemy from savage to client.

Dislodging the Domino Metaphor

Self-fashioned as a foreign-policy realist, Nixon became the thirty-seventh president of the United States in part because of his commitment to end the war in Vietnam.[66] During his campaign, he pledged action to address domestic challenges and "a new policy for peace abroad."[67] That policy included Vietnam, of course, but went much further. "We shall not stop there," he said, "we need a policy to prevent more Vietnams." Nixon's new internationalism, later known as détente, meant peaceful negotiation, an open world, and sharing the burden of enforcing the peace with allies.[68] The paradox of espousing the ideal of peace while endorsing the pragmatics of war provided an underlying logic to the president's end-of-war discourse because it asked the nation and the bureaucracy to understand policies that appeared to favor war as part of his efforts to secure a generation of peace.[69]

In spite of the lofty rhetoric, Nixon's adherence to the domino theory demanded victory in Vietnam. This adherence impeded his pledge to end the war because he couldn't withdraw and discuss the danger a communist Vietnam would pose to the region. He also had to grapple with his own convictions about Vietnam's importance, as well as those of the broader community of national-security experts, public advocates, and administrative actors. But Nixon was not without rhetorical options. By the time he ascended to the presidency, public confidence in the domino metaphor and the importance of Vietnam to Asia had begun to slip. Antiwar derision of the theory moderated the claims of proponents as many of the theory's precepts could not hold up under scrutiny.[70] Debate effects rendered the theory as lacking in credibility, and according to Robert Dallek, both Nixon and Kissinger understood the stakes in Vietnam as about national credibility and not about the inevitable spread of communism in the region.[71]

Dedicating significant energy to foreign policy, Nixon gave particular attention to ending the war in Vietnam on terms favorable to the United States, to improving relations with the Soviet Union, and to opening diplomatic relations with the People's Republic of China. He coupled this general discourse of peace with the specific pledge to achieve "peace with honor" in Vietnam, a consistent phrase used from the start of his campaign for the presidency until the final peace agreement had been reached.[72] As Dallek explained, both Nixon and Kissinger believed that "achieving an 'honorable' end to the Vietnam War was America's most compelling need."[73] Their belief was premised on the political fallout of Johnson's inability to win the war and the potential dangers posed by unilateral withdrawal. From the very beginning of his term in office, then, Nixon based his end-of-war strategy on what he perceived would be effective politically at home and would shore up American prestige and credibility abroad.

This rhetorical attitude joined with Nixon's efforts to isolate the foreign-policy bureaucracy from influencing the direction of policy. From the first days of his presidency, Nixon centralized policy planning and development in the Oval Office, relying primarily on the advice and council of National Security Advisor Henry Kissinger. Doing so meant he and Kissinger maintained resolute control over the direction of Vietnam policy and peace negotiations. Toward that end, he chose the completely inexperienced William P. Rogers as his secretary of state precisely because he would pose no obstacle to Nixon's desire to manage policy from the White House.[74] His choice for secretary of defense, Melvin Laird, a budget-savvy member of the House of Representatives, aided this mission. Laird lacked the name recognition and personality of prior secretaries of defense and, in Nixon's estimation, would serve as administrator rather than public spokesperson for the administration's policies. These choices, combined with structural, bureaucratic changes instituted by Nixon and Kissinger, placed big-ticket foreign-policy items—ending Vietnam, negotiations with the Soviet Union over arms reductions, and opening up formal diplomatic relations with the People's Republic of China—fully in Nixon's and Kissinger's hands.[75] While these changes likely impaired his negotiations with the USSR and China, the sum effect of these maneuvers, as John Lewis Gaddis explained, "concentrat[ed] power in the White House to a degree unprecedented since the wartime administration of Franklin D. Roosevelt."[76]

In addition to the sheer control Nixon and Kissinger exercised over foreign policy, the bureaucratic structure of policymaking facilitated the deep penetration of Nixon's war frames across the administration. As Harvey Averch explained, bureaucratic actors rely on paradigms that "motivate their decisions and behavior."[77] Rather than logically connected and formally thought out, these paradigms instead attach belief and actions to a policy orientation. This results in "an incomplete and partial logic connect[ing] strongly held beliefs, assumed and verifiable facts, and forecasts that cannot ever be checked out."[78] Once these views or orientations become ingrained in the thinking of "managers at the top of the bureaucracy," they "cascade downwards and sideways," penetrating every level of decision-making.[79] Institutional actors, individuals whose jobs are embedded in a formal, hierarchal structure, have financial and career incentives to carry on and ensure the execution of the guiding mission of the institution. With the intuitions of the paradigm guiding decisions, agents replicate institutional rules because of an implicit "bias toward reproduction."[80] There are countless examples of this in foreign policy. Samantha Power, for example, explained that the "normal operations of the foreign policy bureaucracy" enable presidents to express concern for victims while essentially ignoring the problem of genocide.[81] And, when institutional channels shift, as they did when Jimmy Carter prioritized human rights, career bureaucrats enact routinized forms or activities to ensure the execution of the newly prioritized mission.[82]

Reluctant to entirely abandon the domino metaphor or dislodge it from its bureaucratic context, Nixon diminished its importance as a rationale or justification for his actions in Vietnam.[83] Publicly, he suggested losing South Vietnam to communism would be immensely discouraging to other nations in Southeast Asia and ominously encouraging to the communist powers.[84] Rather than infer the inevitability of falling dominoes, the rhetoric defined a losing outcome as impacting national confidence or enthusiasm. Privately, even while maintaining a favorable opinion on the theory, he attempted to set it aside. At a National Security Council meeting in 1972, for example, he both endorsed the theory and urged his counselors to ignore it. Stating that a loss in Vietnam would have a "considerable effect on our allies" and damage "our ability to conduct a credible foreign policy," he asked those present to "leave out the domino theory" and instead recognize that "a Communist success would be considered a failure of U.S. policy." Yet, after Vice President Spiro Agnew and George Lincoln, the director of the Office of Emergency Preparedness, stated they "personally believe[d] in the domino theory," Nixon concurred. "I think we all" believe in it, he said, but "the real question is whether the Americans give a damn any more."[85] Tacitly recognizing the theory's public impotence, this example points to the crux of Nixon's problem: he wanted to win in Vietnam, but as public attitudes shifted against the war, the prospect for continuation dwindled.

While the problem for Nixon lay more in the public's understanding of the theory than the theory itself, his use of the domino metaphor dwindled. Intensely sensitive to public attitudes on Vietnam, Nixon backtracked on the metaphor and shifted its meaning. Prior to Nixon, the domino theory invoked the figure of the enemy by blaming South Vietnam's failure to win on "the aggressive thrust . . . [of] an alien hegemonic movement."[86] Conjoined to the notion of an aggressive force, the theory identified "the relative weakness of the Southeast Asian states" as a key factor in the duration of the conflict.[87] When Nixon used the metaphor, he emphasized American credibility as a structural component determinative of peace. In particular, Nixon stressed the importance of the credibility of U.S. security guarantees to regional security. To cut and run, he claimed, would damage the nation's image and undermine efforts he had made "in building a new structure of peace in the world." While cut-and-run in Vietnam "might be good politics," he continued, doing so would "discourage our friends and . . . encourage our enemies." The effect, moreover, would be global, reaching Europe, Asia, the Middle East, and Latin America.[88] These articulations shifted the tenor of the domino metaphor by linking the risk of a Red Spread to the confidence allies and at-risk states had in American credibility and prestige.[89] Shifting the focus from the status of weak, vulnerable nations to American credibility served Nixon's war aims because it rationalized the continuation of American military presence and training—the so-called Nixon Doctrine—and U.S. military and economic support to Southeast Asia. The pivot also displaced the domino theory with construction metaphors and, in the process, erased savage figures of the enemy by branding those activities as a component of a broader process to build a stable structure of peace in the world.

From Dominoes to a Structure of Peace: Nixon's End-of-War Rhetoric

Finessing the contours of the domino metaphor freed Nixon to approach Vietnam with more flexibility. Cultivating a set of construction metaphors to define his efforts in Vietnam, the progress of peace, and international politics generally supplanted the domino theory with an aspirational conception of international politics. Not the first to use construction metaphors—Senator Kennedy claimed, "Vietnam represents the cornerstone of the Free World in Southeast Asia, the keystone to the arch, the finger in the dike"[90]—Nixon's adoption of these metaphors reflected a fundamental shift in the way presidents talked about Vietnam, its significance in the world, and the means by which the United States could extricate itself from the conflict. Figuring the problem of Vietnam and conflict generally as the outcome of flawed designs, plans, or craftsmanship, this new formulation offered Nixon two rhetorical resources for exiting the war. First, construction metaphors supplanted representations of the North Vietnamese by providing Nixon with a vocabulary that could explain the war without resorting to metaphors of savagery. By emphasizing the structural fault lines of international relations themselves, this rhetoric displaced blame for the war from the North Vietnamese, erasing representations of the enemy in the process. This approach to the problem in Southeast Asia also silenced fears of ideological forces intent on toppling weak nations in a chain reaction across the region. Second, construction metaphors infused American policy with a quality of control. The president's commitment to build a structure, more than empty promises to a nation tired of war, reoriented policy toward peaceful international relations, constituting Vietnam as one component of a broader edifice of peace. That edifice, Nixon contended, would stabilize relations and prevent the outbreak of future conflicts. As I will explain, the interconnected network of construction metaphors enabled by this discourse linked security guarantees to American military strength, forward deployment, alliances, and other material forms that constituted a structure.

Paradoxically, prioritizing structure over event elevated the importance of Vietnam as architectural model even while acknowledging its peripheral status. For Nixon, American policy in Vietnam provided the blueprint for his broader designs for U.S. foreign policy. Unlike Korea, where Eisenhower sought to move beyond Korea by refocusing on the true enemy, Nixon needed a positive outcome in Vietnam in order to demonstrate the efficacy of his global plan for peace. Three aspects of his discourse articulated policy shifts in Vietnam as representative of the structure of peace he planned for the world: the phrase "peace with honor" and its derivatives, his rhetoric of Vietnamization, and his depiction of tectonic shifts in international relations. Each of these aspects represented Vietnam as an architectural model or a blueprint for peace. The Vietnam-as-blueprint metaphor demonstrated the structural contributions to peace—burden sharing, negotiation, training and equipping an ally facing a communist adversary, and maintaining the credibility of American commitments—while connecting those elements to the target terrain where they would be applied. By marking Vietnam as both obstacle and model, this discourse diminished the actual importance of the North Vietnamese as antagonists. The enemy wasn't the focus. Only the structure of peace and Vietnam's connection to the president's architectural plan mattered.

During his first year in office, Nixon's discourse of construction manifested with the elaboration of Vietnamization. In addition to laying out a strategy for Vietnam, the policy represented an important step in elaborating the contours, if not the language, of his plan to build a structure of peace in the world. While implemented in Vietnam, the policy evolved into a broader doctrine and served as a blueprint for Nixon's approach to international affairs. First discussing the status of Asia with reporters in Guam in July 1969, Nixon blamed Communist China for "a very aggressive attitude and a belligerent attitude in foreign policy." This posture, he argued, rendered Asia "the greatest threat to peace," requiring a shift in American policy.[91] By September 1969, he expanded on the theme in two separate speeches. The first posited the basis of the president's foreign-policy agenda as "forging a new structure of world stability."[92] The second, an address to the United Nations General Assembly, extended the theme, describing "peace as a process embodied in a structure," and articulating the proper role for the United States as contributing to "the structure of peace."[93]

Proposing a specific, activist form of international relations, each of these speeches explained peace as something built, bit by bit, over a long period of time. Each speech positioned the United States as the agent most crucial to the building. The metaphoric schema identified the president-as-architect, having both the vision and the ability to see what needs doing and to guide others to address the need. For Nixon, these speeches represented a key moment of demarcation in which the world—and particularly Europe—needed to recognize that the postwar era had concluded and that international politics demanded "a process of creative evolution," or, more simply, "other nations [need] to assume a greater share of the responsibility for their own security."[94] As architect, Nixon provided the blueprint for peace, but asked others to build it. Envisioning peace as a continuous activity—as an exhibition of creative evolution—Nixon claimed the complexity of the modern world meant it was "no longer enough to restrain war. Peace must also embrace progress—both in satisfying man's material needs and in fulfilling his spiritual needs."[95] The new structure included a rigid defense of sovereign borders, the "right to develop" without violence, and the right to self-determination free from outside interference.[96] This definition reflected the desires of one of Nixon's core targets, the nonaligned countries, while incorporating the ideological components of his foreign-policy approach. Nations should act with self-restraint toward others, Nixon urged, and they should "assume a greater share of responsibility for their own security." He pledged that the United States would do its part to "encourage local and regional initiatives, to foster national independence and self-sufficiency," and, in the process, contribute to international peace.[97] Far from romancing Kantian ideals of a positive peace, the president's definition reflected the ideological tenets of the Nixon Doctrine while erasing the particular enemy in favor of a more generalized set of parameters for ensuring peace in world affairs. Those parameters included metaphoric descriptions of peace and transcendence from Vietnam enabled by the phrase "peace with honor."

PEACE WITH HONOR

Questions of method shift the focus of war policy from causes to solutions. Nixon put this movement forward in his address accepting the Republican nomination for president in 1968. This speech, in which he pledged to seek an "honorable end to the war in Vietnam," historicized American foreign policy from Washington to the present and thematically connected America's national mission—and Nixon's—as seeking "peace and freedom in the world."[98] The specific phrase "peace with honor," however, appeared to have little content. It wasn't until he became president that the phrase began to accumulate meaning. Becoming a common refrain in his Vietnam rhetoric, "peace with honor" reflected the president's emphasis on process and the need to end the war the right way. Like the architect outlining the basic steps necessary to build a structure from the rubble, Nixon defined "peace with honor" as involving plans for peace, bargaining or negotiating a settlement with the North Vietnamese, and ensuring that the brokered peace prevented the return of violence in the world.[99] By rhetorically investing in the significance of the process, this discourse distanced the president from the day-to-day realities of the conflict, assured the public of an inevitable and favorable outcome, and established the terms under which the United States could conclude the war. His role, as architect of the peace, focused on planning, monitoring and reporting on progress, and hammering out the terms of a final peace accord. Others would serve as the craftsmen. Concurrently, even in the absence of explicit references to the enemy, the president's discourse implied the presence of a rational interlocutor, ready and able to drive a bargain for peace.

Gradually, "peace with honor" came to mean negotiation over the political causes of the conflict and the potential ways to resolve those issues. These definitional moves crystallized in Nixon's remarks commending a peace proposal put forward by South Vietnam's president Nguyen Van Thieu in July 1969. Identifying war in Vietnam as a failure of politics, Nixon contended that only a political settlement could ease the pain of a tortured land. Emphasizing the reasonableness of Thieu's proposal, the president also spoke of the "long series of steps" taken to develop the proposal, American military restraint, and the mutual desire for a settlement.[100] These statements characterized American efforts as reasonable, flexible, and motivated by a desire to end the suffering of the war. While this message shifted the burden of negotiation to the North Vietnamese, implying their willingness to negotiate would demonstrate their true commitment to peace, the primary valence of the address remained on questions of process. As became typical over the course of his presidency, Nixon's procedural rhetoric—embodied most commonly in the phrase "peace with honor"—elevated method over all other concerns.

This overarching emphasis on process reinforced the president-as-architect persona. By beginning from an assumption that he shared a common view with those opposed to the war—that the nation should end the conflict as soon as possible—Nixon defined peace as an outcome of an incremental process on a specific timeline. Like the architect, behind schedule but on task, the discourse of a "just peace" or "peace with honor" facilitated continuation rather than withdrawal because it provided the president with the means to explain delays or changes in the plan while reminding audiences of the ultimate goal. A television interview in January 1971 bears out the point. When asked to list his achievements and failures, the president pointed to foreign policy as his focus and as bearing positive results. While noting the United States had not fully withdrawn from Vietnam, he claimed, "We are on the way out in a way that will bring a just peace, the kind of a peace that will discourage that kind of aggression in the future, and that will build, I hope, the foundation for a generation of peace."[101] This rhetoric fit with the broader metaphoric pattern typifying Nixon's discourse in that it articulated the shared goal of peace while emphasizing the need for following the correct procedures. Doing so would lay a foundation upon which a lasting peace could be built and, in the immediate future, would deter additional proxy wars. Nixon's construction discourse, then, prioritized method over result and linked the war in Vietnam to the broader Cold War context.

As the war stretched on and negotiations floundered, Nixon expressed frustration about the never-ending war. Claiming he had a "plan for peace," his television remarks on January 25, 1972, updated the status of peace talks and blamed the North Vietnamese for intransigence at the negotiating table.[102] Mimicking his approach to public criticism of his handling of the war, this rhetoric once again shifted responsibility for ending the war to the North Vietnamese. Like the architect blaming the contractor for a lack of progress, the message reiterated his plan for peace and his willingness to negotiate those plans. This strategy presented

Nixon as the one with the vision and desire for peace, only to have his plans frustrated by forces outside of his control. But the speech also demonstrated Nixon's reluctance to reinvoke savage imagery to depict the North Vietnamese. Privately, the president ramped up the violence to pressure the enemy to make concessions at the negotiating table. Sometimes referred to as the madman theory, this strategy escalated the material costs of resisting peace overtures. Driven to exhibit toughness in Vietnam and tired of the lack of progress, Nixon wanted to "bomb the hell out of them." But Kissinger and Laird persuaded him to wait.[103] Nixon gave this address after waiting had yielded no tangible results. His frustration with the war collided with his concerns about its effect on his reelection. For that reason, his abandonment of savage metaphors is striking. Throughout the address Nixon criticized the North Vietnamese for their inflexibility and unwillingness to budge on key issues. At each turn, however, the depiction implied an adversary engaged in strategic thinking, seeking to maximize its gains internationally. That is, Nixon's enemy mirrored Nixon's own realist orientation.

Finally, Nixon employed process discourse in service of his end-of-war strategy by articulating the benefits "peace with honor" could confer to global peace. This rhetoric contended that ending the war in the right way would deter future conflicts by demonstrating to allies and adversaries America's commitment to building a structure of peace. While his rationalization echoed the contours of the domino metaphor—shifting focus from weak states to American strength—it also embodied the persona of president-as-architect by emphasizing the structural benefits of peace. In an address to the nation on April 26, 1972, Nixon provided yet another status update about the war, detailing the progress of the troop drawdown and the training effort. Embedded in the message, however, was the clearest statement of his views on Vietnam's implicit link to the broader contest against communism. Explaining "the stakes are not just for South Vietnam, but for the United States and for the cause of peace in the world," Nixon argued the outcome in Vietnam would influence the likelihood of peace in "the Mideast, in Europe, and in other international danger spots." This argument contended that allies and adversaries watched Vietnam, and the outcome would signal the viability of armed conquest in the new era. But rather than replicate a vulgar form of the domino metaphor, the rhetoric mirrored the contours of Nixon's architectural discourse. The new era he envisioned, the so-called structure of peace, required collaboration from allies, the nonaligned, and adversaries. Their collaboration relied on their confidence in America's commitment to peace. His proposals for peace in Vietnam—"peace with honor for both sides," as he put it—embodied the essence of his imagined structure.[104] That is, he envisioned an outcome to the war premised on collective security, negotiation, and fairness to both sides.

Nixon expanded upon this thesis on the campaign trail prior to his reelection in 1972. At a stop in Ashland, Kentucky, for example, he explicitly linked Vietnam and the foundation for peace. "You want to get it over with honor," he contended, "because by ending it in an honorable way, by ending it in the right way, you may lay the foundation for not having another war in that same generation."[105] In a subsequent address, he put the question to the American people in starker terms: "As we approach the end of the war in Vietnam, the great question is whether the end of that war will be only an interlude between wars or the beginning of a generation of peace for the world." Fitting for a reelection campaign, these messages leveraged Nixon's achievements to argue that a second term would enable him to "build toward a generation of peace."[106] Purposefully ambiguous, the discourse of an "honorable peace," or a peace concluded "the right way," ran throughout Nixon's rhetoric as the foremost means for explaining how to foster the conditions necessary for an extended period of international tranquility. The strategic erasure in this rhetoric—abstracting definitions of peace and his administration's strategy for forcing Vietnamese concessions at the negotiating table— dodged public concerns about Nixon's decision to escalate the war as a means for seeking peace. Instead of recognizing those concerns, construction metaphors displaced them by asserting Vietnam's foundational importance to a broader structure of peace. By implication, this rhetoric contextualized and justified the administration's strategy for achieving the ultimate goal.

On the eve of the election, Nixon's final argument to the American people returned to Vietnam and his structure for peace. Claiming a breakthrough in negotiations, Nixon stated that "there are still some details that I am insisting be worked out and nailed down."[107] The sudden appearance of "peace with honor," he continued, signaled the real possibility of "a lasting peace," for Vietnam and the world.[108] The consummate architect, Nixon's pivot from Vietnam to the world enacted a novel form of erasure—the erasure of sides. Instead of recognizing the battle between the democratic South and the communist North, fundamentally distinct political orientations, and continuing challenges at the negotiating table, this rhetoric amalgamated the complexity of the war into a single plane. Doing so compressed the dissensus that had typified four years of negotiations into the simple matter of nailing down a few final details, something Nixon would oversee. This rhetoric shifted focus from issues related to identity, ideology, facts of the battle, and material disagreements, vacating the figure of the enemy in the process, to Nixon's thesis that the proper process, vision, and leadership would produce peace. By trusting in Nixon's architectural vision, the logic went, peace could be achieved in Vietnam and beyond.

Public discussion about the need for an honorable conclusion to the war echoed across the foreign affairs bureaucracy. As a procedural discourse, it penetrated both Vietnam policy and other components of Nixon's foreign-policy deliberations. In addition to providing consistent updates on his plans to end the war, behind the scenes, the administration worked in overdrive to design the goals, metrics, and outcomes necessary to exit the war. A series of memos and internal documents refer to those designs as plans, suggesting they were blueprints for peace. Kissinger's memos written in anticipation of Nixon's address on the Paris peace talks in January 1972 explained that the current plan "builds on the negotiating principles already established in the public record."[109] Included in the documents is a letter Nixon sent to Chairman Brezhnev of the USSR, explaining that his public comments detailed "a new plan for peace."[110] The point here isn't so much the content of those plans—American negotiating positions evolved over the course of the war—but rather the continuous articulation, publicly and privately, of the administration's plans for peace. Those articulations laid out specific steps—schedules—programmatically establishing a step-by-step process for building the peace.

A component of that discourse articulated the end of the war—as well as the resolution of any international controversy—as a bargain or a settlement. Secretary of State Rogers's brief in anticipation of Nixon's visit to China explained one of the PRC's demands as "mov[ing] the US toward a settlement in Korea on terms at least mildly favorable to the North Koreans."[111] Nixon, in a private letter to Brezhnev, expressed a mutual desire "in moving toward a settlement in the Middle East."[112] And, in terms of Vietnam, the administration worried about the political benefits of a final settlement. Al Haig, in a memo to Kissinger, worried about who would get "credit for the settlement" and how it would impact Nixon's reelection campaign.[113] Kissinger, in private conversations with Nixon, routinely referred to the end of the war as a bargain to settle.[114] In a top-secret cable sent to Haig and the White House on October 22, 1972, Kissinger stressed that "military people [have] to recognize when the time for a settlement" arrives. A follow-up cable sent several hours later reiterated that "the settlement was sound." Ambassador Bunker sent his own cable to Haig on the same evening, expressing a common "purpose to make peace together."[115]

The consistent reliance on the word "settlement"—a ubiquitous term in diplomatic discourse—to describe the end of the war reflects the continuity of the metaphoric economy across the administration. Implying the finalization of a bargain—or closing on a property—the metaphor distanced officials from the on-the-ground outcome of the peace deal. At the same time, the metaphor provided its own impetus. Settlements imply two or more sides, engaged in arduous negotiations, out of which no party will truly be satisfied. But, the great effort undertaken to reach a settlement provides incentives for acceptance. And, indeed, the pressure implied by the metaphor appeared explicitly in Kissinger's discourse. A separate cable from Bunker quoted Kissinger as telling President Thieu, "We have fought for four years, have mortgaged our whole foreign policy to the defense of your country." Like the contractor upset at the client for altering the terms of the deal, the cable went on to blame Thieu for not speaking openly and for having wasted "four days in making plans on how to proceed."[116] Two months later, in a cable from Nixon to Kissinger, the president repeated the phrasing, urging Kissinger to "press for a settlement."[117] Shortly after, Kissinger warned George Carver Jr. about the South Vietnamese attitude toward "the implementation of any settlement."[118] These internal conversations and documents speak to the consistency of this metaphoric form across the key players in the peace process in the final year of America's involvement in the war. But they also demonstrate how the focus on procedures echoed within a bureaucratic structure, mimicking without precisely replicating public discourse.

This procedural discourse penetrated other components of Nixon's foreign-policy process. A memo from John Scali, the ambassador to the United Nations, to the president recommended a media briefing prior to visiting China to dampen expectations. The briefing would clarify that the purpose of the visit "is to open a dialogue with China's leaders, not to lay out a blueprint for solving all of Asia's problems." Scali's concern related to press coverage, not strategy. The danger, he wrote, was that a newsman might explain the visit as "aimed at ending the war in Vietnam."[119] While Kissinger vetoed the briefing, Scali's memo implied the Nixon administration believed ending Vietnam and opening diplomatic relations with China formed a component of their blueprint for peace. Indeed, a follow-up memo from Secretary Rogers to the president confirmed the significance of restoration of diplomatic relations as "contribut[ing] to the evolution of a more stable world balance of power."[120] Conceiving of international relations as radically unstable—and the establishment of diplomatic relations as a stabilizing force—replicated the architectural discourse by stressing the need for structure. This rhetoric characterized foreign leaders, even those espousing hostile ideologies, as rational interlocutors and the outbreak of conflict as a failure of communication. Pointing to the ways the foreign affairs bureaucracy envisioned their task, this discourse connected to and overlaid Nixon's actual policies toward Vietnam.

FROM VIETNAMIZATION TO ASIA

Nixon's construction discourse began in his inaugural when he briefly mentioned his core foreign-policy goal as seeking to "strengthen the structure of peace." This structure, he indicated, would be served by expanding international arms control and boosting economic assistance for "the poor and the hungry."[121] This initial goal, articulated as a single line in a long speech outlining his plan for governing, flourished over time into a fuller discourse. Guided by an idiom of construction metaphors, Nixon articulated each face of the conflict and peace process in terms of "plans," "structures," and "building" or "constructing." He also used terms like "cornerstone" or "keystone," referents to the significance of a single moment or event in the broader architecture of peace his administration sought to spread across the globe. By far the most common metaphoric expression, however, was Nixon's reliance on the phrase "structure of peace." This phrase appeared in his discourse prior to his presidency and continued to shape and frame his approach to world politics, including his end-of-war discourse in Vietnam.

While Nixon's initial speeches about Vietnam and Asia did little more than sketch out his plan, the Vietnamization speech focused on and clarified the doctrinal shift in American foreign policy. In the speech, Nixon posed two possibilities for extricating the nation from Vietnam: precipitate withdrawal, or training and equipping the South Vietnamese while gradually drawing down the American presence. Claiming the first option would result in disaster for South Vietnam, Nixon argued immediate withdrawal would "result in a collapse of confidence in American leadership" and undermine "the cause of peace." Invoking the domino metaphor, he claimed the ultimate outcome would be more war.[122] While the Vietnamization speech has been rightfully criticized for its deceptive rhetoric, the policy it enacted had actually been de facto policy in Vietnam for twenty years. The French called it "*jaunissement* or, 'yellowing,'" Kennedy's military advisors justified greater U.S. involvement on the need to better train the South Vietnamese, and Johnson claimed that better-trained South Vietnamese forces would enable America's withdrawal.[123] As Olson and Roberts put it, "the only difference in 1969 was that the United States had little choice" but to go all in on training the Vietnamese because Nixon had campaigned on ending the war, and the strength of the antiwar movement raised the political stakes of failure.[124]

But the Vietnamization speech did more than just announce a policy that had long been in effect. Rationalizing the gradual withdrawal from Vietnam, Nixon claimed that Vietnamization represented "a plan which will end this war in a way that will bring us closer to . . . a just and lasting peace." In providing guiding principles—maintaining treaty commitments, shielding allies from aggressive nuclear powers, and providing "military and economic assistance when requested"—the speech resolved to move United States policy away from directly defending all nations of the free world. In what would become known as the Nixon Doctrine, the policy sought to distribute responsibility for the defense against communism because, the president argued, "the defense of freedom is everybody's business not just America's business."[125] The transactional logic of this claim—that security was the product of mutual enterprise between like-minded nations—proposed a new model for peacemaking. This new model argued for ending the war by empowering South Vietnam's economic, military, and political independence. Envisioning U.S. assistance as transactional, in which economic and military expenditures became fair exchange for mutual defense and regional stability, reorganized the effort in Vietnam around a plan premised on deterrence, allies and adversaries, and nation-building. Applying that model more broadly, the speech equipped bureaucratic actors with a new lexicon for explaining policy. And indeed, after the speech, "Nixon administration decisionmakers all began speaking of how well the Vietnamization program was going." The policy model put forth by the Doctrine played an instrumental role in this reorganization because it detached internal debates from questions of tactics and instead guided the management of the war and the approach to international relations generally with a paradigmatic orientation.[126]

With the implementation of Vietnamization, Nixon pointed to advancements in the training and arming program to demonstrate that his strategy would eventually bring the conflict to an amenable conclusion. That strategy yielded its first force reduction in June 1969, when the president claimed "the progress of the training program and the equipping program" had brought the South Vietnamese into their own as a military force.[127] This rhetoric omitted any recognition of the role or existence of the enemy. Left vacant was any signification of who South Vietnam needed defending against or, more importantly, a description of the challenge represented by the North Vietnamese. Instead, by isolating progress in the training and equipping program as the sole factor that determined the timeline for American withdrawal, this rhetoric reduced the complexity of the problem to one of logistics. Dismissing the role of the adversary also rendered on-the-ground assessments of South Vietnam's training and their ability to defend national territory unnecessary. Military readiness assumed the nation could defend itself from anyone. Finally, the absence of an antagonist shifted responsibility for the outcome of the war onto South Vietnam, even as it claimed the lion's share of the credit for the U.S. military and Nixon himself.

Nixon's explanation of incremental reductions in U.S. forces (from 549,000 to 69,000 between 1969 and 1972) contributed to this rhetoric of progress. He announced the first troop reduction in September 1969, promising the return of 60,000 soldiers by the end of the year. Depicting U.S. efforts as benevolent and diplomatic, the speech offered evidence that his "administration has made major efforts to bring an end to the war."[128] Ticking off a series of actions taken—from "renounc[ing] an imposed military solution" to "offer[ing] to negotiate"—the address pointed to his incremental approach while eradicating the figure of the enemy, the enemy's motive, or the enemy's role in the peace. Instead, Nixon referenced the North Vietnamese as the "other side," explaining "it is difficult to communicate across the gulf of 5 years of war," a flourish that displaced enemy motive and agency for the continuation of the war to the scene of the war itself.[129] That is, Nixon's description of his incremental approach resituated responsibility for the conclusion of the war on his administration, deflecting attention from North Vietnamese actions on the battlefield and at the negotiating table. Rhetorically removing the North Vietnamese, ironically, invited blame for his inability to end the war.

As architectural model, however, Vietnamization was but one example of the shift in direction enacted by the Nixon Doctrine. As the president explained in early 1971, "We are encouraging countries to participate fully in the creation of plans and the designing of programs . . . Before, we often acted as if our role was primarily one of drawing up and selling American blueprints. Now, we must evoke the ideas of others and together consider programs that meet common needs."[130] Synecdochically representing Vietnamization as a prefabricated model for his policy program, Nixon simplified the complexity of the international system by promoting a singular representation above all others.[131] Simultaneously, this rhetoric depicted the problem of Vietnam specifically, and peace generally, as a result of a lack of planning rather than one of antagonism. Binding Nixon to Vietnamization via an architectural discourse outlining a global structure for peace, this speech marked the end of the era of singular American leadership. In place of hegemonic leadership, Nixon-as-architect asked allied nations to join him in a collective endeavor. That is, Nixon's construction discourse distributed the tasks of design and assembly across and among U.S. allies. Justifying this shift by explaining the transition of allied economies in the post–World War II era, he claimed the United States no longer needed to play a singular role in the preservation of the peace. Rather, peace could not emerge "unless other nations help to fashion it."[132] Vietnamization, then, signaled a broad shift in strategy his administration would undertake.

To underscore the significance of the changes Nixon proposed to U.S. foreign policy, he released a 40,000-word document in February 1970 titled "Foreign Policy for the 1970s: A New Strategy for Peace." This document, Nixon claimed, was the first of its kind and constituted the "most comprehensive statement on foreign and defense policy ever made." At publication, he held a press briefing with Henry Kissinger to emphasize its strategic necessity given "the world situation as it is today."[133] The rhetoric of the report extended and amplified the construction metaphor guiding and directing Nixon's foreign-policy vision by noting Vietnam's significance while displacing the war as the focus of American foreign policy. Arguing that "the whole system of international politics was changing," the document identified the challenge as how to respond to systemic change. Vietnam fit into that challenge, of course, but the opening stanzas demarcated the mission as greater than just the difficulty in Vietnam. Positing the unifying theme of the document as building a "durable structure of international relationships which inhibits or removes the causes of war," Nixon elaborated on three core principles that formed the foundation of this structure of peace: partnership (by which he meant burden sharing), military strength, and "a willingness to negotiate." Each of these foundational principles composed the basic structure by which "international disputes can be settled and clashes contained."[134] The body of the document sought to apply these principles to the geographic regions in the world, but ended up spending a great deal of space rehashing Vietnamization and the status of negotiations with the North Vietnamese. At each point, the document restated Vietnam's importance to a "just peace," for Vietnam and the world. In doing so, it positioned Nixon's Vietnam policy as the architectural model or schematic that demonstrated the wisdom of the document's policy shift.

Nixon updated the document a year later and, upon its release, took the opportunity to describe his foreign-policy strategy in detail. While he touched on all of the major regions of the world, Vietnam dominated the radio address. Topically, the speech streamlined Nixon's foreign policy into three core components: getting out of Vietnam, changes in policy to address a changing world, and efforts to "build a lasting peace." Linguistically, it extended and amplified the construction metaphors typifying Nixon's discourse by mimicking the syntax of an architectural update. After describing reductions in U.S. troops, in casualties, and in expenditures, he argued that the "success of the allied operations against the enemy sanctuaries in Cambodia" and "this year's disruption of the Ho Chi Mihn Trail in Laos" proved the effectiveness of his Vietnamization strategy. But, by posing each aspect of American policy as an achievement—a benchmark in the gradual movement to empower the

South Vietnamese to take responsibility for their own security—the report embodied the form of the project manager. Peace, as something materialized over a long period of time and after much handiwork, emerged
in stages. Like an architect pointing to advances in the construction of
an edifice, Nixon claimed these achievements proved "we have come a
long way."[135] They also implied there was still a long way to go.

Embodying the persona of the architect distanced the president
from the particulars of the policy by emphasizing process over details.
To that end, Nixon stated, "it matters very much how we end this war,"
and again proposed that ending the war in the right way raised the odds
of a permanent peace. By this logic, all of his endeavors in Vietnam,
including escalation of the conflict, represented "efforts to build a lasting peace." These efforts, Nixon explained, were worth doing because
"the right way out is crucial to our changing role in the world and to
peace in the world." Vietnamization—the proof of concept of the Nixon
Doctrine—demonstrated the efficacy of burden sharing as a means to
collectively "build the peace." As Nixon put it, "no single nation can
build a peace alone; peace can only be built by the willing hand—and
minds—of all."[136] In this way, peace-building in Vietnam synecdochically
represented both example and model, demonstrating the capacity of
Nixon's strategic reformation of American foreign policy and validating
his vision for America's role in the world.

Holding out alliances as structural models had long been part of
Nixon's rhetorical repertoire. In expression of his general premise, he
spoke early in his first term of the necessity for "forging a new structure
of world stability in which the burdens as well as the benefits are fairly
shared—a structure that does not rely on the strength of one nation but
that draws strength from all nations."[137] This message, delivered to an
audience of U.S. governors, positioned alliances as crucial to his vision
for peace because, by sharing the burden, all nations could be stronger
at a lowered cost. Even if the United States bore the major costs of security, alliances served as force multipliers in times of conflict. Beyond
burden sharing, however, Nixon's discourse emphasized strength as the
outcome of collective security. Once again extending a relational theory

of security—that positive relations between nations act as incentives for peaceful endeavors like trade—this rhetoric further submerged representations of savagery in world affairs. Dispossessing antagonists of agency, this theory reasserted the significance of the scene as the critical factor to security.

Nixon's international trips provided the president opportunities to expand upon this relational theory of security. Stressing the importance of allied cooperation, burden sharing, and talking with adversaries, he inflated the importance of alliances to the structure of peace. "When we talk about the structure of peace," he said, "we must realize that the most indispensable element is maintaining with our allies and our friends . . . the strength that will deter potential aggression."[138] Spoken on a trip to Europe, this rhetoric articulated a vision of international relations premised on deterrence and the rational-actor theory of politics. Alliances mattered, he suggested, because they signaled to adversaries the seriousness of American and allied commitment to mutual defense. Antagonists, as rational actors, would read collective strength and commitment as warnings of the consequences of adventurism, preventing attacks because of the surety of the response. Representing collective security as a crucial structural element upon which the peace could be built, he stressed the need for "negotiations, if possible, with those who might be our potential opponents, and . . . with nonaligned nations."[139] As with Vietnam, Nixon's foreign-policy discourse emphasized negotiation, relationship building, and burden sharing as vital to the construction of an edifice of peace.

While Nixon's initial ruminations about the importance of alliances did not directly touch upon the conflict in Vietnam, he connected the dots in 1971. In a policy address to Congress, he claimed that Vietnam—and Vietnamization in particular—demonstrated a central truth of burden sharing. After discussing certain program benchmarks, he argued, "We can meet our security assistance objectives effectively only if we link our efforts closely with those of our friends and thereby build the foundations for peace in partnership with them."[140] Again the construction metaphor served as the key link between Vietnam and the rest of the world. Beyond mere burden sharing, Vietnamization involved bilateral cooperation and coordination toward collective goals—defeating the communists. By isolating this component of Vietnamization and offering it as a model, Nixon deepened his definition of the foundation of peace to include coordination and cooperation between allies. Vietnam, in this iteration, served as a model for how to coordinate efforts. And, according to Nixon, the stability of the foundation relied on this type of cooperation.

When pivoting from Asia to Europe, Nixon accented the significance of the role NATO played in "the structure of peace."[141] Identifying it as the preeminent structure that secures the peace in Western Europe, Nixon lamented the absence of similar edifices across the globe. Previously, he posited NATO as the most successful institution or "alliance in the history of the world," to back up his claims about the need to extend the structure to Asia.[142] Ennobling NATO, he held the organization up as a model that merited replication. But, given systemic shifts in international affairs and particular details of Asia, the new structure required new innovations and designs. Indeed, from his remarks at Guam in 1969 to late in his presidency, Nixon focused on Asia, contending that the region represented the key source of danger to the prospects of a long peace. Wrapping up his remarks about the significance of NATO and the trajectory of U.S. foreign policy, Nixon returned to this theme. Erecting a new edifice of peace in Asia required "the right degree of American involvement—not too much and not too little" in order to "evoke the right response from our other partners on this globe in building for our children the kind of world they deserve: a world of opportunity in a world without war."[143] This Goldilocks strategy for U.S. leadership—applying just the right amount of influence to the collective plans for peace—served Nixon's approach to international relations because it highlighted the need for other nations to do more. It also simplified the negotiating task by eliding significant regional variances and excluding concerns from nonaligned nations in the region.

Nixon reiterated these principles on the occasion of his return from a visit to the Soviet Union in 1971. Extolling the prospects of détente with the Soviets and his success in negotiating arms reductions, he spoke of the continuing need for strong alliances as a backstop against renewed aggression. Again, his rhetoric reaffirmed the importance of alliances as "the foundation on which all of our other initiatives for peace and security in the world must rest."[144] This rhetoric, appearing apart from his Vietnam discourse, connected directly to his exit strategy by positing trust and confidence as central to the longevity of alliances. As he put it, "We are ending the war in Vietnam, but we shall end it in a way which will not betray our friends, risk the lives of the courageous Americans still serving in Vietnam, break faith with those held prisoners by the enemy, or stain the honor of the United States of America."[145] Ending Vietnam in the "right way," then, implicated more than just Southeast Asia. It implicated the world because the world would take note of the nation's response to adversity. To abandon Vietnam, Nixon's logic suggested, risked undermining the Atlantic Alliance and all of Europe. While one can read this rhetoric as a shade of the domino theory of international politics, it also speaks to the logic of architecture. A poorly laid foundation jeopardizes the entire edifice. Equally, when different structures become interlinked, faulty construction in one can endanger them all. Nixon's end-of-war rhetoric embodied these theses by pointing to method over outcome. That is, for Nixon, global shifts in the structure of politics combined with interlocking security alliances required a consistent attitude from the United States because only such consistency could provide a stable foundation upon which alliances could be based.

Nixon expanded upon this thesis in his remarks celebrating the nation's independence. Positing Vietnam as one component of his strategy to construct an edifice of peace in the world, he claimed, "We are all aware that a real structure of peace cannot be built on good will alone. Its foundation must be the resolution of those basic national differences which can lead to war. The United States is doing everything in its power to lay down that kind of foundation for peace. It is in this cause that I have traveled to Peking and Moscow, worked for a just peace in Vietnam, acted to check the nuclear arms race, moved to revitalize our alliances."[146] For Nixon, his approach to Vietnam reflected an ethos, a way of doing business, which oriented the totality of American foreign policy under his watch. Concluding Vietnam, in this sense, didn't close the chapter in Southeast Asia or signal an end to American leadership in the region. Rather, it reasserted American leadership as central to facilitating the resolution of differences. Figuring Vietnam as foundational to that approach to the world raised the stakes of the peace talks because it made Nixon's entire blueprint for peace contingent upon successful diplomatic resolution.

At the same time that Nixon's discourse articulated a new vision for the world premised on engineering certain structural elements—mainly alliances, treaties, economic growth, and diplomatic negotiations—it also erased the filaments of savagery present in public articulations of the enemy in Vietnam. As previously mentioned, Nixon's discourse of peace distanced the president from depictions of the Vietnamese. From his Vietnamization speech to the end of the war, he rarely spoke about the North Vietnamese at all. And when he did, he usually spoke of their intransigence or perfidy at the negotiating table. As such, the enemy in Nixon's end-of-war discourse appeared as an adversary to be pressured into peace, rather than an uncivilized force out for blood. Nixon's end-of-war discourse further erased the figure of the enemy by shifting from scene to situation. Rather than recuperate the enemy or relocate the origin of savagery, Nixon explained structural fault lines in international relations as the source of war. This explanation undermined latent claims positing communism as a force that pushes against the dominoes, and situated the credibility of U.S. security guarantees as determining the fate of each and every domino. The rhetoric also linked metaphors of construction to the remnants of the domino theory by implying that structural reinforcement could prevent future dominoes from falling. Articulating the solution to conflict as a structural realignment to shore up the international system and prevent future wars, however, required a more intense disquisition.

A FOREIGN POLICY FOR A CHANGING WORLD

Claims about a fundamental reordering of international relations composed a key component of Nixon's rationalization for a new structure of peace. On numerous occasions, the president spoke about the changing international system, the return of Europe to the world stage, the shift in power from the United States to communist states, the evolving role for U.S. leadership, and the global shift away from imperial politics. Those depictions prioritized structure over event to organize the very logic of the Nixon Doctrine itself, providing the principal pivot that justified the Doctrine. His second annual foreign-policy report defined these shifts and explained the implications for American policy. Describing the postwar era as comprised of "American predominance . . . overwhelming U.S. military strength [and] . . . Communist solidarity," Nixon argued his presidency coincided with a new era, one that would be typified by global partnership. These tectonic shifts in the structure of international relations themselves, he contended, empowered Europe to play a greater role in its own security just as the rise of "multipolar Communism" warranted "negotiation with different Communist countries." For Nixon, these systemic changes in international politics required "an enduring structure of peace," one that would institute "a new and stable framework of international relationships." Holding a distinctly liberal orientation, Nixon's new structure would emphasize coexistence and accommodation as a means for avoiding future violent conflicts. This discourse again distanced the president from tropes of savagery—both in terms of Vietnam and the broader Cold War contest opposing the expansion of communism—by demarcating a shift from the domino theory to a theory of politics premised on collective security, cooperation, and negotiation. His strategy, the logic went, sought to remedy systemic imbalances related to failures of communication, negotiation, mutual respect, and burden sharing. Once built, this architecture of peace would stave off the reemergence of war.[147] Demarcating the 1970s as a new era of international relations placed the international system in the foreground and implied that international conflict derived from systemic factors, rather than differences in ideology, governance, or ambition. In that way, his discourse deprioritized savagery as a force in international relations, recessing, if not erasing the figure of savagery itself.

While the exact shape and form of this new framework never materialized—Nixon provided no architectural schematics or model beyond Vietnamization to depict his vision for international relations—the broader point is that he wielded this depiction of a changing international order to rationalize his emphasis on the process of ending the war in Vietnam. As previously discussed, the radio address summarizing his second annual foreign-policy message emphasized the need to end the war in Vietnam "the right way."[148] The actual message laid out a staged process as the basis of his exit strategy. The gradual drawdown of American troops coupled with training and arming the South Vietnamese, the report claimed, both aided the immediate war context and contributed to the construction of his structure of peace. Linking Vietnam to his articulation of global contextual changes, Nixon claimed the first step in building this structure "is to still the sound of war." Ending war, he continued, was the "core of our new foreign policy," because only by ending conflict could the nation lead the new global partnership. This partnership, moreover, in "its fullest extension encompasses adversaries as well as friends." Here Nixon's erasure of the enemy performs a doubling effect by minimizing the significance of the details of the Vietnam War—ignoring the enemy completely and the difficult negotiations to end the conflict—while also reworking the figure of communist enemies into mere adversaries. Those adversaries, he contended, should be brought into the circle of communication, negotiation, and cooperation. This discourse, the essence of his program of détente, made sensible his emphasis on process because it explained the prospects of relationship building as related to confidence—allied confidence in U.S. security guarantees and adversary confidence in America's willingness to be honest and fair. Once again embodying the president-as-architect persona, Nixon urged patience with his plans for peace since "it will take many years to shape the new American role."[149]

The embodied persona of president-as-architect, moreover, shifted the presidential role away from that of global policeman. Enacting both functionalist and artistic components, the architect persona—in contrast to the policeman—merged a responsibility for public safety with an idealistic goal of erecting a lasting edifice that could prevent the outbreak of war (functional) and inspire a deeper, more permanent form of positive peace (artistic). As architect, Nixon attended to even the smallest, most peripheral details to ensure the sustainable fabrication of a structure of peace. That involved the production and updating of plans—in Vietnam and globally—and the gradual unveiling of completed components of the structure over the life of the project. But, even while demanding continuous monitoring of every stage of his project for peace, this shift in presidential persona displaced Nixon's primary emphasis from the day-to-day management of the war to the broad, interconnected vision of peace that he sought to construct in the world. Noting his policy's success in "winding down the war," Nixon claimed, "Our fundamental goal is deeper. It is to get at the roots of crises and to build a durable structure of international relationships."[150] These statements—equating his end-of-war policy to a form of excavation—reinforced Nixon's construction discourse by referencing the efforts required to clear the terrain prior to beginning the construction of an edifice of peace. They also, however, introduced indeterminacy into his Vietnam policy because construction often requires demolishing preexisting structures, uprooting trees or landscaping in the process, and powering down the demolition equipment in order to build more impressive structures from the rubble. As architecture is both art and science, the embodied persona provided the president with a flexible attitude toward the conflict and an idiom that could rationalize exiting Vietnam, even on unsatisfactory terms.

The focus on the structure also explained international tensions and proposed solutions to those tensions. By 1972, his now annual report to Congress on foreign policy reiterated the importance of structure as the organizing principle of the Nixon Doctrine. It depicted the world shifting in a new direction, requiring a new strategy to achieve the peace.[151] This message, along with a follow-up in 1973, placed all of his achievements—from détente with the Soviets to diplomatic relations with China—in the broader setting of a shifting international context. Embedding Vietnam in the global picture deemphasized the conflict by giving presence to the scenic elements of international relations. The problems were not of design, he insisted, but of execution. By prioritizing structure over event, this scenic orientation homogenized and abstracted the enemy by explaining that structural fault lines drove belligerents to war. Thus, even though an actual enemy existed on the field of battle, their motives derived not from savage designs or ideological antagonisms but rather from disruptions to the international system itself.

As Nixon's first term neared its conclusion, he began to speak about the efforts required to ensure his achievements lasted. Having coordinated his trip to China to coincide with his campaign for reelection, he revisited his actions abroad, depicting those actions as contributing to a foundation upon which his edifice of peace would be built. He articulated this thesis in his "Look to the Future" address—a sort of closing argument for his campaign—just days before his reelection. Dividing his attention between domestic issues and foreign policy, the president pondered the necessity of continuation to ensure the world actually built the lasting peace he envisioned. The speech confided to the American people that his desire for a lasting peace was his central motivation for reelection. "Above all," he claimed, "I want to complete the foundations for a world at peace—so that the next generation can be the first in this century to live without war and without the fear of war."[152] Articulating this desire for peace via the construction metaphor, Nixon pretended he had already built a stable foundation for peace—a significant achievement in its own right—to justify the need to carry on. After all, laying the foundation is merely the first major achievement in erecting an enduring structure.

Ever focused on process, this speech continued Nixon's emphasis on method over result while embodying the persona of president-as-architect. Peace has to be built, constructed, restored, but as architect, Nixon knew small details in the early stages determined the stability of the foundation upon which an edifice of peace could be built. As he put it, "The details can make the difference between an agreement that collapses and an agreement that lasts."[153] Nixon claimed that intricately linked to the stability of the structure, meticulous attention to detail had "restored peace at home," would produce a stable framework of peace in Vietnam, and was already "restoring peace abroad."[154] Expanding the metaphoric economy to include actions that might renovate, rather than completely rebuild certain relationships, the restoration metaphor synced with the array of construction metaphors populating the president's discourse. This discourse plugged all of Nixon's efforts—détente with the USSR, diplomatic relations with China, and his gradual efforts to end the war in Vietnam—into a broader matrix that proved foundational to his efforts to finally build a structure that could end war once and for all.

Explicitly claiming that peace could not arise in the presence of savagery, Nixon's rhetoric implied that only forcing a favorable and lasting outcome in Vietnam could establish a stable foundation for his structure of peace in Asia. This thesis materialized within the bureaucracy as an intense concern to prevent South Vietnamese collapse after the war. Transcripts from an extended conversation involving Nixon, Kissinger, General Alexander Haig, Nguyen Phu Duc (special advisor to President Thieu), and Tran Kim Phuong (the Vietnamese ambassador to the United States) noted the united desire "to prevent the collapse of South Vietnam." While the memo does not explicitly adopt the language of construction beyond this usage, the rationale for a cease-fire is premised on the same argumentative lines as Nixon's public discourse. The enemy, in the memo, is figured as communists who "did not respect paper" and instead "understood bombs and mines and the U.S.'s resolve." Pointing to Johnson's grave mistake in suspending bombing in 1968, the memo identified South Korea as the model by which peace could sustain. "The situation was the same in Vietnam," the president stated, warning that post-settlement incursions by the North Vietnamese "would run a mortal risk." This rhetoric mirrored the administration's thesis that peace is achieved via a combination of military strength and consultation with allies. Throughout the conversation, Nixon and Kissinger spoke about the necessity of maintaining military force and the credibility of American commitments, while also maintaining close diplomatic contact with the South Vietnamese. At one point, Nixon elaborated on the difference between hardware and software, with the former signifying steel and bombs, the latter communication and diplomacy. Constructing peace on a foundation of military deterrence and constant communication, he implied, would ensure the North Vietnamese did not violate the terms of the agreement.[155]

Additionally, Nixon's embodiment of the persona of the architect runs throughout the conversation. At each stage, Nixon positions himself as the master force behind the peace deal's design. He told his Vietnamese counterparts that the "words [General Haig and Dr. Kissinger] spoke were President Nixon's words." Kissinger "would be pronouncing President Nixon's words . . . Kissinger would be told directly . . . Nixon would issue his final instructions" and Kissinger would carry them out. While all authority flows from the president, the conversation established a hierarchy that fit with the logic of an architectural firm. Nixon designed the peace; Kissinger implemented his designs. Monitoring and addressing the elements that would undermine the structure could remedy South Vietnamese objections to the terms. Like an architect seeking to reassure a wary buyer of a half-built structure, Nixon's and Kissinger's pledges to maintain the peace with economic and military assistance amounted to a hard sell. Asking the South Vietnamese to understand the hard reality of American domestic politics, Nixon claimed his hands were tied and that without a final agreement Congress would cut off war funds. The war had to end, on Nixon's terms, and as quickly as possible, and South Vietnam had to sign on to the deal on the table. Ultimately, Nixon and Kissinger acted from the position of inevitability: the American role in "the war was going to be settled" with or without South Vietnam.[156]

Nixon's Second Inaugural perhaps best exhibits the coherence of the metaphoric economy typifying the president's fixation with structure. Claiming that "4 years ago, America was bleak in spirit, depressed by the prospect of seemingly endless war abroad," Nixon used the address to contextualize the progress in negotiations in Vietnam and to link that progress to the broader context of the Cold War. Warning that the "peace we seek in the world is not the flimsy peace which is merely an interlude between war, but a peace which can endure for generations," he emphasized the advances he had made in Vietnam and with the Soviets and Chinese. The promise of those achievements justified continued efforts to "bring down the walls of hostility . . . and to build in their place bridges of understanding." Pledging to "build a structure of peace in the world in which the weak are as safe as the strong," Nixon promised his second term would seek the "noblest endeavor." He would "build such a peace" by erecting a "structure . . . that can last."[157] Once again, metaphors of construction explained the events of the war and the achievements of his administration. By portraying his second mandate as an endorsement of his strategy, Nixon envisioned the world as a site for remodeling. The message urged patience, but also offered the American people an aspiration that patience would yield a beautiful result. Above all, however, he had to resolve the conflict in Vietnam.

Cementing the Foundation of Peace after Vietnam

Over the course of his presidency, Nixon offered few specifics about what actually composed a stable foundation for peace, but two strands or theses stand out: military strength and alliances. For both, resolving the war in Vietnam would prepare the site for the molding of a durable foundation. After the war, the president revisited these theses to highlight the continued need for military and diplomatic engagement. Nixon's address on January 23, 1973, announcing the end of hostilities, signaled the president's pivot from Southeast Asia to the world. Again the construction metaphor served as the engine enabling that pivot. Claiming that "ending the war is only the first step toward building the peace," Nixon urged both North and South Vietnam to "see . . . that this is a peace that lasts, and also a peace that heals," before shifting to the contributions the deal made to the world. He claimed the agreement "not only ends the war in Southeast Asia but contributes to the prospects of peace in the whole world."[158] Again "peace with honor" performed the symbolic work necessary to rationalize his argument. Vietnam mattered to the

world, not just because of its ending, but because of the way it ended—
by tough, honest negotiation that ensured both allies and adversaries
would perceive the seriousness of America's commitment to building a
lasting peace.

In a follow-up speech, Nixon returned to the phrase "peace with
honor" to finesse the lingering elements of the domino metaphor. He
claimed ending the war in "the right way, peace with honor," signaled
to "our allies in Europe, the Japanese, and other allies, the Thais and so
forth, and to potential adversaries, that the United States is a dependable
ally."[159] This statement emphasized Nixon's belief in credibility as the key
determinant of the propensity for international conflict. He backstopped
that view by historicizing his management of Vietnam. Claiming that
"the perspective of history" would confirm his view that "the easy way
out . . . would have eroded and possibly destroyed" the credibility of
U.S. security guarantees, Nixon drew the argument to its conclusion.
Taking the easy way out risked producing a precarious structure prone
to erosion or destruction. Credibility mattered, then, because it staved
off the aggressive intentions of those opposed to liberal democracy and
solidified the structure of peace.[160]

Further, Nixon pointed to successful negotiations as evidence that
strength could provide incentives for peace. Nixon pushed the country
to maintain the course he had plotted by suggesting "we would not have
made the progress toward lasting peace that we have made in this past
year unless we had had the military strength that commanded respect."
Even as Watergate endangered his political life, he stressed the need
for domestic "support . . . for keeping the strength." Linking peace in
Vietnam to the broader context of East-West competition, Nixon warned
that any reduction in military might would increase the risk of war as
the other side would seek to exploit American weakness with force. This
view of international politics—suggesting a delicate equilibrium of force
could keep the peace—reflected the incoherence of Nixon's views, particularly near the end of his presidency. Starkly ignoring the national
mood opposing the use of force abroad (what later became known as the
Vietnam Syndrome), Nixon acted as if American exit from the war had

been a complete success. Indeed, the president doubled down on this discourse when he claimed Vietnam proved that "the chance for building a new structure of peace in the world would be irreparably damaged, and free nations everywhere would be living in mortal danger" if the United States cut its military.[161] While one can argue the president's inability to grapple with the failure in Vietnam reveals one reason his discourse of peace failed, the broader purpose here is to recognize Nixon's consistent use of construction metaphors to depict peace. Nixon, as hackneyed architect seeking investors for a failing edifice, continued to sound the call for constructing the peace even as his political life neared its end.

Nixon, of course, had publicly prepared for a postwar reduction in military spending by linking military strength to the foundation of peace. This discourse appeared within the context of the larger metaphorical ecosystem and laid out the president's views on the necessity of military power. At first, he stressed the difficulty of the task, telling war veterans that "building a lasting peace is not easy," because a multitude of threats continued to challenge the prospects for peace.[162] In this assessment, these threats existed because of structural failures, and only the presence of American military might could stabilize the system and forestall the eruption of violence. As he put it at West Point in 1971, "American strength is the keystone in the structure of peace."[163] The metaphoric choice fit. In architectural terms, keystones are the final supports that ensure the structure doesn't collapse. By linking intersections of arched girders, keystones enable a structure to bear weight, even while they experience less stress than the other components of the structure. They are also visible, decorative elements that, by nature of structural need, center the attention of the viewer. By naming American military strength the keystone, Nixon implied the necessity of strength as both symbol and support. That is, Nixon's representation of military might explicitly pointed to its visibility as deterrent. As if allaying the fears of American audiences, Nixon's insistence on military strength suggested that American military might should be seen rather than used. These representations, similar to Eisenhower's criticism of Truman's handling of Korea, implied that Vietnam had been a mistake because it wasted

American military resources in active combat. While Nixon did not connect those dots as explicitly as Eisenhower, this rhetoric synced with his depictions of the 1970s as "a turning point in modern history."[164] Recognizing the significance of the moment, he claimed, required a reprioritization of U.S. foreign policy toward deterrence, negotiation, and collective security.

Nixon's discourse also managed the implicit contradiction between arming for war while aspiring for peace by articulating the apparent oppositions as actually interlocking components of a broader structural approach to international relations. Noting the collective aspiration "for a time when military strength will be unnecessary," he attenuated that desire with the realist conclusion that "we shall maintain the preparedness which is essential to protect the peace."[165] In Nixon's view, vast arsenals that could utterly destroy the world served the need for balance between the two sides. Implicitly linking this discourse to the logic of mutually assured destruction, he claimed an imbalance in armaments "increases the danger of war," but that "when both sides reduce their forces together do we truly serve the cause of peace."[166] These claims may have upset antiwar activists, but they fit a postwar tradition in which "war preparation became embedded in the rhetoric of preserving peace."[167] Appraising American military might as a foundational element of a broader structure that could foster the conditions for peace, the logic presumed a time when disarmament would be possible, even as it pushed to maintain vast and destructive arsenals.

Having established peace as a goal, and military might as a mechanism to achieve that goal, Nixon's discourse followed a binary pattern of argument that typified his approach to controversy. Defining his central task as to "make America remember this truth: The strength that commands respect is the only foundation on which peace among nations can ever be built," he defined the controversy as having only two sides, one of which was obviously impossible.[168] In this instance, the choice fell between strength and weakness. His view dissevered the notion that arms buildups (races) could cause war, instead positing that war derived from unregulated "conflicts of vital interest."[169] This discourse served his broader purpose because it, again, implied the need for a global structure that could manage international competition—the clashes generated by competition over vital interests. Military strength, Nixon argued, provided a foundational basis by which adversaries would take the nation and its commitment to peace seriously. Strength, in Nixon's worldview, pushed nations toward cooperation.

A final component of this discourse articulated the foundation for peace as an attitude Nixon's policies sought to evoke in American citizens. This vision for a world without war, a reinvigoration of presidential principles dating from at least Woodrow Wilson, called for national investiture in an orientation to world politics. That orientation extended the definition of "strength" beyond mere military might to constitute citizens as participants in a collective process to build peace abroad. Recalling old tropes about the differences between positive and negative peace, Nixon claimed the quest for peace "poses the deep question of whether a nation, without some external threat to unite and motivate it, can find a higher inspiration to lift us all above the mire of softness and stagnation and division and decay."[170] A stable foundation for peace, he argued, required maintaining American military might, but also a collective desire to strive for something more beautiful and enduring than a virtual cease-fire between East and West. Calling on the "Spirit of '76," he explained, "the great challenge of peace is for each of us individually and for all of us as 'one nation under God,' to rededicate ourselves . . . to the American Dream." Doing so would establish peace as "our moral equivalent," enabling the nation to "move into a generation of peace." It would give the nation purpose, filling the void created by the absence of a stable enemy. Rather than lethargy, Nixon asked Americans to engage "in a great enterprise, to build . . . a generation of peace, something that Americans have not enjoyed in this century." This discourse articulated the challenge posed by Vietnam and its ending as deeply embedded in the national consciousness. In observance of the best means for exiting the war, Nixon complicated the question by posing the postwar era as one in need of an alternative vision that could drive international politics. This question, he claimed, was more serious than the challenge of Pearl

Harbor because "25 years after World War II—we have been through
Korea; we are finishing Vietnam; we are looking toward the time when
we will have peace."[171] Furnishing the American people with purpose,
Nixon's end-of-war discourse claimed that national unity composed a
key element of the foundation for peace because only a unified people
could provide the president with the backing necessary to stand firm in
the world.

National unity, as a foundational component, justified the president's policy approach, even as it displaced the figure of savagery in
Vietnam.[172] As a substitute vocabulary, focusing on unity erased the
events of Vietnam—the very source of disunity—as well as the details of
negotiations, the character of American allies and adversaries, and the
role of China and the Soviet Union in supporting the North Vietnamese.
In each major address and foreign-policy document, Nixon articulated
the challenge of peace in terms of how the United States oriented itself
to the world, to the region, and to Vietnam. And, by placing Vietnam
in a continuum stretching from World War II to 1970, the president
introduced historical time as a key factor in understanding—and displacing—the events in Southeast Asia. Historicizing the postwar era
as a series of events foreshadowing systematic changes to international
relations emphasized the epochal nature of conflict, deprived Vietnam
of its uniqueness, and flattened the character and agency of the Viet
Cong. While not entirely exculpatory, locating the cause of the war as
structural rather than ideological suppressed North Vietnam's role and
responsibility for the war.

After Vietnam, Nixon maintained the persona of chief architect even
as he subtly shifted his account of the conflict's role in the structure of
peace. When toasting the prime minister of the United Kingdom in
1973, he claimed he was "one of the prime architects of the new Europe
. . . an indispensable foundation for what we hope will be a new world,
because it will contribute to that new world in which peace" will reign.
Continuing, he linked global peace efforts to his own role as architect.
Noting the historic year, Nixon explained "a trip to Peking, a trip to
Moscow, the end of a long and difficult war in Vietnam" all "mark[ed] a

watershed where we move now to the works of peace."[173] By connecting the three events, Nixon identified them as benchmarks in the broader organizational shift he sought to orchestrate in international affairs. As achievements, moreover, they demonstrated that the construction of an enduring structure of peace had begun, even if they had not materialized formal alliances.

The occasion of South Vietnam's president Nguyen Van Thieu's visit to California evoked an additional attempt to characterize Vietnam as one step forward in the broader architectural plan. In welcoming remarks, Nixon declared the war as over but the job of peace ongoing. Once again relying on the construction metaphor, Nixon claimed, "building a peace after 25 years of war" presented difficulties, but that joint efforts "toward the building of peace" would move Southeast Asia—and by implication the world—"forward in building the lasting peace, the real peace that we have fought together for and that now we want all of our people to live for."[174] This rhetoric embodied the president-as-architect persona by speaking to the necessity of clearing away the rubble of war prior to laying a foundation for peace. Figuring war as demolition, Nixon implied that had been the easy part. The real challenge came in the postwar environment.

Nixon pointed to the presence of stable alliances in Europe and Northeast Asia to support his claims that formal security arrangements could assuage allied fears about communist expansion and signal to communist powers the collective will of democratic nations. This rhetoric employed the construction metaphor to justify continued engagement with allies and adversaries:

Communism had taken various forms; our alliances had stabilized the European and Northeast Asian environments; and we had laid the foundations for negotiation. We had to decide together not only what we were against, but what we were for. Peace required the ending of an ongoing war. Our approach to the Vietnam conflict and our shaping of a new foreign policy were inextricably linked. Naturally, our most urgent concern was to end the war. But we had to end it—or at least our

involvement—in a way that would continue to make possible a responsible American role in the world.[175]

By retelling the story of American involvement in Vietnam, Nixon
linked the outcome in Vietnam to the broader structure of international
relations. Again utilizing a strict binary form of argument—either capitulate to the communists or choose Vietnamization—Nixon emphasized
the alliance-building capacity of his policy approach. Vietnamization
"reassured our allies," he claimed, and served as more than a simple
model for American policy. Instead, it served as the evidence for the
reliability of American commitments. As an attempt to frame postwar
understandings of the war, this rhetoric represented Vietnam and the
long-term potential of American military engagement in Southeast Asia
as essentially equivalent to the relative tranquility instituted by the Korean Armistice.

Peace in Vietnam also doubled the meaning of the foundation metaphor. On the one hand, the negotiated settlement reinforced Nixon's
view of international politics by suppressing the particulars of the
conflict and replacing them with a broad set of principles explaining
the outbreak of war and the restoration of peace. On the other hand,
the foundation metaphor spoke to the prospect of erecting an edifice of
peace beyond Vietnam. Like a newly framed house, peace in Vietnam
was fragile and required continued maintenance and vigilance.[176] Cor-
doning off the area to protect it from outside perpetrators would cement
a structural base from which broader edifices could emerge. Paradoxically, identifying Vietnam as a foundational element adjacent to other
areas in need of architectural management increased, rather than diminished, the Southeast Asian nation's importance at the end of the war.
As Nixon wrote to Congress in 1973, "there cannot be a global structure
of peace while conflict persists in Indochina."[177] This statement, in his
fourth report to Congress on U.S. foreign policy, highlighted Vietnam's
significance to international tranquility. Having failed to construct a
Southeast Asian security alliance, the report employed ambiguous language to discuss the types of lasting arrangements that could ensure

mutual defense against aggression. The prose pointed to a network of alliances that had guided and could continue to guide America's approach to the region. Absent formal security arrangements, the term "alliance" referred to the basic tenets of the Nixon Doctrine—arming and training countries friendly to the United States. Claiming the Nixon Doctrine had been applied to many Asian nations, he stressed that his administration had achieved "a more balanced American role in security arrangements in Asia, an increase in the capacity and willingness of our alliance partners to carry heavier burdens of responsibility for their own protection, and a more equitable sharing of the material and personal costs of security."[178]

After hostilities ended and all U.S. troops returned home, Nixon revisited the thematic displacement of Vietnam. Extolling his commitment to "build a structure of peace for the whole world," the president noted the big news of ending the war in Vietnam, before claiming that the more important news was his visits to Moscow and Peking.[179] These missions contributed more to the structure of peace, he argued, because they decreased the likelihood of "confrontation with the Soviet Union or with the People's Republic of China."[180] This rhetoric reflected a secondary displacement of Vietnam's importance. In concert with his articulation of savagery as an outcome of structural faults in international relations themselves, the rhetoric reprioritized attention to the gravest of fault lines from which catastrophic rupture could occur. Much like an architect identifying different weak points in a sizable edifice, Nixon's postwar rhetoric articulated Vietnam as a location in the structure that had already been shored up. As such, it could be dismissed in favor of the bigger challenge.

Construction discourse and the president-as-architect persona reappeared on the occasion of Kissinger's Nobel Prize announcement. An internal memo written by David Gergen lamented the failure to also name Nixon, claiming, "In fact, the foundation for Dr. Kissinger's efforts were laid by a President who has been without peer in the art of foreign policy." Describing the Nobel Prize as an outcome of "the President's quest for a lasting peace in the world," Gergen went on to suggest the world should "credit the architect as well as the carpenter."[181] Kissinger's acceptance address, read by Thomas R. Byrne, U.S. ambassador to Norway, laid out the tenets of political realism before reiterating the U.S. goal of "building a structure of peace."[182] For his part, Nixon publicly congratulated Kissinger on the prize, crediting him with "laying the groundwork for peace."[183] The consistent message—inside and outside the administration—posited American efforts in terms of construction and figured the president-as-architect.

Nixon's self-fashioning as an agent of peace became increasingly ardent in the wake of Watergate and his struggle to retain his hold on the presidency. In a news conference announcing Kissinger's nomination as the next secretary of state, the president claimed outgoing Secretary of State William Rogers had presided over "one of the most successful eras of foreign policy in any administration in history—an era in which we ended a war, the longest war in American history; an era, in addition, in which we began to build a structure of peace, particularly involving two great powers, the People's Republic of China and the Soviet Union." Here, Vietnam appeared as peripheral to the structure, but given the intensity and longevity of the conflict, its resolution enabled Nixon to build structural correctives. Reiterating the construction metaphor, Nixon credited Rogers as "one of the major architects of" the administration's foreign policy. This press conference, held in the midst of the Watergate investigation, obviously frustrated the president. After attempting to direct the conversation toward Kissinger, foreign policy, and his desire for peace, he received an extended series of questions related to the scandal and his role in it. Urging the nation to "move on from Watergate," Nixon interrupted a reporter to make the following statement:

> We have had 30 minutes of this press conference. I have yet to have, for example, one question on the business of the people, which shows you how we are consumed with this. I am not criticizing the members of the press, because you naturally are very interested in this issue, but let me tell you, years from now people are going to perhaps be interested in what happened in terms of the efforts of the United States to

build a structure of peace in the world . . . Now, our goal is to move forward then, to move forward to build a structure of peace. And when you say, do I consider resigning, the answer is no, I shall not resign. I have 3½ years to go, or almost 3½ years, and I am going to use every day of those 3½ years trying to get the people of the United States to recognize that, whatever mistakes we have made, that in the long run this Administration, by making this world safer for their children, and this Administration, by making their lives better at home for themselves and their children, deserves high marks rather than low marks. Now, whether I succeed or not, we can judge then.[184]

Nixon's harangue sought to reframe the conversation between the president and the press via the tenets of the construction metaphor. The ploy failed, of course. The rest of the press conference involved only a single non-Watergate question. The scandal could not be ignored, after all. But Nixon's resort to the president-as-architect persona as a shield against scandal speaks to its deep entrenchment in his psyche and his administration's approach to politics. His efforts to build a structure of peace, he contended, mattered more than whatever had unfolded at Watergate and after.

Nixon continued along these lines into 1974, even with his resignation around the corner. Now, however, he alternated between claiming the need to build a structure and asserting that the foundation had been set. In his 1974 State of the Union, for example, he argued that evolving and improving allied relations "is a cornerstone of the structure of peace we are seeking to build," positing the moment as "an opportunity we may never have again to create a structure of peace solid enough to last a lifetime and more."[185] Four months later, his Memorial Day radio address extended this theme, avowing, "Only today . . . for the first time in this century do we live in a time when, thanks to past sacrifices, a real chance exists for lasting peace—peace built not on vain hopes and good intentions, but on solid, realistic foundations."[186] Like the architect, behind schedule and desperate to keep the contract, Nixon sought to persuade Congress and the American people that despite his flaws, he was still the man for the job. He had, he contended, made the foundation for peace real.

Implying the construction of a more significant edifice as the next step for peace, Nixon raised the end of Vietnam as the key source of evidence for his approach to international relations. Now, however, he linked peace in Vietnam to the Middle East, China, and the Soviet Union. The meaning of these events, he claimed, demonstrated that "our hopes for a lasting peace are brighter than at any time in living memory, because we now have a structure of peace and we are carefully working to strengthen it."[187] Even while claiming the structure existed, his rhetoric unified the components of the foundation metaphor into a single synthesis. Warning of the danger of relaxing, Nixon claimed, "Lasting peace can be achieved only through lasting awareness, lasting preparedness, and lasting strength, both physical and moral. As America and other nations have learned only too well through experience, weakness invites aggression and aggression triggers war."[188] This rhetoric, enthymemetically acknowledging domestic opposition to Nixon and his Doctrine, interspersed the themes of military might, national unity, and allied support to urge for continuation. But, having failed to create a NATO for Asia, Nixon's rhetoric shifted again, identifying the European alliance as the "cornerstone of this Nation's foreign policy."[189]

Several weeks later, at a meeting in Brussels, he extended the argument. Toasting the president and king of Belgium, Nixon spoke about the "goal of a permanent and just peace." Perhaps because of the setting, his remarks centered on NATO's importance in "building a structure of peace, not only for Europe and the Atlantic community but for all the world." Beyond merely establishing a global mission for NATO, an ambitious shift in its own right, Nixon characterized national leaders as "architects of peace." He claimed the "builders of peace are their ministers, the foreign ministers, and all the others around this table who devote their lives to the art of diplomacy, to carrying out whatever programs or policies will contribute to a goal of peace." He concluded his remarks by toasting the architects and the builders aspiring to "a world of peace."[190]

Subtly figuring himself as the principal architect, Nixon's toast sought to constitute a collective mission.

The President-as-Architect, the Policy Arena, and the Absent Savage

While Nixon's embodiment of the president-as-architect persona shifted figures of the enemy from ideological force to tough customer, it did not facilitate victory in Vietnam. In spite of his efforts, the communist forces of North Vietnam violently unified the country in 1975, effectively closing U.S.-Vietnamese relations for almost twenty years. Moreover, Nixon's Vietnam policy was a disaster for the people of Vietnam, Cambodia, and Laos, not to mention American soldiers pressed into military service. The war's legacy hung over the country and the military like a black cloud—the so-called Vietnam syndrome—and may have impeded American leadership during the 1970s. And while his end-of-war rhetoric facilitated the erasure of the underlying savage motivations for fighting the Viet Cong, the premise of the rhetoric identified the construction of a structure of peace in Asia as the end goal. That structure would look something like NATO and serve a similar stabilizing force in Asia, connecting both sides of the world in a singular network of security, encircling the communist powers in the process. But he didn't get his security architecture. He couldn't build his structure.

These failures do not, however, signal rhetorical impotence. In fact, Nixon's construction discourse fundamentally altered the terms under which the Cold War's disputes could be litigated. The domino theory implied the existence of a savage force—communism—ever present and eager to push into new territory. Nixon's shift away from the domino theory displaced the implicit (and at times explicit) figure of the enemy with a network of metaphors organized around the notion of construction. This metaphoric economy refigured diplomacy, conflict, and war as features of an anarchic international system lacking the proper structures necessary for a sustained peace. In Vietnam, Nixon erased the figure of the Viet Cong entirely by absorbing the enemy into the broad metaphoric economy of construction. The dominant trope used to depict the North Vietnamese across the administration, stretching from his First Inaugural to his resignation, was that of the intransigent bargainer, seeking to hammer out a deal that included more land (property) and control over that land (ownership rights). The North Vietnamese, in Nixon's discourse, appear not as a monolithic communist force out for conquest, but rather as a hard-driving customer willing to purchase peace on very specific terms. In doing so, Nixon's discourse echoed Roosevelt's contention of the international system as a great neighborhood, shifted enemies from barbaric savages to unruly prospective clients interested in purchasing new edifices of peace.

While Nixon's rhetoric focused primarily on the importance of diplomacy, dialogue, and open relations, Secretary Rogers's briefing on China in anticipation of the president's visit emphasized the territorial components of the international scene. China sought the "withdrawal of all US forces on China's periphery," as well as to prevent "Taiwanese independence or movement into the Japanese orbit."[191] This language typifies foreign-policy discourse—scholars often point to the orientational fixation that notions of center and periphery impose on understandings of international power.[192] But it also equated national territory and spheres of influence to property. That equation—comprehending territory as the site for diplomatic, economic, and military intervention—coordinated metaphoric depictions of the world under the master metaphor of construction. Nixon repeated the contours of the metaphor during his visit. In his toast to Chairman Mao, he spoke about division as the source of "the great problems in the world," and used the figure of the Great Wall of China to reason that "a wall can protect us, or a wall can divide us."[193] Here the figure of a wall—an edifice constructed to preserve the peace—demarcated a division between properties, but not as the source of conflict in the world. Instead, it implied that physical partitions between properties were normal, useful even, but that diplomatic division was the actual genesis of conflict. The real problem, Nixon inferred, was the lack of friendly relations between neighbors, something that could be resolved by regular communication.[194]

Embodying a persona reflects more than the adoption of a particular rhetoric. It speaks to a wholesale orientation toward the world. For Nixon, inhabiting the persona of architect coincided with the proliferation of construction metaphors across his discourse, demonstrating the continuity of the discourse and the importance it holds to understanding his approach to politics. For example, in a brief message to Congress in 1972 related to arms control, Nixon described progress with the Soviets before positing the United States as "among the principal architects of a convention banning the development, production and stockpiling of biological weapons and toxins."[195] Nixon also justified changes in trade policy along the lines of the construction metaphor. In proposing the Trade Reform Act of 1973, the president claimed the true importance of the bill was that it would "reduce international tensions and strengthen the structure of peace." The first major section of the speech elaborated on this claim. Titled "Strengthening the Structure of Peace," the section claimed efforts had already "begun to erect a durable structure of peace in the world from which all nations can benefit." Nixon warned that "this structure of peace cannot be strong, however, unless it encompasses international economic affairs" because economic stagnation could erode or otherwise destabilize the political and security ties that formed the foundation for peace. Connecting the need for legislation in the context of a changing world order, Nixon closed by arguing that his reform "helps us build a peaceful, more prosperous world."[196] Energy policy also connected to the structure of peace. Addressing the Congress on April 18, 1973, he linked the energy challenge to every nation and urged Congress to approve his energy policy in order to "strengthen the structure of peace we are seeking to build in the world."[197] On another occasion, he credited his secretary of the treasury, John Connally, as the architect of his administration's economic policy.[198]

From arms control to trade, energy, and economics, these vignettes demonstrate the way the persona of the architect permeated a wide variety of policy areas, serving as the argumentative fulcrum to explain, justify, and rationalize those policies. In each case, the architect persona attempted to link policy with admirable goals. And while it is tempting to declare Nixon's rhetorical strategy a failure—after all, he habitually misled the American public about the war, the peace agreement failed to guarantee democratic governance of the South, and Nixon fled the White House on the eve of impeachment—his rhetoric achieved measured outcomes. He opened diplomatic relations with China, reduced tensions with the Soviet Union, negotiated an arms deal, and established an emergency hotline designed to facilitate communication in times of crisis, all of which reduced the likelihood of global war. Nixon also presided over the practical end of the domino metaphor and, in the process, rearticulated international relations as requiring multilateral leadership based in alliances and diplomacy. All of these are rhetorically significant accomplishments.

Still, his effort to rework public understandings of the Cold War didn't sustain. Perhaps because of the gravitational force of the Manichean dichotomy framing the conflict or because of the rise of Ronald Reagan and his commitment to speak the language of war to achieve policy goals, détente ended with Carter. The 1980s witnessed the resurgence of the savage frame and a return to conflictual relations with the Soviets. However, Nixon's policy approach toward an unwinnable conflict, embodied in his Vietnamization program, would become important again.

CHAPTER 4

The Disembodied Savage

BARACK OBAMA AND THE PERPETUITY
OF NATIONAL VIOLENCE

———— • ————

B arack Obama's rise to the presidency generated optimism that the nation would finally end the wars in Iraq and Afghanistan. George W. Bush's surge had failed to arrest the insurgency in Iraq. The Status of Forces agreement he negotiated with Iraq requiring the U.S. military to depart the country by the end of 2011 signaled the end of efforts at democratization.[1] And, after close to 100,000 Iraqi civilians killed and U.S. casualties topping 4,000, public support for the war had declined precipitously, with only 38 percent supporting the conflict, by one estimate.[2] Military progress in Afghanistan had also stalled. The opium trade had helped fund the Taliban's resurgence and al-Qaeda had returned in numbers.[3] Public support had begun to wane from its all-time high of 87 percent in 2003. By 2010, the majority wanted out.[4] Obama touched on these developments in the democratic primary in 2008, claiming that Iraq was a diversion, Afghanistan the neglected war.[5] He pledged to end the war in Iraq and refocus on Afghanistan in order to combat the danger posed by terrorism.[6] These statements elevated expectations that the United States would end its military misadventure but, like Nixon's, Obama's inherited foreign-policy disaster proved difficult to resolve and harder still to rationalize.

Upon assuming the presidency, Obama's principal foreign-policy task involved the articulation of a new strategy capable of concluding the occupations while accounting for enduring security concerns. This task posed a fundamentally different challenge than the previous conflicts examined in this book for two reasons. First, Afghanistan and Iraq represented only one stage of the extended struggle Bush called the War on Terror, or what Zbigniew Brzezinski has called "expeditionary military operations in hostile territories."[7] These interventions represented the first and most painful phase of wartime—engaging separate theaters of operations with a singular goal—to eliminate al-Qaeda. Second, and more problematically, in the years after 9/11, representations of the terrorist organization as a global force led the Bush administration to reprogram U.S. foreign policy to prioritize preemptive military operations. As one commentator put it, "strategies for combating those threats had, in fact, *become* the dominant theme of American foreign policy, distorting the country's grander goals, preoccupying its leaders, and blinding it to greater opportunities."[8] Thus, even as Obama explained his strategy for withdrawing from Iraq and Afghanistan, he also sought to address prevalent fears posed by terrorism and expound upon American efforts to protect the nation from the threat.

In this chapter, I argue that Obama's campaign to justify an exit from Iraq and Afghanistan hinged upon rhetorically restructuring the enemy from an embodied presence to a disembodied absence. At the end of previous conflicts, presidential metaphors of the enemy extended corporeal terms to describe the Other as victim, competitor, or bargainer. These shifts facilitated the recuperation or elision of the enemy in national discourse, while postulating a postwar mission for U.S. foreign policy. Like his predecessors, Obama leveraged public conceptions about the war to diminish the significance of Iraq and Afghanistan, end combat operations, and withdraw the majority of American forces from those theaters of operation. This strategy sought to reconceptualize public understandings of the nation's security challenges, the changing nature of war, and the problem of confronting substate, transnational actors with a simplified political vernacular. In contrast to the tradition of end-of-war rhetoric, this vernacular cloaked the enemy's identity in mystery, emphasizing the disembodied structures utilized by secretive, mobile fighting forces—safe havens and networks—as sites of intervention. Rather than reckon with depictions of the enemy, this discourse diffused and distributed the danger across time and space, deterritorializing and disembodying the agents responsible for American insecurity. In failing to banish discourses of terror, Obama's strategy constituted a rhetorical force that unified disparate notions about war and insecurity into a conceptual framework that extended fears about the potential for future attacks from bodies that exist but cannot be identified. This redefinition of the nature of security threats in the twenty-first century suppressed questions related to deliberation, war powers, and other procedural or legal controversies in favor of an ultimate necessity to secure the nation against additional attacks. In doing so, Obama reduced the postwar question to a narrow band related to the efficacy and necessity of continued military engagement against terrorism.

Obama did not author the discourse of the disembodied enemy. Rather, he streamlined it over the course of his presidency. His rhetoric of the enemy suppressed attention to bodies, characteristics, nationalities, and identities by focusing on the disembodied structures that enable terrorist operations. The initial phase of this discourse focused almost exclusively on terrorist safe havens and the incapacity of occupation and pacification to address forces that transited between governed and ungoverned spaces. While Bush identified Afghanistan and Iraq as terrorist sanctuaries to justify invasion and occupation, Obama pointed to the likelihood that transient enemies could construct new sanctuaries across the globe to justify deconfliction. Alluding to the problem of the ungoverned region between Afghanistan and Pakistan (the Federally Administered Tribal Area or FATA) and the ease with which al-Qaeda and the Taliban transited outside the established zones of conflict to avoid U.S. forces, Obama underscored the futility of occupation and democratization. He redefined the American mission as rooting out safe havens and depriving the enemy of sanctuaries or bases from which they could plan and launch attacks on U.S. forces. Recentering national attention on the sites that fluid enemies inhabit compressed understandings of how to address security challenges, and posited terrorism as the primary, and permanent, source of danger in the twenty-first century. Instead of abandoning Bush's thesis of the enemy, restructured Obama's administration restructured those views, aligned them with prevailing national-security discourse, and advanced a military strategy premised on speed and agility as the best response to a highly motile, disembodied enemy whose presence is felt, if not seen.

In addition to focusing on location, Obama's depiction of the enemy as mobile, anonymous, and concealed distanced his strategy from attacking enemy bodies and instead targeted the interconnections that enabled those bodies to conduct attacks on the United States and its allies. After 9/11, the Bush administration had extended archetypal approaches to war by identifying specific enemies—even issuing playing cards with the enemy's identity—under the assumption that eliminating al-Qaeda's leadership would undermine its organizational structure and enable the United States to claim victory.[9] By the time Obama became president, however, the insurgencies in Iraq and Afghanistan had revealed the futility of this strategy. Not only did American presence inspire individuals to join insurgent and terrorist groups, but the continuation of violence implied that a warfighting strategy premised on taking and holding territory could never result in victory.[10] While Obama didn't completely abandon the take-and-hold counterinsurgency strategy, and in many ways the underlying logic of destabilizing enemy organizations with leadership attacks continued to guide policy, he gradually suppressed the terrorists-as-bodies elocution. Instead, he emphasized the mobile, anonymous, and concealed nature of the danger. With the exception of Osama bin Laden, representations of specific terrorist bodies morphed into the figure of a constantly replaceable body, moving between governed and ungoverned spaces, orchestrating acts of violence. Confronting such a danger required a shift in strategy, one that deemphasized the actual bodies that conducted violence in favor of the interconnections—the networks—that enabled those bodies to conduct terror.

Featuring safe havens and networks as primary targets of intervention enabled a metaphoric economy of the disembodied enemy that undermined the rationale for military invasion, regime change, and democracy promotion by force while recasting the basic role or persona of the president. Bush's focus on state sponsors had typified his persona of the cowboy, corralling the herd, protecting them from the danger posed by evil states, and meting out frontier justice.[11] Having self-fashioned the persona as the governor of Texas and in his campaign for the presidency, Bush "chopped wood on his ranch, wore jeans and a cowboy hat, and spoke in the plain patois of a cowboy."[12] His post-9/11 speeches built on this persona and "cultivated the image of the sheriff running villains out of a global Dodge City."[13] Claiming "we're going to smoke them out" and that "there's an old poster out West that said, 'wanted, dead or alive,'" this discourse constituted the American mission as out to apply the law to lawless domains.[14] By 2003, media references to Bush as a cowboy president had become ubiquitous.[15] Typifying the way this rhetoric staged the conflict as a showdown between the sheriff and the outlaw in the run-up to the Iraq War, CNN ran a program titled "Showdown: Iraq fram[ing] the situation as a dramatic, final confrontation, a reckoning between Iraq and an unnamed opponent."[16] Dick Cheney publicly endorsed the persona, Colin Powell pointed to Bush's cowboy instincts, and the Bush-as-cowboy mythos spread across print media and academic inquiry.[17] While the specific focus on Bush-as-cowboy faded as Iraq descended into quagmire, the orientational implications of Bush's embodiment of lawman continued to impact the direction of his war policy. American justice would bring the law to a lawless frontier, mostly by force.

Obama's warnings about the fracturing of the state and the rise of disembodied enemies spreading across the globe reworked the national role from lawman to watchman, constantly on the lookout for danger. Rather than seek to impose the law, Obama's end-of-occupation discourse—enacted via a disembodied figure of the enemy transiting between sovereign and ungoverned spaces—implied a fundamental inability to bring order to international disorder. The implied persona of the watchman situated American power as necessary for protection, and induced American foreign policy to remain ever ready to selectively use force to counter the dangers posed by terrorism. In particular, the persona offered the national-security bureaucracy a rationale for counterterrorism, even after the president formally abandoned the phrase "War on Terror."[18] Emergent over the course of his presidency, the watchman persona provided a policy frame that could satisfy bureaucratic inclinations to continue Bush's counterterrorism policies while mollifying public desires to end the wars in Iraq and Afghanistan. It also assuaged Obama's desire to disentangle the nation from long-term occupation and reduce the political, social, and economic costs of war.

Obama's articulation of a disembodied enemy had its roots in the Bush administration's depiction of the terrorists responsible for the attacks on 9/11. Bush's rhetorical structuring of America's response to 9/11 and the evolution of that discourse over his term in office provides a point of departure. While many of the essential components of Obama's rhetoric are present in Bush's discourse, Obama streamlined the rhetoric of the enemy to instill a notion of placelessness as the proximate site for war, initially by identifying the FATA between Afghanistan and Pakistan as a so-called no man's land providing safe haven for terrorists, before moving to entirely delink terrorists from sovereign territorial boundaries. The network metaphor enacted the war-space as always already existing and not existing at once, in what Brian Massumi referred to as "the suddenly irrupting, locally self-organizing, systemically self-amplifying threat of a large scale destruction . . . indiscriminate; coming anywhere, as out of nowhere, at any time."[19] Rather than extend the state of exception to produce a politics of perpetual crisis, however, Obama's refiguring of the enemy and embodiment of the president-as-watchman persona normalized political violence as a tool of statecraft. Disembodying and distributing the danger made threats endemic, requiring permanent preparation for prevention, response, and retribution, "annex[ing] the civilian sphere to the conduct of war."[20] This dynamic became a defining vector for U.S. foreign policy and American political culture, foreshadowed the rise of the Islamic State of Iraq and the Levant (ISIL), and portends a new cycle of enemy construction in the twenty-first century.

9/11, War, and the (Dis)Embodied Savage

George W. Bush's rhetorical response to the events of 9/11—his declaration of a War on Terror—involved the nation in a long-term national struggle to prevent additional attacks. Addressing what he considered a reconstituted international context on September 20, 2001, Bush told the nation that "enemies of freedom committed an act of war against our country." He explained that they come from many countries, "are trained in the tactics of terror," and are "sent back . . . to plot evil and destruction." They do this, he asserted, because "they hate our freedoms." Demurring to make explicit who "they" were, Bush spoke of the enemy as "a radical network of terrorists, and every government that supports them." Starting with al-Qaeda, he declared the war would "not end until every terrorist group of global reach has been found, stopped, and defeated."[21] Ostensibly seeking to identify the perpetrators and their motives in order to justify military intervention, the address instead obscured the enemy's identity. With the exception of Osama bin Laden, Bush described an enemy heard but not seen, felt but unknown. Conjuring images of a phantasmic force, constantly probing America's defenses, the rhetoric tapped into national fears about the vulnerability to additional attacks by converting "the enemy into something not just foreign, not just inhuman, but noncorporeal"—fear itself.[22]

Departing from the wars discussed in this book, Bush's rhetoric of savagery decentered the enemy body as a site for intervention. From World War II to 9/11, presidents classified the enemy on the basis of national identity—as German, Japanese, Korean, Chinese, Soviets, or Vietnamese—implicitly invoking the nation as person metaphor to

contextualize the national attitude toward the enemy.[23] Representing
the state and its enemies in biological and etiologic terms, the nation-
as-person metaphor enacts a discursive economy that defines international relations, threats to national security, and the appropriateness
of the country's response in relation to a fictive body. Routing end-of-
war discourse around figures of a mythic body, this discourse enables
recuperative or ameliorative rhetorics to explain and justify America's
post-conflict policies. Bush's rhetoric departed from this tradition by
dissociating representations of the enemy from national origin or ideological affiliation and portraying terrorists as stateless, sworn to the terrorist organizations, and out to construct a new, religious caliphate to
replace the Westphalian order. These depictions, as Jennifer Eagan has
suggested, produced an afterimage of a nameless, disembodied enemy
that, over time, resolved into "disembodied *types* of people for audiences
of the 'distant spectator.'"[24] Disembodied representations merged with
the proliferation of "representations, or simulations, in political rhetoric,
mass media spectacle, and the panoply of other representational forms
that made the events feel pervasive at the time."[25] This new synthesis
of the enemy, then, served as an enduring source of fear in American
political life because it shifted public feelings of invulnerability from the
outside world and "forced [the United States] to question its sense of
power and security."[26]

Representing the enemy as a disembodied force shattered the myth
that Cold War security structures could ensure the long peace and justified two policy avenues.[27] First, the ethos of the disembodied enemy
penetrated the legal and policy bureaucracy to justify an aggressive
military response to terrorism. Practically, this meant focusing on state
sponsors—principally Afghanistan—and nations that housed terrorist organizations, wittingly or not. Bush pointed to this development
in remarks at the Pentagon on September 17, 2001, where he branded
the terrorist a "different type of enemy," one not bounded by national
identity or borders.[28] Faced with a nontraditional enemy, the nation
would respond with a global campaign to eradicate terrorism wherever
it might be found. The September 18, 2001, Authorization for the Use of

Military Force (AUMF) enacted a legal basis for this strategy. It granted the president the authority to act "against those nations, organizations, or persons he determines planned, authorized, committed, or aided the terrorist attacks that occurred on September 11, 2001."[29] And a covert CIA document "called for an antiterror campaign in eighty countries." As John W. Dower recalled, the approach "reflected this reality of an amorphous, ubiquitous, place-shifting, shape-shifting, name-shifting enemy."[30] Formalizing the enemy as disembodied extended a unique juridical regime that governed the conduct of a war on a transnational force. John Yoo, a Justice Department lawyer, argued that confronting a stateless enemy not defined by national identity and not identifiable by uniforms warranted applying "the laws of war to al-Qaeda" or any other terrorist organization.[31] Enabling a counterterrorism policy that addressed even low-risk threats with overwhelming force, what Ron Suskind called the "One Percent Doctrine," the crucial feature of Bush's war sought "to find the terrorists, wherever they might be, and stop them."[32] But, having synthesized a radically flexible definition of terrorism to potentially include anyone linked to al-Qaeda or affiliates with the urgency of the moment, the administration advanced a theory of the enemy that rendered moot distinctions between combatants and noncombatants.

The second policy avenue focused attention on domestic vulnerability to additional terrorist attacks. Simultaneously highlighting the unknowable "identity and location of terrorists," as the Office of Management and Budget put it in 2003, and the potential that "thousands of dangerous killers . . . are now spread throughout the world like ticking timebombs," as Bush said in 2002, the rhetoric warned of the tentacular reach of terrorist organizations that remained veiled in shadows, present but unknown, and raised the specter of additional attacks absent immediate and continuous remedies.[33] Invoking what Mary L. Dudziak has called a "concept of wartime," Bush induced the nation into an exceptional state justifying a wide variety of actions, up to and including sacrifices to personal freedoms in the name of security.[34] At the level of policy, it justified vast increases in airport security measures, public information campaigns such as "see something, say something," the color-coded terror-threat-level indicators overlaid constantly on cable news channels, and domestic surveillance and law-enforcement measures.[35] The motive force of an unseen, unknowable enemy drove these decisions across Bush's terms and beyond.

Speaking of the enemy in disembodied terms did not expunge representations of enemy bodies from public discourse, of course. Rather, it shifted the materialization of those bodies to after death or capture. Usually led by the media, these representations presented profiles of the agents who orchestrated the brutal acts, publishing shots of their faces, video footage of their bodies in motion, or otherwise representing the terrorist in terms of specific bodily figures. For Bush's part, his administration spoke about seeking to understand the terrorist's motive and to "know" that which had previously been unknowable. This information—mostly biographical in content—flashed across our televisions, appeared in print media, and took its place in presidential statements about the enemies, the events they orchestrated, and the continuing danger they posed. The retelling of the story of Richard Reid, the so-called Shoe Bomber, in Bush's 2002 State of the Union Address bears out the point. As Bush explained, "An airline flight attendant spotted a passenger lighting a match. The crew and passengers quickly subdued the man, who had been trained by Al Qaida and was armed with explosives. The people on that plane were alert and, as a result, likely saved nearly 200 lives."[36] Here, the enemy has a name, a face, and a history that can only be known after the fact. But the portrayal remained flat. Reid, in Bush's telling, had no motive beyond terror itself. Instead, he was a cruel and evil man, only stopped because of the heroism of the crew and passengers. The contrast between the terrorist and the people underlined the need for publics to remain aware of the potential danger posed by a relentless, if unknowable enemy. Stories like these claimed that acts of terror became the enemy's voice, a whisper in the dark, in which great violence wrought upon others provided evidence of the continuing danger. Just as the terrorists of 9/11 had announced their presence with the roar of jet engines, the cacophony of explosions, and the wrecked fuselages, twisted steel beams, and charred concrete, Bush renewed collective fears about terrorism by warning that inaction would embolden terrorists to speak their terrible language once again.

While powerful in structuring national understanding of the danger and justifying aggressive military intervention, the language of the disembodied enemy produced a practical challenge for concluding the War on Terror. Terrorism had provoked, in Bush's parlance, a national emergency on a generational scale justifying "a war on a nameless, stateless, formless enemy." The response had expanded the war to include new groups, new locations, and to account for new types of weapons, making it "hard to see how that war would ever end."[37] As Michael Lind recounted, the quick victory over the Taliban led the president to shift focus from stateless terrorists back to rogue states.[38] The most notable example of that shift came with Bush's claim that an axis of evil—Iraq, Iran, and North Korea—was the driving force behind national insecurity.[39] Incongruous with his own definition of the enemy, the linguistic reorientation marked a commitment to ground troops, invasion, and occupation—so-called nation-building. Thus, even though Bush and many of his colleagues had outlined the parameters of a disembodied enemy—and used the network metaphor to contextualize the national-security challenge—the president continued to lead the war as if it were bounded by territory containing an enemy with a specific, definable identity.

The incongruity present in Bush's rhetoric—simultaneously depicting a mobile, secretive enemy and an enemy with permanent bases in Afghanistan and Iraq—generated criticism about his handling of the problem. Outside of government, public commentators like Mary Kaldor, Marc Sageman, Harvey Kushner, Michael Kenney, Robert J. Bunker, in addition to countless others, offered lengthy narratives explaining the uniqueness of the present war and how fighting transnational terrorist organizations differed from traditional war strategies.[40] Disparate in arguments, these texts constituted a vernacular for understanding the War on Terror—or war in the era of nonstate actors more generally—as one in which states had to judiciously exercise military, economic, and political force to control, contain, and disrupt the organizational conduits that make terror possible. As one scholar explained, the conflict required understanding terrorism as a methodology, not an ideology and aligning strategy to that challenge.[41] By the time Obama became president and national emergency had given way to quagmire, these texts had shifted public definitions of the enemy, conceptions about the meaning of terrorist violence, and policy needs away from Bush's preemptive war doctrine. Instead, the figure of the disembodied enemy had become interwoven with war discourse, complicating Obama's ability to rationalize an end to the wars in Iraq and Afghanistan and limiting the military's options for combating the enduring danger posed by terrorism.

BARACK OBAMA AND THE REITERATION
OF THE DISEMBODIED ENEMY

Stuck with two wars he pledged to end, challenging conditions in Iraq and Afghanistan, and limited policy options, much of Obama's first year in office focused on reframing and restructuring national policies related to the War on Terror. Internally, these efforts took the form of a policy debate pitting advocates of occupation and reconstruction against those favoring counterterrorism. The stakes of this debate were huge. Not only would the outcome determine all aspects of policy toward Afghanistan, including everything from troop deployments to reconstruction, but it also implicated perceptions of national vulnerability to terrorism itself. Many inside and outside of government worried that failing to curtail the danger posed by al-Qaeda by leaving terrorist sanctuaries in Afghanistan and beyond risked affording terrorist groups the space and opportunity necessary for planning and orchestrating new attacks. For these reasons, a central axis of those deliberations asked fundamental questions about the nature of the enemy and the national mission.[42]

Obama's public comments framed and structured these deliberations by reviving depictions of the enemy as an inchoate, disembodied force that could pop up anywhere, at any time, and wreak grave damage on the United States and its allies. Structurally, his thesis of the enemy enacted many of the components of Bush's early characterizations, particularly in terms of regionalizing the danger and delinking al-Qaeda from the territory they inhabited. But, distinct from Bush, Obama streamlined the rhetoric of the enemy by abandoning depictions of state-based dangers entirely. That is, Obama's rhetoric deterritorialized and disembodied the danger while pointing to the need for a new, agile counterterrorism strategy up to the task of responding to a mobile and secretive fighting force. Initially justifying withdrawal from Iraq in order to attend to the resurgent power of al-Qaeda in Afghanistan, this rhetoric rationalized a new orientation toward terrorism itself. As a disembodied danger, lacking in a corporeal identity and spread across much of the world, terrorism could never be defeated. Without victory, terrorism became a perpetual danger with no hope of abatement.

Resonant with the erasure of the North Vietnamese, Obama's disembodied enemy represented a novel shift in the way the nation considers international danger. Nixon shifted the focus from the specific enemy to the general structure of international relations, effectively removing the figure of the enemy as the central axis upon which the conflict should be understood. Far from disembodying the enemy, Nixon's movement from actor to scene freed the North Vietnamese from culpability for the conflict, paving the way for a conclusion and the eventual recuperation of relations. That discourse acknowledged the enemy's existence, claimed they were not responsible for the war, and forgot them. In Obama's rhetoric, the disembodied enemy continued to materially exist and endanger national security, even as representations lacked bodily descriptions that typify end-of-war discourse. This rhetoric amplified, rather than reduced the danger posed. Unseen, unknown, and unknowable, the disembodied enemy imperiled the nation via its anonymity. No president could summarily end a war in the midst of such peril.

This streamlined discourse of the enemy underwrote Obama's end-of-war rhetoric by redefining the international scene in which substate or transnational antagonists appear. This shift rationalized disengaging from Afghanistan because, as Obama contended, occupation could not contain mobile, nomadic irregular armed forces that transit across territory to conduct operations before slipping back into hiding amidst the civilian population. His address at the National Defense University on

March 12, 2009, established the rhetorical shift that would come to define his administration. In the address, Obama claimed that vast changes in the political economy of the globe had produced new dangers, requiring new strategies up to the task of confronting mobile, deterritorialized enemies. Emblematic of his end-of-war rhetoric, the message blurred and erased the defining characteristics of the enemy, elevating the figure of a diffuse, disembodied antagonist, who was nimble, could transit "freely across borders . . . to do great harm," and was unaffiliated with any particular nation. These factors—mobility and concealment—called for the evolution of the nation's military strategy in order to more carefully address the true danger. The unpredictable nature of a disembodied, mobile enemy, moreover, required the nation to "look beyond this conventional advantage" and "develop the new approaches and new capabilities of the 21st century . . . that can help our troops succeed in the unconventional mission that they now face."[43] Even while acknowledging the enduring challenges in Afghanistan, Pakistan, and Iraq, the address elaborated the rationales that would justify his decision to end combat operations and shift the war mission from states back to nonstate actors. Conventional strategies could not defeat terrorism. Nor could occupation and democratization remedy the circumstances that induce individuals to resort to terrorist violence. Terrorism would persist, and policies had to adapt to the permanence of insecurity. Signaling the eventual transition from occupation to watch-and-strike, the speech marked the beginning of a new phase in the War on Terror.

A central aspect of this conceptual reorientation regionalized the conflict by emphasizing the ways the enemy utilized the geography of the theater. In April 2009, for example, Obama warned that the previous administration's war strategy had driven al-Qaeda into "the border regions of Afghanistan and Pakistan," enabling the organization to regroup and "threaten every member of NATO."[44] By identifying the challenge in geographic terms, the president intimated that Bush's war had dispersed the danger over a large geographic terrain that, by its very nature, provided innumerable opportunities for sanctuary against allied military forces. Portraying al-Qaeda as unbound "by oceans or by borders drawn on maps," and with ample room to maneuver, augmented the risks posed by an organization that had already reached into the financial heart of America and done significant damage.[45] Bush's war had not defeated al-Qaeda because it had misread the nature of the danger. Consequently, Obama explained, the war had displaced the organization, dispersing the enemy across the region, and intensified their motives to wreak havoc on the West. These factors, he argued, warranted a reconstituted U.S. mission to seek them, chase them, and kill them wherever they may appear. Convergent with prevalent national-security discourse, Obama's claims blurred "distinctions between soldiers and civilians," and made "identifying the enemy . . . an often elusive goal."[46]

Obama's thesis about the shifting, mobile nature of enemies represented al-Qaeda as a globalized organization stretching from North Africa to Southeast Asia and in need of urgent attention. At odds with Bush's stance, he explained, "The terrorists who struck our country on 9/11 plotted in Hamburg, trained in Kandahar and Karachi, and threaten countries across the globe."[47] The rhetoric articulated the threat as continuing and heightened the stakes in devising a global strategy to confront that danger.[48] Reminding the nation "that attack could occur in any nation" and that Afghanistan "is where Al Qaida trains, plots, and threatens to launch their next attack," Obama argued the first step toward that new strategy required on-the-ground improvements in Afghanistan.[49] But, a short-term increase in troops and training efforts only served immediate security goals. The danger posed by al-Qaeda, a danger he claimed "no corner of the globe can wall itself off from," required "shared and persistent efforts to combat fear and want wherever they exist."[50] Instead of representing a benchmark, Obama contended, al-Qaeda's physical absence demonstrated the continuity of the risk they posed—an enemy that could appear at any moment, in any place, with virtually no warning and with deadly consequences. In other words, Obama hyped the danger posed by al-Qaeda while emphasizing the need for collective action to stem the danger posed by terrorism. More than a decade of war and the virtual decimation of al-Qaeda with little appreciable reduction in risk provided all the evidence he needed to sustain the argument.

Seeking to temporarily increase the number of troops in Afghanistan to stabilize the Afghani government, push the Taliban back, and contain al-Qaeda appeared at odds with Obama's campaign pledge to end the wars in Iraq and Afghanistan, however, and generated public and institutional criticism.[51] Publicly, insurgent violence and declining public support for occupation collided with virulent anti-black elements that questioned Obama's intelligence, birthright, wisdom, and leadership.[52] At the same time, bureaucratic inertia and congressional roadblocks reduced and restricted his ability to reprogram the occupations, particularly in terms of his accelerated schedule for ending the war in Iraq.[53] General Stanley McChrystal's public pressure for more troops, and Obama's objections to that plan on the basis it would prolong the occupation, further complicated the president's exit strategy and end-of-war discourse.[54] Inclined toward pragmatic policymaking and the policy flexibility such an attitude engenders, Obama sought a strategy that could facilitate a quick conclusion to the occupation, not extend it indefinitely.[55] For a president preoccupied with resolving a deep economic crisis at home and focused on extending health-care access to all Americans, the politics of the wars also raised political risks above and beyond the realm of foreign policy.

Obama navigated the political terrain by raising the specter of a disembodied, deterritorialized enemy that had to be confronted, first in the FATA, and later anywhere they might appear. The implied mobility enacted by the figure of a disembodied enemy facilitated the president's gradual redirection of attention away from Iraq and Afghanistan and toward American efforts on stopping terrorists everywhere. In speaking of al-Qaeda's operational reach, Obama explained, "These extremists have killed in Amman and Bali, Islamabad and Kabul, and they have the blood of Americans and Russians on their hands."[56] This portrait of al-Qaeda imagined an enemy stretching across much of the world and with an unceasing desire to threaten American and allied interests. Given that capacity, only a global strategy would suffice. Obama made the case on a trip to Europe in July 2009, where he claimed combating terrorism "in Afghanistan is not simply an American issue; it is a world-wide issue." Since "they consider the West to be one undifferentiated set of countries," he explained, their mere existence represented a "threat to people all around the world."[57] Since al-Qaeda made no distinction between the United States and Europe, the claim signaled the need for continued cooperation to combat the threat. It also emphasized the need for allied forces to detach themselves from occupation—to become as mobile as the force they confronted. In Obama's view, insurgency in Afghanistan bogged down the allied forces while inducing mobility in the true enemy. This situation produced policy failure while heightening the risk that terrorists would find or establish new safe havens, plan new terrorist acts, and orchestrate them against the West. Thus, Obama posited the need for a new strategy that could move past fighting insurgency and instead focus on the danger posed by terrorism.

This rhetoric—a sort of transition-to-war rhetoric that posited neither an endgame nor the conditions for victory—rationalized a temporary influx of troops in Afghanistan as a remedy to the reappearance of al-Qaeda. Obama's address at West Point in December 2009, when he announced the troop increase, justified the surge as necessary to improve security in the country and to increase the pressure on al-Qaeda. As he put it, the "group of extremists" that endangered Afghanistan was the same "ruthless, repressive, and radical movement" that threatened the West. The United States had to act because, in addition to threatening Afghanistan itself, al-Qaeda had "retain[ed] their safe havens along the border."[58] Yet, even in rationalizing a troop surge in Afghanistan, identifying the supranational danger posed by terrorism linked Obama's policy to the broader context of a global fight against extremism. Implying the existence of other forms of danger, diffuse and dispersed, required a rethinking of war itself. As Robert L. Ivie has argued, the claim "transposed war into 'a struggle against extremism' in which the United States would 'exercise restraint' in its goals and its means."[59] Even in outlining limitations to American efforts in Iraq and Afghanistan, the message represented twenty-first-century war as unlimited, continuous, and necessitating perpetual American intervention. The disembodied figure of the enemy, then, underwrote both his justification for the surge in Afghanistan and his determination to end the occupations by committing the administration to a theory of the enemy that excluded long-term occupation as an efficacious response to enduring security threats.

Revising the enemy to appear fully disembodied, mobile, and supranational inferred the contours of a new presidential persona capable of responding to the challenge posed by such a danger. Eschewing Bush's preemptive war doctrine, Obama's persona—the watchman—called upon the national-security bureaucracy to prepare for continued danger in the post-occupation era. The resurgent figure of a disembodied enemy played a central role in the elaboration of the persona because it claimed occupation of Iraq and Afghanistan could never stop terrorist organizations and, in fact, might even undermine efforts to combat terrorism. As Obama put it in 2010, terrorist organizations stretched "from South Asia to the Horn of Africa." Such an expansive scope made Afghanistan a sideshow to a global problem.[60] In 2012, he attributed violence in Yemen to al-Qaeda, claiming it proved "there are still terrorists who seek to kill our citizens." The rhetoric extended the belief that al-Qaeda, as a mobile, deterritorialized organization, could appear anywhere, at any time, and perhaps most importantly, with any form of weaponry, "from the conventional to the unconventional."[61]

Beyond the severity of the danger, however, lay the notion of irruption. Obama presumed the existence of more unnamed terrorist organizations that could appear and disappear at any moment. The secretive nature of these organizations justified constant vigilance as the only appropriate response. As he put it in 2013, al-Qaeda's affiliates, "regional groups, some of which are explicitly tied to Al Qaida or that ideology, some of which are more localized," represented an emergent danger.[62] Constitutive of the watchman persona, this rhetoric sustained the nation's commitment to violent intervention after the conclusion of the wars in Iraq and Afghanistan because it implied the success in Afghanistan had increased—rather than reduced—the danger of terrorism.

Born from a central, paradoxical feature of contemporary American war rhetoric—in which military successes heighten dangers rather than lessen them—the embodied persona of the watchman recast the role of government and the management of foreign policy to inhabit a gray zone of neither war nor peace, in which military force would be used in pursuit of limited goals. It also suggested that the United States should disentangle itself from Afghanistan to better face the enduring threat posed by global, secretive, and disembodied enemies intent on causing catastrophe in the U.S.

Disembodied Movements and the Rhetoric of Terrorist Sanctuary

The thesis of the disembodied enemy articulated the persistence of danger in the world and a policy orientation up to the task of containing it. This new idiom delinked the enemy from territory, rearticulated the danger as global, obscured the representations of the antagonist, and emphasized their implicit mobility, diffusion, and anonymity. In doing so, it also yielded a specific focus on the places terrorists inhabit. A persistent vector running through presidential discourse—from Reagan to Obama—represented the enemy in terms of the sanctuaries they utilized to rest, train, and plot attacks. This discourse pledged to know the terrorists in terms of their movements—from sanctuary to the battlefield to the Western world. Constitutive of a national-security vernacular focused on the presence of terrorist hideouts—most often expressed as the safe haven—this discourse contributed to an image of the terrorist as an ethereal enemy, moving from place to place, in search of refuge in order to recruit, plan, and launch attacks. The Reagan administration used the term to link adversarial states to terrorist groups, enabling a host of policy options including military retaliation.[63] George H. W. Bush declared Iraq "a haven for mercenaries and terrorists."[64] Bill Clinton avoided labeling Afghanistan a safe haven and instead named al-Qaeda a "foreign terrorist organization subject to the same sanctions traditionally reserved for state sponsors."[65] Each of these articulations inferred the existence of physical, clandestine spaces, nested in outlaw states and hidden from international authorities. In doing so, this rhetoric blurred distinctions between the state sponsor and the terrorist organization taking up residence, supplying presidents with rationales sufficient to justify military options.

Thus, it is no surprise that the rhetoric of the safe haven constituted one of the primary vehicles by which Bush maintained a state-based approach to the War on Terror. In dozens of speeches and internal documents, his administration referred to the way terrorists use "safe havens to train and plan and hide."[66] Safe havens, in these articulations, appeared as transit points, places of temporary rest and relief. Implicitly defining the enemy as on the move—mobile, deterritorialized, amorphous, and secretive—the term justified Bush's president-as-cowboy persona, on the hunt for the bad guys. It also echoed Nixon's explanation of his decision to expand the Vietnam War into Cambodia by linking al-Qaeda's survivability to cross border refuges. Figuring Afghanistan as one of many safe havens, this rhetoric asked the military to eliminate all places of refuge that harbor terrorists.[67] At the start, his administration articulated the goals as "destroying the terrorist threat and closing the terrorist safe haven along Pakistan's border with Afghanistan."[68] The 2007 National Intelligence Estimate and 2008 Annual Threat Assessment reiterated this contention, arguing that "al Qaeda has established a safe haven in Pakistan."[69] By singling out the FATA region as a unique zone of terrorist refuge, Bush's rhetoric also connoted home. Terrorists had established a permanent base in Afghanistan, Bush contended, and only by "closing the terrorist safe haven along Pakistan's border with Afghanistan" could America become safe.[70] This rhetoric legitimated intervention and occupation, but it also "collaps[ed] the distinction between terrorists and 'state sponsors' . . . naturaliz[ing] a policy of state intervention in response to an attack by a non-state actor" while also "conflat[ing] Al Qaeda and the Taliban."[71] In this way, Bush's articulation of the safe haven, even while extending the parameters of the disembodied enemy, adopted a state-based approach to terrorism, vesting the American mission in regime change, occupation, and reconstruction.

Outside experts warned that Bush's vision was short-sighted and ignored the existence of virtual (or micro) safe havens across the world. Michael F. Scheuer, in the foreword of a volume titled *Denial of Sanctuary*, warned that traditional notions of safe havens "as specific geographic locations" had given way to internetworked sanctuaries that enable terrorists to receive the same benefits of the safe haven while residing in urban areas.[72] Kenneth J. Menkhaus claimed in the same volume that al-Qaeda had found safe haven in the Horn of Africa.[73] And terrorism scholars Jarret Brachman and James J. F. Forest argued that one of the key challenges was to design strategies to address virtual sanctuaries that exist online but perform the same function.[74] As these examples demonstrate, by the end of Bush's second term, consensus outside of government had cohered into a view of al-Qaeda as deterritorialized, with a base in the FATA region, but perpetually on the lookout for additional sanctuaries. In spite of these assessments, critics observed that the Bush administration ignored the sanctuary in the FATA and failed to deliver a comprehensive plan to address the problem.[75]

BARACK OBAMA, TERRORIST SAFE HAVENS, AND THE RECONFIGURATION OF WAR-SPACE

Like Bush, Obama used the rhetoric of the safe haven to direct attention to the danger posed by terrorist hideouts in the FATA. This rhetoric fit with his campaign goal of focusing on the "real" fight against terrorism to win the war against al-Qaeda. For example, in remarks at the State Department the day after his inaugural, he claimed "there is no answer in Afghanistan that does not confront the Al Qaida and Taliban bases along the border."[76] Two weeks later, he reiterated the problem, explaining that the geographic region housed the base used "to launch an attack that killed 3,000 Americans" and provided havens for those still "planning attacks on the U.S. homeland."[77] Extending these claims to justify a temporary increase in U.S. troop deployments to the region, Obama reset the war mission to focus on identifying and destroying those sanctuaries.[78] As he put it in February 2009, safe havens enabled "brazen

attacks from Taliban forces, extremist forces."[79] Since the Bush administration had failed "to root out those safe havens," a task Obama deemed
necessary to "make our mission successful," the United States would
deploy an additional 17,000 troops focused on finding and destroying
terrorist sanctuaries.[80] Discussing the geography of the region and the
ease with which those groups retreated to mountain hideouts that knew
no national borders, Obama redefined the problem in Afghanistan as
supranational, involving multiple geographic locations at once.

This initial foray into the thorny problem of Afghanistan extended
and amplified the idiom of terrorism resonant across the previous seven
presidential administrations. This vernacular isolated the terrorist as a
unique enemy—disembodied, mobile, and clandestine—always on the
move. It also represented the terrorist as the enemy of all, outside of
law, nationality, and civilization itself, a sort of twenty-first-century pi-
ratical engagement, entailing an antagonist in the perpetual hunt for
safe havens from which they can rest, train, and plan their next attacks.
This enemy, as Blackstone put it in his *Commentaries on the Laws of England*,
"has reduced himself afresh to the savage state of nature," severing any
attachment to place and the identity that origins provide.[81] Echoing the
term's historic roots in the discourse of piracy, in which safe havens referred to secretive ports of call, Obama's emphasis on physical sanctuaries further downplayed the importance of any given terrorist.[82] As with
pirates, there would always be more terrorists, but sanctuaries are finite.
Eliminating the sanctuary, then, could neutralize the danger posed by
terrorism.

Retargeting to focus on essentially ungoverned spaces populated
with terrorist sanctuaries shifted strategy away from occupation and pacification to search and strike. But, by compressing vast amounts of difficult terrain spanning parts of Afghanistan, Pakistan, and the FATA into a
single, enclosed domain populated with clandestine refuges reduced the
likelihood of success. The FATA alone measures approximately 10,500
square miles—roughly the same size as Massachusetts—of ungoverned,
difficult mountainous terrain with little to no modern infrastructure.[83]
In addition, the mobility of terrorist groups who hold no attachment to

land and can easily find or construct bases undermined the likelihood of sustainable achievements. And, indeed, as the war stretched on with few positive signs, the administration distanced itself from public conversation about the FATA, opting instead to discuss a warfighting strategy premised on identifying safe havens—sanctuaries predominantly found in ungoverned spaces are often difficult to distinguish from civilian use of land—and destroying them.

Obama managed the challenge of geography and the implausibility of victory in two ways. First, distinguishing between the Taliban, who crossed borders to escape reprisals, and terrorist organizations, who lacked all national affiliations, gradually distanced the American mission from occupation and reconstruction. While Obama initially named al-Qaeda as the principal concern, he also hinted at the existence of other terrorist organizations. For example, in a town hall in April 2009, he claimed his role as Commander in Chief, obligated he ensure "that bin Laden and his cronies are not able to create a safe . . . haven within which they can kill another 3,000 Americans or more."[84] The ambiguity of the term "cronies" foreshadowed the rise of additional groups, tangentially affiliated with the terrorist leader. By July, he claimed al-Qaeda had many affiliates who "have defiled a great religion of peace and justice and ruthlessly murdered men, women, and children of all nationalities and faiths . . . they're plotting to kill more of our people, and they benefit from safe havens that allow them to train and operate, particularly along the border of Pakistan and Afghanistan."[85] Blurring the identity of the enemy—anyone could become a terrorist—Obama's references to an affiliate or extremist implied the existence of additional antagonists, not yet known, also seeking sanctuary. War strategy had to evolve to address dangers known and unknown.

This rhetorical recalibration of the mission also focused American efforts on containing the danger posed by ungovernable spaces across the globe. As with the terrorists themselves, Obama's initial focus on the FATA ceded to a more generalized thesis about terrorist sanctuaries beyond the region. That thesis suggested terrorists would find and use additional ungovernable spaces to plan and orchestrate attacks on

Western forces. Thus, Obama broadened the mission from occupation and democracy promotion to identifying and neutralizing clandestine locations. This movement began with an address in March 2009 announcing his strategy for the region. Referring to the danger from terrorists in Pakistan and Afghanistan, Obama acknowledged the need to continue to support the Afghani government in its quest to defeat the Taliban, but also refocused the true American mission on the threat posed by al-Qaeda. Where Bush had invaded state sponsors, occupied them, and rebuilt them in our image, Obama pinpointed ungoverned spaces as the domain for American military intervention. As he put it, the danger zone stretched from London to Bali and North Africa to the Middle East.[86] Bruce Riedel, the lead author of Obama's initial counterterrorism strategy, later identified al-Qaeda safe havens in Sudan, Afghanistan, and Pakistan, and claimed the enemy sought to "consolidate their safe haven in South Asia while creating new al Qaeda 'franchises' or allies across the Muslim world."[87] Riedel's thesis, reflected in Obama's rhetoric, identified the inherent statelessness of al-Qaeda and noted the ways fighting a transient, nomadic force should alter policy.

Diverging from Bush's discourse by warning of the danger posed by the proliferation of terrorist sanctuaries outside of the war zone, this conceptual reorientation rationalized a policy shift toward a mobile military strategy, detached from the impasses of occupation, reconstruction, and democracy promotion. This discourse reconfigured national strategy and resulted in an increased reliance on remote, unmanned aerial vehicles to reach the enemy by reconfiguring war-space away from Afghanistan in two ways. First, the president's emphasis on sites or locations that enable geographies of violence yielded a strategy premised on the destruction of those material or virtual spaces. War rhetoric almost always derives from the enemy's relationship to place. Those relationships give rise to a vernacular of the enemy that is based in racist representations of the Other and manifests in bodily terms (skin color, angle of one's eyes, and so on). As previously discussed, Obama's disembodied enemy was "known" not by national origin or affiliation, but by the violence they conducted. Focusing on safe havens facilitated this detachment by representing the enemy as a shadowy figure navigating hostile and civilian zones, intent on acts of gruesome violence. In the absence of corporeal representations, however, the geographies of violence endemic in these depictions resolved into the image of the sanctuary. That is, in place of corporeal representations of the enemy, Obama invoked the existence of material structures that enable the enemy's mission and targeted those spaces for state intervention and violence. Claiming terrorism impossible to defeat, material and digital sites of sanctuary became the true target. Sites terrorists use to constitute their organizations, plan their missions, and train the members can be found and destroyed. Blurring distinctions between war zones and civilian spaces, focusing on the vital importance of the safe haven rendered all who participated in the construction and maintenance of such sites as equivalently engaged in the provision of sanctuary to terrorists. As such, everyone from the goat herder to the carpenter could fall under the penumbra of "providing material support for terrorism."

Additionally, mobilizing the concept of "sanctuary" itself pointed to the need for policies that could identify and respond to the appearance of new safe havens. This rhetoric bolstered the case for withdrawing from Iraq and Afghanistan. As Obama put it at the United Nations General Assembly in September 2009, the United States "will permit no safe haven for Al Qaida to launch attacks from Afghanistan or any other nation."[88] He recalled how the refuge Afghanistan had provided to al-Qaeda had enabled the organization to plot the 9/11 attacks, but it also distributed the danger posed by sanctuaries beyond South Asia. Suggesting the likelihood of additional zones of sanctuary diminished the significance of any specific space or combat zone to the enduring struggle against terrorism and justified his global focus. Three months later, at West Point, he claimed, "Since 9/11, Al Qaida's safe havens have been the source of attacks against London and Amman and Bali."[89] Ostensibly referring to sanctuaries in Afghanistan and Pakistan, the ambiguous statement invited the prospect of safe havens elsewhere, especially in consideration of the great reach of al-Qaeda. That reach implicated the nation in a struggle that far exceeded the fight in Afghanistan, one that required detaching the mission from Afghanistan in order to pursue terrorist organizations around the world. A year later, Obama returned to the theme, claiming, "We have refocused on defeating Al Qaida and denying its affiliates a safe haven."[90] The haven, secretive, hidden, and recuperative, merged with the prospect of affiliates spread across the globe establishing new refuges. For Obama, "the awful loss of life, from 9/11 to Bali" proves "what happens when Al Qaida has safe havens."[91] Echoing Nixon's displacement of Vietnam to focus on the international system, Obama globalized the problem of sanctuaries to urge the nation to look beyond Afghanistan.

Obama's rhetoric of the safe haven redefined the end game in Afghanistan not as defeating the Taliban, but as pushing terrorist organizations out of the country and ensuring they would no longer find welcome. Pledging to keep al-Qaeda on the run so "it's harder for them to train and to plot and to attack," Obama clarified early in his first term that he sought to ensure American security and not win a victory against the Taliban.[92] By May 2010, in an indication of the failure of pacification, he claimed deploying additional troops to Afghanistan would deny "an even larger safe haven for Al Qaida and its affiliates."[93] Distancing the strategy from the Taliban, the declaration signaled that the mission had shifted toward counterterrorism. It also reworked the terms of victory by establishing the destruction of safe havens as the key metric. Focusing on al-Qaeda would suffice because it would push them out of the war zone and frustrate their ability to conduct operations against American targets. More explicitly, he argued, "our core goal" is "focused on disrupting, dismantling, and defeating al Qaida in Afghanistan and Pakistan" and not on defeating the Taliban.[94] While mobility lay at the center of the mission—literally driving al-Qaeda out of Afghanistan and Pakistan—the responsibility for defeating the Taliban and rebuilding the country fell to the Afghani people. The strategy made sense, Obama claimed, "because it is Afghans who must build their nation."[95] By establishing these goals, Obama's rhetoric dissociated the Taliban—anti-Western but not threatening—from al-Qaeda, the true enemy with which there could be no peace. This move delinked al-Qaeda from territory and state by depriving the organization of any formal affiliation with Afghanistan or the insurgent group fighting for control of the country.

The likelihood that terrorists would continue to find or construct new safe havens provided a continuing rationale for violent confrontation and underwrote the production of the president-as-watchman persona. Initially justifying a troop surge in Afghanistan, Obama established the safe haven itself as the primary target of national attention. This rhetorical effort shifted national strategy from occupation and reconstruction to a role premised on surveillance, preparation, and limited military engagements. Yet, since new sanctuaries could appear at any point, anywhere, only a national-security strategy tasked with watching and striking globally could counteract the danger posed by terrorist sanctuaries. Adding to the complexity of focusing on a disembodied structure as a primary target in the War on Terror, Obama's rhetoric expanded war-space to cover half the globe—from Africa to Southeast Asia—as the places where sanctuaries were likely to appear. The inherent mobility of the enemy combined with their need for sanctuaries enmeshed the president in a progressively developing discourse invested in reidentifying the line between those who could be included in the governable order and those who faced the ultimate punishment of execution.

Disembodied Associations and the Terrorist-as-Network Trope

As a disembodied force typified by its corporeal absence, post-9/11 terrorist discourse also claimed to "know" the enemy by their associations—their ways of organizing.[96] This rhetoric expanded the enunciative field that defines terrorism to figure the terrorist as a precarious enemy.[97] As previously discussed, one strand of discourse depicted the terrorist as "evil" or opposed to our "freedoms." This discourse typified the genre of American war rhetoric in that it performed a routine, almost ceremonial form of otherization. Once defined as "evil," the enemy needed no further context, for there could only be one response. But, the War on Terror posed a fundamentally different type of confrontation and gave rise to a new type of enemy—an enemy defined by the instability of its structure. Initially pointing to terrorists opening branches or franchises as part of an extensive set of cross-border interconnections engaged in plotting and orchestrating acts of terrorism, this discourse comprehended terrorists as entrenched in highly structured, bureaucratic, and hierarchical organizations.[98]

Presidential articulations departed from this implicit business model of terrorism and instead figured terrorists as networked agents—individual actors or nodes embedded within what Manuel Castells called the "global network society."[99] With this metaphor deeply ingrained in national-security discourse, analysts first used it to describe terrorism in the 1970s. By 2000, the figure of the network had become the preeminent metaphor in many different domains, but became *doxa* in national-security discourse after 9/11.[100] This shift compounded disembodied representations of the enemy by emphasizing the precarious nature of the associations that enable terrorist planning, training, and attacks. By their very nature, networks are "temporary, dynamic, emergent, adaptive, entrepreneurial, and flexible structures."[101] Those that use networks, then, experience the interconnected possibilities in fluid, impermanent, and pliable ways. For the anonymous troll who flames Reddit with posts about the excesses of late capitalism while sipping a $6 latte at Starbucks, the anonymity of the network enables a particular type of practice not possible in the material world. But it also deemphasizes the importance of any given troll and reveals the network as the provenance of the practice of trolling itself. As there are billions of nodes, framing terrorists-as-networked represented the danger as the network itself, rather than derived from individual cells or agents. As with the Internet troll, this framing enumerated actual terrorists as precarious lives, what Yasmin Jiwani called "lives that do not matter," and diminished the significance of any given individual or node in the network in favor of the phenomenon itself.[102] Reflecting the endemic precarity of the twenty-first century, this facet of the metaphor implied there would always be another troll, another terrorist, another node on the endless grid of digital connection. The network could add or shed bodies as needed.[103] Obviating the need to identify individual terrorists (beyond Osama bin Laden), the network metaphor placed the onus of policy on eliminating the structures that enabled networked communication in the first place.

While gradually inserting elements of precarity into depictions of the enemy, the network metaphor initially reserved space for speakers to employ the figure of the enemy in differential ways. Especially in the first few years of the War on Terror, the imprecision of the content of the metaphor endowed terrorist discourse with elastic representations capable of justifying policies ranging from international police work to invasion and air strikes. Like the rhetoric of the safe haven, which facilitated invasion and occupation prior to retargeting military strategy toward the sites that terrorists inhabit, the articulation of the enemy in terms of digital structures invoked an apparatus of security activities organized around the premise that the enemy could be anyone, anywhere, and always seeking to orchestrate acts of violence upon the West. For Bush, the metaphor infused his discourse of the enemy with fear and urgency to rationalize invasion and occupation becoming yet another component of his call to bring the law to the lawless. For Obama, the lesson of occupation dictated a mobile military strategy premised on the thesis that a truly networked enemy lacked territorial affiliations and had thus survived the violence wrought by American forces in Iraq and Afghanistan by further embedding into digital spaces.

GEORGE W. BUSH, TERRORISM, AND THE NETWORK

In the immediate aftermath of 9/11, Bush popularized the centrality of the network metaphor by defining the purpose of the War on Terror as "defeating 'the' global terror network," claiming on September 20th, "our enemy is a radical network of terrorism and every government that supports them."[104] The conservative Heritage Foundation echoed Bush's frame, designating the global terrorist network as the true threat, and advocated for sustained U.S. military intervention in Afghanistan to uproot and destroy it.[105] As the discourse of the network enmeshed with the Bush administration's terrorism rhetoric, the president singled out the "shadowy networks with no nation or citizens to defend" as a primary target in the War on Terror. Once again declaring the terrorist as the enemy of all, Bush inferred their lack of national affiliations meant they could not be deterred or contained. Only "tak[ing] the battle to the enemy" could ensure American security.[106] The rhetoric reiterated the basic structure of the disembodied enemy—they lay in shadow, could not be identified, and existed outside of the law—while isolating the associational links between and among terrorist organizations both as confirming the enemy's existence and as pointing to a way in which security activities could detect and counteract their efforts.

Eschewing the post-territorial elements of the metaphor, however, the Bush administration articulated the enemy-as-network to rationalize preemptive war. Especially in the initial years after 9/11, the administration's discourse of terror spoke to the explosive potential manifest in transnational terrorist relationships—not because of the qualities or features of internetworked agents, but rather due to the potential for those agents to establish links to rogue states willing to assist in further acts of terror. In concert with the ethos of the safe haven, Defense Secretary Donald Rumsfeld flagged the danger posed by state sponsors of terrorism and terrorist organizations that utilized sanctuaries to plan additional acts of violence. In his discourse, the network metaphor accented the potential for global terrorist networks to acquire weapons of mass destruction due to the intimate relationships they have with terrorist states. Given linkages between the state and the network, he contended, "the only defense is to take the effort to find those global networks and to deal with them as the United States did in Afghanistan."[107] While inaccurate, the thesis added to the Bush administration's rationale for invading Iraq, if not the entire doctrine of preventive war, by articulating terrorist organizations as always already intertwined with rogue states, who Rumsfeld argued would "use terrorist networks to dispense weapons of mass destruction."[108] This description rendered the real danger as the state and relegated the terrorist network to the role of a bit player, the agent capable of implementing rogue designs. Far from the sole voice in the administration, Vice President Dick Cheney also spoke about the threat of a "terrorist network, with ties in Iraq, that threatened the very security of the United States."[109] Cheney echoed those comments in a speech to war veterans, claiming "the al Qaeda network is pursuing" weapons of mass destruction and that "constitutes as grave a threat as can be imagined."[110] In this discourse, the absence of evidence—as in the case of Iraq—didn't discount the intent of networked organizations to use safe havens located in rogue sponsors to acquire and deploy increasingly lethal technologies. Instead, it validated such concerns, verifying the secretive nature of the enemy.

Even while devising strategy premised on representations of enemy networks embedded in specific, actionable territory, the Bush administration acknowledged the nature of a post-territorial contest in which the enemy disregards traditional notions of territory and contiguity. Rumsfeld identified the enemy's very fluidity as their deadliest strength. In organizationally constituted "networks, unburdened by fixed borders, headquarters or conventional forces," he warned, terrorists could easily observe and adapt to the nation's response to 9/11. Revealing fundamental flaws in the proposition to invade and occupy Afghanistan and Iraq, Rumsfeld's rhetoric identified the inherent mobility of the enemy as a crucial factor in the design of a forward-thinking national counterterrorism strategy. As he put it, terrorists "cannot be attacked in a traditional battle" and instead the United States needed "swifter, more lethal ways to fight, including pre-emptive strikes." Because institutions like the Department of Defense are "ponderous and clumsy and slow," Rumsfeld ceded tactical advantage to the terrorists because they could adapt "cheaper, quicker, and for a period" those changes remain invisible.[111]

These two strategic attitudes—pinning policy on invading state sponsors of terrorism while acknowledging terrorists are highly mobile transnational agents—reflected a schism between the administration's rationale for preemptive war and their view of the enemy. At first glance, foregrounding the significance of the state while placing the terrorist network in the background may seem logical. At the level of policy, disrupting the ability of Afghanistan and Iraq—or other state sponsors—to provide safe haven to terrorists should also degrade terrorist capacities.

But, at the level of representation, foregrounding the state isolated "Afghanis" and "Iraqis" as the enemy, rather than the terrorist, and advanced the notion that the enemy's relationship to place took priority over their inherent mobility. This emphasis abandoned a central aspect of the network metaphor—that networks are by nature transnational—and committed the administration to democratization, a policy portfolio at odds with counterterrorism. Democratization seeks to establish permanent governmental and societal institutions that order, manage, and guide politics, policy, and controversy. It presumes the existence of a stable population, with a unifying identity, that seeks a common and collective future. Yet, the figure of the precarious enemy, digitally connected and organized around anti-Western antagonisms rather than the common bonds of national identity and purpose, represented the danger in terms antithetical to democratic solutions. Democratization could never resolve the terrorism problem because denationalized actors lack the spatial affiliations necessary for constituting an identity beyond their ideological orientation. They are not and can never be citizens, thus their grievances can never be managed via democratic procedures. Even though Rumsfeld hinted at this dynamic, the Bush administration continued to prioritize democratization and economic development.

The discrepancy between the administration's rationale for invasion and occupation and the figure of a networked, deterritorialized enemy gradually transmuted Bush's preemptive war doctrine into a recognition that the nature of terrorism required an evolving security doctrine more closely attuned to the nature of the enemy. As Tim Minor insisted, "scholars on the subject feel that states are disadvantaged when attempting to mitigate the success of such actors because of the fluidity that these networks exhibit." Identifying the network as the enemy required addressing the "adaptability, resilience, [the] capacity for innovation and learning, and wide-scale recruitment" inherent in digital connectivity. It also meant devising strategies to address the shapelessness of the organization, as a precarious structure never actually exists and instead is typified by uncertainty and change.[112] While Bush's policies responded slowly to the challenge, envisioning terrorists as engaged in a broad network of interconnected conduits "resolve[d] the disparate intentions of those encompassed under the terrorist label" by lumping together dissimilar groups with often conflicting ideologies under a single frame of terrorist.[113] The fissures between an escalating commitment to democratization and the evolving figure of a precarious enemy detached from territory, however, complicated Bush's ability to escape the wars once Iraq combusted into insurgency and quagmire. Instead, having synthesized terrorism into a singular, internetworked group, the president maintained the continuous cycle of surge and withdrawal until the end of his term in office.

BARACK OBAMA, NODES OF TERROR, AND THE DISEMBODIED ENEMY

By the time Obama became president, most of the culprits responsible for 9/11 were dead or captured, and the occupations had shifted from counterterrorism to scattered attempts to institute governance in ungoverned land. This situation complicated Obama's plans to extricate the nation from Afghanistan because it pitted his campaign pledge to end the war against his institutional responsibility to protect the nation from future attacks. Obama resolved this tension by streamlining and amplifying the terrorist-as-network metaphor to move conceptions of the enemy away from state-based dangers and align policy with the rhetoric of the precarious, disembodied enemy. It became the central means for rationalizing the end to occupation, and he flagged this shift in his inaugural address, observing that "our Nation is at war against a far-reaching network of violence and hatred."[114] But he stopped short of recommending policy to address that danger, instead opting for an extended internal review that set political goals (reducing troop deployments, cutting costs, and ending the conflict) against policy needs (a democratic Afghanistan, security from future attacks).[115] Over time, however, Obama extended the network metaphor to articulate the danger posed by those behind the perpetrators of 9/11, those brimming with terrorist motivations but remotely connected. This shift materialized as a new policy goal to "disrupt, dismantle, and defeat terrorist networks," a metaphor that made the case for a reconfiguration of war strategy from occupation to watch-and-strike.[116] Underwriting the watchman persona, Obama extended the essential premise of the disembodied enemy—a nomadic enemy felt, but not seen—while tapping into the recurrent symbolic economy that shapes the object of terrorism as a permanent, precarious feature of the twenty-first-century security landscape. Defining the danger as the network itself—the "aggregates of ties that individuals have"—rather than individuals, Obama's end-of-war rhetoric proposed a set of tactics to detect their activities, upend their designs, and reduce the enemy's ability to function as an organization.[117]

Initially echoing Bush, Obama claimed a troop surge in Afghanistan was necessary to prevent more attacks "by an Al Qaida network that killed thousands on American soil."[118] But, even while aspiring to defeat the Taliban and al-Qaeda in Afghanistan, he called for dismantling and destroying terrorist networks. These terms typified his rhetoric of the enemy and reflected a terminological choice to sketch the enemy in terms of its associations, as he did at the United Nations in September 2009 when he identified the enemy as "a network that has killed thousands of people of many faiths and nations."[119] While this rhetoric mirrored Bush's, it served a different purpose. For Bush, the term "global terrorist network" narrowed the focus to those organizations capable of launching attacks on the West. The term implicitly recognized that the United States could not stop every level of terrorism in the world and directed efforts toward al-Qaeda and its state sponsors. Obama's course correction broadened the military agenda away from costly interventions that drain national resources and energy from the true target—networks of terror. This shift extended the meaning of the metaphor by isolating the disembodied qualities of the enemy as the central and crucial enduring danger of the twenty-first century. For Obama, al-Qaeda and other terrorist organizations shared a common communicative methodology—the ways they linked transnationally to recruit, fundraise, plan, and orchestrate attacks across the globe. Those commonalities warranted shifts in strategy that would eventually fuse with his call for gradual disengagement and advance the need to remain vigilant against a disembodied but continuous threat.

While not abandoning the occupation of Iraq and Afghanistan, Obama's rhetoric clarified his administration's thinking about the enemy by isolating a policy that sought to disrupt terrorist networks, including the identification and destruction of individual nodes, as a means to reduce the ability of networks to commit mass acts of terror. Directly contravening Bush's persona of the lawman bringing justice to the frontier, Obama's address at West Point in December 2009 pointed to the futility of pacification and argued for additional homeland security measures since "we can't capture or kill every violent extremist abroad." His solution sought to "improve and better coordinate our intelligence so that we stay one step ahead of shadowy networks."[120] Highlighting the president's conviction that networks of terror could never be fully defeated, the address proposed a set of policies designed to quickly respond to the reconstitution of terror networks. As he put it, American strategy had to shift away from intervention and occupation and instead be "nimble and precise in our use of military power."[121] Echoing Rumsfeld, this rhetoric weighed both the danger posed by a disembodied, precarious enemy and the need to continuously watch for security threats across the globe. But, unlike Bush's depiction, Obama's portrayal of the enemy as a networked danger with conduits of communication conducting associational acts across space, time, ideology, and national origin became the principal engine for a shift in policy from occupation to mobile strike.[122]

Falling short of a true end-of-war discourse, Obama's emphasis on the mobility of a disembodied enemy and the incapacity of victory evolved into a theory of international politics that posited that this specific form of political violence would remain a permanent fixture of the twenty-first century. This theory entailed two components. First, unlike the security threats posed by the analog era, in which geographical borders restricted terrorist activities, facilitated tracking, and boosted efforts to counter or prevent acts of terror, figuring the terrorist as a digitally networked force introduced what Michael Hardt and Antonio Negri referred to as "a new regime of time."[123] This regime unbound the terrorist danger from temporal concerns and characterized terrorism as a continuous activity. To put it another way, the network never sleeps—ergo, the danger continues in perpetuity. Beyond depersonalization or deterritorialization, this component of the network metaphor suggested that Western governments had to match the continuous efforts of terrorists with constant vigilance, preparation, and military action. Eventually becoming a key aspect of the watchman persona, this demand for vigilance joined with the fears related to the networked anonymity of the enemy to warn of the grave harm terrorism would pose even after the conclusion of the wars in Iraq and Afghanistan.

Second, dissociating the figure of the enemy from bodies and reassociating it to connectivity itself made ending the War on Terror a practical impossibility. This act of redefinition articulated terrorism not as a feature of an organization or an ideology, but rather as the outcome of a specific set of communication and organizational practices. As the president explained at West Point in May 2010, "This is a different kind of war. There will be no simple moment of surrender to mark the journey's end, no armistice, no banner headline. Though we have had more success in eliminating Al Qaida leaders in recent months than in recent years, they will continue to recruit and plot and exploit our open society . . . pressure on networks like Al Qaida is forcing them to rely on terrorists with less time and space to train. We see the potential duration of this struggle in Al Qaida's gross distortions of Islam, their disrespect for human life, and their attempt to prey upon fear and hatred and prejudice."[124] Challenging national-security experts to recognize and plan for an enduring, generational struggle, Obama's remarks pointed to a set of practices that could never be stopped because they had become an endemic feature of a global communication architecture that defines the twenty-first century. On a par with how actors understood the Cold War, Obama's characterization of this struggle posited disorder and war as the norm for the twenty-first century—a norm that articulated the American mission as one of vigilance, engagement, and limited military action. Connecting to Obama's pledge to end the wars in Iraq and Afghanistan, the address justified shifting away from occupation and democratization in favor of more flexible and less costly options.

OSAMA BIN LADEN AND THE DISEMBODIED ENEMY

Even as Obama articulated the contours of the non-corporeal elements of the network metaphor to disentangle the nation from Iraq and Afghanistan, one terrorist body remained ever present in the national imaginary: Osama bin Laden. The symbolic figure of al-Qaeda, bin Laden escaped capture in 2001 and became a central point of criticism in the 2004 presidential campaign when John Kerry attacked Bush for letting the terrorist leader escape at Tora Bora.[125] As author, funder, and coordinator of terrorist attacks, many inside and outside government considered capturing bin Laden the linchpin to unraveling al-Qaeda's leadership and potential as a terrorist organization.[126] Beyond his importance to al-Qaeda, bin Laden held special significance as an embodied representation of terrorism. While Obama hardly ever described the enemy in corporeal terms, instead opting for the broad outlines of a cruel and savage character disconnected from any visual or textual representation, bin Laden's bearded visage sustained. That is, bin Laden functioned as a condensation symbol for terrorism, invested with a "host of different meanings and connotations" that coordinated the archetypal image of the terrorist and, to American audiences, connected the disembodied features of the terrorist with a tangibly verifiable image.[127] With such an elevated, symbolic significance, many considered the elimination of bin Laden as crucial to collapsing the entire terrorist network. This view reflected a certain type of network thinking, and premised the defeat of al-Qaeda on the prospect of eliminating key nodal points in the terrorist network.

Obama prioritized efforts to find and capture or kill the terrorist leader and, after a long intelligence operation, succeeded on May 2, 2011.[128] This event marked a crucial moment in the elaboration of a disembodied enemy and Obama's end-of-war discourse. Announcing the development in nationally televised remarks, Obama pointed to bin Laden as "Al Qaida's leader and symbol," and claimed his death "mark[ed] the most significant achievement to date in our Nation's effort to defeat Al Qaida." But he also warned, "His death does not mark the end of our effort. There's no doubt that Al Qaida will continue to pursue attacks against us. We must—and we will—remain vigilant at home and abroad."[129] The statement marked a point of departure in the fight against terrorism by emphasizing bin Laden's importance to 9/11 while stressing the continuity of the struggle. It also refigured the symbolic economy of terrorism by "designif[ying] bin Laden as the object of enmity," detaching bin Laden from the discourse of the enemy entirely, and displacing his visage with a corporeal absence.[130] Excising the most important condensation symbol binding visual and verbal representations of the enemy streamlined the discourse of the enemy behind the veil of a disembodied force, conveying the continuous nature of the danger and the need for watchfulness.

Beyond its symbolic efficiency, bin Laden's elimination altered the course of national-security policy by rearranging the content implied by the network metaphor. During the Bush years, the metaphor signaled a specific type of power—the power of individual agents to influence "other social actors in the network," what Castells called "networked power."[131] This version of the metaphor implied a hierarchy in which terrorists populated the network, but key leaders performed specific types of influence to ensure that the interconnected web of affiliations between individual nodes on the network performed its desired function—the orchestration of acts of political violence. The view of the terrorist network-as-hierarchy began to shift in Bush's second term, however, toward a theory of network power as distributed across individuals and digital and geographic space. In particular, McChrystal contended, "it takes a network to defeat a network," a realization that marked the beginning of a shift in military strategy away from attacking terrorist leaders and instead focusing on "dispersion, flexibility, and speed" of American efforts.[132] By prioritizing the hunt for bin Laden, however, Obama had maintained emphasis on the importance of powerful individuals capable of influencing those in the network as well as bridging differences among and between terrorist organizations. Pointing to the elimination of "high ranking Al Qaida and Taliban leaders" provided his war policy with tangible results but maintained the significance of individual terrorist leaders.[133] This aspect of the network-as-hierarchy metaphor undermined counterterrorism strategy by extending the notion that attacking the leadership could contain or disrupt the enemy.

The raid that killed bin Laden shifted the meaning of the metaphor to emphasize a more anonymous, disembodied form of network power—the power related to the "imposition of the rules of inclusion" in the network itself.[134] Since individual users—nodes—may come and go, but the digital infrastructure endures, post–bin Laden depictions emphasized the danger of interconnected milieus while discounting the significance of the individuals that constitute those milieus.[135] Obama pivoted toward this understanding in his address announcing the operation, contending that "the killing or capture of bin Laden" constituted one component of a comprehensive strategy "to disrupt, dismantle, and defeat his network."[136] Eliminating an important node in the network would not topple it. Instead, as he explained, bin Laden's demise disordered the network and impeded the enemy's ability to conduct operations. While Obama claimed later that killing bin Laden brought the nation "closer than ever to defeating Al Qaida and its murderous network," he stressed the perpetuity of the fight.[137] Echoed in subsequent addresses, Obama's version of the network metaphor recentered terrorist power within the network itself, rather than in the individual users or nodes. This movement energized figures of the disembodied savage by constituting the primary danger as connectivity above all else.

Once articulated as a networked danger, delinked from national territory or material space, and principally empowered by digital connectivity, representations of terrorism altered the way government understood the spatial relationships that defined the war in two ways. First, rather than identify specific bodies, the metaphor expressed individual terrorists as nodes in a global communication infrastructure. As a node in a network could literally be anybody, anywhere, this aspect of the metaphor deprived the individual terrorist of substantive content by positing the interconnections themselves as "constitutive of the nodes that they connect." Given the precarious nature of digital habitus, the metaphor inferred the likelihood that terrorists could appear and disappear, converse or lurk, circulate propaganda or other recruiting tools, and otherwise maintain a digital presence while disconnected from the material body.[138] In essence the metaphor accentuated the disembodied features of the enemy by explaining how affiliates use digital communication infrastructures to cloak their identities, to log in and communicate from virtually any location on the globe, and to manage geographic, cultural, and ethnic divergence.[139] This conceptual framework of terrorism, then, distributed the terrorists across the globe, making no distinction between the dusty terrain of Afghanistan and the bustling metropolis of Paris. Instead, it asserted an image of the terrorist as dissimilar in makeup, distributed across the globe, but tapped into a broader system of interconnections. Detaching the enemy from territory, this discourse rendered any attempt to map the enemy a visual convention rather than a cartographic sensibility.[140]

Second, in contrast to the rhetoric of the safe haven, which targeted specific geographic areas for military intervention, the network trope elevated the importance of digital space. Representing the terrorist-as-node signified the presence of a communicative architecture embedded with innumerable nodes, rendering any single node a transit point rather than a spatial location. Isolating the interconnections or links between groups tying together different organizations enabled by networked forms of communication, then, distanced Obama's rhetoric from individual nodes, rendering those bodies less significant in the struggle against terrorism than the interconnected web of associations.[141] The constancy of nodes coupled with the challenge of finding them all warranted a shift in policy to address the connections between nodes. That shift did not diminish the attention to individuals, however. If anything, the metaphoric reorientation escalated that attention, particularly in the form of drone strikes, by seeking "to detect potential threats through a focus on relationships" rather than individuals, and then respond to them. That is, in acknowledging an incapacity to counter lone wolves, Obama sought to disrupt the ability of those wolves to connect with others across the network.[142] In doing so, he sanctioned the watchman persona, an orientation to terrorism that made ending the War on Terror impossible.

TRANSNATIONAL NODES

AND THE IMPOSSIBILITY OF VICTORY

Obama's streamlined meaning of the terrorist-as-network facilitated his appeal to end combat operations in Iraq and Afghanistan, but raised the likelihood that the war against terrorism would continue indefinitely. Manifest in speeches given during the last four years of his presidency, the network metaphor amplified Obama's rendering of the disembodied, precarious enemy; deepened his theory of international relations; and explained the splintering of terrorist groups and the rise of new threats. His speech to the National Defense University on May 23, 2013, typified this discourse. In the address, Obama emphasized the continuing danger posed by terrorists. Presaging the discourse to come, he recognized "that the threat has shifted and evolved from the one that came to our shores on 9/11" and identified the terrorists as "lethal yet less capable Al Qaida affiliates, threats to diplomatic facilities and businesses abroad, homegrown extremists."[143] Displacing Afghanistan, the Taliban, and al-Qaeda from the frame, this rhetoric instead highlighted an implicit element of a networked foe—the ease with which associates or allies appear to fill power vacuums.

Further complicating the end-of-war context, Obama also appealed to scenic elements that he claimed reconfigured problems of international security and America's posture toward emerging threats. His meditations on the danger posed in Afghanistan reiterated the permanence of terrorism in international relations because, as he observed, no one "can promise the total defeat of terrorism."[144] Echoing Eisenhower's rhetorical transference from Korea to the confrontation with communism, Obama implied a broader field of conflict, diminishing the uniqueness of

Afghanistan and shifting the conflict from the domain of war to that of military action. The metaphor implied that strategies of violence would continue even as the theaters of operation shifted away from Afghanistan. Once again deploying the terrorist-as-network metaphor to justify a policy shift, Obama directed the military to "dismantle networks that pose a direct danger to us and make it less likely for new groups to gain a foothold."[145] This rhetoric extended the figure of a disembodied, networked enemy by emphasizing the importance of interconnections between individuals as the key source of danger. In doing so, it made the "boundless global war on terror" an inevitable condition of Obama's presidency and beyond because it posited "specific networks of violent extremists" as the source of American insecurity. He argued that the only way to counter this source of insecurity was to remain "vigilant for signs that these groups may pose a transnational threat" and to engage "a series of persistent, targeted efforts" to destabilize or destroy them.[146] Syncing with the rhetoric of the disembodied enemy, this discourse reoriented foreign policy away from occupation but toward perpetual forms of limited intervention.[147]

The pivot in the National Defense University address—from one terrorist network to the proliferation of diverse but potent multitudes of networks—echoed across Obama's presidency.[148] Several examples bear out the point. His speech to the United Nations General Assembly in September 2013, for example, articulated a view of the world as fragmented and chaotic, one in which the defeat of al-Qaeda in Afghanistan had spread terrorist violence across the globe. As he put it, "Al Qaida has splintered into regional networks and militias . . . [that] pose serious threats to governments and diplomats, businesses and civilians, all across the globe."[149] The message, pragmatic in the elaboration of imperfect but functional choices, reiterated his central thesis of terrorism: networked dangers could not be destroyed, they could only be monitored and reacted to. He added to this thesis at West Point on May 28, 2014, in a speech that precluded invasion and occupation as the appropriate policy. Arguing that the "world is changing with accelerating speed," Obama claimed 9/11 and its aftermath demonstrated "how technology and globalization has put power once reserved for states in the hands of individuals, raising the capacity for terrorists to do harm."[150] Occupation made no sense when faced with transnational and diffuse networks that overlap, can splinter and reconstitute, and resist defeat. Moreover, this phenomenon of diffusion and reconstitution appeared in Afghanistan, where, he claimed, the "principal threat no longer comes from a centralized Al Qaida leadership. Instead, it comes from decentralized Al Qaida affiliates and extremists . . . so we have to develop a strategy that matches this diffuse threat."[151] The same situation played out in Iraq, where Obama identified the challenge posed by a "fluid combination of hardened terrorist . . . where there's vacuums, they're filling it."[152] Obama's representational shift from stable, containable enemies to disembodied, precarious antagonists aligned presidential discourse with prevalent thinking about the enemy.[153] Confronting a disembodied enemy, delinked from the states they inhabit, unrestrained by geography, and sharing a common desire to attack the West required a strategy beyond occupation and democratization.

In sum, the network metaphor served Obama's purpose of articulating a way out of the wars in Iraq and Afghanistan by offering a new source of American insecurity as the target of American attention—the network itself. By identifying the network as the danger, Obama rationalized a policy premised on watching and striking the appearance of nodes on the network, even if those raids violated sovereign boundaries. Confronting a networked enemy required that he "hunt down terrorists and dismantle their networks," wherever they may be found. As with the bin Laden raid, Obama "reserve[d] the right to act unilaterally . . . to take out terrorists who pose a direct threat to us and our allies."[154] Toward that end, Obama declared the war in Iraq over on December 15, 2011, and ended the combat mission in Afghanistan on December 28, 2014.[155] Both declarations represented fine-grained distinctions between war and peace, generating significant public controversy about the continuing use of force after formally ending the wars.[156] And, rather than simplifying his foreign policy, Obama's end-of-war declarations reoriented the nation toward a normalized form of political violence.

The Disembodied Enemy, the President-as-Watchman,
and the Rise of a New Antagonist

Obama's movement from a specific antagonist—embodied in the form of Osama bin Laden—to an indeterminate, disembodied, and non-hierarchical coalition of adversaries underwrote the rise of a presidential persona oriented toward watching and responding to emergent threats. As previously discussed, the metaphoric economy of the terrorist-as-network inferred the need for a strategy based on recognizing and responding to the emergence of danger. By 2014, the watchman persona had passed from nascent political orientation to doctrine, traversing the boundaries of Afghanistan to compose the presidency and the foreign affairs bureaucracy as a regional, if not global sentinel on the lookout for the emergence of terrorism. In specific form, this orientation rationalized targeted air strikes in Syria, Iraq, Afghanistan, Yemen, and a handful of countries in North Africa as the logical response to the appearance of danger. But, as a doctrinal attitude, embodying the persona of the watchman delimited the conflict from the region to the world. After terrorist attacks in Paris and elsewhere, Obama claimed the world had to remain vigilant, everywhere, all the time. He pointed to vigilance as the only means able to "bring the perpetrators of this specific act to justice and to roll up the networks that help to advance these kinds of plots."[157] The rhetoric pointed to the ways the watchman persona entailed the president in immediate action—tracking the perpetrators in order to catch them—and long-term efforts to monitor and destroy the network of actors out to terrorize the West. It also contextualized American withdrawal from Afghanistan as enabling the real mission. As Obama explained in a news conference, "with the combat mission in Afghanistan over," the task turned to "defeat[ing] these terrorist networks" and for helping "Afghan forces to secure their own country and deny Al Qaida any safe haven there."[158] Implicitly shifting focus to a disembodied enemy linked in a broad network of contacts stretching from South Asia to North Africa, the rhetoric epitomized the movement from warfighter to sentinel. The war in Afghanistan had to end, in Obama's mind, not because of a need for reconciliation or negotiated settlement, but because combat operations detracted from the nation's ability to identify and respond to the precarious dangers of the era.

An outcome of a twenty-first-century paradox of insecurity—in which military successes against foreign antagonists increase rather than reduce insecurity—the watchman persona provided an a priori rationale for a more nuanced and focused application of violence in the pursuit of national goals. Similar to Eisenhower's depiction of the global nature of the Cold War, Obama-as-watchman figured the appearance of new terrorist networks and safe havens as imminent, and espoused the need to continuously prepare for danger at home and abroad. The persona enacted what Tom Engelhardt called a "deeper structure of argument and thought that is essential to Washington's vision of itself as a planet-straddling Goliath."[159] That "structure of argument" operationalized sites of training or support for terrorists—in countries like Yemen, Somalia, Libya, and Mali—as examples of the global possibilities available to terrorist networks. Rather than approach those locations as safe havens sponsored by anti-Western nations, as Bush had done, the Obama administration posited that terrorist networks exploited weak states to organize, plan, and orchestrate acts of violence. The State Department's annual threat assessment extended the logic, claiming "al-Qa'ida . . . continued to serve as a focal point of 'inspiration' for a worldwide network of affiliated groups."[160] The report listed sixty-one different terrorist organizations, the vast majority of which fell under the jurisdiction of the War on Terror. A 2016 report coauthored by the State Department and USAID warned that "from Afghanistan to Nigeria, terrorists seek to expand their reach and resonance by exploiting ongoing conflicts and insurgency, joining forces with criminal networks, establishing safe havens in weak and repressive states, and propagating hatred via social media." The enemy described in the report assumed the disembodied form typifying the Obama administration's end-of-war rhetoric. Excessively diverse to the point of defying classification, the report represented the enemy as "violent extremists speaking a variety of languages, born of many races and ethnic groups, and belonging to diverse religions

[who] continue to recruit, radicalize, and mobilize people—especially young people—to engage in terrorist acts."[161] This language distributed the savage across the globe and reasserted the watchman persona as the only remedy to a vague and unclassifiable enemy. It also mirrored that of the Bush era national-security document that had identified an "arc of instability" prior to 9/11 that could jeopardize American interests. In 2004, the unstable zone carried a panoramic sweep stretching from Africa to Southeast Asia. Ten years later, U.S. forces conducted operations in more than 150 countries.[162]

Derived from depictions of diffuse, disembodied antagonists spread across a massive geographic area, the watchman persona articulated a theory of intervention that justified the use of limited military incursions regardless of the location of the threat. This theory tasked the bureaucracy with locating physical spaces where terrorists could construct or solidify their networks. Referring to those spaces as weak countries, Obama contended,

> Terrorists typically are not going to be locating and maintaining bases and having broad networks inside of countries that have strong central governments, strong militaries, and strong law enforcement. By definition, we're going to be operating in places where oftentimes there's a vacuum or capabilities are somewhat low. And we've got to just continually apply patience, training, resources . . . it is a long, arduous process. It is not neat, and it is not simple, but it is the best option that we have. And what we have shown is that we can maintain the kind of pressure on these terrorist networks even in these kinds of difficult-to-operate environments.[163]

This discourse spatialized the domain of American surveillance and intervention by enacting what Janosch Prinz and Conrad Schetter termed "conditioned sovereignty."[164] That is, for Obama, the absence of governance justified surveillance and intervention against "localize[d] nonstate actors" who occupied "ungoverned spaces" that lie between or inside states. Conditioning claims of sovereignty on the basis of the state's capacity to govern, Obama isolated the absence of national authorities as a source of American insecurity. He claimed that states unwilling or unable to act against terrorist safe havens or networks ceded sovereign control over that space to forces capable of intervention. Mapping the discourse of conditioned sovereignty by isolating scenic elements that impede national authorities from containing terrorism, this rhetoric underwrote his decision to authorize the raid that killed bin Laden and became a centerpiece of the national mission to "root out terrorist networks" and deprive killers of a safe haven.[165] In essence, Obama warned that states incapable of preventing terrorists from camping out in their territory—as was the case with bin Laden in Pakistan—had no legal recourse to object to American intervention. Enmeshing policy in a relation between digital and analog space, this discourse reinforced the veracity of the watchman persona. The scope of the task required patience, over a long time period, but also continuous attention to the types of situations and remedies that could prevent the appearance of terrorist networks or safe havens.[166]

While the watchman persona reoriented governmental attitudes toward Afghanistan, its most direct and immediate impact appeared in Iraq. As Obama put it in a press conference in 2014, "this is an area that we've been watching . . . what we've seen over the last couple of days indicates the degree to which Iraq is going to need more help."[167] Presaging the rise of ISIL and his administration's focus on defeating the new enemy, this statement justified additional assistance to Iraq on the basis that Obama had watched and assessed the rise of a new danger.[168] He later clarified that those assessments included observing "foreign fighters and jihadists gathering in Syria and now in Iraq, who might potentially launch attacks outside the region against Western targets and U.S. targets."[169] These initial statements flourished into a more fully embodied discourse as ISIL became entrenched in Iraq and Syria, threatening to undermine the bulk of U.S. efforts in the region. They also signaled the way the watchman persona reordered the national bureaucracy after Afghanistan.

THE RISE OF ISIL AND THE INCARNATE WATCHMAN

While Obama-as-watchman reported on a number of potential dangers early in his second term, the rise of ISIL from the remnants of al-Qaeda in Iraq, and its expansion to cover territory in Syria, Iraq, and Libya drew the majority of the president's attention.[170] Obama publicly addressed the organization for the first time seven months after its appearance. Labeling it as the most important of the "al Qaida affiliated groups threatening Iraq," a joint statement by Obama and Iraqi prime minister Nuri al-Maliki set the stage for how to confront the organization. Designating the group as an al-Qaeda affiliate brought any potential policy decision under the umbrella of the AUMF, meaning that Obama would not need congressional approval to use military force. But the statement warned of the need to aggressively counter extremist networks of all varieties.[171] Again, identifying one network buttressed the notion that there were additional networks. By June 2014, policymakers worried that ISIL endangered the United States and its allies via direct attacks in the region or by copycat attacks in Western Europe and the U.S.[172] The president warned journalists that ISIL "could pose a threat eventually to American interests."[173] The specter of a potent, violent organization justified American military intervention, he contended, to compensate for the failure of Iraqi security forces. Stating that his policy would prevent ISIL from "gain[ing] a foothold inside of Iraq," Obama characterized the mission as emblematic of his counterterrorism endeavors, which were oriented at preventing terrorist organizations from "establish[ing a] safe haven" anywhere in the world.[174] But, reintervention risked undermining Obama's claim to have ended the war in Iraq, jeopardizing his legacy as well as inviting partisan sniping from both the right and the left.[175]

Upsetting Obama's thesis of the enemy as a disembodied force, spread across the globe, ISIL revealed cracks in the president's end-of-war discursive strategy. When he depicted the new antagonist in archetypal terms by claiming ISIL's ruthless campaign had revealed their barbaric character, citing mass executions and the enslavement of Yazidi women, the president gave valence to the agents of terror as a prototypical savage force.[176] This risked undermining the essence of the disembodied enemy because it gave texture to the figure of a specific enemy, rooted in a specific place, seeking to take and hold specific territory. These initial depictions, however, gave way to more generalized figures of the enemy that, once again, emerged from the network metaphor. ISIL "is terrorizing the people of Syria and Iraq and engaging in unspeakable cruelty," Obama explained at a White House Summit on Extremism in 2015, but the danger existed across the world. As he put it, "ISIL-linked terrorists murdered Egyptians in the Sinai Peninsula, and . . . in Libya . . . [and] Beyond the region, we've seen deadly attacks in Ottawa, Sydney, Paris, and now Copenhagen."[177] Even while pointing to the barbarity of the acts, the rhetoric disembodied the enemy by implying the organization behind these attacks shared a central fundamental power—the network. Thus, in spite of its new appellation, Obama's rhetoric defined ISIL as al-Qaeda re-networked, a hidden enemy visible anew, but maintained by digital interconnectivity that traverses time and space.

While public accounts of ISIL iterated the organization as structured, bureaucratic, and governing a specific territory, Obama figured the terrorist organization as a particularly large splinter group, sustained by internetworked communication infrastructures. This splintered force, rather than having a specific organizational structure—a hierarchy—was composed of a "network of killers who are brutalizing local populations."[178] Specifically pushing back against inferences that ISIL looked like a state-based enemy, bound to specific territory, Obama argued, "This is not conventional warfare. We play into the ISIL narrative when we act as if they're a state and we use routine military tactics that are designed to fight a state . . . That's not what's going on here."[179] These comments reframed Obama's definition of the enemy as emblematic of the disembodied savage. Contrary to the organizational structure implied by its name, ISIL demonstrated how networked forces could appear in disorganized national space and conduct acts of great violence. ISIL itself, the president contended, "grew stronger amidst the chaos of war in Iraq and then Syria," facilitated by internetworked communication that "erases the distance between countries."[180] Thus, rather than depicting ISIL as a hierarchical governing body, intent on administering territory in Iraq and Syria, Obama concluded they were just another networked force, exploiting ungoverned spaces for political ends.

Administration officials extended the network splintering thesis to enlace the conflict with ISIL in a broader frame about the international danger posed by disembodied enemies. Susan Rice contended in the 2015 National Security Strategy that "the enemy has evolved" because they have been decimated by U.S. efforts. The irony of success, then, is "the diffusion of the threat—to al-Qa'ida affiliates, ISIL, local militias, and home-grown violent extremists."[181] The finding of the splintering of terrorist networks, she argued, meant the nation needed better strategic and tactical decision-making, primarily in the form of targeted drone strikes. General Sean MacFarland explained allied efforts as succeeding at "put[ting] pressure on the enemy's terror networks."[182] Secretary of Defense Ash Carter, even when using cancer metaphors to describe ISIL, reiterated the danger as "ISIL's network of foreign fighters—networks we are determined to destroy."[183] He issued a statement justifying an increase in U.S. forces, claiming the extra capabilities would "help disrupt ISIL's terrorist networks in Iraq and beyond."[184] Secretary of State John Kerry pledged the "United States will continue to work closely . . . with partners on every single continent in order to defeat vicious terrorist networks, particularly those of Daesh and al-Qaida."[185] Each of these statements identified ISIL's network as one of many enduring security challenges. Those challenges manifested with the specific problem in Iraq and Syria as well as the terrorist and criminal networks that continued to endanger Afghanistan.[186]

Obama's depiction of ISIL galvanized the watchman persona by defining the threat as global, delinked from national territory or affiliation, and embedded in digital networks and ungoverned spaces. Pointing to deadly attacks in North Africa and the Middle East, he warned of "a growing ISIL presence in Libya and attempts to establish footholds across North Africa, the Middle East, the Caucasus, and Southeast Asia," in addition to attacks in Ottawa, Sydney, France, and Copenhagen.[187] At the United Nations in September 2015, he claimed "ISIL's tentacles reach into other regions."[188] Later he worried that "ISIL has been able to dig in" to zones of low or no governance and "have shown themselves to be resilient, and they are very effective through social media and have been able to attract adherents not just from the areas in which they operate, but in many of our own countries."[189] This rhetoric spoke to the organization's reach—stretching across most of the world—but also to its structure. ISIL was an internetworked, caustic ideological force intent on acts of violence; thus, anti-terrorist strategy had to address the transience of mobile networks. Capitalizing on the implicit connection to the rhetoric of sanctuary, this view reiterated the specialized discourse of ungovernable zones populated with terrorist safe havens to justify a policy of monitoring and response. But, given the despacialization of digital connectivity, the watchman policy had to extend beyond the Middle East, beyond ungoverned territory, in order to "disrupt terrorist networks and thwart attacks, and to smother nascent ISIL cells that may be trying to develop in other parts of the world."[190] Rather than articulate ISIL as a specific regional threat tied to a specific territory, and with a known identity and hierarchy, this rhetoric posed the problem in terms of a disembodied enemy, embedded in covert, clandestine networks. Obama's declaration that "we will degrade and ultimately destroy this barbaric terrorist organization" makes sense in this context.[191] Given the nature of the disembodied enemy, only disrupting the network could contain the danger.

While the watchman persona prescribed a general orientation for the national-security bureaucracy, it also yielded a specific policy outcome: a permanent U.S. military presence in Afghanistan. Seemingly at odds with the idea of going after a highly mobile terrorist network, the base in Afghanistan served as a strategic platform from which the military could observe and attack. As Obama reasoned when he announced his decision to retain 15,000 troops on October 15, 2015, "we've always known that we had to maintain a counterterrorism operation in that region in order to tamp down any reemergence of active Al Qaida networks or other networks that might do us harm."[192] Characterizing the base as an outpost designed to respond to terrorist networks, Obama rooted the policy decision in his thesis of the enemy. The United States needed a base for monitoring and responding to always existing secretive agents lurking in analog and digital spaces. This rhetoric rationalized a permanent presence in Afghanistan, as well as other theaters of operation, while diminishing the uniqueness of ISIL as a terrorist force. That is, in Obama's terms, ISIL proved the truth of his theory of the enemy. The enduring security challenge of the twenty-first century demanded a postwar strategy of surveillance and response—a manifestation of the watchman persona—due to the permanent presence of a disembodied enemy, cloaked in digital space and existing beyond the war-space that defined the struggle against ISIL. In this context, permanent bases served as outposts from which military forces could watch and strike emergent dangers.

A final aspect of the watchman persona posited that even defeating ISIL entirely wouldn't remedy the threat since the genesis of the danger sprang from the network itself. The watchman persona, then, reflected a permanent reorientation of government policy to address future dangers. Obama spoke to this at a press conference in November 2015, explaining "once this network is destroyed—and it will be—there may be others that pop up in different parts of the world, and so we're going to have to continue to take seriously how we maintain the infrastructure that we've built to prevent this."[193] When faced with an invincible condition—the eternal disembodied enemy—the persona of the president-as-watchman appeared the only reasonable response. Even after the best efforts to dismantle their networks or otherwise impede their operations, "they still pose a threat . . . because they still operate in areas between Pakistan and Afghanistan, or more prominently right now, in Yemen, that are hard to reach."[194] Evoking the central truth of his theory of the enemy, Obama's statement pointed to continuity of the danger and the necessity of unceasing American efforts to contain it. It also revealed the ultimate pivot—the war could never be won. No policy could stop every extremist from killing people. The network—digital and physical—represented a crucial, permanent terrain for policies to restrict terrorist funding, undermine terrorist organizations, and disrupt their attempts at communication, propaganda, and recruitment. This conception oriented the national-security bureaucracy toward "unbounded global surveillance designed to trace networks whatever their geo-spatial location," instantiating the persona of the watchman across government agencies tasked with conducting activities to fight terror.[195]

FROM WATCHMAN TO WHAC-A-MOLE

Articulating the U.S. mission as that of watchman—duty bound to monitor and respond to the emergence of terror threats—may have saved the nation from catastrophic military adventurism, but it provided no solution to political violence. Instead, embodying the persona primed the bureaucracy to launch targeted strikes as the response to a mobile, agile, and disembodied danger. Shifting national violence from the ground to the air, this strategy made the use of targeted strikes a central feature of the nation's national-security strategy, risking what some critics called "permanent war."[196] Even as Obama dodged many of the legal and ethical questions related to drone strikes, he argued that counterterrorism was a more effective and less costly approach to insecurity.[197] He made the case in his commencement address at West Point in 2014, where he argued that "a strategy that involves invading every country that harbors terrorist networks is naïve and unsustainable." This argument hinged upon two factors. First, Obama presented his policy options in a strict binary—either he could authorize invasion, or he could employ a counterterrorism policy of limited engagement. Binary arguments, by nature, define situations in terms of two possibilities while excluding alternatives. For Obama, a policy of drone strikes was the inevitable outcome of insecurity. Warning that "just because we have the best hammer does not mean that every problem is a nail," the president's binary choice made counterterrorism—drone strikes—seem like the more reasonable option. Second, the justification for this binary choice stemmed entirely from representations of the disembodied enemy. Decentralized terrorists networks and the extremists they recruit, he explained, retain "power once reserved for states . . . raising the capacity of terrorists to do harm."[198] Fragmented, decentralized networks of individuals who transited across governed and ungoverned territory required rapid, mobile responses. Drone strikes provided that. Invasion did not.

Over the final years of his presidency, this argument resolved into the metaphor of the Whac-A-Mole. For Obama, the metaphor represented the terrorist as the mole and military invasion as the whac. Deploying the metaphor to warn against perpetual war, he contended that invasion and occupation couldn't stop terrorism because disembodied antagonists have no connection to territory, readily move away from military forces, and are deeply rooted in digital spaces. Invasion only risked bogging the nation down in cycles of occupation and insurgency, raising human and financial costs while undermining the military's ability to find and confront the agents of insecurity. Commenting on the rise of terrorism in Yemen, for example, he stated that "our efforts to go after terrorist networks inside of Yemen" rely on cooperating with allies rather than deploying ground troops, because "the alternative would be for us to play Whac-A-Mole every time there is a terrorist actor inside of any given country, to deploy U.S. troops. And that's not a sustainable strategy."[199] He repeated this refrain when justifying lethal air operations against ISIL, claiming ground operations would stretch the United States thin because "we'll be playing Whac-A-Mole, and there will be a whole lot of unintended consequences that ultimately make us less secure."[200] Within the penumbra of the network metaphor, combating terrorism required a mobile strategy, focused on digital and analog spaces that provide enemies the safe havens they need to organize. Invasion and occupation could never contain terrorist danger.

Yet, as a vehicle to convey the inefficacy of ground troops, Obama's Whac-A-Mole metaphor never made sense. While referring to the terrorist as the never destroyed but often whacked "mole" may have served as a useful vehicle for describing the way terrorists continue to pop up around the world, and for conveying the gravitational pull that observing danger places upon the presidential bureaucracy, invasion and occupation involve much greater commitments than mere "whacks." Rather, counterterrorism itself, in which a watchful military whacks terrorists with drone strikes but never arrests the cause of terrorism, more accurately fit the metaphoric logic. Even while using the metaphor to resist ground deployments, then, Obama authorized a policy that mirrored the metaphor's entailments. His claims about U.S. air strikes on ISIL bear out the point. After noting that air strikes had caused ISIL to shift tactics to increase attacks on the West, he argued the air campaign was "destroying ISIL's networks" and blocking Syria from "maintain[ing] a safe haven to train and plot attacks against us." Referencing economic, territorial, and intelligence strategies, he warned that ISIL's "twisted ideology" will motivate new groups and heighten the "risk in getting sucked into the kind of global Whac-A-Mole where we're always reacting to the latest threat or lone actor."[201] Indeed, Obama's warning had already come to fruition. As he put it in February 2016, "Every day, our air campaign—more than 10,000 strikes so far—continues to destroy ISIL forces, infrastructure, and heavy weapons. ISIL fighters are learning that they've got no safe haven. We can hit them anywhere, anytime, and we do."[202] As an embodiment of the watchman persona, Obama's discourse on air strikes positioned the United States as a global force, ever present and ready to use force without hesitation. This rhetoric mirrored depictions of the enemy itself and signaled the completion of the strategic shift posited the previous December. When faced with highly mobile, secretive terrorist organizations capable of global reach, the nation's response required a highly intrusive, mobile military strategy with instantaneous, global potential to whack at danger wherever it might appear. And, with military success came a need for renewed vigilance "in our homeland" and in places like Europe.[203] In a refrain that reappeared in Obama's discourse for the rest of his term, this rhetoric reiterated understandings of terrorist networks as horizontally distributed, virtually leaderless, and ever mobile.[204] Near instantaneous kinetic lethality was the only apt response when faced with such dangers.

Finally, Obama's embrace of the watchman persona made the Whac-A-Mole a permanent feature of his presidency and beyond because it offered a politically salient alternative to occupation. Once he articulated terrorism as an enduring challenge, one that would last beyond ISIL or al-Qaeda because, as Obama put it, the "networks will probably sustain themselves," he had little choice but to expand the drone strike program.[205] And, indeed, his administration accelerated the drone program because it "saw the unmanned, robotic aircraft as an ideal way of killing enemies in remote parts of the world."[206] Authorizing more than ten times the number of strikes as Bush, the policy showed no signs of abating, in spite of significant criticism.[207] Given the embedded watchman persona, the risks of terrorists setting up shop in weak states, and the downside of direct military invasion, the drone policy fulfilled the twin desires of permanent vigilance and rapid response without significant commitments of personnel or the exposure to danger those commitments involve. For a president who had pledged to end America's involvement in the wars in Iraq and Afghanistan, it also represented a means for him to come close to keeping that promise.

War Ever After and the Rhetorical Legacy of a Disembodied Savage

Rhetoric constructs the world, but it doesn't invent it. Obama, one of the finest orators of his generation with a deep reservoir of rhetorical possibilities, couldn't wield discursive magic to escape the violence of terrorism because some things transcend even the power of the president. Faced with the prospect of a war that cannot be won, huge numbers of ground troops deployed in two theaters of war, massive blowback from the citizens of Iraq and Afghanistan, and a domestic context in which everything he said and did invoked virulently racist opposition, Obama failed to orchestrate the full withdrawal, instead drawing down troop deployments from 180,000 to 8,400 at the end of his presidency.[208] And, in spite of his claim that "this war, like all wars, must end," he left office with an extensive military presence in Syria, Iraq, and Afghanistan.[209] Instead of exit, Obama's rhetoric blurred the features of the enemy, isolated their disembodied enablers—the safe haven and the network—and elevated a figure of a precarious enemy. By figuring the United States as global sentinel, searching for a disembodied enemy, and armed and willing to act, Obama oriented the nation toward continuing the national violence at the same time he yearned for it to end. Marking a cruel optimism that would flourish in the latter half of his second term, his conviction that he would end national violence, then, registered an attachment to victory that sustained the war effort in Afghanistan and beyond while distancing the nation from a peaceful conclusion.[210]

His end-of-war rhetoric, moreover, signaled a comprehensive shift in how the nation imagined and addressed its enemies. Taking the form of the watchman persona—a representation that accentuates the movement from occupation to rapid, violent response to emergent dangers—this reconfiguration of the U.S. military mission envisioned war as an activity primarily pitting sovereign states against non-sovereign agents. Implying that states at war no longer seek to conquer and annex territory and instead act against disembodied constructs, this shift served the logic of exception and emergency that provides the basic rationale for modern sovereign power.[211] But, unlike the period immediately after 9/11, in which a national crisis warranted an exceptional response, the watchman routinized exceptional forms of violence as a normal feature of statecraft in the post-9/11 era. Reflecting a post-biopolitical apparatus Achilles Mbembe called "necropolitics," this new regime of military power sought to manage the precarity of danger in the twenty-first century by applying regimes of governance normally associated with death into spaces ungovernable in life. Circulating across the national-security bureaucracy, this necropolitical logic of the enemy produced a trajectory for postwar policy premised on the global mobility of military operations.[212] Whacking the mole never felt so good and useless at the same time.

While the potential for global military operations to worsen on-the-ground situations across much of the Muslim world has generated ethical and practical challenges, advancing limited military engagement as a core component of U.S. foreign policy represents continuity, rather than interruption. By one estimate, "between 1800 and 1934, U.S. Marines staged 180 landings abroad" as part of the nation's commitment to employing force to achieve national goals, a tradition revived after the

Cold War with interventions in Somalia, Haiti, Bosnia, and Kosovo.[213] By returning foreign policy to its tradition of managing international problems with diplomacy and limited military actions, Obama marked Bush's policy of democratization-by-force an anomaly. This shift undermined the credibility of those in government committed to regime change—the so-called neoconservatives—and brought the presidency into agreement with the national-security bureaucracy about how best to confront the danger posed by terrorism. The result is a legacy of violence, but with less exposure to American troops. Relying primarily on airpower dramatically reduced the number of U.S. casualties—a 60 percent decline by one estimate—with the numbers dropping even lower during the American air campaign against ISIL.[214] This shift failed to satisfy partisans on both the right and the left, however, instead inviting condemnation, with some attacking its efficacy and others claiming Obama bombed children.[215] Even so, the number of foreign casualties inflicted by Obama's drone war is measured in the hundreds or thousands, a remarkable reduction in war deaths compared to the Bush years.[216]

While it is tempting to evaluate this policy shift favorably, especially in contrast to the wreckage wrought by the Bush administration, comparative-advantage thinking produces three specific problems. First, it conceals the error replication consistent across the War on Terror. Both presidents defined terrorism in disembodied terms. Those definitions represented the enemy as a corporeal absence—an identity—undermining any and all attempts to negotiate or reincorporate the body into the international body politics. Efforts to reincorporate transnational enemies who hold no claim to sovereign power may be impossible given the nation's disinterest in recognizing such claims, but it's certainly impossible when transnational bodies cannot even be identified. The logic of the disembodied enemy, then, centralized the answer to terrorism in an institutional arrangement reliant on military might. While Obama's shift from states to non-state actors may have produced smaller echoes of violence, it still failed to apprehend the diffuse and ephemeral nature of the power wielded by the enemy. In fact, much like Nixon during Vietnamization, Obama's shift from ground deployments to air power sought to close the war by expanding it. While Obama's shift orchestrated a policy of violence short of war but far from peaceful, the central truth, as he claimed on several occasions, is that networks of terror cannot be defeated with the application of military power—either overwhelming force or targeted strikes.

Second, the rhetorical restructuring of the enemy facilitated the emergence of a necropolitical logic of statecraft by defining the enemy of the twenty-first century as the product of intranational conflict, a lack of governance, and the rise of despatialized digital networks. This discursive realignment penetrated the national-security bureaucracy to prioritize a counterterrorism strategy focused on rapid response and minimal deployments. Once organized as such, bureaucratic inertia and agency commitment to better identify and destroy potential terrorists prior to their acts of terrorism became the norm.[217] With permanent outposts established in Iraq, Afghanistan, and countless countries across North Africa, the military's reach has expanded to the point that it can watch and confront the precarious enemy anywhere in the world, in real time. The elasticity of the definition of the disembodied enemy increased the likelihood that the nation will amplify efforts to confront all dangers that appear to be terrorism with kinetic lethality.

Finally, the comparative advantage between Obama and Bush depends on subsequent presidents acting like Obama—with limited application of force, justified under specific protocols. Even the most ardent defenders of Obama acknowledged the potential for future presidents to display less restraint in America's drone wars. And, indeed, Donald Trump's ascension to the presidency has borne out this warning. Given that metaphoric trajectories sustain across presidential administrations, as well as Trump's disinclination to arrest or restrain national policy toward terrorism, and his affinity to invoke archetypal representations of the terrorist as evil, barbaric, and uncivilized, the Trump administration reveals the danger of empowering articulations of the enemy as disembodied, precarious, and constantly searching for ways to hurt the West.[218] Mostly adopting Obama's frames, Trump has employed the rhetoric of the safe haven and the network metaphor to reinvigorate depictions of

ISIL and to justify ignoring the ethical and procedural limits enacted by the Obama administration.[219] While Trump's use of these metaphors appears haphazard, speed bumps of the superhighway of a more generalized rhetoric of insecurity spoken by a man disinterested in details, they underline the continuity in how the presidency itself is oriented toward twenty-first-century insecurity. In fact, soon after assuming office, he delegated "authority to field commanders" while maintaining Obama's commitment to partnership, air strikes, and training and arming.[220] The continuity of counterterrorism strategy across administrations of polar ideological opposites points to bipartisan and universal conceptions of the enemy and the attendant necropolitical strategies of managing violence in the twenty-first century. The deep penetration of this discourse across the national-security bureaucracy makes it difficult to see an alternative to a necropolitical foreign policy, no matter who holds the office of the presidency.

CHAPTER 5

The Eternal Savage

WAR, THE GLOBALIZATION OF VIOLENCE, AND THE SOVEREIGN POWER OF THE PRESENT

——— •◆• ———

For much of the nation's history, the country has believed it holds an exceptional place in world affairs. From the Monroe Doctrine to what C. Vann Woodward called "the era of free security," nineteenth-century Americans assumed the moral superiority of the United States established a unique and powerful role for the nation in world affairs.[1] By the 1890s, national power caught up with those convictions. The Spanish-American War inaugurated the nation into an epoch of invincibility by reinvigorating belief in the nation's indomitable character as a marker of its right to lead. Advocates evoked American belief in its own excellence, above and beyond all other nations, in racial terms. As Theodore Roosevelt put it in the lead-up to the war, "all the great masterful races have been fighting races." Taking on the Spaniards would enable America to take her place as "equal of the best."[2] Beating one of the great European powers—even one in decline—signaled the nation's rise as an international power, a force to be reckoned with, surprising the

British and giving rise to a number of war heroes, one of whom would go on to become president of the United States.[3] Without prescribing the nature of leadership, the Spanish-American War produced a protean narrative, what Evan Thomas termed "a foundation stone of American exceptionalism," establishing the ethos of America as "better—somehow more decent—than that of other nations."[4] Potent enough to gloss over the extended insurgency in the Philippines, the narrative justified a range of often conflicting policy initiatives including American intervention in World War I, the genesis and rejection of the League of Nations, Franklin Roosevelt's push to involve the country in World War II, the construction of the postwar security architecture—including the United Nations, NATO, and the Bretton Woods economic structure—U.S. military efforts in Korea, and finally, the gradual escalation in Vietnam.

The stalemate in Korea marked the beginning of the end of the epoch of invincibility, raising the prospect that American power had finite limits. Eisenhower's rhetorical restructuring of the war—shifting the focus from North Korea to the Soviets—finessed understandings of the war, relegated the region to a single part of the great power game between East and West, and attributed the failure of American policy to an external enemy. Rather than apprehend limits to American power after Korea, though, Eisenhower's rhetorical transference of savagery doubled down on the prospect that American leadership could reconstitute the world as it saw fit. What Korea started, Vietnam finished. The idea of unparalleled, invincible American power crashed down as a small nation bought its colonial freedom with an unwavering commitment to guerrilla tactics. With defeat undeniable, Nixon's resignation, and the national desire to move on, the end of the Vietnam War moved American power into a new epoch, one marked by limited military engagements to achieve minimal gains. Chastened, American leaders resisted the urge to promote democracy by force or otherwise engage in deploying U.S. military troops in arenas of national struggle, opting instead for indirect measures.[5] The end of the Cold War ostensibly represented a break in that cycle. From Francis Fukuyama's claim about the end of history to George H. W. Bush's decision to evict Iraq from Kuwait in the first Gulf

War, faith in the unparalleled capabilities of U.S. military power began to return.[6] Even the hiccups in Somalia and the Balkans couldn't disrupt Bill Clinton's search for a vocabulary that could characterize the nation's mission in the post–Cold War era or obsession with defining America's next grand strategy.[7] Instead, the nation's foreign-policy elite sensed a moment of transition from great-power rivalry to unipolar hegemonic leadership—an opportunity, as some had it, to finally remake the world in America's image.[8]

But, as Chris Hayes has written, "The wolf is always at the door. It just changes its clothing."[9] September 11, 2001, brought that wolf into the open and marked the beginning of a third epoch in which security goals would be pursued with military intervention, occupation, democracy promotion by force, and quagmire. This time called a War on Terror, American foreign policy once again confronted the prospect of failure. The Bush administration, seeking to navigate a deteriorating situation, returned to the Civil War–era claim that only internal division and strife could stop American military power—a claim that formed a key component of the so-called troop surge in 2007. But, like Truman, Eisenhower, Johnson, and Nixon, escalation failed to win the war, leaving that challenge to Obama. Grappling with a new, twenty-first-century version of the epoch of invincibility, Obama identified limits to American power even as he proved incapable of orchestrating a complete exit from Iraq and Afghanistan. Identifying those limits, however, did not arrest what some have called the militarization of American foreign policy.[10] In fact, reliance on military strategies to address international issues appears to be in favor, leaving many to wonder if we are witnessing the gradual decline of American diplomatic power and the aftermath of how a culture that believes in its own invincibility confronts its limitations.

This backdrop structures the problem of executive power, an increasingly violent foreign policy, and the idea of perpetual war. While the content of the rhetorical endeavors of the twenty-first century resemble those used across the nation's history, many view the War on Terror as a blanket endorsement that enables political leaders to continue to pursue the culprits of 9/11, potentially forever.[11] Terming this outcome "endless war," scholars have warned of both the perpetuation of war that appears to "have no temporal limits," and the inability of state violence to achieve the types of lasting material gains that could result in an end to hostilities.[12] The cultural implications of this near permanent condition, some warn, normalizes war and "promotes passivity at home while perpetuating destruction abroad."[13] Fearing that post-9/11 rhetorical vectors involve quiescent tropes that minimize citizen engagement in war, both as a deliberative event at home and in direct participation abroad, scholars warn that speed, technology, and distance from war have stifled the effects of war on the body and, as a result, "shield war from critique and interruption."[14] Joining those in political science, law, and history who have warned of the possibility, if not probability, of war becoming a permanent condition, communication scholars have identified a consistency of presidential discourse across the Bush and Obama presidencies that reiterates resonant fear and rage lingering in the afterimage of 9/11 to abbreviate deliberation down to who to strike next.[15] The conversation about the hazards incurred by a runaway executive, empowered with time-honored rhetorical appeals, has raised the possibility that the nation's conception of international politics leaves the world "on a perpetual brink of peace. Or war."[16]

The rhetorical legacy articulated in this book complicates concerns about the perpetual expansion of presidential military power and an increasingly violent American foreign policy. The War on Terror—the principal focus of national violence—does not invoke a stable figure of the enemy. In abeyance to the tradition of enemy-making, the shift from embodied to disembodied representations of danger marked a movement in how the nation imagines and addresses security threats. Unmooring foreign-policy discourse from stable representations of the enemy, Obama's rhetoric provided a "generalized or free-floating drive of control and domination" as motive for continual action.[17] While not exclusive to the War on Terror, this destructuring of the enemy envisioned a contest pitting sovereign states against non-sovereign agents—insurgents, terrorists, and criminal organizations. Displacing a stable figure of the enemy with the need for global security or the preservation of "global social and economic order" as ends to be achieved by policy, Obama's discourse converted this war from a specific, bounded struggle into a form of continuous violent action because, as Michael Hardt and Antonio Negri put it, "one cannot win such a war, or, rather, it has to be won again every day."[18]

Additionally, the War on Terror does not articulate its goals in terms of victory over an enemy fighting force. Obama abandoned that goal in 2010 when he made clear that the security challenge would continue for a generation or longer. In the place of victory, the goal has become stability—routine acts of lethal forms of violence its method. This shift in goals has also shifted the presidential subject from commander in chief to the watchman—a representation that accentuates the movement from occupation to rapid, violent response to emergent dangers. Implying that states no longer seek to conquer and annex territory and instead act against disembodied constructs, this shift serves the logic of exception and emergency and provides the basic rationale for modern sovereign power—the power to "dictate who may live and who must die."[19] It also provides an archive of rationales for presidents seeking to justify military action since, as David Chandler put it, "interventions can be rewritten as morally and strategically well designed, merely coming unstuck on their overestimation of the capacity of the target populations."[20] While this approach may backfire by exposing the liberal order's incapacity to create possibilities for economic opportunity, political freedom, and conflict resolution, routine forms of violence now hold a defined place in American foreign policy.

Those concerned with the perpetual aspects of war have resisted the idea that wars are bounded spaces that have discrete beginnings and endings. Instead, advocates emphasize the quotidian violence of foreign-policy-making and the essential similarity between the policies of peace and war. This strategy proposes extending the vernacular of war to the "constant military presence" and "horrific, state-sponsored violence [that] is happening nearly all over, all the time, and . . . is perpetuated by military institutions and other militaristic agents of the state." Doing so, advocates contend, would isolate the "omnipresence of militarism" and undermine the "false belief that the absence of declared armed conflicts *is* peace, the polar opposite of war."[21] These efforts seek to make the term "war" irrelevant, a demarcation with no essential meaning, and reimagine resistance to national violence outside the confines of a temporal imagination. Concerned about the cyclical nature of antiwar protests that respond to specific moments, this approach worries that seeing war as an event authorizes political action in response to specific instances of violence while ignoring ongoing, everyday violence. Antiwar protests, then, *enable* militarism because they register opposition to a specific abrogation of order and tranquility while permitting everyday forms of structural violence to continue.[22] The failure to apprehend the daily devastating effects of militarism, according to this thesis, instills complacency, and "undermines democratic vigilance" by ceding agency to the event, rather than identifying specific actions taken by national leaders to make such events possible. The starting point for this strategy recognizes war as a perpetual and routine policy orchestrated by national leaders.[23] Constitutive of a more engaged and politically activated public, this approach to state-based violence implies the necessity and capacity of civic action in restraining presidential war-making.

Unfortunately, the movement to reframe war as process rather than event, encapsulated in the phrase "perpetual war," inadequately addresses both what is happening and the politics surrounding those things. At its root, the term "war" refers to a distinct legal category that invokes specific deliberative procedures. Wars are fought against states; they are formally or informally declared; and they require congressional authorization.[24] One only has to witness discussions about the security dangers posed by North Korea, Iran, and Russia; congressional comments about the president's ability to act against those nations; and the far-flung concern that the president could Tweet the nation into war. Advocates from the president to the national-security staff to the press all speak the language of war—a language that extends archetypal figures of the enemy to assess motive, represents the international situation with a vernacular of security, and discusses the legal hurdles the president has to overcome to sanction hostilities. While the specifics related to the actors, scenes, and technology have altered, public discussion of state-based dangers have reproduced this class of security discourse, in an almost unaltered form. Critics of war discourse simply cannot abandon categorical notions of war because of the perpetuity of state violence in the Middle East, South Asia, and North Africa. To do so would be to miss the opportunity to continuously level criticism at presidents who extend the savage idiom as a constitutive resource when articulating international problems and policies.

Additionally, the militarization of American foreign policy operates at a different register. Its targets are, for the most part, non-state actors—individuals and organizations designated by the State Department as "terrorists"—that the national-security bureaucracy deems a problem with no viable solution other than lethal force. Targeting individuals, rather than states, invokes and applies the laws of war in ways that run counter to the tradition of state conflict, leading critics to worry about the implications this new legal regime has for combatants, noncombatants, property, and prisoners.[25] That does not mean the violence should receive less scrutiny or incur fewer legal protections. To the contrary, recognizing that two distinct processes are afoot heightens the need for extended engagement and scrutiny of American foreign policy by public actors empowered to criticize the consolidation of foreign-policy-making in the domain of the security bureaucracy. But, the form of violence conducted in the so-called drone wars is distinct from war and merits its own vernacular.

Beyond categorical aspects, the perpetual war thesis also adopts a historical amnesia by assuming the current phase of state-sanctioned violence is a new feature of American foreign policy when, in fact, it is the norm. Beginning with the violent occupation of Indian lands, a continuously bloody foreign policy spanning over one hundred years, the United States has used various forms of military force to pursue policy goals.[26] The twentieth century began with the occupation of Hawaii, Puerto Rico, and the Philippines, marking the continuity of policies of systemic violence after the close of the frontier. In Latin America alone, the United States suppressed insurgency in Cuba, orchestrated the creation of Panama, and sponsored coups in Nicaragua, Honduras, Chile, and Guatemala. Presidents also sponsored or supported military coups in Iran and Indonesia, intervened in Vietnam, and have supplied millions of military materiel to Afghanistan and Iraq, among other nations. These policies do not reflect perpetual war, even while they have incurred significant human casualties. For example, 4,200 Americans and over 20,000 Filipinos perished during the three-year occupation of the Philippines from 1899 to 1902, yet no one would call it a war. These interventions, instead, have been cloaked in a "rhetoric of intervention" in which presidents conceal national motivations, deny direct involvement, or defend the country's pure motives to mask base motivations for military action.[27] It is important to recognize not only that violence has typified American statecraft, but that political leaders have articulated that violence as anything but war. Responding to such a rhetoric requires a vernacular more precise than that offered by antiwar discourse, no matter whether one figures war as event or process.

Rather than characterize counterterrorism policy and its affiliates as a form of perpetual war, the episodic violence of the first two decades of the twenty-first century should be distinguished as two distinct forms of action: nation-state war and the sporadic, but violent imposition of a specific type of sovereign power. While the goals of the first form have already been elaborated, America's ongoing military adventurism seeks a juridical, rather than political solution to the problem of terrorism. That is, it seeks to impose a sovereign dominion upon vast sections of the world not premised on demarcating territory to be administrated via democratic (or otherwise) institutions, but rather by governing bodies, their movements and mortalities. Necropolitics, a governing logic engineered to facilitate the permanent management of insecurity, life and death, and the attendant regimes of surveillance, arose from the elevation of indeterminacy as a central feature of the present era.[28] Circulating through the national-security bureaucracy, this logic of the enemy produced a trajectory for postwar policy premised on the global mobility of military operations.[29] Given the likelihood that climate change will entrench inequities between the developed and developing world, exacerbate refugee crises, and spark additional waves of anti-imperial violence, one can reasonably expect the continuity of American foreign-policy violence.

To be clear, there is nothing new about continuously "violating the sovereignty of non-Western polities."[30] As stated previously, it is what the country has done for hundreds of years when facing Indian nations, pirates, or sovereign states opposed to American interests. Now, however, the necropolitical logic that governs American military intervention seeks to sustain an eroding liberal international order via the violent disruption of antagonist organizations deemed most responsible for challenging Western hegemony. In distinction from the period immediately after 9/11, which fused crisis and insecurity to warrant an exceptional response to terrorism, the underlying impulse of American power is governed by the desire to respond to threats with rapid, lethal action rather than extended intervention. The primary consequence of this ontology of violence comes in the form of statecraft that, as Brian Massumi put it, makes this new sovereign order felt in two ways. First, it affects individuals across much of the world by threatening to act wherever a security threat can be identified. That is, actors across the globe have to account for the possibility they could be targeted with lethal action, even if they fall outside the scope of terrorism. Second, the imposition of a violent, sovereign order requires routine operations because, as Massumi put it, "it has to introduce itself into each situation into which it moves."[31] At the level of structure, the logic of necropolitical sovereignty infers that power unused is not power at all. Thus, the combination of potential and actual sovereign power combined with the conviction of its necessity provides the impetus for continuation, even as direct exposure of threats to American territory increasingly declines.

Given the awesome cultural, political, and bureaucratic incentives to enact a necropolitical logic of sovereignty and the president's participation in directing postwar energies toward managing insecurity with violence, one may conclude that, as currently configured, America's relationship with war appears inevitable, unbreakable, and permanent. And while the prospect for disrupting the continuity of national violence may

appear distant, we should recall that war "is always contingent on specific structures and human agents situated in specific temporal-spatial
contexts." National violence and war culture may appear, at a glance,
to be permanent fixtures of American culture, but the contingency of
violence means war is neither "stable nor predictable."[32] The practices of
violence are historically linked and built upon prior experiences. Confronting the perpetual production of enemies and the security apparatus
that follows represents a herculean task of sustained, active political action by mass publics committed to a more equitable world. But it also
requires presidential leadership.

Rhetorics of War and Peace and the Nascent Enemy

In spite of efforts to displace and refigure representations of the enemy,
efforts that have significantly shifted the metaphoric economy employed
to represent danger after war, presidential rhetoric heralding peace in the
post–World War II era has contained the seeds of future warfare. Wittingly or not, presidents have constituted metaphoric personae that have
structured the ways institutions understand and respond to insecurity at
the end of hostilities. Those shifting representations have reconstituted
an American mission after war by invoking a nascent figure of the enemy,
one that continues to dominate American foreign-policy discourse. The
continuity of the nascent enemy in presidential rhetoric refocuses national attention on the next danger, militarizes foreign policy, and accents
the role presidents and the language of peace play in the cyclical aspect
of war. Presidential end-of-war discourse establishes the terms that frame
and shape the basis for the next war because presidents desire peace, but
only certain kinds and under certain conditions. Rather than illuminate
a true discourse of peace, I point to a vast and flexible repertoire from
which presidents can draw to articulate the enemy in ways that serve
American power. The form and trajectory of that discourse depends on
the ideology, skill, and attitude of the president, but the continuity of
insecurity as an iconic, persuasive vehicle present across different eras

of political leadership speaks to an underlying epistemology of security, otherization, and American exceptionalism.

While the potential for rehumanizing discourses to raise the prospects of peace in global affairs persists, presidents have opted for discursive strategies that reify, rather than undermine, the epistemology of security. This rhetoric facilitates transitions out of war even as the plasticity of representations of the enemy refocuses public and bureaucratic perspectives on international insecurity in ways that increase, rather than reduce the likelihood of subsequent conflicts. Truman's reassessment of Germany and Japan as diseased bodies reasserted a theory of nations-as-bodies; raised the likelihood there would be another disease, another vulnerable mind for toxic ideology to contaminate or brainwash; and structured the conflict between the United States and the Soviet Union. Eisenhower's solution, shifting the metaphoric frame from disease to competition, rationalized the cease-fire with North Korea, but proved equally imperfect. Articulating international relations as a great game, with many players on the board, elevated the significance of communist incursion in Southeast Asia and compelled American intervention in Vietnam. In spite of Nixon's duplicitous escalation into Cambodia and Laos, his eventual movement from game theory to architecture similarly failed to solve the problem of a foreign policy premised on containment. And, Obama's movement to represent the enemy as a disembodied, mobile force, detached from nation and territory, represented insecurity as a permanent fixture of the twenty-first century and ensured the continuity of the War on Terror during his presidency and beyond.

Beyond these shifts in representation, presidents have attempted to manage the paradox between peace and hegemonic leadership by making policy promises that vastly exceed their abilities to implement. Arriving with prefabricated policy agendas they seek to enact, regardless of the practical or political challenges those goals may incur, their public pronouncements frame or structure public understandings of controversy while constraining and undermining their policy program. With the possible exception of Truman—whose promise of unconditional surrender led to the utter destruction of Japan—each president discussed in this book failed to make good on his proclamations. Eisenhower's declaration that he will go to Korea, for example, pegged his immediate foreign-policy goal as extracting the nation from war, even though, as president, he had no control over the direction of armistice negotiations. In failing to reset the competition between the United States and the Soviet Union, moreover, his end-of-war rhetoric ensured the continuation of hot proxy wars between East and West. Nixon's pledge to win in Vietnam weighed upon his foreign policy, opened his administration to visceral domestic criticism, and contributed to the unraveling of his presidency. George W. Bush suffered a similar outcome with his declaration of mission accomplished after the initial stage of combat operations in Iraq. Equally, Obama's pledge to close Guantanamo and win the war in Afghanistan made for a good campaign platform, but it didn't address the sticky problems related to the prison facility, insurgency, and nation-building.

In many respects, these observations reflect vast and deep limitations on presidential foreign-policy-making power. Much scholarship implies, if not explicitly argues, that presidents have great latitude to organize end-of-war policy as they see fit. In contradistinction, this book considers the president as a significantly constrained policy agent. Echoing Fred Charles Iklé's iconic warning that "those with power to start war frequently come to discover that they lack the power to stop it," presidents have struggled to manage the discursive constraints imposed by the rhetoric of savagery, even as they have modified that discourse to create new possibilities in the postwar era.[33] Some of those constraints are material—belligerents have to agree to negotiate, make concessions, and otherwise establish the conditions for ending hostilities. Others exist because, to borrow from Michael Shapiro, presidential end-of-war rhetoric "draws from the archive of the already said."[34] Presidents don't have all the answers—their unique position doesn't automatically confer advantages above and beyond other public actors because, in addition to material factors, they face rhetorical constraints of their own making. Presidents grapple with the problem of peace by articulating a path forward at the end of war that narrows the domain of policymaking.

This balance between constraints and opportunities serves as a useful starting point for thinking about presidential power, war, and the possibilities of an antiwar politics. With presidents enjoying increasingly lax constraints on their ability to use force abroad, and public attitudes favorable to the continued militarization of American foreign policy, it is crucial to speculate about the possibilities of a rhetoric of peace that could demilitarize U.S. foreign policy. Unfortunately, absent significant rethinking of the nation's role in the world, the complex of security and national interest will prioritize policy choices that make future confrontation with new antagonists likely. Presidential end-of-war rhetoric plays a key role in this process because it reflects systematic ideas that underwrite the goals and practices of American foreign policy. The tangled skein that ensnares presidents, what Claudia Aradau termed the "sovereign logic of security," establishes the "elimination of enemies" as a principal goal of foreign policy and integral to American national identity.[35]

In addition to the gravitational force security plays on presidential end-of-war discourse, presidents leave most policy details to the foreign affairs bureaucracy, trusted advisors, and the executive staff. The bureaucratization of policy problematizes efforts to slow the war drive because the circulation of presidential metaphors of the enemy function as a sort of negative feedback loop on the president and the policy agenda. Presidents are both authors and audiences of the discourse that circulates around the presidency. That discourse guides how presidents conceive of the international situation and articulate the domain of possible solutions. While I have argued in this book that a president is one of the most lucid confederates of the postwar policy agenda, uniquely capable of articulating the language of savagery to manage contextual and material changes to the international system, the presidential voice encompasses a wide domain of administrative actors who may speak in ways that constrain or disrupt presidential initiatives to foster the conditions for peace. Sometimes, as with Dick Cheney, Donald Rumsfeld, and Paul Wolfowitz, those actors serve in subsequent administrations, bringing old arguments to new situations with disastrous outcomes.[36] At other times, as with Obama, those actors wait out the end of a president's term in office and seek the policy they desired all along.[37]

Additionally, since most policy decisions are vastly more complex than presidents assert in public, bureaucratic proximity determines the likelihood that the president receives materials and information that could drive policy decisions. Paul Nitze's reframing of internal opposition to NSC-68 to characterize it as favorable, for example, contributed to Truman's belief that the State Department was united behind containment.[38] Similarly, John Foster Dulles's proximity to Eisenhower helped convince the president to adopt aggressive nuclear-deterrent strategies toward the Soviet Union and China.[39] Kissinger acted as a buffer between Nixon and the Cabinet, a factor that only intensified after he became secretary of state as well.[40] And, Obama's personal disdain for Richard Holbrooke kept the primary advocate for negotiating with the Taliban away from the White House, allowing military voices to dominate the president's purview.[41] Ultimately, every president enters the office believing they can dominate the bureaucracy and enforce their will. But, without exception, every president leaves office having succumbed to the institution.

For these reasons, presidents will likely continue to articulate political violence as a continuous enterprise, inextricably linked to securing and maintaining American power in the world. That does not mean that leadership is irrelevant, language is fundamentally incapable of taming the war beast, or that self-fulfilling prophecies actually self-fulfill. Cultural, ideological, institutional, and rhetorical pressures do not render presidents powerless. Nor is it a given that future presidents will understand and articulate security challenges in ways similar to the presidents described in this volume. Focusing on the rhetorical components of the end of war demonstrates how presidents shackle policy to an administrative logic of security by condensing the prospects of peace to a specific set of national interests they identify as preconditions to permanent peace. But it also points to roads not taken, the possibilities for rhetorical invention yet to be exploited. Rhetoric, after all, is the domain of invention and there are always possibilities, even if, as Michael Howard put it, peace "is certainly a far more complex affair than war."[42] While it may be tempting to suggest the impossibility of a rhetorical cure to war in an era of imperial decline, no rhetoric is insoluble. The real question, then, is what can rhetoric do? Or, more appropriately, what can presidents make rhetoric do?

If there is potential for future presidents to break the cycle described, it is likely in having better awareness of the language choices used to articulate the policy problems posed by the end of war. Presidents should recognize the political, cultural, and policy downsides to articulating policy in terms of threat and insecurity. Rhetoric has consequences. It enables presidents to articulate policies, to explain the makeup of the world, to orient the nation to that world, and to rationalize their own leadership. Because presidential speech is ecumenical in orientation—a blended form of genera that can be more or less eloquent but is always coextensive with the way people think—it establishes a textual authority that guides all other discourse about war. And, by reflecting a "corresponding form of character" back upon the speaker in the form of a persona, presidential end-of-war rhetoric materially entangles the presidency in a logic that defines the war preparation as necessary for peace.[43] As long as the underlying premise of (in)security serves as the guiding principle for U.S. policy, better metaphors—better rhetoric—will not fix the incommensurable idea of peace under empire.

Rather than forward securitized rationales, presidents should refrain from unambiguous public promises about ending war and instead ponder the rhetorical possibilities of a desecuritizing discourse. Such a discourse would be "informed by the principles of universality and recognition" that emphasize democratic, inclusive, and emancipatory attitudes toward the Other.[44] It would humanize America's adversaries, not by portraying them as victims of an external evil, but by situating political violence as a product of complex motivations, contexts, and interests. Doing so would emphasize the inalienable right to life of all people, even above security demands. This approach would resolve the inherent tension between presidential speech that blames foreign leaders for war while justifying policies that cause the people to suffer.

Truman's decision to drop the atom bomb on Hiroshima and Nagasaki stands out as a prototypical example. Even as he warned the Japanese to throw down arms and evacuate their cities, he tasked the military to use weapons that would incur mass civilian casualties. As is the case for most of the nation's adversaries, Japan was not a democracy. The citizens of Japan had little, if any control over national policy. Presidents should recognize that people living in nondemocratic states not only are incapable of altering the politics of their nations, but also are the parties who suffer most deeply in times of war. Rather than recycle old tropes at the end of war to extend the mission into peacetime, a desecuritizing discourse would emphasize the humanitarian consequences of militaristic foreign policies and focus on civilians and the sanctity of all life. Shifting away from the need for absolute security to emphasize humanitarian concerns might liberate presidents from the rhetorical constraints of the securitized discourse that typifies end-of-war contexts.

An additional element of a desecuritizing discourse would emphasize violence and war as a last resort. Franklin D. Roosevelt's visceral description of war at Chautauqua, New York, in 1936 serves as a powerful example. In the address, Roosevelt claimed to have seen war, and went on to describe "blood running from the wounded . . . men coughing out their gassed lungs . . . the dead in the mud . . . cities destroyed . . . children starving . . . the agony of mothers and wives." The speech emphasized the terribleness of war, the impact it has on everyone, while avoiding any discussion of an enemy or culpability. Far from glorifying war, Roosevelt hated it and pledged to author policies that would "make clear that the conscience of America revolts against war." Even while acknowledging it was beyond his power to "keep war from all Nations," Roosevelt represented war as a last, terrible resort.[45] The speech is instructive not just because of its visceral, humanitarian representation of war, but also because he delivered it in a moment when the world appeared headed toward war. Japan had invaded Manchuria in 1931, Hitler had risen to power on a wave of nationalist sentiment, the Spanish Revolution had already involved France and Germany, and Italy had conquered Ethiopia. In short, in a moment when the League of Nations had failed to keep the peace and global war appeared possible, Roosevelt rejected war as a legitimate form of policy. While such an attitude could not prevent the return of war, it raised the threshold of national violence by educating the nation about the true stakes of conflict.

Still, even if rhetoric like Roosevelt's may deglamorize war, over-investing in presidential rhetorical power is inadvisable. Presidents always have to be ready to use military force to defend the nation. It's part of the job, literally written into the text of the Constitutional mandate. Similarly, presidents struggle to avoid the perpetual and dangerous compulsion of narratives of insecurity. The nascent enemy is too deeply embedded in American culture and reigns in bureaucratic settings geared toward determining threat levels for a wide array of potential antagonists. One only has to recall Obama's quip after a security briefing in 2008 that he's "worried about winning this election," given the "dubious tools to keep [catastrophe] from happening," to understand the context presidents enter into.[46] Even candidates who express commitments to diplomacy and negotiated settlements of disputes feel the cultural, political, and bureaucratic pressures to securitize foreign policy. Those pressures restrict and restrain the way they can articulate problems and solutions. In the best case, presidents manage those constraints by displacing single-minded forms of securitization with a rhetoric emphasizing the nation's highest ideals as guideposts for postwar policy, as was the case with Roosevelt's Four Freedoms address. But even those choices have downsides since escalating the significance of universal ideals also extends absolutist principles that underwrite future clashes with nations or peoples who do not share those ideals. And so the cycle repeats.

Assessing Contemporary Efforts to Resist War

On the Friday after 9/11, Barbara Lee stood before the House of Representatives as the lone voice in opposition to granting President Bush unlimited power to respond to the attack with military force. Expressing profound sadness about the events that transpired three days earlier, she stated she would vote against the Authorization for Military Force against Terrorists (AUMF) because "military action will not prevent further acts of terrorism against the United States." Rather, putting the nation on a war footing, she warned, endangered the innocents and noncombatants that live in the war zone, while bringing the nation closer to "the evil that we deplore."[47] Intensely cognizant of the way the terrorist attack had reshaped national and global politics, Lee knew the statement came with significant risks. She was called a "traitor . . . un-American and an accomplice of the terrorists."[48] Still, nine days later she doubled down with an editorial in the *San Francisco Chronicle* arguing the resolution was a blank check and that she "could not support such a grant of war-making authority to [the] president" because military action would entangle the nation in a complex web of violence that would be difficult to escape. The consequences of such authority "would put more innocent lives at risk."[49] Eighteen years later, after more than forty-one military actions in nineteen countries, Lee introduced legislation to repeal the AUMF. In her brief remarks, she stated, "Congress has abdicated its constitutional responsibility to debate and vote on matters of war and peace," and it was past time to "repeal this blank check for war."[50] The text of the legislation sought to end the "open-ended authorization for the use of military force," claiming presidential interpretation of the AUMF was "inconsistent with the authority of Congress to declare war."[51] Passing the House but stalling in the Senate, the scene would repeat in 2017.[52]

Lee's strategy—connecting pragmatic rationales with moral ones—is common for antiwar discourse. American political history is replete with mainstream opposition to war, not to mention presidential discourses of peace. John Lowell's antiwar pamphlets that he distributed across New England during the War of 1812, for example, called James Madison's "unnecessary and ruinous war" the latest aspect of his policy of perpetual war. Typical for the era, the document parsed the constitutional and legal rationale for the war, arguing that Madison had no basis to request a war declaration from Congress.[53] Abraham Lincoln, as congressman, issued a series of spot resolutions to challenge President Polk on his claim that

Mexico had entered U.S. territory and attacked American soldiers.[54] The legal argument didn't halt the war, but it did raise the possibility that the United States had started the war for unjust cause, incurring political costs for the president.[55] In opposing the war with Spain, William Jennings Bryan warned of the risks of imperialism as a driving force for policy.[56] Eugene Debs opposed World War I on the grounds that it was the product of the ruling class, and that the people "have never yet had a voice in either declaring war or making peace."[57] Innumerable speeches opposed the Vietnam War, perhaps most famously when Martin Luther King Jr. warned of "a society gone mad on war." In pointing to the cruel irony of drafting black men to fight for freedoms in South Vietnam that they did not enjoy at home, he argued the war proved that the "greatest purveyor of violence in the world today: my own government." Taking the form of cultural criticism, King argued, "Vietnam is but a symptom of a far deeper malady within the American spirit."[58]

This brief review highlights two strands of antiwar criticism. One strand of opposition to American war-making has focused on systemic critique. This discourse has located the source of America's violent foreign policy in its imperialist orientation. Present in one form or another over the course of American history, the anti-imperial argument in the contemporary era reached its zenith in 2003, but has largely disappeared since.[59] The other strand is procedural. It focuses on the justice of the cause, the legal aspects of moving the nation to war, and the abuse of executive authority. This approach extends legal arguments parsing the "facts" of the case—much the way opposition to the war in Iraq highlighted George W. Bush's deceit about weapons of mass destruction in Iraq—to raise claims related to the abuse of executive authority. This strand does not indict the ethics of war itself; rather it debates the justice of the specific case. Thus, one can imagine that if Iraq had had an actual WMD program, the public would have supported the war in Iraq, the way they supported the war in Afghanistan.

Unfortunately, the bulk of antiwar activism in contemporary times avoids systemic critique in favor of procedural approaches. Excluding Lee's rhetoric, most calls to end or revise the AUMF seek to submit the

violence of American foreign policy to congressional deliberation and
oversight. For example, the libertarian CATO Institute claimed the time
had come to "recognize the original authorization had run its course,
sunset it, leaving adequate time . . . for the president to make the case for
any new authorization he thinks is needed."[60] Similarly, the liberal Center for American Progress (CAP) advocated for congressional oversight
as the remedy to endless war. In spite of expressions of concern about
endless war, neither organization considered the possibility of ending
war as a primary tool of statecraft. Instead, both documents warned
about the incoherence of Donald Trump's strategy and the need for more
precise strategies to address the security risks incurred by terrorism. For
example, the CAP report worried that Trump's incoherence and ambivalence was contributing to endless wars, and that most proposals to revise
the "AUMF would enshrine endless war as the norm." The report called
for an extensive assessment by Congress to check presidential authority,
raise public understanding about the war, and improve the prospects of
victory.[61] Similarly, the CATO report called for sunsetting the AUMF
in the interest of public accountability. Without an AUMF, their report
argued, the president would have to "make the case [for war] to the
people's representatives and secure authorization for the war in the way
the Constitution envisioned."[62]

The CATO and CAP documents reflect the shape of contemporary
policy debates about the War on Terror. Both express concern about
the prospect of endless war. Both emphasize the importance of constitutional mechanisms to restrain presidential power and the necessity of
keeping the American people informed about the war. Reflecting the
republican ideal that an informed citizenry can check presidential power
and improve decision-making, both propose public accountability as the
remedy to the War on Terror—including where it is being fought, against
whom, and to what end. But, unlike with Lee's critique, neither report
objects to the War on Terror in principle. Rather, they express concerns
that the War on Terror isn't being fought the right way, and that public—congressional—oversight would improve the prospects for victory.

The beneficent case for American power, framed and shaped by liberal notions of freedom, human rights, and economic opportunity, is in the mainstream for antiwar discourse. The Washington, DC–based nonprofit organization Win Without War bears out the point. According to its mission statement, the organization advocates for a progressive foreign policy premised in the demilitarization of U.S. foreign policy. Writing politics-as-competition into the title of the organization, the mission statement suggests military strategies don't improve national security and urges an end to endless wars. Yet, the hegemonic role of the nation goes without challenge. Claiming "our values do not stop at water's edge," the document prioritizes the United States' role "to uplift and reinforce all peoples' desire for dignity, prosperity, and self-determination," a goal to be achieved "by building a global movement for change rooted in solidarity and our shared values of justice, equality, and security for all."[63] Admirable in principle, the message reiterates the basic tenets of democracy promotion and economic development that have defined American foreign policy for decades. That is, it premises demilitarization of U.S. foreign policy on the ability of the nation to satisfy economic, political, and security goals via other means. In doing so, it exhibits the problem of presidential peace rhetoric. Even when expressing an unequivocal opposition to war as a form of statecraft, it elaborates a national attitude toward the world based in universal notions of democracy, human rights, and capitalist economics. Those notions, combined with America's belief in its right to lead, entangle the nation in a host of accords, treaties, and institutions that make clashes inevitable because not all nations share the same values and not all goals can be achieved via diplomacy. Far from anti-imperialist, contemporary peace rhetoric is imperialism repackaged, couched in the rhetoric of the Enlightenment, and consistent with the rhetorical patterns that have long justified American influence in the affairs of others.

These examples shed light on the strategic flaws inherent in the rhetoric of those opposing war. All three organizations espouse deeply problematic notions that information deficits contribute to the perpetuation of war and that public accountability could alter the policy trajectory in ways that improve the prospects for victory. To begin with, these views locate the source of perpetual war in presidential power. By leveraging the republican ideal of public accountability, they imply that the American people are less interested in war than the president and would act to restrain presidential war-making power as a result. The evidence of American attitudes toward war indicts this assumption. The deep penetration of war culture in popular culture via video games, violent movies, and public events that glamorize military technology have diminished public opposition to war. Robert L. Ivie perhaps put it best when he stated, "The United States is strongly predisposed toward violence and deeply motivated to rationalize war as the work of peace."[64] The cultural disconnect between a sanitized military fetish, the actual features of violence, and widespread notions that war serves the interests of peace makes publics more likely to respond to security discourse with support for military action.

Additionally, notions about the power of deliberation fail to apprehend the unique rhetorical power of the presidency in framing and shaping public understandings of international insecurity. Scholars have long worried about presidential maneuvers (often rhetorical ones) undermining the constitutional order that deferred war-making power to Congress. These studies have contended that presidents neutralize institutional and normative constraints on presidential war-making by identifying and demonizing enemies, rhetorical acts that compel the nation to war. Pointing to the inherent power of the savage idiom, critics have pointed to the facility with which presidents can launch a war, on the flimsiest grounds, and the inability of Congress or the public to constrain such actions. In the twentieth century alone, those appeals have justified attempts to assassinate foreign leaders, sponsor coups, and weaponize militant groups who espouse a pro-American ideology. Conceding that the basic pattern of presidential war rhetoric has continued unaltered over the course of the nation's history, critics mark presidential war appeals as a key source of presidential power that has contributed to the militarization of American foreign policy, even as they wish for elusive procedural remedies that have no hope of passing and wouldn't restrain presidential speech if they did.[65]

Moreover, public accountability assumes that congressional over-sight would shed light on rarely seen aspects of U.S. foreign policy and distribute that information to mass publics in ways that would stimulate antiwar activism. Yet, the vast majority of U.S. foreign policy exists under the radar, rarely subject to congressional scrutiny or public de-liberation. Instead, as demonstrated in this volume, presidents task the bureaucracy with developing policies to resolve security concerns via a range of activities that often include violence. Frequently shielded by the secrecy afforded by the CIA and DOD, presidents rarely have to make public cases for these strategies of blood. And, even when deliberation in public or Congress has sought to restrict presidential latitude, as in the case of Ronald Reagan's support for the Contras, they have gotten their way, with minimal consequences.[66] Without changing this funda-mental dynamic, no amount of congressional scrutiny will create lasting restraints on presidential action.

Finally, and perhaps most importantly, congressional oversight wouldn't significantly restrict the president's ability to conduct military operations against organizations and individuals classified as terrorists because presidents have already shaped the postwar context in ways that enable political violence as a normalized form of statecraft. Dislodging the state from its militarist foreign policy requires sustained activism beyond congressional scrutiny because of the deep penetration of the rhetoric of security in the post-9/11 era. The enduring figure of a dis-embodied antagonist had elevated the importance of self-protection as the pinnacle guidepost in policy decision-making, risking the expansion of "the security realm endlessly, until it encompasses the whole social and political agenda."[67] The inextricable link between security and ter-rorism means that any utterance of one also invokes the other, rational-izing a host of policies that run counter to America's founding ideals. From drone strikes to violations of personal space in airport security, the color-coded terror alert system, "see something, say something," and the infinite number of other ways anxiety about terrorism lodged itself in cultural artifacts, public memory, and public deliberation, the logic of security governs the nation's orientation to foreign policy more

generally. Given the expansion and penetration of this ontology of security and the ways this logic has conditioned Americans to apprehend
violent forms of statecraft as an a priori necessity for safety, constituting
a viable opposition to the militarization of American foreign policy is
an encompassing problem requiring more than public accountability
and oversight. The ultimate cruel optimism of contemporary American
foreign-policy discourse may not be the quest for peace. Rather, it might
be the idea that democratic deliberation can remedy the problem of violent statecraft.

Toward a Sustained Antiwar Politics

While entrenched beliefs about the need for juridical strategies to manage insecurity makes sustained opposition challenging, maintaining
distinctions between formal wars and the militarization of American
foreign policy offers a way forward by refocusing criticism from specific
incidents to the generalized problem of power and leadership. The critique leveled by this book demonstrates that imperial politics produce
recurring cycles of otherization, threat construction, and political violence that may exceed even the president's vast power. It happens every
day, destroying lives, countries, and the environment. Expecting solutions to that problem to come from the president, even one committed
to ending wars, reinforces a textual authority centered on the necessity of
presidents threading the needle of peace, when ideological, institutional,
and discursive factors render such things impractical. Overinvesting in
the potentialities of the presidency risks undermining the coalitional
politics necessary to generate a forceful resistance by displacing the citizen in favor of the executive. Rather than remaining entrapped by the
discourses of security and policy that prefigure public discourse about
foreign policy, activists should seek to displace, upset, and otherwise
destabilize those discourses. While the contours of that resistance have
yet to be elaborated, possibilities for sustained criticism remain.

The notion of a sustained opposition to violent statecraft may seem abnormal to contemporary audiences, but there is significant historical precedent. During the Cold War, peace activists in the United States and beyond militated against the rise in tensions between the U.S. and the Soviet Union, the proliferation of nuclear weapons, and the dangers posed by a world preparing for the next war. While those advocates could not halt the Cold War, many employed strategies focused on specific issues or instances of violence. Beyond Vietnam, which has received inordinate attention from scholars, advocates also leveraged global relationships to oppose nuclear testing. As Petra Goedde recalled, those strategies emphasized a common humanity shared across the globe and identified the ways nuclear testing affected everyone. Her examination of peace movements during the Cold War demonstrates how the rhetoric of peace "became a key tool [for political leaders] in the cultural and political battles of the Cold War," and galvanized "a redoubled effort to develop and expand a politics of peace."[68] While the impact of collaborations that cut across the Iron Curtain to constitute a global coalition for peace remains unclear, Goedde credits the domestic anti-testing movement for pushing John F. Kennedy to focus on the environmental impacts related to nuclear testing, resulting in the Nuclear Test Ban Treaty of 1963.[69] Goedde's text illuminates the ways specific, targeted forms of advocacy can impact policy outcomes while more comprehensive, radical critiques do not. Similarly, J. Michael Hogan's examination of the anti-nuclear movement underlines the failure of eloquent rhetoric that audiences perceive as "radical, irrational, alien, and condescending."[70] Rhetoric always has an audience, and it is incumbent on those who oppose the imperial practice of American foreign policy to find one capable of sustained public engagement.

Given the incentives for presidents to continue to discuss American leadership, political violence, the sources of insecurity, and national enemies in inconsistent and ambiguous ways, citizens have an obligation to become educated about foreign policy in ways they have never previously been. Principally, citizens need to develop a rhetorical sensitivity to foreign-policy rhetoric and "its sheer predictability."[71] Recognizing that presidential end-of-war rhetoric inevitably resuscitates the logics and rationalities of war in postwar eras would prepare citizens to "take a step to the side" and consider such rhetoric as a continuous discourse authored by empire. The crucial point here, as Michael Steudeman described, is that such a "step aside" would disrupt the seamlessness of the discursive encounter, raising both cognitive and affective uncertainties. This disruptive moment would recognize that the rhetorics of war, peace, and empire have already infiltrated and penetrated public discussions of war and its aftermath, as they always do.[72] Seeing "new" calls for war as part of an ongoing discursive enterprise to center and prioritize American power and security above all other concerns would liberate audiences from the unique power of the rhetoric. A rhetorically sensitive audience would identify the narrow space between war rhetoric and rhetorics of peace, note the inherent conflation between the two, and inculcate an attitude of suspicion about interlocutors advancing arguments beyond "no more war."[73] This attitude—or rhetorical sensitivity—does not posit resistant discourse within the domain of rational, critical debate. Nor does it assert that "the people" endorse war because of ignorance and imply that good decision-making is a product of cognition. Rather, rhetorical sensitivity to national violence acknowledges the stickiness of discourses of empire and the means by which they affectively manage public attitudes toward security, threat, and international relations. Inculcating rhetorical sensitivity, ultimately, seeks to demystify presidential appeals by imbuing audiences with awareness of the rhetorical contexts generative of discourses of empire.

Part of this project involves recognizing national violence as both product and process. Proponents of the perpetual-war thesis warn that viewing war as an eruption and an abnormal abrogation of peaceful times "essentialize[s] both its origins and its function," ignores the permanence of violence, and deprives citizens of intellectual mechanisms for resisting state-based violence. When violence "becomes part of the expectation of living," they contend, citizens lack the means for parsing the discursive mechanisms constitutive of the violent episteme.[74] But just as we can't solely envision war as event, we also can't only imagine it as process. In the current era, perhaps always, wars are image events. They draw press attention and public interest. The decision to move the nation to war requires rhetorical energy that normalized political violence does not.[75] Discourses resistant to specific forms of military invasion and conquest have a rhetorical history and legacy. Blurring the distinction between war and the violent conduct of foreign policy risks effacing the historic power of antiwar discourse and undermining the cohesive elements that discourse sustains. Simply, generating and sustaining citizen opposition to wars against Iran, North Korea, or any other nation may prove easier given the errors made in Iraq, the memory of antiwar activism stretching from 1812 to the present, and the specificity of the enemy. Instead of choosing to see war either as event or as process, an attitude of rhetorical sensitivity would comprehend that empire is productive of both. Violence is both a continuous process and an event orchestrated by political elites in pursuit of national goals. Resistance to violent statecraft means recognizing the continuous presence of violence, the nuanced forms it takes, and the intricacies of rationalizations articulated in service of an imperial, necropolitical power.

A citizenry infused with this class of rhetorical sensitivity would have responded to Obama's Nobel Prize speech—where he put forth a rigorous justification for war—by opposing, rather than praising, the president's foreign-policy agenda. A rhetorically sensitive citizenry would have recognized that the ways Obama articulated the enemy made distinguishing between civilians and combatants near impossible. A rhetorically sensitive citizenry would have realized that referring to the deaths of thousands of citizens as collateral damage covered over the real, life-altering circumstances of being targeted by American military power. A rhetorically sensitive audience would have comprehended Obama's discourse of security as old wine in a new bottle. And, a rhetorically sensitive citizenry would have acted against a policy agenda that killed thousands of innocents, served as propaganda for terrorist recruitment, and concealed the paltry security gains achieved. Ultimately, a discourse is only as good as its practical application, and had an engaged coalition of citizens pushed back against the War on Terror, Obama might have been forced to answer the truly tough questions about his policies in ways that might have altered the trajectory of the nation.[76] By ceding the ground to the president—because of partisanship, among other reasons—American political culture enabled Obama to cloak his discussion of the enemy in ambiguous or disembodied terms and avoid more nuanced and complex conversations about war and foreign policy.[77]

Resistant voices also need to recognize that wars cannot be concluded by executive fiat. Beyond the constraints and incentives previously discussed, presidents increasingly defer decision-making to a matrix of military and national-security offices. As previously discussed, contemporary concerns have focused on the hazy legal standing and political challenges related to motivating citizen action against the War on Terror. These concerns largely ignore bureaucratic shifts designed to ensure that political violence continues, even if the wars officially end. Delegation to military decision-makers conceals deliberations about the war and restricts conversations to classified, interagency domains. It also distributes the power to define the nation's enemies in ways that make accountability difficult if not impossible. The faceless bureaucracy largely operates on its own, with little outside oversight, and the task of tracing, analyzing, and critiquing key definitions is essentially impossible at present.[78] Deferring the conversation about national enemies to the national-security bureaucracy poses a real danger to public deliberation and accountability of America's war state because presidents can respond to opposition by pointing to procedures and protocols embedded in layers of secret and opaque agencies.

Ultimately, the prospects for peaceful international policy depend upon thickening public deliberative culture in ways that enable, rather than curtail, the ways of understanding national adversaries.[79] To date, Representative Lee's approach has been an outlier, rather than in the mainstream. If advocates wish to make any lasting impact on the direction of national-security discourse and the violent trajectory of American foreign policy, they would be wise to shift her critique to the center. Absent sustained resistance from intersectional coalitions bound together by the promise of justice, equality, and a desire for peace, it is difficult to see an end to American war culture and the militarization of U.S. foreign policy.

Notes

———•◆•———

PREFACE

1. H. G. Wells, *The War That Will End War* (New York: Duffield & Company, 1914), 11.
2. See BBC News, "The War to End All Wars," November 10, 1998, http://news.bbc.co.uk/2/hi/special_report/1998/10/98/world_war_i/198172.stm; and Edwin Stepp, "A War to End All War," *Vision* (Spring 2014), https://www.vision.org/history-the-great-war-can-a-war-end-all-war-33.
3. Woodrow Wilson, "Address to the Nation," April 16, 1917, American Presidency Project.
4. Audrey Cohan and Charles F. Howlett, "Global Conflicts Shattered World Peace: John Dewey's Influence on Peace Educators and Practitioners," *Education and Culture* 33, no. 1 (2017): 59–60.
5. Woodrow Wilson, "Address to a Joint Session of Congress Concerning the Terms of Armistice Signed by Germany," November 11, 1918, American Presidency Project.

6. Charles H. Grasty, "Forces at War in Peace Conclave: Ralph Pulitzer Sees Influence at Work for a 'Sinister Peace,'" *New York Times*, January 18, 1919.

7. Arthur Derrin Call, "Ninety-Two Years of Age," *Advocate of Peace through Justice* 82, no. 6 (1920): 180.

8. Wells, *The War That Will End War*, 8–9.

9. Franklin D. Roosevelt, "Fireside Chat," September 3, 1939, American Presidency Project.

10. Robert L. Ivie, "Presidential Motives for War," *Quarterly Journal of Speech* 60 (1974): 337–45; Robert L. Ivie, "Images of Savagery in American Justifications for War," *Communication Monographs* 47 (1980): 279–94; and Robert L. Ivie, "Literalizing the Metaphor of Soviet Savagery: President Truman's Plain Style," *Southern Speech Communication Journal* 51 (1986): 91–105.

11. Robert L. Ivie, "The Metaphor of Force in Prowar Discourse: The Case of 1812," *Quarterly Journal of Speech* 68 (1982): 241.

12. James K. Polk, "Special Message to Congress on Mexican Relations," May 11, 1846, American Presidency Project.

13. William McKinley, "Message to Congress Requesting a Declaration of War with Spain," April 11, 1898, American Presidency Project.

14. See Robert L. Ivie, *Dissent from War* (Bloomfield, CT: Kumarian Press, 2007).

15. See Andrew J. Polsky, *Elusive Victories: The American Presidency at War* (New York: Oxford University Press, 2012).

16. Ivie, *Dissent from War*, 60.

17. Michael S. Sherry, *In the Shadow of War: The United States since the 1930s*, 2nd ed. (New Haven, CT: Yale University Press, 1997), ix.

18. Sherry, *In the Shadow of War*, 7.

19. James T. Sparrow, *Warfare State: World War II Americans and the Age of Big Government* (New York: Oxford Books, 2011), 5–6; Kelly Denton-Borhaug, *U.S. War Culture, Sacrifice and Salvation* (Oakville, CT: Equinox, 2011); and Roger Stahl, *Militainment, Inc: War, Media, and Culture* (New York: Routledge, 2010).

20. Sherry, *In the Shadow of War*, x–xi.

21. For three exceptions, see Robert L. Ivie, "Obama at West Point: A Study in Ambiguity of Purpose," *Rhetoric & Public Affairs* 14, no. 4 (2011): 727–59; Robert E. Terrill, "An Uneasy Peace: Barack Obama's Nobel Peace Prize Lecture," *Rhetoric & Public Affairs* 14, no. 4 (2011): 761–79; and Joshua Reeves and Matthew S. May, "The Peace Rhetoric of a War President: Barack Obama and the Just War Legacy," *Rhetoric & Public Affairs* 16, no. 4 (Winter 2013): 623–50.

22. Roger J. Spiller, "Six Propositions," in *Between War and Peace: How America Ends Its Wars*, ed. Col. Matthew Moten (New York: Free Press, 2011), 11.

23. See Spiller, "Six Propositions," 4; Ivie, "Obama at West Point," 727–28; and David Zarefsky, *President Johnson's War on Poverty* (Tuscaloosa: University of Alabama Press, 1986), 5.

24. Feargal Cochrane, *Ending Wars* (Malden, MA: Polity Press, 2008), 4–5.

25. While not all authors point to the linguistic challenges of ending war, scholarship has begun to identify discursive challenges as inextricably linked to the political and policy difficulties that accompany efforts to end war. See Fred Charles Iklé, *Every War Must End*, 2nd rev. ed. (New York: Columbia University Press, 2005); Dan Reiter, *How Wars End* (Princeton, NJ: Princeton University Press, 2009); Gideon Rose, *How Wars End: Why We Always Fight the Last Battle* (New York: Simon & Schuster, 2010); and Peter Turchin, *War and Peace and War: The Rise and Fall of Empires* (New York: Plume Books, 2007). See also Jeremy Engels, *Enemyship: Democracy and Counter-Revolution in the Early Republic* (East Lansing: Michigan State University Press, 2010).

26. George Bush, "Address to the Nation Announcing Allied Military Action in the Persian Gulf," January 16, 1991, American Presidency Project. For a close reading of the metaphoric clusters constitutive of Bush's rhetoric of savagery, see Benjamin R. Bates, "Audiences, Metaphors, and the Persian Gulf War," *Communication Studies* 55, no. 3 (2004): 447–63.

27. See Michael Osborn and Douglas Ehninger, "The Metaphor in Public Address," *Speech Monographs* 29 (1962): 223–34; Michael Osborn, "Archetypal Metaphor in Rhetoric: The Light-Dark Family," *Quarterly Journal of Speech* 53, no. 2 (1967): 115–26; Michael Osborn, "The Evolution of the Archetypal Sea in Rhetoric and Poetic," *Quarterly Journal of Speech* 63

(1977): 347–63; and Michael Osborn, "The Trajectory of My Work with Metaphor," *Southern Communication Journal* 74, no. 1 (January–March 2009): 79–87.

28. Political realism is an intellectual tradition with roots in Ancient Greece. In contemporary times, E. H. Carr's criticism of political idealism stimulated the development of postwar political realism rooted in the definition and pursuit of national interests. See "Political Realism in International Relations," *Stanford Encyclopedia of Philosophy* (May 24, 2017); Hans Morgenthau, *Politics among Nations: The Struggle for Power and Peace* (Boston: McGraw-Hill, 1993); and J. Peter Pham, "Political Realism, the Economy, and the National Interest," *American Foreign Policy Interests* 33, no. 1 (2011): 47–48.

29. Political realists warn these entanglements pose specific dangers to American power. See John J. Mearsheimer, "The False Promise of International Institutions," *International Security* 19, no. 3 (1994–1995): 5–49.

30. See, for example, Barry Posen, *Restraint: A New Foundation for U.S. Grand Strategy* (Ithaca, NY: Cornell University Press, 2014).

31. I am cognizant, of course, that it is difficult to say the war in Afghanistan ever truly ended.

32. For example, the United States forced enemies to surrender in the Revolutionary War, the Mexican-American War, Spanish-American War, and World War I. The War of 1812 resulted in a limited deal that sustained antagonisms between England and the United States. The Indian Wars produced outcomes that precluded a lasting agreement between the parties.

33. Chris J. Cuomo, "War Is Not Just an Event: Reflections on the Significance of Everyday Violence," *Hypatia* 11, no. 4 (Fall 1996): 30–45.

34. As of this writing, Obama's presidential archive has yet to open.

35. Joshua M. Scacco and Kevin Coe, "The Ubiquitous Presidency: Toward a New Paradigm for Studying Presidential Communication," *International Journal of Communication* 10 (2016): 2014–37.

36. Jeffrey K. Tulis, *The Rhetorical Presidency* (Princeton, NJ: Princeton University Press, 1987). I expand on these themes in Stephen J. Heidt,

"Introduction: The Study of Presidential Rhetoric in Uncertain Times: Thoughts on Theory and Practice," in *Reading the Presidency: Advances in Presidential Rhetoric*, ed. Stephen J. Heidt and Mary E. Stuckey (New York: Peter Lang, 2019), 1-20.

37. See Samuel Kernell, *Going Public: New Strategies of Presidential Leadership* (Washington, DC: CQ Press, 2007). On the use of administrative strategies, see Vanessa B. Beasley, "The Rhetorical Presidency Meets the Unitary Executive: Implications for Presidential Rhetoric on Public Policy," *Rhetoric & Public Affairs* 13, no. 1 (2010): 7-36.

38. Martin J. Medhurst, "Introduction," in *Before the Rhetorical Presidency*, ed. Martin J. Medhurst (College Station: Texas A&M University Press).

39. See, for example, John M. Murphy, *John F. Kennedy and the Liberal Persuasion* (East Lansing: Michigan State University Press, 2019).

40. For a comprehensive discussion of these issues, see Heidt, "Introduction: The Study of Presidential Rhetoric in Uncertain Times," 1-19.

41. Roderick Hart, *The Sound of Leadership: Presidential Communication in the Modern Age* (Chicago: University of Chicago Press, 1987), 14-17.

42. See, for example, Elizabeth N. Saunders, *Leaders at War: How Presidents Shape Military Interventions* (Ithaca, NY: Cornell University Press, 2011).

43. Murphy, *John F. Kennedy and the Liberal Persuasion*, 23.

44. Heidt, "Introduction: The Study of Presidential Rhetoric in Uncertain Times," 7.

45. Robert Asen, "Introduction: Rhetoric and Public Policy," *Rhetoric & Public Affairs* 13, no. 1 (2010): 1-6. Steven R. Goldzwig, "LBJ, the Rhetoric of Transcendence, and the Civil Rights Act of 1968," *Rhetoric & Public Affairs* 6, no. 1 (2003): 25-54. Trevor Parry-Giles, "Resisting a 'Treacherous Piety': Issues, Images, and Public Policy Deliberation in Presidential Campaigns," *Rhetoric & Public Affairs* 13, no. 1 (2010): 37-64. Megan Foley, "From Infantile Citizens to Infantile Institutions: The Metaphoric Transformation of Political Economy in the 2008 Housing Market Crisis," *Quarterly Journal of Speech* 98, no. 4 (2012): 386-410; and Stephen J. Heidt, "Presidential Rhetoric, Metaphor, and the Emergence of the Democracy Promotion Industry," *Southern Communication Journal* 78, no. 3 (2013): 233-55. Beasley, "The Rhetorical Presidency Meets the Unitary

Executive." David S. Birdsell, "George W. Bush's Signing Statements: The Assault on Deliberation," *Rhetoric & Public Affairs* 10, no. 2 (2007): 335–60. Mary E. Stuckey, *Jimmy Carter, Human Rights, and the National Agenda* (College Station: Texas A&M University Press, 2008); and Stephen J. Heidt, "Presidential Power and National Violence: James K. Polk's Rhetorical Transfer of Savagery," *Rhetoric & Public Affairs* 19, no. 3 (2016): 365–96.

46. Michel Foucault, *Discipline and Punish: The Birth of the Prison*, trans. Alan Sheridan (New York: Vintage Books, 1995); and Wendy Brown, "American Nightmare: Neoliberalism, Neoconservatism, and De-Democratization," *Political Theory* 34, no. 6 (December 2006): 690–714.

47. Ned O'Gorman, *Spirits of the Cold War* (East Lansing: Michigan State University Press, 2011), 7.

48. O'Gorman, *Spirits of the Cold War*, 16.

49. Karlyn Kohrs Campbell, "Agency: Promiscuous and Protean," *Communication and Critical/Cultural Studies* 2 (2005): 5. Cited in O'Gorman, *Spirits of the Cold War*, chap. 1, n. 30.

50. Edward Said, *Orientalism*, 25th anniversary ed. (New York: Vintage Books, 1994), 23.

51. Stuckey, *Jimmy Carter, Human Rights, and the National Agenda*, xxviii.

52. Michel Foucault, *The Archeology of Knowledge*, trans. A. M. Sheridan Smith (New York: Vintage Books, 2010).

53. Said, *Orientalism*, 239.

54. O'Gorman, *Spirits of the Cold War*, 15.

55. O'Gorman, *Spirits of the Cold War*, 236.

56. Stephen J. Heidt, "The Presidency as Pastiche: Atomization, Circulation, and Rhetorical Instability," *Rhetoric & Public Affairs* 15, no. 4 (2012): 630.

57. See Brandon Rottinghaus, *The Provisional Pulpit: Modern Presidential Leadership of Public Opinion* (College Station: Texas A&M University Press, 2010).

58. Stuckey, *Jimmy Carter, Human Rights, and the National Agenda*, 112.

59. Chantal Mouffe, "Citizenship and Political Identity," *October* 61, The Identity in Question (Summer 1992): 28.

60. Michael J. Shapiro, *Violent Cartographies: Mapping Cultures of War* (Minneapolis: University of Minnesota Press, 1997), 59.

61. See Carl Schmitt, *The Concept of the Political* (Chicago: University of Chicago Press, 2007), 26.

62. Engels, *Enemyship.*

63. Said, *Orientalism.*

64. Mary E. Stuckey, *Defining Americans* (Lawrence: University Press of Kansas, 2004).

65. Robert L. Ivie, "Images of Savagery in American Justifications for War," *Communication Monographs* 47 (1980): 281. See also Robert L. Ivie, "Fire, Flood, and Red Fever: Motivating Metaphors of Global Emergency in the Truman Doctrine Speech," *Presidential Studies Quarterly* 29, no. 3 (1999): 570–91.

66. William L. Nothstine, "'Topics' as Ontological Metaphor in Contemporary Rhetorical Theory and Criticism," *Quarterly Journal of Speech* 74 (1988): 151.

67. Osborn and Ehninger, "The Metaphor in Public Address," 228.

68. Kathleen Hall Jamieson, "The Metaphoric Cluster in the Rhetoric of Pope Paul VI and Edmund G. Brown, Jr.," *Quarterly Journal of Speech* 66 (1980): 54.

69. Ronald Walter Greene, "Another Materialist Rhetoric," *Critical Studies in Mass Communication* 15 (1998): 27.

70. Thomas Lemke, "'The Birth of Bio-politics': Michel Foucault's Lecture at the College de France on Neo-liberal Governmentality," *Economy and Society* 30, no. 2 (May 2001): 191.

71. Foley, "From Infantile Citizens to Infantile Institutions," 403.

72. Leah Ceccarelli, *On the Frontier of Science: An American Rhetoric of Exploration and Exploitation* (East Lansing: Michigan State University Press, 2013), 77.

73. Karlyn Kohrs Campbell and Kathleen Hall Jamieson, *Presidents Creating the Presidency: Deeds Done in Words*, 2nd ed. (Chicago: University of Chicago Press, 2008), 234–35.

74. "A Report to the National Security Council—NSC 68," April 12, 1950, President's Secretary File, Truman Papers, Truman Library, 4, 7.

75. Nicholas Thompson, *The Hawk and the Dove: Paul Nitze, George Kennan, and the History of the Cold War* (New York: Henry Holt & Company, 2009), 9.

Chapter 1. The Recivilized Savage:
Harry Truman and the Victory of the Good War

1. Lawrence Verria and George Galdorisi, *The Kissing Sailor* (Annapolis, MD: Naval Institute Press, 2012).

2. See Robert Hariman and John Luis Lucaites, *No Caption Needed: Iconic Photographs, Public Culture, and Liberal Democracy* (Chicago: University of Chicago Press, 2007).

3. James Alvin Huston, *The Sinews of War: Army Logistics, 1775–1953* (Washington, DC: U.S. Government Printing Office, 1966), 561–62.

4. Patti Clayton Becker, *Books and Libraries in American Society during World War II: Weapons in the War of Ideas* (New York: Routledge, 2005), 193.

5. Cabinet Meeting Minutes, August 16, 1945, Matthew J. Connelly Papers: Notes on Cabinet Meetings I, Truman Papers, Truman Library.

6. Gary A. Donaldson, *American Foreign Policy: The Twentieth Century in Documents* (New York: Longman Press, 2003), 116.

7. These concerns existed inside and outside government. See, for example, Norman Thomas, "Arming against Russia," *Annals of the American Academy of Political and Social Science* 241 (September 1945): 67–71; Frederick L. Schuman, "A Diagnosis of the Big Three Problem," *New York Times*, June 30, 1946; and Ronald D. Lipschutz, *Cold War Fantasies: Film, Fiction, and Foreign Policy* (Lanham, MD: Rowman & Littlefield Publishers, 2001), 16.

8. Roosevelt had been attuned to the likelihood of strategic rivalry between the United States and the USSR and had pointed to Soviet designs for Poland as evidence of communist desires to develop a sphere of influence in Europe. See Warren F. Kimball, *The Juggler: Franklin Roosevelt as Wartime Statesman* (Princeton, NJ: Princeton University Press, 1994), 90; Michael Dobbs, *Six Months in 1945: FDR, Stalin, Churchill and Truman—from World War to Cold War.* (New York: Alfred A. Knopf, 2012); David M. Kennedy, "Culture Wars: The Sources and Uses of Enmity in American History," in *Enemy Images in American History*, ed. Ragnhild Fiebig-von Hase and Irsula Lehmkuhl (New York: Berghahn Books, 1997), 807–8.

9. Dobbs, *Six Months in 1945*, 196.

10. Tsuyoshi Hasegawa, *Racing the Enemy: Stalin, Truman, and the Surrender of Japan* (Cambridge, MA: Belknap Press of Harvard University Press,

2005), 269–70.

11. Harry S. Truman, "Statement by the President Announcing the Use of the A-Bomb at Hiroshima," August 6, 1945, American Presidency Project.

12. Lipschutz, *Cold War Fantasies*, 27–28; and Robert P. Newman, *Truman and the Hiroshima Cult* (East Lansing: Michigan State University Press, 1995), 28, 95.

13. Konrad H. Jarausch, *After Hitler: Recivilizing Germans, 1945-1995* (New York: Oxford University Press, 2006), 5.

14. Jarausch, *After Hitler*, 6.

15. For more about the Morgenthau Plan, see Michael Beschloss, *The Conquerors: Roosevelt, Truman, and the Destruction of Hitler's Germany, 1941-1945* (New York: Simon & Schuster, 2002), 233; and Jarausch, *After Hitler*, 6.

16. This challenge grew as American failure to persuade Germans of their culpability for the war contributed to the anti-German hawks' position. See Byron Price to the President, November 9, 1945, President Secretary's File: Historical File, 1924–1953, Box 196, Folder 10: Germany—Postwar, Truman Papers, Truman Library.

17. Andrew J. Polsky, *Elusive Victories: The American Presidency at War* (New York: Oxford University Press, 2012), 171.

18. John Dower, *War without Mercy: Race and Power in the Pacific War* (New York: Pantheon Books, 1986), 137.

19. Gideon Rose, *How Wars End: Why We Always Fight the Last Battle* (New York: Simon & Schuster, 2009), 94. See also Polsky, *Elusive Victories*, 171. This challenge produced difficulty for Truman's desire to finesse definitions of "unconditional surrender." See Hasegawa, *Racing the Enemy*, 51–56.

20. The gendered "man" here is intentional as the image referenced, typical for the genre, clearly exhibited masculine features. As far as this author is aware, these types of racialized images only displayed women in helpless positions, at the point of being raped or violated by the beastly Japanese. That is, in addition to being raced, images of savagery were also gendered. See Sam Keen, *Faces of the Enemy*; Dower, *War without Mercy*; and Kennedy, "Culture Wars," 353–55.

21. For an explanation of how naming the enemy contributed to the internment of Japanese Americans, see Gordon Nakagawa, "'No Japs

Allowed': Negation and Naming as Subject-constituting Strategies
Reflected in Contemporary Stories of Japanese American Internment,"
Communication Reports 3, no. 1 (Winter 1990): 22–27. While policymakers
were generally not interested in exterminating the Japanese entirely,
talk about the possibility is more than apocryphal. The British
committed extensive propaganda resources to convince their troops
to kill the Japanese, generating significantly greater animus against
the Asian enemy than even that against the Germans, who had been
bombing London continuously. See Tim Moreman, *The Japanese and the
British Commonwealth Armies at War, 1941–45* (London: Routledge, 2013),
103–5. And, the Japanese themselves needed to be convinced that the
Americans had no interest in exterminating their race, partially because
the Japanese government had spent years pointing to American atrocities
and the internment of Japanese Americans as evidence of the country's
exterminationist desires. See David C. Earhart, *Certain Victory: Images of
World War II in the Japanese Media* (Armonk, NY: M.E. Sharpe, 2009), 366–
70. Finally, there were voices in the Roosevelt administration, principally
Admiral William Leahy, Roosevelt's chief of staff, as well as other
lower-level functionaries, who favored what would now be considered
genocide of the Japanese people. The view held sway with the American
public, with polls showing continued support for the extermination of
the Japanese even after the war formally concluded. See Dan Reiter,
How Wars End (Princeton, NJ: Princeton University Press, 2009), 111.
Those voices did not represent U.S. government policy, however, as
Truman was careful to explain that victory did not mean extermination
of the Japanese people, and Acheson authored a memo expressing the
importance of publicly communicating that the U.S. would not seek to
exterminate the Japanese after a peace deal concluded. See Hasegawa,
Racing the Enemy, 70, 328.

22. Reiter, *How Wars End*, 111.

23. Rose, *How Wars End*, 119.

24. David Campbell, *Writing Security: United States Foreign Policy and the Politics of
Identity*, rev. ed. (Minneapolis: University of Minnesota Press, 1998), 143.

25. As one scholar put it, "to depict societies, states and/or nations as a *body*

is a metaphoric framing that has a long and famous pedigree" stretching from "pre-Socratic thinking" to the present. See Andreas Musolff, *Metaphor, Nation and the Holocaust: The Concept of the Body Politic* (New York: Routledge, 2010), 4.

26. Claire Rasmussen and Michael Brown, "The Body Politic as Spatial Metaphor," *Citizenship Studies* 9, no. 5 (2005): 470–71.

27. Conceptions of the doctor-patient relationship in the 1940s differed greatly from contemporary understandings. At the time, doctors performed a paternalistic role that looked at and treated the whole patient, rather than individual symptoms. This "paternalistic" form of medicine might not have been terribly effective, but it held great cultural power. In recognition of that power, cigarette companies employed actors to dress up as doctors and "recommend" specific brands. Physician recommendations also sparked a surge in tonsillectomies, an unnecessary procedure for most adolescents; concern that minor ailments like flat feet could indicate serious problems; the popularization of electroshock treatments for improving mental health; and attention to cancer, among other things. In sum, when Truman channeled the persona of the doctor, he also conveyed a sort of authoritarian, paternalistic ethos. See Mark Siegler, *The Three Ages of Medicine and the Doctor Patient Relationship* (Barcelona: Monographs of the Victor Grifols i Lucas Foundation, 2011), 13–14, https://www.fundaciogrifols.org; David J. Rothman, *Strangers at the Bedside: A History of How Law and Bioethics Transformed Medical Decision Making* (New York: Basic Books, 1991); Bryan Sisk, Richard Frankel, Eric Kodish, and J. Harry Isaacson, "The Truth about Truth-Telling in American Medicine: A Brief History," *Permanente Journal* 20, no. 3 (2016): 215–19; and Martha N. Gardner and Allan M. Brandt, "'The Doctors' Choice Is America's Choice': The Physician in US Cigarette Advertisements, 1930–1953," *American Journal of Public Health* 96, no. 2 (2006): 222–32.

28. Siegler, *The Three Ages of Medicine and the Doctor Patient Relationship*, 13–14.

29. David J. Rothman, *Strangers at the Bedside: A History of How Law and Bioethics Transformed Medical Decision Making* (New York: Basic Books, 1991), 1.

30. See Douglas T. Stuart, *Creating the National Security State: A History of the Law*

That Transformed America (Princeton, NJ: Princeton University Press, 2008), 1–3.

31. See Loch K. Johnson, ed., *Strategic Intelligence: Understanding the Hidden Side of Government* (Westport, CT: Praeger Security International, 2007), 220–21.

32. Roger Dingman, "Truman's Gift: The Japanese Peace Settlement," in *Northeast Asia and the Legacy of Harry S. Truman: Japan, China, and the Two Koreas*, ed. James I. Matray (Kirksville, MO: Truman State University Press, 2012), 55.

33. Murray Edelman, *Constructing Political Spectacle* (Chicago: University of Chicago Press, 1988), 78.

34. Harry S. Truman, "Address before a Joint Session of the Congress," April 16, 1945, American Presidency Project.

35. James K. Polk, "Third Annual Message," December 7, 1847, American Presidency Project.

36. William McKinley, "Second Annual Message," December 5, 1898, American Presidency Project.

37. Jason Flanagan, *Imagining the Enemy: American Presidential War Rhetoric from Woodrow Wilson to George W. Bush* (Claremont, CA: Regina Books, 2009).

38. Polsky, *Elusive Victories*, 155.

39. Dobbs, *Six Months in 1945*, 237.

40. Roosevelt, quoted in Flanagan, *Imagining the Enemy*, 72.

41. Harry S. Truman, "Broadcast to the American People Announcing the Surrender of Germany," May 8, 1945, American Presidency Project.

42. Harry S. Truman, "Messages to Allied Leaders and to General Eisenhower on the Surrender of Germany," May 8, 1945, American Presidency Project.

43. Harry S. Truman, "The President's News Conference," May 15, 1945, American Presidency Project.

44. See Anthony Rhodes, *Propaganda: The Art of Persuasion: World War II* (New York: Chelsea House Publishers, 1976); William L. O'Neill, *A Democracy at War: America's Fight at Home and Abroad in World War II* (Cambridge, MA: Harvard University Press, 1995); Clayton Laurie, *The Propaganda Warriors* (Lawrence: Kansas University Press, 1996); Allan Winkler, *The Politics of Propaganda: Office of War Information, 1942–1945* (New Haven, CT: Yale

University Press, 1978); Robert Heide and John Gilman, *Home Front America: Popular Culture of the World War II Era* (Chronicle Books, 1995); and Gerd Horten, *Radio Goes to War: The Cultural Politics of Propaganda during World War II* (Berkeley: University of California Press, 2002).

45. Harry S. Truman, "Joint Report with Allied Leaders on the Potsdam Conference," August 2, 1945, American Presidency Project.

46. J. Samuel Walker, *Prompt and Utter Destruction: Truman and the Use of Atomic Bombs against Japan*, rev. ed. (Chapel Hill: University of North Carolina Press, 2004), 20-21.

47. See Office of War Information, "The Job Ahead: Japan," Fact Sheet No. 322 (March 26, 1945), President Secretary's File: Historical File, 1924–1953, Box 198, Truman Papers, Truman Library.

48. Office of War Information, "V-E Day and After," Fact Sheet (April 6, 1945), p. 2, President Secretary's File: Historical File, 1924–1953, Box 198, Truman Papers, Truman Library.

49. Harry S. Truman, "Broadcast to the American People Announcing the Surrender of Germany," May 8, 1945, American Presidency Project.

50. Harry S. Truman, "Radio Address to the American People after the Signing of the Terms of Unconditional Surrender by Japan," September 1, 1945, American Presidency Project.

51. Harry S. Truman, "Radio Address to the Members of the Armed Forces," September 2, 1945, American Presidency Project.

52. Harry S. Truman, "Statement by the President on the Surrender of German Forces in Italy," May 2, 1945, American Presidency Project.

53. Rasmussen and Brown, "The Body Politic as Spatial Metaphor," 480.

54. Joshua Gunn, "The Rhetoric of Exorcism: George W. Bush and the Return of Political Demonology," *Western Journal of Communication* 68, no. 1 (Winter 2004): 18.

55. Harry S. Truman, "Statement by the President Calling for Unconditional Surrender of Japan," May 8, 1945, American Presidency Project.

56. Truman, "Statement by the President Calling for Unconditional Surrender of Japan," May 8, 1945.

57. Truman, "Statement by the President Calling for Unconditional Surrender of Japan," May 8, 1945.

58. Truman, "Statement by the President Calling for Unconditional Surrender of Japan," May 8, 1945.

59. Harry S. Truman, "Special Message to the Congress on Winning the War with Japan," June 1, 1945, American Presidency Project.

60. There remains significant historical controversy related to Truman's motivation to drop the bomb. Robert Newman contends that Truman's primary motivation—perhaps sole motivation—derived from concerns that no other means could force Japanese concession and save millions of lives. Still, he doesn't entirely discount the possibility that Soviet entry into the war may have played a role in the decision. See Newman, *Truman and the Hiroshima Cult*, 35, 37–38, 42–43; Robert P. Newman, with David Deifell, *Invincible Ignorance in American Foreign Policy: The Triumph of Ideology over Evidence* (New York: Peter Lang Publishing, 2013), 1–17; Richard B. Frank, *Downfall: The End of the Imperial Japanese Empire* (New York: Penguin Books, 2001); and Sadao Asada, "The Shock of the Atomic Bomb and Japan's Decision to Surrender—A Reconsideration," *Pacific Historical Review* 67, no. 4 (1998): 477–512. Others remain convinced that the threat of Soviet intervention in August 1945 spurred Truman to action. See Andrew J. Rotter, *Hiroshima: The World's Bomb* (London: Oxford University Press, 2008); and Ronald Takaki, *Hiroshima: Why America Dropped the Atomic Bomb*, repr. (New York: Back Bay Books, 1996). Indeed, Henry Stimson's journal entries appear to confirm that the likelihood of great power rivalry had already entered Truman's calculus by July 1945. See United States Department of State, *Foreign Relations of the United States: Diplomatic Papers: The Conference of Berlin (The Potsdam Conference), 1945*, vol. 2 (Washington, DC: Government Printing Office, 1960), 1373.

61. Harry S. Truman, "Radio Report to the American People on the Potsdam Conference," August 9, 1945, American Presidency Project.

62. Truman, "Radio Report to the American People on the Potsdam Conference," August 9, 1945.

63. Emperor Hirohito, "Accepting the Potsdam Declaration, Radio Broadcast," August 14, 1945, online at https://www.mtholyoke.edu/acad/intrel/hirohito.htm.

64. Harry S. Truman, "Proclamation 2660—Victory in the East—Day of

Prayer," August 16, 1945, American Presidency Project.

65. Truman, "Proclamation 2660—Victory in the East—Day of Prayer," August 16, 1945.

66. Harry S. Truman, "Radio Address to the American People after the Signing of the Terms of Unconditional Surrender by Japan," September 1, 1945, American Presidency Project.

67. Michael Osborn, *Michael Osborn on Metaphor and Style* (East Lansing: Michigan State University Press, 2018), 235.

68. Osborn, *Michael Osborn on Metaphor and Style*, 242.

69. Osborn, *Michael Osborn on Metaphor and Style*, 242.

70. See Siegler, *The Three Ages of Medicine and the Doctor Patient Relationship.*

71. Siegler, *The Three Ages of Medicine and the Doctor Patient Relationship*, 13–14.

72. Truman, "Radio Report to the American People on the Potsdam Conference," August 9, 1945.

73. Dingman, "Truman's Gift: The Japanese Peace Settlement," 51.

74. Harry S. Truman, "Radio Address to the Members of the Armed Forces," September 2, 1945, American Presidency Project.

75. Harry S. Truman, "Statement of Policy, Approved by the President, Relating to Post-War Japan," September 22, 1945, American Presidency Project.

76. Truman, "Statement of Policy, Approved by the President, Relating to Post-War Japan," September 22, 1945.

77. Harry S. Truman, "Address in Chicago on Army Day," April 6, 1946, American Presidency Project.

78. Truman, "Address in Chicago on Army Day," April 6, 1946.

79. While only explicitly identifying Germany in this quote, the next question asked if this would "apply to the Japanese." Truman answered, "it certainly will." See Harry S. Truman, "The President's News Conference," August 16, 1945, American Presidency Project.

80. Arthur H. Vandenberg, "American Foreign Policy," U.S. Congress, Senate, *Congressional Record*, 79th Cong., 1st sess., 165–67.

81. "Directive to Commander in Chief of the United States Forces of Occupation Regarding the Military Government of Germany (Joint Chiefs of Staff Directive 1067), April 1945," *Foreign Relations of the United*

States, vol. 3 (Washington, DC: Department of State, 1945), 484.

82. See Takushi Ohno, "United States Policy on Japanese War Reparations, 1945–1951," *Asian Studies* 13, no. 3 (1975): 23–45.

83. Robert Trumbull, "Hirohito Promises Japan a Recovery: Opening Diet, Emperor Talks of 'Glory,' Not Surrender—Allied Reporters Attend," *New York Times*, September 5, 1945, 1.

84. James F. Byrnes, "Texts of Byrnes Statement and U.S. Policy on Reparations and Aid to Germany," *New York Times*, December 12, 1945, 2.

85. Burton Crane, "Japan's Recovery Has Not Been Fast," *New York Times*, December 31, 1946, 7.

86. "Summary of State Department's Position of European Recovery Plan," August 26, 1947, Subject File, Clifford Papers, Truman Papers, Truman Library.

87. Harry S. Truman, "Address in New York City at the Opening Session of the United Nations General Assembly," October 23, 1946, American Presidency Project.

88. Harry S. Truman, "Address in New York City at the Opening Session of the United Nations General Assembly," October 23, 1946, American Presidency Project.

89. In many ways, this obligation mimics the rhetorical patterns established in the postcolonial era. See Alison Brysk, Craig Parsons, and Wayne Sandholtz, "After Empire: National Identity and Post-Colonial Families of Nations," *European Journal of International Relations* 8, no. 2 (2002): 274.

90. Harry S. Truman, "Special Message to the Congress Presenting a 21-Point Program for the Reconversion Period," September 6, 1945, American Presidency Project.

91. Derek S. Reveron, Nikolas K. Gvosdeve, and Mackubin Thomas Owens, *US Foreign Policy and Defense Strategy: The Evolution of an Incidental Superpower* (Washington, DC: Georgetown University Press, 2015), 179–80.

92. Harry S. Truman, "Address before a Joint Session of the Congress," April 16, 1945, American Presidency Project.

93. Memorandum for the President, by John McCloy, April 26, 1945, Harry S. Truman Papers, Harry S. Truman Library, Independence, MO, President's Secretary's File, Box 178; Stimson Diary, May 4–16, 1945,

Truman Papers, Truman Library.

94. Harry S. Truman, "Letter to Heads of War Agencies on the Economic Situation in the Liberated Countries of Northwest Europe," May 22, 1945, American Presidency Project.

95. Harry S. Truman, "Radio Report to the American People on the Potsdam Conference," August 9, 1945, American Presidency Project.

96. Truman well understood the alliance could not sustain. Divisions between the U.S. and the Soviets on topics like German reparations, the status of Poland, and the postwar future of Germany made clear the allies would never see eye to eye. See Terry Charman, "How the Potsdam Conference Shaped the Future of Post-War Europe," Imperial War Museums (January 10, 2018), https://www.iwm.org.uk/history/how-the-potsdam-conference-shaped-the-future-of-post-war-europe.

97. Truman, "Radio Report to the American People on the Potsdam Conference," August 9, 1945.

98. Memorandum by the Secretary of State to President Truman, February 22, 1946, in *Foreign Relations of the United States, 1946*, vol. 8, *The Far East* (Washington, DC: U.S. Government Printing Office, 1971).

99. Memorandum by the Secretary of State to President Truman, February 27, 1946, in *Foreign Relations of the United States, 1946*, vol. 8, *The Far East* (Washington, DC: U.S. Government Printing Office, 1971), 150.

100. Truman, "Address before the Governing Board of the Pan American Union," April 15, 1946.

101. Harry S. Truman, "The President's News Conference," February 7, 1946, American Presidency Project.

102. Harry S. Truman, "Special Message to the Congress on Extension of the Second War Powers Act," January 31, 1947, American Presidency Project.

103. Harry S. Truman, "Address in New York City at the Opening Session of the United Nations General Assembly," October 23, 1946, American Presidency Project.

104. Truman, "Address in Chicago on Army Day," April 6, 1946.

105. Truman, "Address in Chicago on Army Day," April 6, 1946.

106. Harry S. Truman, "Address in New York City at the Opening Session of the United Nations General Assembly," October 23, 1946, American

Presidency Project.

107. Harry S. Truman, "Address in San Francisco at the Closing Session of the United Nations Conference," June 26, 1945, American Presidency Project.

108. Truman, "Address in San Francisco at the Closing Session of the United Nations Conference," June 26, 1945.

109. Roosevelt prefigured this orientation when he exhorted the Axis powers to "abandon the philosophy, and the teaching of that philosophy, which has brought so much suffering to the world." See Franklin D. Roosevelt, "State of the Union Address," January 7, 1943, American Presidency Project.

110. Office of War Information, "The Job Ahead: Japan," 4–5.

111. Office of War Information, "The Job Ahead: Japan," 5.

112. Harry S. Truman, "Remarks at the Pemiscot County Fair, Caruthersville, Missouri," October 7, 1945, American Presidency Project.

113. Truman, "Remarks at the Pemiscot County Fair, Caruthersville, Missouri," October 7, 1945.

114. Harry S. Truman, "Address on Foreign Policy at the Navy Day Celebration in New York City," October 27, 1945, American Presidency Project.

115. See Michael J. Hogan, *A Cross of Iron: Harry S. Truman and the Origins of the National Security State, 1945-1954* (New York: Cambridge University Press, 1998), 2.

116. Truman, "Address in Chicago on Army Day," April 6, 1946.

117. Truman, "Address before the Governing Board of the Pan American Union," April 15, 1946.

118. Truman, "Address in Chicago on Army Day," April 6, 1946.

119. *The End of the War in the Pacific: Surrender Documents in Facsimile* (Washington, DC: National Archives Publication, 1945), 5; PSF: Historical File, Box 197: Japanese Surrender, Truman Papers, Truman Library.

120. Harry S. Truman, "Statement of Policy, Approved by the President, Relating to Post-War Japan," September 22, 1945, American Presidency Project.

121. Truman, "Statement of Policy, Approved by the President, Relating to

Post-War Japan," September 22, 1945.

122. Truman, "Statement of Policy, Approved by the President, Relating to Post-War Japan," September 22, 1945.

123. Truman, "Statement of Policy, Approved by the President, Relating to Post-War Japan," September 22, 1945.

124. Proclamation Defining Terms of Japanese Surrender, Issued at Potsdam, July 26, 1945, http://www.ndl.go.jp/constitution/e/etc/c06.html.

125. Harry S. Truman, "Address before the Governing Board of the Pan American Union," April 15, 1946, American Presidency Project.

126. Truman, "Address before the Governing Board of the Pan American Union," April 15, 1946.

127. Truman, "Address before the Governing Board of the Pan American Union," April 15, 1946.

128. Truman, "Address in New York City at the Opening Session of the United Nations General Assembly," October 23, 1946.

129. Truman, "Address in New York City at the Opening Session of the United Nations General Assembly," October 23, 1946.

130. Truman, "Address in New York City at the Opening Session of the United Nations General Assembly," October 23, 1946.

131. Bryon Price to the President, November 28, 1945, PSF: Historical File, Box 196, Folder 4, Truman Papers, Truman Library.

132. George Atcheson Jr., The Acting Political Advisor in Japan (Atcheson) to President Truman, January 4, 1946, in *Foreign Relations of the United States, 1946*, vol. 8, *The Far East* (Washington, DC: U.S. Government Printing Office, 1971).

133. Report by the State-War-Navy Coordinating Subcommittee for the Far East, January 8, 1946, in *Foreign Relations of the United States, 1946*, vol. 8, *The Far East* (Washington, DC: U.S. Government Printing Office, 1971).

134. Max Bishop, of the Office of the Political Advisor in Japan, to the Secretary of State, April 10, 1946, in *Foreign Relations of the United States, 1946*, vol. 8, *The Far East* (Washington, DC: U.S. Government Printing Office, 1971).

135. "M'Arthur Pleased with Year's Gains," *New York Times*, January 1, 1947, 15.

136. James F. Byrnes to the President, September 2, 1946, PSF: Presidential

Speeches, Longhand Notes, Box 42, Truman Papers, Truman Library.

137. Wesley W. Widmaier, "Constructing Foreign Policy Crises: Interpretive Leadership in the Cold War and War on Terrorism," *International Studies Quarterly* 51 (2007): 785–86.

138. Truman's control of the occupation functioned as an extension of MacArthur's appointment as Allied Supreme Commander and enabled the executive branch to operate in almost complete freedom from congressional scrutiny. Richard Neustadt implies as much with his explanation of MacArthur's role in the Korea conflict. See Richard E. Neustadt, *Presidential Power and the Modern Presidents: The Politics of Leadership from Roosevelt to Reagan* (New York: Free Press, 1990), 12. Truman's relationship with Senator Arthur Vandenberg and the perception produced by rhetoric espousing the value of "bipartisan foreign policy" facilitated this power by effectively shielding Truman's actions abroad from significant congressional scrutiny. See Arthur M. Schlesinger Jr., *The Imperial Presidency* (New York: First Mariner Books, 2004), 130–32. Gerald Astor shows how Truman managed to institutionalize war organizations into civilian agencies like the Central Intelligence Agency and the National Security Council. See Gerald Astor, *Presidents at War: From Truman to Bush, the Gathering of Military Power to Our Commanders in Chief* (Hoboken, NJ: John Wiley & Sons, 2006), 49–50.

139. See Robert L. Ivie, "Fire, Flood, and Red Fever: Motivating Metaphors of Global Emergency in the Truman Doctrine Speech," *Presidential Studies Quarterly* 29, no. 3 (1999).

140. Flanagan, *Imagining the Enemy*, 76.

141. Thomas R. Maddux, "Red Fascism, Brown Bolshevism: The American Image of Totalitarianism in the 1930s," *Historian* 40 (1977): 86; and Les K. Adler and Thomas G. Paterson, "Red Fascism: The Merger of Nazi Germany and Soviet Russia in the American Image of Totalitarianism, 1930s–1950s," *American Historical Review* 75, no. 4 (1970): 1046–64.

142. Robert Mann, *Wartime Dissent in America: A History and Anthology* (New York: Palgrave Macmillan, 2010), 103. See also Petra Goedde, *The Politics of Peace: A Global Cold War History* (New York: Oxford University Press, 2019), 52.

143. Melvin P. Leffler, *The Struggle for Germany and the Origins of the Cold War*

(Washington, DC: German Historical Institute, 1996), 13.

144. Flanagan, *Imagining the Enemy*, 77; Robert L. Messer, *The End of an Alliance: James F. Byrnes, Roosevelt, Truman, and the Origins of the Cold War* (Chapel Hill: University of North Carolina Press, 1982), 135-36.

145. Flanagan, *Imagining the Enemy*, 83.

146. Truman, "Address on Foreign Policy at the Navy Day Celebration in New York City."

147. Michael S. Sherry, *In the Shadow of War: The United States since the 1930s* (New Haven, CT: Yale University Press, 1995), 126.

148. Denise Bostdorff, *Proclaiming the Truman Doctrine: The Cold War Call to Arms* (College Station: Texas A&M University Press, 2008), 36.

149. Longhand Draft Letter from President Harry S. Truman to Secretary of State James Byrnes, January 5, 1946, PSF, Truman Papers, Truman Library.

150. Arnold A. Offner, *Another Such Victory: President Truman and the Cold War, 1945-1953* (Stanford, CA: Stanford University Press, 2002), 132.

151. The speech is reproduced and the event recounted in Donaldson, *American Foreign Policy*, 116-22.

152. Tony Judt, *Postwar: A History of Europe Since 1945* (New York: Penguin Books, 2005), 110.

153. Harry S. Truman, "Special Message to the Congress on Greece and Turkey: The Truman Doctrine," March 12, 1947, American Presidency Project.

154. See Anne Pierce, *Woodrow Wilson and Harry Truman: Mission and Power in American Foreign Policy* (Westport, CT: Praeger Publishers, 2003), 167-99; Elizabeth Edwards Spalding, *The First Cold Warrior: Harry Truman, Containment, and the Remaking of Liberal Internationalism* (Lexington: University Press of Kentucky, 2006), 61-80; Denis M. Bostdorff, *Proclaiming the Truman Doctrine: The Cold War Call to Arms* (College Station: Texas A&M University Press, 2008); John Lewis Gaddis, *Strategies of Containment: A Critical Appraisal of American National Security Policy during the Cold War* (Oxford: Oxford University Press, 2005), 22-23; and Michael J. Hogan, *A Cross of Iron: Harry S. Truman and the Origins of the National Security State, 1945-1954* (New York: Cambridge University Press, 1998), 11-12.

155. Arthur H. Vandenberg, "Soviet Pressure, a World Peril, Delivered to the United States Senate, April 8, 1947," *Vital Speeches of the Day* 13, no. 13 (April 14, 1947): 391.

156. See Walter Lippmann, *The Cold War: A Study in U.S. Foreign Policy* (New York: Harper, 1947).

157. Ivie, "Fire, Flood, and Red Fever," 579.

158. Harry S. Truman, "The President's Special Conference with the Association of Radio News Analysts," May 13, 1947, American Presidency Project.

159. Truman, "The President's Special Conference with the Association of Radio News Analysts," May 13, 1947.

160. Harry S. Truman, "Remarks and Question and Answer Period with the National Conference of Editorial Writers," October 17, 1947, American Presidency Project.

161. *Development of Foreign Reconstruction Policy*, March–July 1947, ca. September 1947, Subject File, J. M. Jones Papers, 13, Truman Papers, Truman Library.

162. Dean Acheson, "The Requirements of Reconstruction" (May 18, 1947), *Department of State Bulletin*, vol. 16, no. 411 (Washington, DC: U.S. Government Printing Office, 1947), 991.

163. Dean Acheson, "An Address at Wesleyan University," June 15, 1947, *The Development of the Foreign Reconstruction Policy of the United States, March–July 1947* (Washington, DC: U.S. Government Printing Office, 1947), 8.

164. George C. Marshall, "European Initiative Essential to Economic Recovery: Remarks by the Secretary of State," June 15, 1947, *Department of State Bulletin* 16, no. 392 (Washington, DC: U.S. Government Printing Office, 1947): 1159–60.

165. Ferald J. Bryan, "George C. Marshall at Harvard: A Study on the Origins and Construction of the 'Marshall Plan' Speech," *Presidential Studies Quarterly* 21, no. 3 (1991): 489–502.

166. The Marshall Plan Speech, George C. Marshall Foundation, http://marshallfoundation.org/marshall/the-marshall-plan/marshall-plan-speech.

167. Report on Radio Reaction to Under Secretary Acheson's Speech at

Cleveland, Mississippi on May 8, 1947, Dean Acheson Papers: Speech and Articles File, Box 134, Truman Papers, Truman Library.

168. Joseph M. Jones to Walter Lippmann, May 7, 1947, Subject File: J. M. Jones Papers, Truman Papers, Truman Library.

169. Report on Radio Reaction to Under Secretary Acheson's Speech at Cleveland, Mississippi on May 8, 1947.

170. Harry S. Truman, "Radio Address to the American People on the Special Session of Congress," October 24, 1947, American Presidency Project.

171. Harry S. Truman, "Annual Message to the Congress on the State of the Union," January 7, 1948, American Presidency Project.

172. Truman, "Annual Message to the Congress on the State of the Union," January 7, 1948.

173. Harry S. Truman, "Address in the Chicago Stadium," October 25, 1948, American Presidency Project.

174. Truman, "Address in the Chicago Stadium," October 25, 1948.

175. Truman, "Address in the Chicago Stadium," October 25, 1948.

176. Truman, "Address in the Chicago Stadium," October 25, 1948.

177. Harry S. Truman, "Address in Miami at the American Legion Convention," October 18, 1948, American Presidency Project.

178. Harry S. Truman, "Statement by the President on the Termination of the State of War with Japan," April 28, 1952, American Presidency Project.

179. Harry S. Truman, "Proclamation 2673—Thanksgiving Day, 1945," November 12, 1945, American Presidency Project.

180. Schlesinger Jr., *The Imperial Presidency*, 6–7.

181. Ivie, *Democracy and America's War on Terror*, 140.

Chapter 2. The Mobile Savage: Harry Truman, Dwight Eisenhower, and Stalemate in Korea

1. James I. Matray, "Introduction: Mild about Harry—President Harry S. Truman's Legacy in Northeast Asia," in *Northeast Asia and the Legacy of Harry S. Truman: Japan, China, and the Two Koreas*, ed. James I. Matray (Kirksville, MO: Truman State University Press, 2012), 7–8.

2. Matray, "Introduction," 9–10.

3. Losing China posed political and policy challenges. Politically,

Republicans used Chinese communism to portray Truman as an ineffective leader in face of what they saw as an international emergency. The policy challenges were even more dire. Rebuilding Japan depended on the existence of a Chinese market for Japanese goods. With communist China closing its doors to the West, and Japanese goods, Truman's reconstruction plan faced crisis. Both of these factors raised the importance of Korea as both democratic outpost and economic market. See Justin Hart, *Empire of Ideas: The Origins of Public Diplomacy* (New York: Oxford University Press, 2013), 142–45. Larry Blomstedt, *Truman, Congress, and Korea: The Politics of America's First Undeclared War* (Lexington: University Press of Kentucky, 2016), 55–57.

4. Denise Bostdorff, *The Presidency and the Rhetoric of Foreign Crisis* (Columbia: University of South Carolina Press, 1994), 30.

5. The North Koreans enjoyed a massive advantage in soldiers at the start of the war with a force size between 150,000 and 200,000 men compared to South Korea's approximately 65,000 combat soldiers, and that difference almost saw South Korea wiped out before the U.S. could enter the war. See Allen R. Millet, *The Korean War: The Essential Biography* (Dulles, VA: Potomac Books, 2007).

6. Robert Mann, *Wartime Dissent in America: A History and Anthology* (New York: Palgrave Macmillan, 2010), 118–19.

7. H. W. Brands, *The General vs. the President: MacArthur and Truman at the Brink of Nuclear War* (New York: Doubleday, 2016), 3–9.

8. Robert J. MacMahon, "The Cold War in Asia: Toward a New Synthesis," *Diplomatic History* 12, no. 3 (1988): 316–17.

9. Elizabeth Stanley, *Paths to Peace: Domestic Coalition Shifts, War Termination and the Korean War* (Stanford, CA: Stanford University Press, 2009), 5.

10. Harry S. Truman, "Statement by the President on the Violation of the 38th Parallel in Korea," June 26, 1950, American Presidency Project.

11. Far East: Invasion of Republic of Korea, June 28, 1950, Subject File: Korea, Papers of George M. Elsey, Truman Papers, Truman Library.

12. Steven Casey, "Harry Truman, the Korean War, and the Transformation of US Policy in East Asia, June 1950–June 1951," in *Northeast Asia and the Legacy of Harry S. Truman: Japan, China, and the Two Koreas*, ed. James I.

Matray (Kirksville, MO: Truman State University Press, 2012), 197.

13. Casey, "Harry Truman, the Korean War, and the Transformation of US Policy in East Asia," 197.

14. Dan Reiter, *How Wars End* (Princeton, NJ: Princeton University Press, 2009), 77.

15. William Stueck, "Conclusion," in *The Korean War in World History*, ed. William Stueck (Lexington: University Press of Kentucky, 2004), 184–85.

16. Stanley, *Paths to Peace*, 9–10.

17. See Karlyn Kohrs Campbell and Kathleen Hall Jamieson, *Presidents Creating the Presidency: Deeds Done in Words* (Chicago: University of Chicago Press, 2008).

18. See Jason C. Flanagan, *Imagining the Enemy: American Presidential War Rhetoric from Woodrow Wilson to George W. Bush* (Claremont, CA: Regina Books, 2009), 97–105.

19. See Leland M. Griffin, "When Dreams Collide: Rhetorical Trajectories in the Assassination of President Kennedy," *Quarterly Journal of Speech* 70, no. 2 (1984): 111–31.

20. See Stephen J. Heidt, "Presidential Power and National Violence: James K. Polk's Rhetorical Transfer of Savagery," *Rhetoric & Public Affairs* 19, no. 3 (2016): 365–95.

21. Stanley Sadler, *The Korean War: No Victors, No Vanquished* (London: UCL Press, 2003), 39–40.

22. Harry S. Truman, "The President's News Conference," June 29, 1950, American Presidency Project.

23. Steven Casey, *Selling the Korean War: Propaganda, Politics, and Public Opinion in the United States, 1950–1953* (Oxford: Oxford University Press, 2008), 28. Robin Santos Doak, *The Korean War* (Milwaukee, WI: World Almanac Library, 2007), 19.

24. Blomstedt, *Truman, Congress, and Korea*, 57. Harry S. Truman, "Radio and Television Address to the American People on the Situation in Korea," July 19, 1950, American Presidency Project.

25. Truman, "The President's News Conference," June 29, 1950.

26. Halford Ross Ryan, *U.S. Presidents as Orators: A Bio-Critical Sourcebook* (Westport, CT: Greenwood Press, 1995), 174.

27. Notes from National Security Council Meeting, June 29, 1950, Subject File: Korea, Papers of George M. Elsey, Truman Papers, Truman Library.

28. Blomstedt, *Truman, Congress, and Korea*, 33.

29. The Korean War quashed any doubts about the logic of containment as the central organizing principle of the Cold War. See Michael Lind, *The American Way of Strategy: U.S. Foreign Policy and the American Way of Life* (New York: Oxford University Press, 2006), 126.

30. Christopher B. Strain, *The Long Sixties: America, 1955-1973* (Malden, MA: Wiley Blackwell, 2017), 8.

31. Harry S. Truman, "Letter to the Speaker Transmitting Supplemental Estimate of Appropriations for Military Assistance," August 1, 1950, American Presidency Project.

32. Truman, "Letter to the Speaker Transmitting Supplemental Estimate of Appropriations for Military Assistance," August 1, 1950.

33. Supplemental Appropriation Act of 1951 (September 27, 1950), 64 Stat. 1063.

34. Harry S. Truman, "Address before the Midcentury White House Conference on Children and Youth," December 5, 1950, American Presidency Project.

35. Deborah Cowen, *The Deadly Life of Logistics: Mapping Violence in Global Trade* (Minneapolis: University of Minnesota Press, 2014), 5.

36. Carlo Galli, *Political Spaces and Global War*, trans. Elisabeth Fay (Minneapolis: University of Minnesota Press, 2010), 4.

37. Harry S. Truman, "Address in San Francisco at the War Memorial Opera House," October 17, 1950, American Presidency Project.

38. Truman understood, of course, that the Soviet Union was the true danger and the source of war in Korea. But, he urged congressional leaders and those in his administration to stay silent about the Soviet role in order to preserve diplomatic options. See Notes from Meeting with Congressional Leaders, June 27, 1950, Subject File: Korea, Papers of George M. Elsey, Truman Papers, Truman Library; President Truman's conversations with George M. Elsey, June 26, 1950, Subject File: Korea, Papers of George M. Elsey, Truman Papers, Truman Library; Telegram from Walworth Barber to Secretary of State, June 25, 1950, Subject File:

Korea, Papers of George M. Elsey, Truman Papers, Truman Library; and Notes from National Security Council Meeting, June 29, 1950, Subject File: Korea, Papers of George M. Elsey, Truman Papers, Truman Library.

39. Harry S. Truman, "Statement by the President upon Signing Bill Continuing the Military Aid Program," July 26, 1950, American Presidency Project.

40. Harry S. Truman, "Radio and Television Report to the American People on the National Emergency," December 15, 1950, American Presidency Project.

41. Harry S. Truman, "Radio Report to the American People on Korea and on U.S. Policy in the Far East," April 11, 1951, American Presidency Project.

42. There is a long history of legal jurisprudence speaking to this understanding of criminal conspiracies. See, for example, Byron K. Elliot and William F. Elliot, *A Treatise on the Law of Evidence: Crimes, Equity, Admiralty, Courts-martial* (Indianapolis, IN: Bobbs-Merrill Company, 1905), 191–92.

43. See Peter Gilles, *The Law of Criminal Conspiracy*, 2nd ed. (Sydney, Australia: Federation Press, 1990), 176.

44. Harry S. Truman, "Annual Budget Message to the Congress: Fiscal Year 1952," January 15, 1951, American Presidency Project.

45. Harry S. Truman, "Address at a Dinner of the Civil Defense Conference," May 7, 1951, American Presidency Project.

46. Harry S. Truman, "Radio and Television Address to the American People on the Mutual Security Program," March 6, 1952, American Presidency Project.

47. Those possibilities include what might be referred to today as "nation-building," as well as the construction of military alliances in Asia.

48. Truman, "Letter to the Speaker Transmitting Supplemental Estimate of Appropriations for Military Assistance," August 1, 1950.

49. Casey, *Selling the Korean War*, 97.

50. Truman was disinclined to use nuclear weapons at any rate. See Brands, *The General vs. the President*, 4–5, 222–23; Lester H. Brune and Robin Hingham, eds., *The Korean War: Handbook of the Literature and Research* (Westport, CT: Greenwood Press, 1996), 299–306; and Martin V. Melosi,

"Harry S. Truman and the Origins of the Nuclear Arms Race," in *Nuclear Energy and the Legacy of Harry S. Truman*, ed. J. Samuel Walker (Kirksville, MO: Truman State University Press, 2016), 90–92.

51. Max Hastings, *The Korean War* (London: Guild Publishing, 1987), 91.

52. Harry S. Truman: "Rear Platform and Other Informal Remarks in Minnesota, North Dakota, and Montana," September 29, 1952, American Presidency Project.

53. Harry S. Truman, "Telegram to General Marshall on the Strength of the U.S. Armed Forces," March 21, 1951, American Presidency Project.

54. Truman, "Telegram to General Marshall on the Strength of the U.S. Armed Forces," March 21, 1951.

55. This was a strange claim since everyone jockeyed for Eisenhower. Equally strange, World War II and the rise of communism had made backbenchers out of the isolationists.

56. Harry S. Truman, "Address before the Woman's National Democratic Club," November 20, 1951, American Presidency Project.

57. Harry S. Truman, "Annual Message to the Congress on the State of the Union," January 9, 1952, American Presidency Project.

58. Truman, "Annual Message to the Congress on the State of the Union," January 9, 1952.

59. Truman, "Annual Message to the Congress on the State of the Union," January 9, 1952.

60. Michael S. Mayer, *The Eisenhower Years* (New York: Facts on File, 2010), vii.

61. See Martin Medhurst, *Dwight D. Eisenhower: Strategic Communicator* (Westport, CT: Greenwood Press, 1993), 38–39, 43–44.

62. Still, this declaration likely swung the election decisively in his favor. See Evan Thomas, *Ike's Bluff: President Eisenhower's Secret Battle to Save the World* (New York: Little, Brown and Company, 2012), 11.

63. Thomas, *Ike's Bluff*, 70.

64. Lewis K. Gough to Dwight D. Eisenhower, November 18, 1952, Confidential Memorandum, Official File, Box 727, Folder 196: Korea, Government and Embassy of, 1952–1953, Eisenhower Presidential Library.

65. John Foster Dulles to Dwight D. Eisenhower, November 20, 1952,

Official File, Box 727, Folder 196: Korea, Government and Embassy of, 1952–1953, Eisenhower Presidential Library.

66. Dulles to Eisenhower, November 20, 1952.

67. Casey, *Selling the Korean War*, 344.

68. Casey, *Selling the Korean War*, 342–43.

69. Louis Fisher, *Presidential War Power*, 3rd rev. ed. (Lawrence: University Press of Kansas, 2013), 116.

70. Eisenhower, quoted in Elizabeth N. Saunders, *Leaders at War: How Presidents Shape Military Interventions* (Ithaca, NY: Cornell University Press, 2011), 65.

71. Saunders, *Leaders at War*, 65.

72. Michael P. Marks, *Metaphors in International Relations Theory* (New York: Palgrave Macmillan, 2011), 30.

73. Abdul Karim Bangura, "International Relations," in *Unpeaceful Metaphors*, ed. Abdul Karim Bangura (New York: Writer's Press Club, 2002), 205.

74. See Martin J. Medhurst, "Eisenhower and the Crusade for Freedom: The Rhetorical Origins of a Cold War Campaign," *Presidential Studies Quarterly* 27, no. 4 (1997): 646–61.

75. Elmer E. Schattschneider, *The Semisovereign People: A Realist's View of Democracy in America*, intro. David Adamy, rev. ed. (Boston: Cengage Learning, 1975), xvii, 16, 39.

76. Michael P. Manks, *The Prison as Metaphor: Re-imagining International Relations* (New York: Peter Lang Publishing, 2004), 53–56.

77. Ann E. Cloud, "Sporting Metaphors: Competition and the Ethos of Capitalism," *Journal of Philosophy in Sport* 34 (2007): 52.

78. Cloud, "Sporting Metaphors," 55–56.

79. Paul Chilton and George Lakoff, "Foreign Policy by Metaphor," in *Language and Peace*, ed. Christina Schaffne and Anita L. Wenden (London: Taylor & Francis e-Library, 2005), 47–48.

80. Bangura, "International Relations," 212–13.

81. Eisenhower earned renown as a game player and strategist prior to becoming Supreme Allied Commander Europe. As a young army officer, he played and then coached football. He was also a committed golfer, playing an estimated eight hundred rounds during his presidency. But

his lasting reputation was that of a "card shark," which originated from "his West Point days," where he played poker. Evan Thomas recounted how Eisenhower "won so often and so much . . . that he had to quit poker altogether to avoid a reputation for fleecing his fellow officers." Later in life, he became an avid bridge player, a game that involved the same skill set he practiced in the presidency: "reading minds, weighing options (his own and others'), thinking ahead, and concealing his intentions." And, in fact, his staff secretary General Andrew Goodpaster attributed Eisenhower's leadership skills to his ability and inclination to "work to multiple objectives" at the same time. See Jean Edward Smith, *Eisenhower in War and Peace* (New York: Random House, 2012), 23–27, 30–31; and Thomas, *Ike's Bluff*, 14–15, 40–42.

82. John Foster Dulles to Dwight D. Eisenhower, "Victory with Honor in Korea," November 20, 1952, Official File, Box 727, Folder 196: Korea, Government and Embassy of, 1952–1953, Eisenhower Presidential Library.

83. Dwight D. Eisenhower, "Inaugural Address," January 20, 1953, American Presidency Project.

84. Dwight D. Eisenhower, "Annual Message to the Congress on the State of the Union," February 2, 1953, American Presidency Project.

85. Dwight D. Eisenhower, "Joint Statement Following Discussions with Prime Minister St. Laurent of Canada," May 8, 1953, American Presidency Project.

86. Dwight D. Eisenhower, "The President's News Conference," March 19, 1953, American Presidency Project.

87. Dwight D. Eisenhower, "The President's News Conference," March 23, 1955, American Presidency Project.

88. Carl Von Clauswitz, *On War*, trans. Col. J. J. Graham, new and rev. ed., intro. Col. F. N. Maude, 3 vols. (London: Kegan Paul, Trench, Trubner & Co., 1918), vol. 1.

89. Douglas MacArthur, "Memorandum on Ending the Korean War" (December 14, 1952), 2, John Foster Dulles Papers, Box 8, Korea Folder, Eisenhower Presidential Library.

90. John Foster Dulles to Dwight D. Eisenhower, November 26, 1952, Memorandum on The Korean War, John Foster Dulles Papers, Box 8,

Korea Folder, Eisenhower Presidential Library.

91. Dulles to Eisenhower, November 26, 1952, Memorandum on The Korean War.

92. Dulles to Eisenhower, November 26, 1952, Memorandum on The Korean War.

93. Dulles to Eisenhower, November 26, 1952, Memorandum on The Korean War.

94. John Foster Dulles, "Address by the Honorable John Foster Dulles, Secretary of State, over the Coast to Coast Facilities of the Columbia Broadcasting System and CBS Television," January 27, 1953, McCardle Papers, Box 6, Folder: Dulles Speeches 1953, Eisenhower Presidential Library.

95. Dwight D. Eisenhower, "Annual Message to the Congress on the State of the Union," January 7, 1954, American Presidency Project.

96. Michael Ledeen, "Bridge, Not Chess, Is the Ultimate War Game," *Wall Street Journal*, May 17, 2015.

97. Dwight D. Eisenhower, "Address at the Columbia University National Bicentennial Dinner, New York City," May 31, 1954, American Presidency Project.

98. Eisenhower, "Address at the Columbia University National Bicentennial Dinner, New York City," May 31, 1954.

99. See David A. Nichols, *Ike and McCarthy: Dwight Eisenhower's Secret Campaign against Joseph McCarthy* (New York: Simon & Schuster, 2017); David Plotke, *Building a Democratic Political Order: Reshaping American Liberalism in the 1930s and 1940s* (New York: Cambridge University Press, 1996), 348–51; and Larry Ceplair, *Anti-communism in Twentieth-century America: A Critical History* (Santa Barbara, CA: Praeger Press, 2011), 145–48.

100. Dwight D. Eisenhower, "The President's News Conference," March 17, 1954, American Presidency Project.

101. Dwight D. Eisenhower, "Address at Annual Dinner of the American Society of Newspaper Editors," April 21, 1956, American Presidency Project.

102. Eisenhower, "Address at Annual Dinner of the American Society of Newspaper Editors," April 21, 1956.

103. John Foster Dulles and Walter S. Robertson, "Report to the Nation by the Honorable John Foster Dulles, Secretary of State, and the Honorable Walter S. Robertson, Assistant Secretary of State," July 17, 1953, McCardle Papers, Box 1, Folder: Korea Truce Negotiations, Eisenhower Presidential Library.

104. See Alan K. Henrikson, "FDR and the 'World-Wide Arena,'" in *FDR's World: War, Peace, and Legacies*, ed. David B. Woolner, Warren F. Kimball, and David Reynolds (New York: Palgrave Macmillan, 2008), 35–36, 39; and, more generally, Jeremy Black, "Geographies of War: The Recent Historical Background," in *The Geography of War and Peace: From Death Camps to Diplomats*, ed. Colin Flint (New York: Oxford University Press, 2005), 19–21.

105. Dwight D. Eisenhower, "Toasts of the President and President Bayar at the Turkish Embassy," January 29, 1954, American Presidency Project.

106. This rhetoric reflects the cartographic sensibilities of the age. See Timothy Barney, *Mapping the Cold War: Cartography and the Framing of America's International Power* (Chapel Hill: University of North Carolina Press, 2015).

107. Dwight D. Eisenhower, "Radio and Television Address to the American People Announcing the Signing of the Korean Armistice," July 26, 1953, American Presidency Project.

108. I should note that, as a Republican, on the verge of celebrating the 100th anniversary of the founding of the Republican Party, Eisenhower's use of Lincoln was not surprising. Two months later, he would more fully commemorate the founding of the Party and Lincoln's leadership. See Dwight D. Eisenhower, "Address at the New England "Forward to '54" Dinner, Boston, Massachusetts," September 21, 1953, American Presidency Project.

109. John Foster Dulles, "Welcome by Secretary of State John Foster Dulles to the Eighth Annual Boys Nation to the Department of State," July 27, 1953, McCardle Papers, Box 6, Folder: Dulles Speeches 1953, Eisenhower Presidential Library.

110. John Foster Dulles, "Address by the Honorable John Foster Dulles, Secretary of State, Made in General Debate of the United Nations Assembly," September 17, 1953, McCardle Papers, Box 6, Folder: Dulles

Speeches 1953, Eisenhower Presidential Library.

111. John Foster Dulles, "The Moral Initiative," November 18, 1953, McCardle Papers, Box 6, Folder: Dulles Speeches 1953, Eisenhower Presidential Library.

112. Dwight D. Eisenhower, "Address at the Republican Precinct Day Rally, Denver, Colorado," October 8, 1954, American Presidency Project.

113. Dwight D. Eisenhower, "Address at Eisenhower Day Dinner Given by the Citizens for Eisenhower Congressional Committee for the District of Columbia," October 28, 1954, American Presidency Project.

114. Eisenhower, "Address at Eisenhower Day Dinner Given by the Citizens for Eisenhower Congressional Committee for the District of Columbia," October 28, 1954.

115. Dwight D. Eisenhower, "Address at Annual Dinner of the American Society of Newspaper Editors," April 21, 1956, American Presidency Project.

116. Eisenhower, "Address at Annual Dinner of the American Society of Newspaper Editors," April 21, 1956.

117. Eisenhower, "Address at Annual Dinner of the American Society of Newspaper Editors," April 21, 1956.

118. Dwight D. Eisenhower, "Address to the Third Special Emergency Session of the General Assembly of the United Nations," August 13, 1958, American Presidency Project.

119. Dwight D. Eisenhower, "Annual Message to the Congress on the State of the Union," January 7, 1954, American Presidency Project.

120. Dwight D. Eisenhower, "Address at the Columbia University National Bicentennial Dinner, New York City," May 31, 1954, American Presidency Project.

121. Eisenhower, "Address at the Columbia University National Bicentennial Dinner, New York City," May 31, 1954.

122. David Halberstam, *The Coldest Winter: America and the Korean War* (New York: Hyperion, 2007), 648.

123. Emma Chanlett-Avery, *U.S.-South Korean Alliance: Issues for Congress,* (Washington, DC: Congressional Research Service Report No. IF11388, December 10, 2019).

124. Dwight D. Eisenhower, "Special Message to the Senate Transmitting the Mutual Defense Treaty between the United States and the Republic of Korea," January 11, 1954, American Presidency Project.

125. Eric Setzekorn, "Eisenhower's Mutual Security Program and Congress: Defense and Economic Assistance for Cold War Asia," *Federal History* (2017): 8–9.

126. Dwight D. Eisenhower, "Special Message to the Congress on the Mutual Security Program," June 23, 1954, American Presidency Project.

127. Eisenhower, "Special Message to the Congress on the Mutual Security Program," June 23, 1954.

128. Eisenhower, "Special Message to the Congress on the Mutual Security Program," June 23, 1954.

129. Eisenhower, "Address at Annual Dinner of the American Society of Newspaper Editors," April 21, 1956.

130. Eisenhower, "Address at Annual Dinner of the American Society of Newspaper Editors," April 21, 1956.

131. Eisenhower, "Address at Annual Dinner of the American Society of Newspaper Editors," April 21, 1956.

132. Andreas Wenger, *Living with Peril: Eisenhower, Kennedy, and Nuclear Weapons* (Lanham, MD: Rowman & Littlefield Publishers, 1997), 13, 16.

133. Dwight D. Eisenhower, "Address 'The Chance for Peace' Delivered before the American Society of Newspaper Editors," April 16, 1953, American Presidency Project.

134. Eisenhower, "Address 'The Chance for Peace.'"

135. Robert L. Ivie, "Dwight D. Eisenhower's 'Chance for Peace': Quest or Crusade?" *Rhetoric & Public Affairs* 1, no. 2 (1998): 227.

136. See Ned O'Gorman, "Eisenhower and the American Sublime," *Quarterly Journal of Speech* 94, no. 1 (February 2008): 44–72; Ira Chernus, *General Eisenhower: Ideology and Discourse* (East Lansing: Michigan State University Press, 2002); Ira Chernus, *Eisenhower's Atoms for Peace* (College Station: Texas A&M University Press, 2002); Medhurst, *Dwight D. Eisenhower*, 73–92; and Martin Medhurst, "Eisenhower's 'Atoms for Peace' Speech: A Case Study in the Strategic Use of Language," *Communication Monographs* 54, no. 2 (June 1987): 204–20.

137. Dwight D. Eisenhower, "Address at the Republican Precinct Day Rally, Denver, Colorado," October 8, 1954, American Presidency Project.

138. Eisenhower, "Address at Annual Dinner of the American Society of Newspaper Editors," April 21, 1956.

139. Eisenhower, "Address at Annual Dinner of the American Society of Newspaper Editors," April 21, 1956.

140. Dwight D. Eisenhower, "Remarks at the Governors' Conference, Seattle, Washington," August 4, 1953, American Presidency Project.

141. Dwight D. Eisenhower, "The President's News Conference," May 12, 1954, American Presidency Project.

142. Conference in President's Office, May 28, 1954, John Foster Dulles Papers, Box 9, Folder: Indochina, Eisenhower Presidential Library.

143. Dwight D. Eisenhower, "Address at the Columbia University National Bicentennial Dinner, New York City," May 31, 1954, American Presidency Project.

144. John Foster Dulles, "Address before the Forty-Fifth Annual Convention of Rotary International," June 10, 1954, John Foster Dulles Papers, Box 9, Folder: Indochina 1953–1954, Eisenhower Presidential Library.

145. Dwight D. Eisenhower, "Address at the Illinois State Fair at Springfield," August 19, 1954, American Presidency Project.

146. Dwight D. Eisenhower, "Radio and Television Address to the American People on the Achievements of the 83d Congress," August 23, 1954, American Presidency Project.

147. Dwight D. Eisenhower, "Special Message to the Congress on the Mutual Security Program," March 13, 1959, American Presidency Project.

148. Eisenhower, "Special Message to the Congress on the Mutual Security Program," March 13, 1959.

149. Eisenhower, "Special Message to the Congress on the Mutual Security Program," March 13, 1959.

150. Eisenhower, "Special Message to the Congress on the Mutual Security Program," March 13, 1959.

151. Dwight D. Eisenhower, "Address at the Gettysburg College Convocation: The Importance of Understanding," April 4, 1959, American Presidency Project.

Chapter 3. Erasing the Savage: Richard Nixon, the Architecture of Peace, and the Eternal Vietnam

1. Hal Bochin, *Richard Nixon: Rhetorical Strategist* (New York: Greenwood Press, 1990), 58.

2. Bochin, *Richard Nixon*, 62.

3. Robert Mann, *Wartime Dissent in America: A History and Anthology* (New York: Palgrave Macmillan, 2010), 135.

4. Bochin, *Richard Nixon*, 63.

5. Richard Nixon, "Address to the Nation on the Situation in Southeast Asia," April 30, 1970, American Presidency Project.

6. Quoted in Jeffrey Kimball, *Nixon's Vietnam War* (Lawrence: University Press of Kansas, 1998), 146.

7. Bochin, *Richard Nixon*, 66; and Mann, *Wartime Dissent in America*, 136.

8. Marilyn B. Young, *The Vietnam Wars, 1945-1990* (New York: HarperCollins, 1991), 263–66.

9. See Frank Ninkovich, *Modernity and Power: A History of the Domino Theory in the Twentieth Century* (Chicago: University of Chicago Press, 1994).

10. Historians agree that Vietnam became Nixon and Kissinger's obsession. Here I point to the rhetorical component of that obsession.

11. Roopali Mukherjee, "Antiracism Limited," *Cultural Studies* 30, no. 1 (2016): 50.

12. Richard Morris and Mary E. Stuckey, "'More Rain and Less Thunder': Substitute Vocabularies, Richard Nixon, and the Construction of Political Reality," *Communication Monographs* 64 (1997): 141.

13. Mary E. Stuckey, "The Donner Party and the Rhetoric of Westward Expansion," *Rhetoric & Public Affairs* 14, no. 2 (2011): 232.

14. Robert L. Ivie, "Metaphor and the Rhetorical Invention of Cold War 'Idealists,'" in *Cold War Rhetoric: Strategy, Metaphor, and Ideology*, ed. Martin J. Medhurst, Robert L. Ivie, Philip Wander, and Robert L. Scott (East Lansing: Michigan State University Press, 1997), 105.

15. Mary E. Stuckey, *The Good Neighbor: Franklin D. Roosevelt and the Rhetoric of American Power* (East Lansing: Michigan State University Press, 2013), 167–200.

16. Truman referred to the delegates of the United Nations conference as the

"architects of the better world." See Harry S. Truman, "Address to the United Nations Conference in San Francisco," April 25, 1945, online by Gerhard Peters and John T. Woolley, American Presidency Project.

17. Jennifer L. Milliken, "Metaphors of Prestige and Reputation in American Foreign Policy and American Realism," in *Post-Realism: The Rhetorical Turn in International Relations*, ed. Francis A. Beer and Robert Hariman (East Lansing: Michigan State University Press, 1996), 227.

18. Richard M. Nixon, "Asia after Viet Nam," *Foreign Affairs* 46 (October 1967): 113.

19. Carol K. Winkler, *In the Name of Terrorism: Presidents on Political Violence in the Post-World War II Era* (Albany: State University of New York Press, 2006), 20–21.

20. Matthew Muspratt and H. Leslie Steeves, "Rejecting Erasure Tropes of Africa: *The Amazing Race* Episodes in Ghana Counter Postcolonial Critiques," *Communication, Culture & Critique* 5 (2012): 536.

21. Bruno Latour, *We Have Never Been Modern*, trans. Catherine Porter (Cambridge, MA: Harvard University Press, 1993), 77–78.

22. See Kenneth Burke, "(Nonsymbolic) Motion/(Symbolic) Action," *Critical Inquiry* 4, no. 4 (Summer 1978): 809–38.

23. Muspratt and Steeves, "Rejecting Erasure Tropes of Africa," 536.

24. Stuart Hall, "Culture, Community, Nation," *Cultural Studies* 7, no. 3 (1993): 362.

25. Nicholas P. De Genova, "Migrant 'Illegality' and Deportability in Everyday Life," *Annual Review of Anthropology* 31 (2002): 427.

26. Richard Nixon, "Address to the Nation Making Public a Plan for Peace in Vietnam," January 25, 1972, American Presidency Project.

27. Thomas Fiddick, "Beyond the Domino Theory: The Vietnam War and Metaphors of Sport," *Journal of American Culture* 12, no. 4 (1989): 79.

28. Lyndon Johnson, quoted in Ronnie Dugger, *The Life and Times of Lyndon Johnson* (New York: W.W. Norton, 1982), 370–71.

29. Frank Cormier, *LBJ: The Way He Was* (Garden City, NY: Doubleday and Company, 1971), 186.

30. Fiddick, "Beyond the Domino Theory," 82.

31. Richard M. Nixon, *Six Crises* (Garden City, NY: Doubleday and

Company, 1962), 173.

32. William C. Westmoreland, *A Soldier Reports* (Garden City, NY: Doubleday and Company, 1976), 112.

33. Paul Chilton, *Security Metaphors: Cold War Discourse from Containment to Common House* (New York: Peter Lang, 1996), 124.

34. Fiddick, "Beyond the Domino Theory," 81.

35. Rodney P. Carlisle, *Encyclopedia of Play in Today's Society*, vol. 1 (Thousand Oaks, CA: Sage Publications, 2009), 180.

36. Ruud van Dijk, ed., *Encyclopedia of the Cold War* (New York: Routledge, 2008), 268-69.

37. Jerome Slater, "The Domino Theory and International Politics: The Case of Vietnam," *Security Studies* 3, no. 2 (Winter 1993/94): 186-87.

38. Slater, "The Domino Theory and International Politics," 187.

39. Ninkovich, *Modernity and Power*, 68.

40. Ninkovich, *Modernity and Power*, 117-18.

41. Slater, "The Domino Theory and International Politics," 218.

42. James S. Olson and Randy Roberts, *Where the Domino Fell: America and Vietnam, 1945-1990* (New York: St. Martin's Press, 1991), 29.

43. Norman A. Graebner, "Myth and Reality: America's Rhetorical Cold War," in *Critical Reflections on the Cold War: Linking Rhetoric and History*, ed. Martin J. Medhurst and H. W. Brands (College Station: Texas A&M University Press, 2000), 25.

44. Slater, "The Domino Theory and International Politics," 186. John Lewis Gaddis, *Strategies of Containment: A Critical Appraisal of American National Security Policy during the Cold War*, rev. and expanded ed. (New York: Oxford University Press, 2005), 89-90.

45. Quoted in Frederick Logevall, *Embers of War: The Fall of an Empire and the Making of America's Vietnam* (New York: Random House, 2012), 222.

46. Milliken, "Metaphors of Prestige and Reputation," 219.

47. David L. Anderson, "Dwight D. Eisenhower and Wholehearted Support of Ngo Dinh Diem," in *Shadow of the White House: Presidents and the Vietnam War, 1945-1975*, ed. David L. Anderson (Lawrence: University Press of Kansas, 1993), 43.

48. Gary R. Hess, "Commitment in the Age of Counterinsurgency:

Kennedy's Vietnam Options and Decisions, 1961–1963," in Anderson, *Shadow of the White House*, 81.

49. Sandra C. Taylor, "Lyndon Johnson and the Vietnamese," in Anderson, *Shadow of the White House*, 115.

50. Quoted in Young, *The Vietnam Wars*, 206.

51. Graebner, "Myth and Reality," 32–33.

52. Olson and Roberts, *Where the Domino Fell*, 31.

53. Mark Atwood Lawrence, *The Vietnam War: A Concise International History* (New York: Oxford University Press, 2008), 96.

54. Nicholas Thompson, *The Hawk and the Dove: Paul Nitze, George Kennan, and the History of the Cold War* (New York: Henry Holt and Company, 2009), 201.

55. Logevall, *Embers of War*, 222.

56. Young, *The Vietnam Wars*, 28–29, 31.

57. Young, *The Vietnam Wars*, 31.

58. Jeffrey K. Kimball, "'Peace with Honor': Richard Nixon and the Diplomacy of Threat and Symbolism," in Anderson, *Shadow of the White House*, 153.

59. Kimball, "Peace with Honor," 152–53.

60. Kimball, "Peace with Honor," 153.

61. Quoted by Edwin E. Moise, "The Domino Theory," in *Encyclopedia of American Foreign Policy*, 2nd ed., vol. 1, ed. Richard Dean Burns, Alexander DeConde, and Fredrik Logevall (New York: Charles Scribner's Sons, 2002), 557.

62. Quoted by Moise, "The Domino Theory," 551.

63. Sandra Scanlon, "The Conservative Lobby and Nixon's 'Peace with Honor' in Vietnam," *Journal of American Studies* 43, no. 2 (2009): 260–61.

64. Jeffrey P. Kimball, *To Reason Why: The Debate about the Causes of U.S. Involvement in the Vietnam War* (Eugene, OR: Resource Publications, 1990), 70.

65. Mary E. Stuckey, "Competing Foreign Policy Visions: Rhetorical Hybrids after the Cold War," *Western Journal of Communication* 59 (Summer 1995): 216.

66. Gaddis, *Strategies of Containment*, 272. Nixon claimed publicly to base policymaking "on an evaluation of the world as it is." See Richard Nixon,

"Annual Message to the Congress on the State of the Union," January 22, 1970, American Presidency Project.

67. Rick Perlstein, *Nixonland: The Rise of a President and the Fracturing of America* (New York: Scribner, 2008), 435.

68. Richard Nixon: "Address Accepting the Presidential Nomination at the Republican National Convention in Miami Beach, Florida," August 8, 1968, American Presidency Project.

69. Richard Nixon, "Address on the State of the Union Delivered before a Joint Session of the Congress," January 20, 1972, American Presidency Project.

70. Moise, "The Domino Theory," 558.

71. Robert Dallek, *Nixon and Kissinger: Partners in Power* (New York: HarperCollins, 2007), 115.

72. Kimball, "Peace with Honor," 153.

73. Dallek, *Nixon and Kissinger*, 105.

74. Dallek, *Nixon and Kissinger*, 83.

75. Dallek, *Nixon and Kissinger*, 84–86.

76. Gaddis, *Strategies of Containment*, 273.

77. He defines a "model" as "an interlocking network of argument." See Harvey Averch, *The Rhetoric of War: Language, Argument, and Policy during the Vietnam War* (Lanham, MD: University Press of America, 2002), 4.

78. Averch, *The Rhetoric of War*, x.

79. Averch, *The Rhetoric of War*, xi.

80. J. C. Lammers and J. B. Barbour, "An Institutional Theory of Organizational Communication," *Communication Theory* 16 (2006): 365.

81. Samantha Power, *A Problem from Hell: America and the Age of Genocide* (New York: Basic Books, 2013), 508.

82. Mary E. Stuckey, *Jimmy Carter, Human Rights, and the National Agenda* (College Station: Texas A&M University Press, 2009), xvi.

83. As late as 1972 he claimed that "defeat in Vietnam would encourage this kind of aggression all over the world . . . world peace would be in grave jeopardy." Richard Nixon, "Address to the Nation on the Situation in Southeast Asia," May 8, 1972, American Presidency Project.

84. Quoted by Moise, "The Domino Theory," 558.

85. Memorandum for the President's Files, May 8, 1972, NSC Files, Box 998, Alexander M. Haig Chronological Files, Haig Memcons, January–December 1972 [2 of 3], Nixon Presidential Materials, National Archives.

86. Jerry Mark Silverman, "The Domino Theory: Alternatives to a Self-Fulfilling Prophecy," *Asian Survey* 15, no. 11 (1975): 916.

87. Silverman, "The Domino Theory," 916.

88. Richard Nixon, "Remarks on Accepting the Presidential Nomination of the Republican National Convention," August 23, 1972, American Presidency Project.

89. Concerns about prestige dominated the remainder of his end-of-war discourse. See Milliken, "Metaphors of Prestige and Reputation," 217.

90. John F. Kennedy, "America's Stake in Vietnam" (June 1, 1956), John F. Kennedy Pre-Presidential Papers, National Archives, https://research.archives.gov/id/193152.

91. See Richard Nixon, "Informal Remarks in Guam with Newsmen," July 25, 1969, American Presidency Project.

92. Richard Nixon, "Address at the National Governors' Conference," September 1, 1969, American Presidency Project.

93. Richard Nixon, "Address before the 24th Session of the General Assembly of the United Nations," September 18, 1969, American Presidency Project.

94. Nixon, "Address before the 24th Session of the General Assembly of the United Nations," September 18, 1969.

95. Nixon, "Address before the 24th Session of the General Assembly of the United Nations," September 18, 1969.

96. Nixon, "Address before the 24th Session of the General Assembly of the United Nations," September 18, 1969.

97. Nixon, "Address before the 24th Session of the General Assembly of the United Nations," September 18, 1969.

98. Richard Nixon, "Address Accepting the Presidential Nomination at the Republican National Convention in Miami Beach, Florida," August 8, 1968, American Presidency Project.

99. I should note here that many have taken issue with Nixon's phrase "peace with honor," labeling it a guise by which to hide his escalation of the war.

See Larry Berman, *No Peace, No Honor: Nixon, Kissinger, and Betrayal in Vietnam* (New York: Free Press, 2001), 221–39.

100. Richard Nixon, "Statement on the July 11 Speech of President Thieu of the Republic of Vietnam," July 11, 1969, American Presidency Project.

101. Richard Nixon, "'A Conversation with the President,' Interview with Four Representatives of the Television Networks," January 4, 1971, American Presidency Project.

102. Richard Nixon, "Address to the Nation Making Public a Plan for Peace in Vietnam," January 25, 1972, American Presidency Project.

103. Olson and Roberts, *Where the Domino Fell*, 246.

104. Richard Nixon, "Address to the Nation on Vietnam," April 26, 1972, American Presidency Project.

105. Richard Nixon, "Remarks in Ashland, Kentucky," October 26, 1972, American Presidency Project.

106. Richard Nixon, "Radio Address on Foreign Policy," November 4, 1972, American Presidency Project.

107. Richard Nixon, "Remarks on Election Eve," November 6, 1972, American Presidency Project.

108. Nixon, "Remarks on Election Eve," November 6, 1972.

109. Memo from Henry A. Kissinger to Ambassador Watson, Paris (January 24, 1972), Folder [7] President's January 25, 1972 Speech Vietnam [2 of 3], Box 125, NSC Files, Vietnam Subject Files, Nixon Presidential Materials, National Archives.

110. Draft Letter to Chairman Brezhnev from the President, President's January 25, 1972 Speech Vietnam [2 of 3], Box 125, NSC Files, Vietnam Subject Files, Nixon Presidential Materials, National Archives.

111. The Scope of the Agreement in Peking, [Visit of Richard Nixon President of the United States to the People's Republic of China February 1972, Briefing Papers Mr. Haldeman 3 of 3], H.R. Haldeman, White House Special Files [WHSF], Staff Materials and Special Files [SMOF], Richard Nixon Presidential Library and Museum. Rogers used the term in other situations too. For example, in a memo to the president at the very beginning of Nixon's first term, he wrote of the shared desire among all parties involved in Vietnam to "reach a settlement of the war."

See William Rogers to the President, Subj: Evening Report, January 23, 1969, NSC Files, Presidents Daily Briefings, Box 1, Folder [1] President's Daily Briefs, January 1–27, 1969, Richard Nixon Presidential Library and Museum.

112. Letter from President Nixon to Soviet General Secretary Brezhnev, December 18, 1972, NSC Files, President's Trip Files, Box 495, Dobrynin/Kissinger, vol. 14, Nixon Presidential Materials, National Archives.

113. Al Haig, "Memorandum for Henry Kissinger Re: Cease-fire and Political Settlement, June 28, 1972," Folder [5] Haig Chron—June 1–30, 1972 [1 of 2], Box 993, National Security Council Files, Haig Chron. Files, Richard Nixon Presidential Library and Museum.

114. See Douglas Brinkley and Luke A. Nichter, *The Nixon Tapes: 1971–1972* (New York: Houghton Mifflin Harcourt, 2014), 394.

115. Henry A. Kissinger to General Haig, Re: Vietnam, October 22, 1972, WHSF: SMOF: H.R. Haldeman, Box 180, Folder [NCS—Top Secret], Richard Nixon Presidential Library and Museum.

116. Kissinger to Haig, Re: Vietnam, October 22, 1972.

117. President Nixon to Henry A. Kissinger, December 7, 1972, HAK Office Files, Box 27, HAK Paris Trip TO HAK 1–100 December 3–13, 1972, Richard Nixon Presidential Library and Museum.

118. Memo with attachments, Richard T. Kennedy to Richard Campbell for Kissinger, December 21, 1972, NSC Files, Vietnam Country Files, Box 162, Folder [4] Vietnam, December 1972, Richard Nixon Presidential Library and Museum.

119. Pre-China Briefing, January 31, 1972, WHSF: SMOF, [China 2 of 2]: H.R. Haldeman, Richard Nixon Presidential Library and Museum.

120. The Scope of the Agreement in Peking, [Visit of Richard Nixon President of the United States to the People's Republic of China February 1972, Briefing Papers Mr. Haldeman 3 of 3], H.R. Haldeman, WHSF: SMOF, Richard Nixon Presidential Library and Museum.

121. Richard Nixon, "Inaugural Address," January 20, 1969, American Presidency Project.

122. Richard Nixon, "Address to the Nation on the War in Vietnam,"

November 3, 1969, American Presidency Project.

123. Olson and Roberts, *Where the Domino Fell*, 219–20.

124. Olson and Roberts, *Where the Domino Fell*, 220.

125. Nixon, "Address to the Nation on the War in Vietnam," November 3, 1969.

126. Averch, *The Rhetoric of War*, 8.

127. Richard Nixon, "Remarks Following Initial Meeting with President Thieu at Midway Island," June 8, 1969, American Presidency Project.

128. Richard Nixon, "Statement on United States Troops in Vietnam," September 16, 1969, American Presidency Project.

129. Nixon, "Statement on United States Troops in Vietnam," September 16, 1969.

130. Richard Nixon, "Second Annual Report to the Congress on United States Foreign Policy," February 25, 1971, American Presidency Project.

131. See Mark P. Moore, "Making Sense of Salmon: Synecdoche and Irony in a Natural Resource Crisis," *Western Journal of Communication* 67, no. 1 (Winter 2003): 74–96; Mark P. Moore, "The Cigarette as Representational Ideograph in the Debate over Environmental Tobacco Smoke," *Communication Monographs* 64 (March 1996); Mark P. Moore, "Life, Liberty, and the Handgun: The Function of Synecdoche in the Brady Bill Debate," *Communication Quarterly* 42, no. 4 (Fall 1994): 434–47; Mark Moore, "Constructing Irreconcilable Conflict: The Function of Synecdoche in the Spotted Owl Controversy," *Communication Monographs* 60 (September 1993); Barry Brummett, "Gastronomic Reference, Synecdoche, and Political Images," *Quarterly Journal of Speech* 67 (1981): 138–45; and Arnie Madsen, "The Synecdochic and Metonymic Processes and the Political Image Construct," in *Argumentation and Values: Proceedings of the Ninth SCA/AFA Conference on Argumentation*, ed. Sally Jackson (Annandale, VA: Speech Communication Association, 1995).

132. Richard Nixon, "Second Annual Report to the Congress on United States Foreign Policy," February 25, 1971, American Presidency Project.

133. Richard Nixon, "Remarks to Reporters at a Briefing on the Foreign Policy Report to the Congress," February 18, 1970, American Presidency Project.

134. Richard Nixon, "First Annual Report to the Congress on United States

Foreign Policy for the 1970's," February 18, 1970, American Presidency Project.

135. Richard Nixon, "Radio Address about Second Annual Foreign Policy Report to the Congress," February 25, 1971, American Presidency Project.

136. Nixon, "Radio Address about Second Annual Foreign Policy Report to the Congress," February 25, 1971.

137. Richard Nixon, "Address at the National Governors' Conference," September 1, 1969, American Presidency Project.

138. Richard Nixon, "Remarks to Reporters Summarizing His European Trip," October 4, 1970, American Presidency Project.

139. Nixon, "Remarks to Reporters Summarizing His European Trip," October 4, 1970.

140. Richard Nixon, "Special Message to the Congress Proposing Reform of the Foreign Assistance Program," April 21, 1971, American Presidency Project.

141. Richard Nixon, "Radio Address about Second Annual Foreign Policy Report to the Congress," February 25, 1971, American Presidency Project.

142. Richard Nixon, "Remarks on Arrival at the NATO Southern Command in Naples, Italy," September 30, 1970, American Presidency Project.

143. Nixon, "Radio Address about Second Annual Foreign Policy Report to the Congress," February 25, 1971.

144. Richard Nixon, "Address to a Joint Session of the Congress on Return from Austria, the Soviet Union, Iran, and Poland," June 1, 1972, American Presidency Project.

145. Nixon, "Address to a Joint Session of the Congress on Return from Austria, the Soviet Union, Iran, and Poland," June 1, 1972.

146. Richard Nixon, "Address to the Nation Announcing Plans for America's Bicentennial Celebration," July 4, 1972, American Presidency Project.

147. Richard Nixon, "Second Annual Report to the Congress on United States Foreign Policy," February 25, 1971, American Presidency Project.

148. Nixon, "Radio Address about Second Annual Foreign Policy Report to the Congress," February 25, 1971.

149. Nixon, "Second Annual Report to the Congress on United States Foreign Policy," February 25, 1971.

150. Nixon, "Second Annual Report to the Congress on United States Foreign Policy," February 25, 1971.

151. Richard Nixon, "Radio Address about the Third Annual Foreign Policy Report to the Congress," February 9, 1972, American Presidency Project.

152. Richard Nixon, "Address to the Nation: 'Look to the Future,'" November 2, 1972, American Presidency Project.

153. Nixon, "Address to the Nation: 'Look to the Future,'" November 2, 1972.

154. Nixon, "Address to the Nation: 'Look to the Future,'" November 2, 1972.

155. Memorandum of Conversation between President Nixon; Dr. Henry A. Kissinger; General Alexander M. Haig, Jr.; Nguyen Phu Duc; and Tran Kim Phuong, Ambassador to the United States, November 29, 1972, President's Files, NSC Files, Box 859, Folder Camp David—Sensitive—Vol. 22, Richard Nixon Presidential Library and Museum.

156. Memorandum of Conversation between President Nixon; Dr. Henry A. Kissinger; General Alexander M. Haig, Jr.; Nguyen Phu Duc; and Tran Kim Phuong.

157. Richard Nixon, "Oath of Office and Second Inaugural Address," January 20, 1973, American Presidency Project.

158. Richard Nixon, "Address to the Nation Announcing Conclusion of an Agreement on Ending the War and Restoring Peace in Vietnam," January 23, 1973, American Presidency Project.

159. Richard Nixon, "Remarks about United States Relations with Europe," February 15, 1973, American Presidency Project.

160. Nixon, "Remarks about United States Relations with Europe," February 15, 1973.

161. Richard Nixon, "Address to the Nation about Vietnam and Domestic Problems," March 29, 1973, American Presidency Project.

162. Richard Nixon, "Remarks at the Veterans of Foreign Wars Annual Convention, in Dallas, Texas," August 19, 1971, American Presidency Project.

163. Richard Nixon, "Remarks to the Corps of Cadets at the United States Military Academy in West Point, New York," May 29, 1971, American Presidency Project.

164. Nixon, "Remarks to the Corps of Cadets at the United States Military

Academy in West Point, New York," May 29, 1971.

165. Nixon, "Remarks to the Corps of Cadets at the United States Military Academy in West Point, New York," May 29, 1971.

166. Nixon, "Remarks to the Corps of Cadets at the United States Military Academy in West Point, New York," May 29, 1971.

167. Petra Goedde, *The Politics of Peace: A Global Cold War History* (New York: Oxford University Press, 2019), 13.

168. Nixon, "Remarks at the Veterans of Foreign Wars Annual Convention, in Dallas, Texas," August 19, 1971.

169. Nixon, "Remarks at the Veterans of Foreign Wars Annual Convention, in Dallas, Texas," August 19, 1971.

170. Nixon, "Remarks at the Veterans of Foreign Wars Annual Convention, in Dallas, Texas," August 19, 1971.

171. Nixon, "Remarks at the Veterans of Foreign Wars Annual Convention, in Dallas, Texas," August 19, 1971.

172. I should also note that his call for unity cannot be delinked from his attempt to hold onto power in the face of public investigations into his administration that eventually forced his resignation. Nixon was nothing if not self-serving.

173. Richard Nixon, "Toasts of the President and Prime Minister Heath of the United Kingdom," February 1, 1973, American Presidency Project.

174. Richard Nixon, "Remarks of Welcome to President Nguyen Van Thieu of the Republic of Vietnam at San Clemente, California," April 2, 1973, American Presidency Project.

175. Richard Nixon, "Fourth Annual Report to the Congress on United States Foreign Policy," May 3, 1973, American Presidency Project.

176. Nixon, "Fourth Annual Report to the Congress on United States Foreign Policy," May 3, 1973.

177. Nixon, "Fourth Annual Report to the Congress on United States Foreign Policy," May 3, 1973.

178. Nixon, "Fourth Annual Report to the Congress on United States Foreign Policy," May 3, 1973.

179. Richard Nixon, "Remarks at the Veterans of Foreign Wars National Convention, New Orleans, Louisiana," August 20, 1973, American

Presidency Project.

180. Nixon, "Remarks at the Veterans of Foreign Wars National Convention, New Orleans, Louisiana," August 20, 1973.

181. Speeches requested by Ken Clawson, October 18, 1973, WHCF: SMOF: David Gergen, Messages File, Presidential Statements, Box 58, Folder Statement: Nobel Peace Prize 10/73 [OA 13481], Richard Nixon Presidential Library and Museum.

182. Henry Kissinger, "Acceptance Address," December 10, 1973, https:// www.nobelprize.org.

183. Richard Nixon, "Statement about the Selection of Henry A. Kissinger as Corecipient of the Nobel Peace Prize for 1973," October 16, 1973, American Presidency Project.

184. Richard Nixon, "The President's News Conference," August 22, 1973, American Presidency Project.

185. Richard Nixon, "Annual Message to the Congress on the State of the Union," January 30, 1974, American Presidency Project.

186. Richard Nixon, "Radio Address on Memorial Day," May 27, 1974, American Presidency Project.

187. Nixon, "Radio Address on Memorial Day," May 27, 1974.

188. Nixon, "Radio Address on Memorial Day," May 27, 1974.

189. Nixon, "Radio Address on Memorial Day," May 27, 1974.

190. Richard Nixon, "Toasts of the President and King Baudouin of Belgium at a Luncheon in Brussels," June 26, 1974, American Presidency Project.

191. The Scope of the Agreement in Peking, [Visit of Richard Nixon President of the United States to the People's Republic of China February 1972, Briefing Papers Mr. Haldeman 3 of 3], H.R. Haldeman, WHSF: SMOF, Richard Nixon Presidential Library and Museum.

192. See Stuckey, "Competing Foreign Policy Visions"; and Karlyn Kohrs Campbell, "Agency: Promiscuous and Protean," *Communication and Critical/ Cultural Studies* 2 (2005): 6–7.

193. Toast Proposed by Richard Nixon, China President's Talks with Mao and Chou En-Lai February 1972 [TS 2 of 2] (1 of 3), HAK Files, NSC Files, Richard Nixon Presidential Library and Museum.

194. See Michelle Murray Yang, "President Nixon's Speeches and Toasts

during His 1972 Trip to China: A Study in Diplomatic Rhetoric," *Rhetoric & Public Affairs* 14, no. 1 (Spring 2011): 19.

195. Richard Nixon, "Message to the Congress Transmitting Annual Report of the United States Arms Control and Disarmament Agency," February 10, 1972, American Presidency Project.

196. Richard Nixon, "Special Message to the Congress Proposing Trade Reform Legislation," April 10, 1973, American Presidency Project.

197. Richard Nixon, "Special Message to the Congress on Energy Policy," April 18, 1973, American Presidency Project.

198. Richard Nixon, "Remarks at a Buffet Dinner at the Texas Ranch of John B. Connally," September 22, 1972, American Presidency Project.

CHAPTER 4. THE DISEMBODIED SAVAGE: BARACK OBAMA AND THE PERPETUITY OF NATIONAL VIOLENCE

1. Terry H. Anderson, *Bush's Wars* (New York: Oxford University Press, 2011), 213.

2. "Public Attitudes toward the War in Iraq: 2003–2008," Pew Research Center (March 19, 2008), http://www.pewresearch.org/2008/03/19/public-attitudes-toward-the-war-in-iraq-20032008.

3. Tim McGirk, "Behind the Taliban's Resurgence in Afghanistan," *Time*, September 16, 2009. See also Hassan Abbas, *The Taliban Revival: Violence and Extremism on the Pakistan-Afghanistan Border* (New Haven, CT: Yale University Press, 2014), 168–70.

4. Chris Good, "When and Why Did Americans Turn against the War in Afghanistan?," *The Atlantic*, June 22, 2001.

5. Anthony R. DiMaggio, *Selling War, Selling Hope: Presidential Rhetoric, the News Media, and U.S. Foreign Policy since 9/11* (Albany: State University of New York Press, 2015), 33.

6. See, for example, Obama's explanation of the two wars during the first two presidential debates: Presidential Candidates Debates, "Presidential Debate at the University of Mississippi in Oxford," September 26, 2008; and Presidential Candidates Debates, "Presidential Debate at Belmont University in Nashville, Tennessee," October 7, 2008, American Presidency Project.

7. Zbigniew Brzezinski, *Strategic Vision: America and the Crisis of Global Power* (New York: Basic Books, 2013), 67.

8. David E. Sanger, *Confront and Conceal: Obama's Secret Wars and Surprising Use of American Power* (New York: Broadway Paperbacks, 2013), xvi. Italics in original.

9. The identification of the terrorist manifest, in particular, in the form of "most wanted" playing cards became desirable collectibles at home, but also gave an image to the enemy that Bush's rhetoric mostly did not. See Lisa Burgess, "Buyers Beware: The Real Iraq 'Most Wanted' Cards Are Still Awaiting Distribution," *Stars and Stripes*, April 17, 2003.

10. See Petter Nesser, "Jihadism in Western Europe after the Invasion of Iraq: Tracing Motivational Influences from the Iraq War on Jihadist Terrorism in Western Europe," *Studies in Conflict & Terrorism* 26, no. 4 (2006): 323–42.

11. David Zarefsky, "George Bush Discovers Rhetoric: September 20, 2001, and the U.S. Response to Terrorism," in *The Ethos of Rhetoric*, ed. Michael J. Hyde (Columbia: University of South Carolina Press, 2004), 143, 145.

12. Kiku Adatto, *Picture Perfect: Life in the Age of the Photo Op* (Princeton, NJ: Princeton University Press, 2008), 32.

13. Karen Jones and John Wills, *The American West: Competing Visions* (Edinburgh: Edinburgh University Press, 2009), 110.

14. Brian Knowlton and International Herald Tribune, "Terror in America/'We're Going to Smoke Them Out': President Airs His Anger," *New York Times*, September 19, 2001.

15. Jones and Wills, *The American West*, 110.

16. Jack Lule, *Globalization and Media: Global Village of Babel* (Lanham, MD: Rowman & Littlefield Publishers, 2012), 106.

17. Adatto, *Picture Perfect*, 34; Ilan Peleg, *The Legacy of George W. Bush's Foreign Policy: Moving beyond Neoconservatism* (Boulder, CO: Westview Press, 2008), 158; B. Mazid, "Cowboy and Misanthrope: A Critical (Discourse) Analysis of Bush and Bin Laden Cartoons," *Discourse & Communication* 2, no. 4 (2008): 433–57; and S. Renshon, "Presidential Address: George W. Bush's Cowboy Politics: An Inquiry," *Political Psychology* 26, no. 4 (2005): 585–614.

18. See Jai Singh and Ajay Singh, "The War on Terror—Over?" *Small Wars Journal* (August 28, 2012).

19. Brian Massumi, "National Enterprise Emergency: Steps toward an Ecology of Powers," in *Beyond Biopolitics: Essays on the Governance of Life and Death*, ed. Patricia Ticineto Clough and Craig Willse (Durham, NC: Duke University Press, 2011), 20.

20. Massumi, "National Enterprise Emergency," 20.

21. George W. Bush, "Address before a Joint Session of the Congress on the United States Response to the Terrorist Attacks of September 11," September 20, 2001, American Presidency Project.

22. Jesse Kavadlo, *American Popular Culture in the Era of Terror: Falling Skies, Dark Knights Rising, and Collapsing Cultures* (Santa Barbara, CA: Praeger Press, 2015), 59.

23. George Lakoff, "Metaphor and War, Again," *Alternet*, March 17, 2003, https://www.alternet.org.

24. Jennifer E. Eagan, "Enforced Homogeneity or Mutual Difference? Luce Irigaray, the War on Terrorism, and International Peace," in *Philosophical Perspectives on the "War on Terrorism,"* ed. Gail M. Presbey (New York: Rodopi Press, 2007), 44; and Donileen R. Loseke, "Examining Emotion as Discourse: Emotion Codes and Presidential Speeches Justifying War," *Sociological Quarterly* 50, no. 3 (Summer 2009): 503.

25. David Holloway, *Cultures of the War on Terror: Empire, Ideology, and the Remaking of 9/11* (Montreal: McGill-Queen's University Press, 2008), 4–5.

26. Feargul Cochrane, *Ending Wars* (Malden, MA: Polity Press, 2008), 129.

27. Richard Clarke, who served three presidents as part of the National Security Council staff, appears to agree with this assessment. He argues that even as the paradigm shifted to address non-state actors, the strategies used resembled "regime change" instead of "search-and-destroy" operations. See Richard A. Clarke, *Against All Enemies: Inside America's War on Terror* (New York: Free Press, 2004), 274.

28. George W. Bush, "Remarks to Employees in the Pentagon and an Exchange with Reporters in Arlington, Virginia," September 17, 2001, American Presidency Project.

29. The Authorization for the Use of Military Force, Public Law 107–40,

September 18, 2001.

30. John W. Dower, *The Violent American Century: War and Terror since World War II* (Chicago: Haymarket Books, 2017), 88–89, 91.

31. Jack McDonald, *Enemies Known and Unknown: Targeted Killings in America's Transnational War* (Oxford: Oxford University Press, 2017), 64.

32. Ron Suskind, *The One Percent Doctrine: Deep inside America's Pursuit of Its Enemies since 9/11* (New York: Simon & Schuster, 2006), 62–63.

33. *2003 Report to Congress on Combating Terrorism* (Washington, DC: Office of Management and Budget, 2003), 18; and George W. Bush, "Address before a Joint Session of the Congress on the State of the Union," January 29, 2002, American Presidency Project.

34. Mary L. Dudziak, *War-Time: An Idea, Its History, Its Consequences* (New York: Oxford University Press, 2013), 105.

35. Holloway, *Cultures of the War on Terror*, 4–5.

36. Bush, "State of the Union," January 29, 2002.

37. Rosa Brooks, *How Everything Became War and the Military Became Everything: Tales from the Pentagon* (New York: Simon & Schuster, 2016), 12.

38. Michael Lind, *The American Way of Strategy: U.S. Foreign Policy and the American Way of Life* (New York: Oxford University Press, 2006), 140.

39. Bush, "State of the Union," January 29, 2002.

40. See Mary Kaldor, *Global Civil Society* (Malden, MA: Polity Press, 2003); Marc Sageman, *Understanding Terror Networks* (Philadelphia: University of Pennsylvania Press, 2004); Harvey W. Kushner, *Holy War on the Home Front: The Secret Islamic Terror Network in the United States* (New York: Penguin, 2004); Michael Kenney, *From Pablo to Osama: Trafficking and Terrorist Networks, Government Bureaucracies, and Competitive Adaptation* (University Park: Pennsylvania State University Press, 2007); and Robert J. Bunker, *Networks, Terrorism and Global Insurgency* (New York: Routledge, 2005).

41. Cochrane, *Ending Wars*, 135.

42. Bob Woodward, *Obama's Wars* (New York: Simon & Schuster, 2010), 475, 487.

43. Barack Obama, "Remarks at the National Defense University," March 12, 2009, American Presidency Project.

44. Barack Obama, "The President's News Conference in Strasbourg," April

4, 2009, American Presidency Project.

45. Barack Obama, "The President's Weekly Address," April 4, 2009, American Presidency Project.

46. Wendy Kozol, *Distant Wars Visible: The Ambivalence of Witnessing* (Minneapolis: University of Minnesota Press, 2014), 8.

47. Obama, "The President's Weekly Address," April 4, 2009.

48. It also specifically identified Pakistan as a hub for the training and planning, a theme he would take up again after Bin Laden's execution.

49. Obama, "The President's Weekly Address," April 4, 2009.

50. Obama, "The President's Weekly Address," April 4, 2009.

51. Rajiv Chandrasekaran, *Little America: The War within the War for Afghanistan* (New York: Bloomsbury Publishing, 2013), 9.

52. Michael R. Gordon, *The Endgame: The Inside Story of the Struggle for Iraq, from George W. Bush to Barack Obama* (New York: Vintage Books, 2013), 523; and Ta-Nehisi Coates, "My President Was Black: A History of the First African American White House—and of What Came Next," *The Atlantic* (January/February 2017).

53. Jack Goldsmith, *Power and Constraint: The Accountable Presidency after 9/11* (New York: W.W. Norton & Company, 2012), 5–19; and Gordon, *The Endgame*, 538, 560.

54. DiMaggio, *Selling War, Selling Hope*, 34–35.

55. Martin S. Indyk, Kenneth G. Lieberthal, and Michael E. O'Hanlon, *Bending History: Barack Obama's Foreign Policy* (Washington, DC: Brookings Institution, 2012), 7, 11, 14–15.

56. Barack Obama, "Remarks at a Graduation Ceremony at the New Economic School in Moscow, Russia," July 7, 2009, American Presidency Project.

57. Barack Obama, "Remarks Following a Meeting with Prime Minister Jan Peter Balkenende of the Netherlands and an Exchange with Reporters," July 14, 2009, American Presidency Project.

58. Barack Obama, "Remarks at the United States Military Academy at West Point, New York," December 1, 2009, American Presidency Project.

59. Robert L. Ivie, "Obama at West Point: A Study in Ambiguity of Purpose," *Rhetoric & Public Affairs* 14, no. 4 (2011): 730.

60. Barack Obama, "Remarks to the United Nations General Assembly in New York City," September 23, 2010, American Presidency Project.

61. Barack Obama, "Commencement Address at the United States Air Force Academy in Colorado Springs, Colorado," May 23, 2012, American Presidency Project.

62. Barack Obama, "The President's News Conference," October 8, 2013, American Presidency Project.

63. Carol K. Winkler, *In the Name of Terrorism: Presidents on Political Violence in the Post-World War II Era* (Albany: State University of New York Press, 2006), 70–71.

64. Quoted in Winkler, *In the Name of Terrorism*, 100.

65. Winkler, *In the Name of Terrorism*, 135.

66. George W. Bush, "Remarks to the United Nations General Assembly in New York City," November 10, 2001, American Presidency Project.

67. Bush, "Address before a Joint Session of the Congress on the United States Response to the Terrorist Attacks of September 11."

68. Kristen E. Boon, "Terrorism: Commentary on Security Documents," in *Global Issues*, vol. 103, *Terrorism*, ed. Kristen Boon, Aziz Huq, and Douglas C. Lovelace Jr. (New York: Oxford University Press, 2009), 158.

69. Boon, "Terrorism," 134.

70. Boon, "Terrorism," 158.

71. Jack Holland, *Selling the War on Terror: Foreign Policy Discourses after 9/11* (London: Routledge, 2013), 109.

72. Michael F. Scheuer, "Foreword," in *Denial of Sanctuary: Understanding Terrorist Safe Havens*, ed. Michael A. Innes (Westport, CT: Praeger Press, 2007), vii–viii.

73. Kenneth J. Menkhaus, "Constraints and Opportunities in Ungoverned Spaces: The Horn of Africa," in Innes, *Denial of Sanctuary*, 76.

74. Jarret Brachman and James J. F. Forest, "Exploring the Role of Virtual Camps," in Innes, *Denial of Sanctuary*, 135.

75. Boon, "Terrorism," 138.

76. Barack Obama, "Remarks at the State Department," January 22, 2009, American Presidency Project.

77. Barack Obama, "The President's News Conference," February 9, 2009,

American Presidency Project.

78. See, for example, Obama's clarification after meeting with NATO leaders: Barack Obama, "The President's News Conference with Chancellor Angela Merkel of Germany in Baden-Baden, Germany," April 3, 2009, American Presidency Project.

79. Barack Obama, "Interview with Master Sergeant Rusty Barfield of the Pentagon Channel," February 27, 2009, American Presidency Project.

80. Obama, "The President's News Conference," February 9, 2009.

81. William Blackstone, *Commentaries on the Laws of England (1765-1769)*, electronic ed. (https://lonang.com/library/reference/blackstone-commentaries-law-england), book 4, chap. 5, 71–72. Special thanks to Rob Mills for directing my attention to this source.

82. For more on the origins of the safe haven metaphor and its linkages to the sea: Martin Jay, "Diving into the Wreck: Aesthetic Spectatorship at the Fin-de-siècle," *Critical Horizons* 1, no. 1 (2000): 93–111.

83. Sahar Said, "The Unwanted Federally Administered Tribal Areas," *Foreign Policy Association* (September 3, 2013), https://foreignpolicyblogs.com/2013/09/03/the-unwanted-federally-administered-tribal-areas.

84. Obama misspoke and said "safe heaven" before correcting himself. I have omitted "heaven" for clarity's sake. See Barack Obama, "Remarks at a Town Hall Meeting and a Question-and-Answer Session in Arnold, Missouri," April 29, 2009, American Presidency Project.

85. Obama, "Remarks at a Graduation Ceremony at the New Economic School in Moscow, Russia," July 7, 2009.

86. Barack Obama, "Remarks on United States Military and Diplomatic Strategies for Afghanistan and Pakistan," March 27, 2009, American Presidency Project.

87. Bruce Riedel, *The Search for Al Qaeda: Its Leadership, Ideology, and Future* (Washington, DC: Brookings Institution, 2010), 11, 49, 86, 121.

88. Barack Obama, "Remarks to the United Nations General Assembly in New York City," September 23, 2009, American Presidency Project.

89. Obama, "Remarks at the United States Military Academy at West Point, New York," December 1, 2009.

90. Obama, "Remarks to the United Nations General Assembly in New York

City," September 23, 2010.

91. Barack Obama, "The President's News Conference with Prime Minister Julia E. Gillard of Australia in Canberra, Australia," November 16, 2011, American Presidency Project.

92. Barack Obama, "Remarks to United States and Coalition Troops at Bagram Air Base, Afghanistan," March 28, 2010, American Presidency Project.

93. Barack Obama, "The President's News Conference with President Hamid Karzai of Afghanistan," May 12, 2010, American Presidency Project.

94. Barack Obama, "Remarks on United States Military and Diplomatic Strategies for Afghanistan and Pakistan," December 16, 2010, American Presidency Project.

95. Obama, "Remarks on United States Military and Diplomatic Strategies for Afghanistan and Pakistan," December 16, 2010.

96. Charlotte Heath-Kelly, "Forgetting ISIS: Enmity, Drive and Repetition in Security Discourse," *Critical Studies on Security* (2017): 11.

97. Michel Foucault, *Archeology of Knowledge: And the Discourse on Language* (New York: Vintage Books, 1982), 99.

98. The metaphors are ubiquitous. See, for example, Carlos Munoz, "Obama Faces Resurgent al Qaeda in 2014," *The Hill*, January 1, 2014.

99. Manuel Castells, *Communication Power* (New York: Oxford University Press, 2009), 49.

100. Janet Fulk, "Global Network Organizations: Emergence and Future Prospects," *Human Relations* 54 (2001): 91–99.

101. Cynthia Stohl and Michael Stohl, "Networks of Terror: Theoretical Assumptions and Pragmatic Consequences," *Communication Theory* 17 (2007): 106.

102. Yasmin Jiwani, "Trapped in the Carceral Net: Race, Gender, and the 'War on Terror,'" *Global Media Journal: Canadian Edition* 4, no. 2 (2011): 18.

103. Luke Howie and Perri Campbell, *Crisis and Terror in the Age of Anxiety: 9/11, the Global Financial Crisis and ISIS* (London: Palgrave Macmillan, 2017), 46.

104. Stohl and Stohl, "Networks of Terror," 98; and Bush, "Address before a Joint Session of the Congress on the United States Response to the Terrorist Attacks of September 11," September 20, 2001.

105. James Phillips, "Uproot Bin Laden's Terrorist Network and Taliban Allies in Afghanistan," *Heritage Foundation Executive Memorandum* 776 (September 17, 2001).

106. George W. Bush, "Commencement Address at the United States Military Academy in West Point, New York," June 1, 2002, American Presidency Project.

107. Donald Rumsfeld, Press Conference, June 6, 2002, http://www.nato.int/docu/speech/2002/s020606g.htm.

108. Quoted in Ron Robin, *The Cold World They Made: The Strategic Legacy of Roberta and Albert Wohlstetter* (Cambridge, MA: Harvard University Press, 2016), 295.

109. Shirley Anne Warshaw, *The Co-Presidency of Bush and Cheney* (Stanford, CA: Stanford University Press, 2009), 218.

110. "Full Text of Dick Cheney's Speech," *The Guardian*, August 27, 2002. He continued this theme throughout his term and after leaving office. See Richard B. Cheney, "Remarks," May 21, 2009, https://www.aei.org/research-products/speech/remarks-by-richard-b-cheney.

111. Thom Shanker, "Traces of Terror; Rumsfeld's Search for a Way to Fight a New Type of Foe," *New York Times*, September 4, 2002.

112. Tim Minor, "Attacking the Nodes of Terrorist Networks," *Global Security Studies* 3, no. 2 (2012): 5.

113. Winkler, *In the Name of Terrorism*, 169.

114. Barack Obama, "Inaugural Address," January 20, 2009, American Presidency Project.

115. Bob Woodward argued the bureaucracy constrained Obama's policy review with what he called "the ghosts of the Vietnam and Iraq wars." He meant that the military bureaucracy could not be trusted "to Get It Right," because they would always produce force estimates, war planning and gaming, and timelines that fit their goals to the exclusion of the political and economic realities of conflict. In other words, bureaucracies bureaucratize conflict. If you task the bureaucracy with offering a plan for war, they'll give you a plan for war. Had Obama gone with "give me a plan to withdraw from Afghanistan in 2011," he might have ended up with different options. Instead, he asked the bureaucracy to do

something it wasn't designed to do: plan a troop increase and decrease at the same time. End goals have a huge impact on the performance of the task. Because he was dealt a bad hand by the bureaucracy, he could either tinker with it (deployment speed, troop configuration, and absolute numbers of troops) or reject it entirely. There was no possibility of rethinking the strategy from scratch, as he professed to desire, because he tasked military leaders to think about how to get to peace when they are trained and equipped to think only of a narrow definition of "winning." This ideological incapacity of the military left Obama in the position of pushing for political goals (an exit, reduced costs, etc.) rather than policy goals. See Woodward, *Obama's Wars*, 643–44.

116. Barack Obama, "Remarks at the Fifth Annual Meeting of the Clinton Global Initiative in New York City," September 22, 2009, American Presidency Project. Obama also referred to the Taliban in the same vein. See Obama, "The President's News Conference with President Hamid Karzai of Afghanistan," May 12, 2010.

117. Mark Erickson, "Network as Metaphor," *International Journal of Criminology and Sociological Theory* 5, no. 2 (August 2012): 915.

118. Obama, "Remarks at a Town Hall Meeting and a Question-and-Answer Session in Strasbourg," April 3, 2009.

119. Obama, "Remarks to the United Nations General Assembly in New York City," September 23, 2009.

120. Obama, "Remarks at the United States Military Academy at West Point, New York," December 1, 2009.

121. Obama, "Remarks at the United States Military Academy at West Point, New York," December 1, 2009.

122. See Stohl and Stohl, "Networks of Terror," 93–124; and Michael Stohl, "US Homeland Security, the Global War on Terror and Militarism," in *The Marketing of War in the Age of Neo-Militarism*, ed. Kostas Gouliamos and Christos Kassimeris (New York: Routledge, 2012), 113–14.

123. Michael Hardt and Antonio Negri, *Commonwealth* (Cambridge, MA: Belknap Press of Harvard University Press, 2009), 146.

124. Barack Obama, "Commencement Address at the United States Military Academy in West Point, New York," May 22, 2010, American Presidency

Project.

125. George W. Bush, "Presidential Debate in Coral Gables, Florida," September 30, 2004, American Presidency Project.

126. See, for example, Rob Schultheis, *Hunting Bin Laden: How Al-Qaeda Is Winning the War on Terror* (New York: Skyhorse Press, 2008), 32; Charles V. Peña, *Winning the Un-war: A New Strategy for the War on Terrorism* (Washington, DC: Potomac Books, 2007).

127. David Zarefsky, *President Johnson's War on Poverty* (Tuscaloosa: University of Alabama Press, 2005), 3, 10–11.

128. Greg Miller, "CIA Spied on bin Laden from Safe House," *Washington Post*, May 6, 2011.

129. Barack Obama, "Remarks on the Death of Al Qaida Terrorist Organization Leader Usama bin Laden," May 1, 2011, American Presidency Project.

130. Heath-Kelly, "Forgetting ISIS," 11.

131. Manuel Castells, "A Network Theory of Power," *International Journal of Communication* 5 (2011): 773.

132. Niall Ferguson, "The False Prophecy of Hyperconnection," *Foreign Affairs* (September/October 2017).

133. Obama, "Remarks at the United States Military Academy at West Point, New York," December 1, 2009.

134. Castells, "A Network Theory of Power," 774–75.

135. Martin Coward, "Against Network Thinking: A Critique of Pathological Sovereignty," *European Journal of International Relations* (2017): 13.

136. Obama, "Remarks on the Death of Al Qaida Terrorist Organization Leader Usama bin Laden," May 1, 2011.

137. Barack Obama, "Statement on the 10th Anniversary of the Commencement of United States Military Operations in Afghanistan," October 7, 2011, American Presidency Project.

138. While studies contend that users' digital presence mirrors the individual user's offline personality, the point remains that criminal elements can easily hide behind increasingly sophisticated digital personas. A common example of this is "catfishing," in which an individual creates a fake social-media identity to scam or troll others. See, for example,

Awais Rashid, Alistair Baron, Paul Rayson, Corinne May-Chahal, Phil Greenwood, and James Walkerdine, "Who Am I? Analyzing Digital Personas in Cybercrime Investigations," *Computer* 46, no. 4 (2013): 54–61; and Krystal D'Costa, "Catfishing: The Truth about Deception Online," *Scientific American*, April 25, 2014, https://blogs.scientificamerican.com/anthropology-in-practice/catfishing-the-truth-about-deception-online.

139. Mary McEvoy Manjikian, "From Global Village to Virtual Battlespace: The Colonizing of the Internet and the Extension of Realpolitik," *International Studies Quarterly* 54, no. 2 (June 2010): 387.

140. Coward, "Against Network Thinking," 13.

141. Coward, "Against Network Thinking," 13.

142. Coward, "Against Network Thinking," 12–13.

143. Barack Obama, "Remarks at National Defense University," May 23, 2013, American Presidency Project.

144. Obama, "Remarks at National Defense University," May 23, 2013.

145. Obama, "Remarks at National Defense University," May 23, 2013.

146. Obama, "Remarks at National Defense University," May 23, 2013.

147. While distinctions between "war" and "military operations" may be immaterial from a legal perspective, my contention here is that Obama's recontextualization of the war reflected an underlying distinction between the two. Invasion, occupation, and democratization reflect a national commitment exceeding the parameters of counterterrorism while incurring human and financial costs. Obama's shift toward limited military operations designed to counter terrorism represented a difference in kind, if not in legal category.

148. For those on the ground, this was hardly a new phenomenon. There were so many of these groups in Iraq that the policy bureaucracy could hardly keep up with them. By one count, 103 different "insurgent groups claim[ed] responsibility for attacks on Americans and Iraqis" over a six-month span in 2005. But it was new for the president to acknowledge this long-public truth. See Dexter Filkins, *The Forever War* (New York: Vintage Books, 2008), 235–36.

149. Barack Obama, "Remarks to the United Nations General Assembly in New York City," September 24, 2013, American Presidency Project.

150. Barack Obama, "Commencement Address at the United States Military Academy in West Point, New York," May 28, 2014, American Presidency Project.

151. Obama, "Commencement Address at the United States Military Academy in West Point, New York," May 28, 2014.

152. Barack Obama, "Remarks on the Situation in Iraq and an Exchange with Reporters," June 19, 2014, American Presidency Project.

153. Jesse Paul Lehrke and Rahel Schomaker, "Kill, Capture, or Defend? The Effectiveness of Specific and General Counterterrorism Tactics against the Global Threats of the Post-9/11 Era," *Security Studies* 25, no. 4 (2016): 732.

154. Barack Obama, "Address before a Joint Session of the Congress on the State of the Union," January 20, 2015, American Presidency Project.

155. Mark Thompson, "U.S. Ends Its War in Afghanistan," *Time*, December 28, 2014.

156. For examples, see Greg Myre, "Pledging to End Two Wars, Obama Finds Himself Entangled in Three," *NPR*, October 15, 2015, http://www.npr.org/sections/parallels/2015/10/15/448925947/pledging-to-end-two-wars-obama-finds-himself-entangled-in-three; Neelesh Moorthy, "Obama Increases U.S. Troops to Remain in Afghanistan Past 2016," *Politifact*, July 6, 2016, http://www.politifact.com/truth-o-meter/promises/obameter/promise/1096/end-war-afghanistan-2014; and Laurel Miller, "A Peace 'Surge' to End War in Afghanistan," *New York Times*, July 23, 2017.

157. Barack Obama, "Remarks on the Terrorist Attack in Paris, France, during a Meeting with Vice President Joe Biden and Secretary of State John F. Kerry," January 7, 2015, American Presidency Project.

158. Barack Obama, "The President's News Conference with Prime Minister David Cameron of the United Kingdom," January 16, 2015, American Presidency Project.

159. Tom Engelhardt, *The American Way of War: How Bush's Wars Became Obama's* (Chicago: Haymarket Books, 2010), 103–4.

160. Department of State, *Country Reports on Terrorism 2014* (Washington, DC: Bureau of Counterterrorism, 2015), 8.

161. Department of State and USAID, *Joint Strategy on Countering Violent*

Extremism (Washington, DC: U.S. Government Printing Office, 2016), 2–3.

162. Dower, *The Violent American Century*, 106–17.

163. Barack Obama, "Remarks with Prime Minister Narendra Modi of India in New Delhi, India, and an Exchange with Reporters," January 25, 2015, American Presidency Project.

164. Janosch Prinz and Conrad Schetter, "Conditioned Sovereignty: The Creation and Legitimation of Spaces of Violence in Counterterrorism Operations in the 'War on Terror,'" *Alternatives: Global, Local, Political* 41, no. 3 (2016): 119.

165. Barack Obama, "Remarks at the Association of Southeast Asian Nations Business and Investment Summit in Kuala Lumpur, Malaysia," November 21, 2015, American Presidency Project.

166. I should note that Obama's notion of "rooting out" networks made little sense. Networks have no "roots." Even if one can imagine the cables and computers that enable network access, the digital era has ensured there are always more "roots." There's always another cell phone, another laptop, another internet café.

167. Barack Obama, "Remarks Following a Meeting with Prime Minister Anthony J. Abbott of Australia and an Exchange with Reporters," June 12, 2014, American Presidency Project.

168. For uniformity, I use the Obama administration's term "ISIL" instead of "ISIS" or "Daesh."

169. Barack Obama, "Remarks on the Situation in Iraq and an Exchange with Reporters," August 9, 2014, American Presidency Project.

170. Christopher M. Blanchard and Carla E. Humud, *The Islamic State and U.S. Policy* (Washington, DC: Congressional Research Service, 2017), n.p.

171. Barack Obama, "Joint Statement by President Barack Obama and Prime Minister Nuri al-Maliki of Iraq," November 1, 2013, American Presidency Project.

172. Hal Brands and Peter Feaver, "Was the Rise of ISIS Inevitable?" *Survival* 59, no. 3 (June-July 2017): 8.

173. Obama, "Remarks on the Situation in Iraq and an Exchange with Reporters," June 13, 2014.

174. Obama, "Remarks on the Situation in Iraq and an Exchange with Reporters," June 13, 2014.

175. Edward Morrisey, "Obama's ISIS Failures," *The Week*, November 17, 2015, http://theweek.com/articles/589272/obamas-isis-failure; and Greg Myre, "Pledging to End Two Wars, Obama Finds Himself Entangled in Three," *NPR*, October 15, 2015, http://www.npr.org/sections/parallels/2015/10/15/448925947/pledging-to-end-two-wars-obama-finds-himself-entangled-in-three.

176. Obama, "Remarks on the Situation in Iraq," August 7, 2014.

177. Barack Obama, "Remarks at the White House Summit on Countering Violent Extremism," February 19, 2015, American Presidency Project.

178. Barack Obama, "The President's News Conference in Belek, Turkey," November 16, 2015, American Presidency Project.

179. Obama, "The President's News Conference in Belek, Turkey," November 16, 2015.

180. Barack Obama, "Address to the Nation on United States Counterterrorism Strategy," December 6, 2015, American Presidency Project.

181. Susan Rice, "Remarks by National Security Advisor Susan Rice on the 2015 National Security Strategy," February 6, 2015, https://obamawhitehouse.archives.gov/the-press-office/2015/02/06/remarks-national-security-advisor-susan-rice-2015-national-security-stra.

182. Euan McKirdy and Barbara Starr, "Ash Carter: U.S. Sending More Troops to Iraq," *CNN*, July 11, 2016.

183. Ash Carter, Statement on "U.S. National Security Challenges and Ongoing Military Operations," Senate Armed Services Committee, September 22, 2016.

184. Ash Carter, Statement from Secretary of Defense Ash Carter on Additional Support to Iraqi Counter-ISIL Efforts, Press Release No: NR-342–16, September 28, 2016, https://www.defense.gov/Newsroom/Releases/Release/Article/958052/statement-from-secretary-of-defense-ash-carter-on-additional-support-to-iraqi-c.

185. Sophie Tatum, "Kerry: US Increasing Counter-terror Work with Bangladesh," *CNN*, August 30, 2016.

186. Department of Defense, *Enhancing Security and Stability in Afghanistan*, December 2016, 1–7, https://media.defense.gov/2018/Dec/20/2002075158/-1/-1/1/1225-REPORT-DECEMBER-2018.pdf.

187. Obama, "Remarks on United States Efforts to Combat the Islamic State of Iraq and the Levant (ISIL) Terrorist Organization and an Exchange with Reporters," July 6, 2015, American Presidency Project.

188. Barack Obama, "Remarks at the United Nations Leaders' Summit on Countering ISIL and Violent Extremism in New York City," September 29, 2015, American Presidency Project.

189. Obama, "Remarks at the United Nations Leaders' Summit on Countering ISIL and Violent Extremism in New York City," September 29, 2015.

190. Obama, "Remarks on United States Efforts to Combat the Islamic State of Iraq and the Levant (ISIL) Terrorist Organization and an Exchange with Reporters," July 6, 2015.

191. Barack Obama, "Remarks at the Veterans of Foreign Wars National Convention in Pittsburgh, Pennsylvania," July 21, 2015, American Presidency Project.

192. Barack Obama, "Remarks on United States Military Strategy in Afghanistan and an Exchange with Reporters," October 15, 2015, American Presidency Project.

193. Barack Obama, "The President's News Conference in Kuala Lumpur, Malaysia," November 22, 2015, American Presidency Project.

194. Barack Obama, "The President's News Conference," December 18, 2015, American Presidency Project.

195. Coward, "Against Network Thinking," 16.

196. Gene Healy, "President Obama's Legacy Is Endless War," *Time*, May 5, 2016.

197. See Mike Aaronson, Wali Aslam, Tom Dyson, and Regina Rauxloh, *Precision Strike Warfare and International Intervention: Strategic, Ethico-legal, and Decisional Implications* (New York: Routledge, 2015); Rosa Brooks, "Drones and the International Rule of Law," *Ethics & International Affairs* 28, no. 1 (2014); and Medea Benjamin, "America Dropped 26,171 Bombs in 2016; What a Bloody End to Obama's Reign," *The Guardian*, January 9, 2017.

198. Obama, "Commencement Address at the United States Military Academy in West Point, New York," May 28, 2014.

199. Obama, "Remarks with Prime Minister Narendra Modi of India in New Delhi, India, and an Exchange with Reporters," January 25, 2015.

200. Obama, "Remarks on United States Efforts to Combat the Islamic State of Iraq and the Levant (ISIL) Terrorist Organization and an Exchange with Reporters," July 6, 2015.

201. Obama, "The President's News Conference at the Pentagon in Arlington, Virginia," August 4, 2016.

202. Barack Obama, "Remarks on United States Efforts to Combat the Islamic State of Iraq and the Levant (ISIL) Terrorist Organization," February 25, 2016, American Presidency Project, https://www.presidency.ucsb.edu/node/315343.

203. Obama, "The President's News Conference with President Mauricio Macri of Argentina in Buenos Aires, Argentina," March 23, 2016, https://www.govinfo.gov/content/pkg/DCPD-201600174/html/DCPD-201600174.htm.

204. See, for example, Barack Obama, "The President's News Conference with Prime Minister David W.D. Cameron of the United Kingdom in London, England," April 22, 2016; and Barack Obama, "Remarks on United States Strategy to Counter the Islamic State of Iraq and the Levant (ISIL) Terrorist Organization at the Department of the Treasury," June 14, 2016, American Presidency Project.

205. Obama, "The President's News Conference at the Pentagon in Arlington, Virginia," August 4, 2016.

206. Dan De Luce, "Obama's Drone Policy Gets an 'F,'" *Foreign Policy*, February 23, 2016.

207. James Downie, "Obama's Drone War Is a Shameful Part of His Legacy," *Washington Post*, May 5, 2016.

208. Amy Belasco, *The Cost of Iraq, Afghanistan, and Other Global War on Terror Operations since 9/11* (Washington, DC: Congressional Research Service, December 8, 2014), 10.

209. Obama, "Remarks at National Defense University," May 23, 2013.

210. See Lauren Berlant, *Cruel Optimism* (Durham, NC: Duke University Press,

2013); and Jennifer Terry, "Introduction to Attachments to War: Violence and the Production of Biomedical Knowledge in Twenty-first Century America," *Catalyst: Feminism, Theory, Technoscience* 2, no. 1 (2016).

211. And here I utilize Mbembe's definition of sovereign power as the power to "dictate who may live and who must die." See Achille Mbembe, "Necropolitics," *Public Culture* 15, no. 1 (Winter 2003): 11, 31.

212. Mbembe, "Necropolitics," 31.

213. Max Boot, *The Savage Wars of Peace: Small Wars and the Rise of American Power*, rev. ed. (New York: Basic Books, 2014), xviii–xix.

214. Edward Delman, "Obama Promised to End America's Wars—Has He?" *The Atlantic*, March 30, 2016.

215. See Crystal Marie Fleming, "There Are Few Things I Can Think of More Ruthless Than Throwing Your Own Pastor under the Bus. Bombing Children, Perhaps. Obama Did Both," https://twitter.com/alwaystheself/status/915652241834545153.

216. See Jessica Purkiss and Jack Serle, "Obama's Covert Drone War in Numbers: Ten Times More Strikes Than Bush," *Bureau of Investigative Journalism*, January 17, 2017, https://www.thebureauinvestigates.com/stories/2017-01-17/obamas-covert-drone-war-in-numbers-ten-times-more-strikes-than-bush. By comparison, an estimated 800,000–1,000,000 foreign fighters and civilians died during the Bush years. See John Tirman, "Bush's War Totals," *The Nation*, January 29, 2009.

217. See Brooks, *How Everything Became War and the Military Became Everything*, 338–42.

218. See Stephen J. Heidt, "Scapegoater-in-Chief: Racist Undertones of Donald Trump's Rhetorical Repertoire," in *The Trump Presidency, Journalism, and Democracy*, ed. Robert Gutsche Jr. (New York: Routledge, 2018); Donald J. Trump, "The President's News Conference with Prime Minister Theresa May of the United Kingdom," January 27, 2017; Donald J. Trump, "Statement on the Death of a United States Servicemember in Yemen," January 29, 2017; Donald J. Trump, "The President's News Conference with King Abdullah II of Jordan," April 5, 2017; Donald J. Trump, "Remarks at the Arab Islamic American Summit in Riyadh, Saudi Arabia," May 21, 2017; Donald J. Trump, "Remarks with Prime

Minister Benjamin Netanyahu of Israel in Jerusalem," May 22, 2017; Donald J. Trump, "Statement on the Terrorist Attacks in Iran," June 7, 2017; Donald J. Trump, "Remarks at the Faith and Freedom Coalition's Road to Majority Conference," June 8, 2017; and Donald J. Trump, "Remarks to Members of the Press with Prime Minister Narendra Modi of India," June 26, 2017, American Presidency Project.

219. See, for example, Donald J. Trump, "Address before a Joint Session of the Congress," February 28, 2017; Donald J. Trump, "Remarks at the Arab Islamic American Summit in Riyadh, Saudi Arabia," May 21, 2017; and Donald J. Trump, "Remarks in Warsaw, Poland," July 6, 2017, American Presidency Project.

220. Brian P. McKeon, "Trump's 'Secret Plan' to Defeat ISIS Looks a Lot Like Obama's," *Foreign Policy*, May 31, 2017.

Chapter 5. The Eternal Savage: War, the Globalization of Violence, and the Sovereign Power of the Present

1. C. Vann Woodward, "The Age of Reinterpretation," *American Historical Review* 66, no. 1 (1960): 3.

2. Evan Thomas, *The War Lovers: Roosevelt, Lodge, Hearst, and the Rush to Empire, 1898* (New York: Hachette Book Group, 2010), 172.

3. Thomas, *The War Lovers*, 60–61, 254.

4. Thomas, *The War Lovers*, 364.

5. Funding anti-communist forces in Nicaragua and Afghanistan, the limited engagements in Grenada and Panama, and the increasing focus on rhetorical dramatism vis-à-vis the Soviet Union are prime examples of how American power sought the same goals but with less direct exposure to American forces.

6. This power relied on allies and coalitions, of course, but the point remains the same. Bush declared the "Vietnam syndrome is over," and media commentators backed him up. See, for example, Harry G. Summers Jr., "Putting Vietnam Syndrome to Rest," *Los Angeles Times*, March 2, 1991; and Dov S. Zakheim, "Is the Vietnam Syndrome Dead? Happily, It's Buried in the Gulf," *New York Times*, March 4, 1991.

7. See Jason Edwards, *Navigating the Post–Cold War World: President Clinton's*

Foreign Policy Rhetoric (Lanham, MD: Lexington Books, 2008).

8. See Christopher Layne and Benjamin Schwarz, "American Hegemony: Without an Enemy," *Foreign Policy* 92 (Autumn 1993): 5–23.

9. Chris Hayes, *A Colony in a Nation* (New York: W.W. Norton & Company, 2017), 135.

10. Ronan Farrow, *War on Peace: The End of Diplomacy and the Decline of American Influence* (New York: W.W. Norton & Company, 2018), 22–23.

11. See Jessica Stern, "Obama and Terrorism: Like It or Not, the War Goes On," *Foreign Affairs* (September/October 2015): 62–70.

12. Mary Dudziak, *War Time: An Idea, Its History, Its Consequences* (New York: Oxford University Press, 2013), 113. See also David Keen, *Endless War? Hidden Functions of the "War on Terror"* (London: Hurst, 2006).

13. Jeremy Engels and William O. Saas, "On Acquiescence and Ends-Less War: An Inquiry into the New War Rhetoric," *Quarterly Journal of Speech* 99, no. 2 (2013): 227.

14. Jessy Ohl, "Nothing to See or Fear: Light War and the Boring Visual Rhetoric of U.S. Drone Imagery," *Quarterly Journal of Speech* 101, no. 4 (2015): 613. See also Jessy J. Ohl, "In Pursuit of Light War in Libya: *Kairotic* Justifications of War That *Just* Happened," *Rhetoric & Public Affairs* 20, no. 2 (Summer 2017): 210.

15. Carl Boggs, *Origins of the Warfare State: World War II and the Transformation of American Politics* (New York: Routledge, 2017); Rosa Brooks, *How Everything Became War and the Military Became Everything: Tales from the Pentagon* (New York: Simon & Schuster, 2016); Rachel Maddow, *Drift: The Unmooring of American Military Power* (New York: Broadway Paperbacks, 2012); Bruce Robbins, *Perpetual War: Cosmopolitanism from the Viewpoint of Violence* (Durham, NC: Duke University Press, 2012); Andrew J. Bacevich, *Washington Rules: America's Path to Permanent War* (New York: Metropolitan Books, 2010); Douglas Kellner, "Postmodern Military and Permanent War," in *Masters of War: Militarism and Blowback in the Era of American Empire*, ed. Carl Boggs (New York: Routledge, 2003), 229–44; and Gore Vidal, *Perpetual War for Perpetual Peace: How We Got to Be So Hated* (New York: Thunder's Mouth Press/Nation Books, 2002). See Michael Lee, "Us, Them, and the War on Terror: Reassessing George W. Bush's Rhetorical Legacy," *Communication*

and Critical/Cultural Studies 14, no. 1 (2017): 3–30.

16. Robert E. Terrill, "An Uneasy Peace: Barack Obama's Nobel Peace Prize Lecture," *Rhetoric & Public Affairs* 14, no. 4 (2011): 774.

17. David Chandler, "War without End(s): Grounding the Discourse of 'Global War,'" *Security Dialogue* 40, no. 3 (2009): 254.

18. Michael Hardt and Antonio Negri, *Multitude: War and Democracy in the Age of Empire* (New York: Penguin Books, 2004), 14.

19. And here I utilize Mbembe's definition of sovereign power. See Achille Mbembe, "Necropolitics," *Public Culture* 15, no. 1 (Winter 2003): 11, 31.

20. Chandler, "War without End(s)," 250.

21. Chris J. Cuomo, "War Is Not Just an Event: Reflections on the Significance of Everyday Violence," *Hypatia* 11, no. 4 (Fall 1996): 31–32.

22. Necati Polat, "Peace as War," *Alternatives* 35 (2010): 336.

23. Dudziak, *War Time*, 136.

24. While the U.S. Congress has only formally declared war five times, Congress has authorized military action on fifteen additional occasions. Similarly, "informal" wars have been initiated by the United Nations Security Council and backed by Congress seven times. The notion that wars are rarely "declared" is unsustainable.

25. See Geoffrey S. Corn, Victor M. Hansen, Dick Jackson, Eric Talbot Jensen, Michael W. Lewis, and James A. Schoettler Jr., *The War on Terror and the Laws of War: A Military Perspective*, 2nd ed. (New York: Oxford University Press, 2015).

26. See Greg Grandin, *The End of Myth: From the Frontier to the Border Wall in the Mind of America* (New York: Henry Holt and Company, 2019), 67, 91–93.

27. Stephen Kinzer, *Overthrow: America's Century of Regime Change from Hawaii to Iraq* (New York: Henry Holt and Company, 2006), 18–21.

28. Mbembe is centrally concerned with what he calls the "generalized instrumentalization of human existence and the material destruction of human bodies and populations." Necropolitics is the term he gives to describe a form of modern sovereign power that "define[s] who matters and who does not, who is disposable and who is not." One of the consequences of this specific form of power is that modern warfare does not seek territorial acquisition. Rather, it "aim[s] to force the enemy into

submission regardless of the immediate consequences, side effects, and 'collateral damage' of the military actions." More generally, his thesis seeks to elaborate a theoretical basis for comprehending the sovereign logic of global, mobile military operations that enact routine forms of violence not to surveil or govern populations, but to routinize their management with death.

29. Mbembe, "Necropolitics," 31.

30. Nick Danforth, "Westphalia to Communicate: Sovereignty, Confusion, and the International Order," *War on the Rocks*, November 1, 2017, https://warontherocks.com/2017/11/westphalia-to-communicate-sovereignty-confusion-and-the-international-order.

31. "Brad Evans Interviews Brian Massumi," *Los Angeles Review of Books*, November 13, 2017; italics in original.

32. Bruce B. Lawrence and Aisha Karim, eds., *On Violence* (Durham, NC: Duke University Press, 2007), 14.

33. Fred Charles Iklé, *Every War Must End*, 2nd rev. ed. (New York: Columbia University Press, 2005), 106.

34. Michael Shapiro, *Violent Cartographies: Mapping Cultures of War* (Minneapolis: University of Minnesota Press, 1997), 172.

35. Claudia Aradau, "Beyond Good and Evil: Ethics and Securitization/Desecuritization Techniques," *Rubikon* (December 2001), http://venus.ci.uw.edu.pl/~rubikon/forum/claudia2.htm.

36. See Ivo H. Daalder and James M. Lindsay, *America Unbound: The Bush Revolution in Foreign Policy* (Washington, DC: Brookings Institution, 2003), 17–34, 50–61.

37. In Obama's case, the military brass sought to step up the military's presence in Afghanistan even as the president publicly committed to ending the war. Prepping a public communication campaign in the final months of 2016 to justify a permanent generational presence in the country, Defense Department actors became increasingly vocal and public after Trump's inauguration. As Ronan Farrow recounted, "the same language cropped up again, this time from Trump surrogates" to justify a massive increase in deployments and an expansion of the mission. See Farrow, *War on Peace*, 201.

38. See Robert Newman, *Invincible Ignorance in American Foreign Policy: The Triumph of Ideology over Evidence* (New York: Peter Lang Publishing, 2013), 47.

39. Office of the Historian, "Foreign Policy under President Eisenhower," in *A Short History of the State Department* (Washington, DC: Department of State, n.d.), https://history.state.gov/departmenthistory/short-history/eisenhower.

40. Office of the Historian, "President Nixon and the NSC," in *A Short History of the State Department* (Washington, DC: Department of State, n.d.), https://history.state.gov/departmenthistory/short-history/nixon-nsc.

41. See Farrow, *War on Peace.*

42. Michael Howard, *The Invention of Peace and the Reinvention of War* (London: Profile Books, 2002), 1–2.

43. Edwin Black, "The Second Persona," *Quarterly Journal of Speech* 56, no. 2 (1970): 110.

44. Claudia Aradau, "Security and the Democratic Scene: Desecuritization and Emancipation," *Journal of International Relations and Development* 7, no. 4 (2004): 3.

45. Franklin D. Roosevelt, "Address at Chautauqua, N.Y.," August 14, 1936, American Presidency Project.

46. Bob Woodward, *Obama's Wars* (New York: Simon & Schuster, 2010), 2, 11.

47. Quoted in Amy Goodman and Denis Moynihan, "'Let Us Not Become the Evil We Deplore,'" *Democracy Now!*, September 16, 2009, www.democracynow.org.

48. Marc Cooper, "Rep. Barbara Lee: Rowing against the Tide," *Los Angeles Times*, September 23, 2001.

49. Barbara Lee, "Why I Opposed the Resolution to Oppose Force," *San Francisco Chronicle*, September 23, 2001.

50. Barbara Lee, "Congresswoman Barbara Lee Introduces AUMF Repeal Legislation," February 14, 2019, https://lee.house.gov/news/press-releases/congresswoman-barbara-lee-introduces-aumf-repeal-legislation.

51. To Repeal Public Law 107–40, 116th Congress, 1st session, https://lee.house.gov/imo/media/doc/LEE_2001%20AUMF_xml.pdf.

52. Matt Fuller and Amanda Terkel, "18 Years Later, the House Finally Repeals the President's 9/11 War Authority," *Huffington Post*, June 19, 2019.

Jeremy Herb, "Senate Rejects Bid to Repeal War Authorizations," *CNN*, September 13, 2017.

53. John Lowell, *Perpetual War, the Policy of Mr. Madison* (Boston: Chester Stebbins, 1812), 10.

54. Abraham Lincoln, Spot Resolutions in the United States House of Representatives, December 22, 1847, National Archives Building, RG 233, Entry 362: Thirtieth Congress, 1847–1849, Records of Legislative Proceedings, Bills and Resolutions Originating in the House, 1847–1849.

55. Ted Gottfried, *The Fight for Peace: A History of Antiwar Movements in America* (Minneapolis: Twenty-First Century Books, 2006), 33–34.

56. William Jennings Bryan, "Imperialism," August 8, 1900, Voices of Democracy, https://voicesofdemocracy.umd.edu/william-jennings-bryan-imperialism-speech-text.

57. Quoted in Robert Mann, *Wartime Dissent in America: A History and Anthology* (New York: Palgrave Macmillan, 2010), 84.

58. Martin Luther King Jr., "Beyond Vietnam," April 4, 1967, https://kinginstitute.stanford.edu/king-papers/documents/beyond-vietnam.

59. See Tom Engelhardt, "What Happened to the Global Anti-War Movement," *Common Dreams*, May 28, 2019, https://www.commondreams.org/views/2019/05/28/what-happened-global-anti-war-movement.

60. Gene Healy and John Glaser, "Repeal, Don't Replace, the AUMF," Cato Institute Policy Report, July/August 2018, https://www.cato.org/policy-report/julyaugust-2018/repeal-dont-replace-aumf.

61. Ken Gude and Kate Martin, *Preventing Endless War Requires Real Congressional Oversight—Not New War Authority*, Center for American Progress, Washington, DC, December 14, 2018, https://www.americanprogress.org.

62. Healy and Glaser, "Repeal, Don't Replace, the AUMF."

63. *Principles of a Progressive Foreign Policy for the United States* (Washington, DC: Win Without War, n.d., https://winwithoutwar.org.

64. Robert L. Ivie, *Democracy and America's War on Terror* (Tuscaloosa: University of Alabama Press, 2005), 5.

65. See Karlyn Kohrs Campbell and Kathleen Hall Jamieson, *Presidents Creating the Presidency: Deeds Done in Words* (Chicago: University of Chicago Press, 2008), 252; and Carol K. Winkler, "Parallels in Preemptive War

Rhetoric: Reagan on Libya; Bush 43 on Iraq," *Rhetoric & Public Affairs* 10, no. 2 (2007): 303–34.

66. Congress sought to restrict Reagan's ability to arm the Contras in Nicaragua with the Boland Amendment. While the Amendment frustrated the president, he resorted to extralegal means to pursue his desired policy. The Iran-Contra scandal may have tarnished his presidency and imprisoned several functionaries, but Reagan ultimately got what he wanted with impunity. See Edward P. Boland, "Amendments for H.R. 2968," 98th Congress H.AMDT.461 (October 20, 1983).

67. Ronnie D. Lipschutz, "Negotiating the Boundaries of Difference and Security at Millennium's End," in *On Security*, ed. Ronnie D. Lipschutz (New York: Columbia University Press, 1995), 213–14. Ole Waever, "Securitization and Desecuritization," in Lipschutz, ed., *On Security*, 48.

68. Petra Goedde, *The Politics of Peace: A Global Cold War History* (New York: Oxford University Press, 2019), 13, 5.

69. Goedde, *The Politics of Peace*, 194.

70. J. Michael Hogan, *The Nuclear Freeze Campaign: Rhetoric and Foreign Policy in the Telepolitical Age* (East Lansing: Michigan State University Press, 1994), 63.

71. Michael Steudeman used this phrase to discuss demagogic rhetoric, but it serves my purposes here given the continuity of the rhetoric of savagery. See Michael J. Steudeman, "Rethinking Rhetorical Education in Times of Demagoguery," *Rhetoric Society Quarterly* 49, no. 3 (2019): 297–314.

72. Steudeman, "Rethinking Rhetorical Education," 307–8.

73. This phrase was Mike Gravel's campaign slogan for his 2020 presidential campaign.

74. Lawrence and Karim, *On Violence*, 11–12.

75. Witness the Obama administration's unwillingness to discuss the aspects of the drone strike program. It was only after significant pushback from both the political left and Republicans in Congress (ostensibly in search of oversight, but rather more focused on fabricating scandal) that Obama released a memo that outlined the procedure for how his government went about authorizing aerial attacks against agents hostile to the United States.

76. I do not see dissent as fulfilling the republican ideal of oversight here. Rather, I mean that civic action against war is likely the only way to force presidents to alter the trajectory of U.S. foreign policy. This form of civic action exists outside of procedural democratic practice. I am more optimistic about the disruptive potential of this form of civic action rather than procedural avenues like voting.

77. A good example of this is found in "Frontline: Obama's War," an episode of the long-running PBS documentary show that aired in late 2009. While not interviewing Obama, the reporting points to his direct control of the Afghan war and its strategy, effectively ceding agency from the generals and other practitioners back onto the executive.

78. Brooks, *How Everything Became War*, 122–23.

79. Robert L. Ivie, *Democracy and America's War on Terror* (Tuscaloosa: University of Alabama Press, 2005), 8–9.

Index